The Role of the State and Accounting Transparency

T0293346

Dr Mohammad Nurunnabi examines the factors that affect the implementation of International Financial Reporting Standards (IFRS) in developing countries and answers these specific research questions:

- What is the relative impact of accounting regulatory frameworks and politico-institutional factors on the implementation of IFRS in developing countries?
- How do cultural factors affect said implementation?
- How does a study of implementing IFRS help to build an understanding of a theory of the role of the state in accounting change in developing countries?

This follows a mixed methodology approach, in which interviews are conducted, IFRS-related enforcement documents and annual reports are evaluated. More than 138 countries have adopted IFRS, yet the International Accounting Standards Board (IASB) does not provide an implementation index. Financial reporting varies by country, even within the area of the world that has apparently adopted IFRS and Nurunnabi offers an important viewpoint that considers the issues of IFRS implementation from various perspectives. This is an invaluable resource for Undergraduate, Masters and PhD students, policy makers (at local, regional and international level) namely the IASB, World Bank, IMF, practitioners and users, giving them the necessary insight into the financial reporting environment and the state's attitude towards accounting transparency. Most importantly, this book contributes to military and democratic political regimes and the Max Weberian view of the theory of the role of the state's attitude towards accounting transparency.

Mohammad Nurunnabi FHEA FRSA FAIA(Acad) is an Associate Professor in Accounting and Chair of the Department of Accounting at Prince Sultan University, Riyadh, Saudi Arabia. He holds a PhD in Accounting (International Financial Reporting Standards – IFRS) with outright pass (no corrections) from the University of Edinburgh, UK. Previously he was a Senior Lecturer in Accounting and Research Leader in the Accounting Group at the University of East London, UK. He also taught in University of Bedfordshire, UK and Edge Hill University, UK. He teaches Advanced Accounting, Accounting Theory, Auditing and Management Accounting. He is an Editorial Member of eight journals and reviewer of 41 journals.

The Role of the State and Accounting Transparency

IFRS implementation in developing countries

Mohammad Nurunnabi

Routledge
Taylor & Francis Group

LONDON AND NEW YORK

First published 2016
by Routledge
2 Park Square, Milton Park, Abingdon, Oxon OX14 4RN

and by Routledge
711 Third Avenue, New York, NY 10017

First issued in paperback 2018

Routledge is an imprint of the Taylor & Francis Group, an informa business

British Library Cataloguing-in-Publication Data
A catalogue record for this book is available from the British Library

Library of Congress Cataloging-in-Publication Data
Nurunnabi, Mohammad.
The role of the state and accounting transparency : IFRS implementation in developing countries / by Mohammad Nurunnabi.
    pages cm
  Includes bibliographical references and index.
  ISBN 978-1-4724-3064-9 (hardback)— ISBN 978-1-4724-3065-6 (ebook)—
  ISBN 978-1-3155-5327-6 (epub)
  1. Accounting—Standards—Developing countries. 2. Financial statements—Standards—Developing countries. 3. Corporations—Accounting—Standards—Developing countries. 4. Environmental responsibility—Developing countries. I. Title.

  HF5616.5.N87 2016
  657.02'18—dc23
  2015029976

ISBN 13: 978-1-138-32012-3 (pbk)
ISBN 13: 978-1-4724-3064-9 (hbk)

Typeset in Baskerville
by Apex CoVantage, LLC

This book is dedicated to my parents, Mohammad Sirazul Islam and Mrs Nurun Nahar, for their love and support throughout my life; my wife, Antara, and daughter, red devils Alfi; to my uncle, Professor Abdul Kayum; and to my grandfather, the late Mohammad Abdul Jabbar Sardar, who taught me how to read and write.

Contents

Figures

Tables

Abbreviations

AAA	American Accounting Association
ABS	Association of Business Schools
ACCA	The Association of Chartered Certified Accountants
ADB	The Asian Development Bank
AGM	Annual General Meeting
AICPA	The American Institute of Certified Public Accountants
AL	The Awami League
ASB	The Accounting Standards Board
ASCPA	Australian Society of Certified Practising Accountants
ASEAN	The Association of Southeast Asian Nations
BAB	Bangladesh Association of Banks
BADC	The Business Accounting Deliberation Council
BAFA	The British Accounting and Finance Association
BaFin	Bundesanstalt für Finanzdienstleistungsaufsicht
BAKSAL	The Bangladesh Krishak Sramik Awami League
BAPLC	Bangladesh Association of Publicly Listed Companies
BAS	Bangladesh Accounting Standards
BB	Bangladesh Bank
BDR	Bangladesh Rifles
BFRS	Bangladesh Financial Reporting Standards
BGB	Border Guard Bangladesh
BGMEA	Bangladesh Garment Manufacturers and Exporters Association
BIGUF	Bangladesh Independent Garment Workers Union Federation
BNP	The Bangladesh Nationalist Party
BOI	Board of Investment
BRC	Banking Reform Committee
BRPD	Banking Regulation and Policy Department of Bangladesh Bank
BSE	Bombay Stock Exchange
BSEC	The Bangladesh Securities and Exchange Commission
BTCL	The Bangladesh Telecommunications Company Limited
BTMA	Bangladesh Textile Mills Association
BTTB	The Bangladesh Telephone and Telegraph Board
CA	Chartered Accountant/Accountancy
CAPA	Confederation of Asian and Pacific Accountants
CDBL	Central Depository Bangladesh Limited
CEO	Chief Executive Officer
CESR	The Committee of European Securities Regulators

CG	Corporate Governance
CIA	The Central Intelligence Agency
CIPFA	The Chartered Institute of Public Finance and Accountancy
CPA	Certified Public Accountant
CPD	Continuing Professional Development
CPE	Continuing Professional Education
CRAB	Credit Rating Agency of Bangladesh
CSE	The Chittagong Stock Exchange
CSI	China Securities Index
DCCI	Dhaka Chamber of Commerce and Industry
DPR	Deutsche Prüfstelle für Rechnungslegung
DSE	The Dhaka Stock Exchange
EAA	The European Accounting Association
EC	European Commission
ECON	The Committee on Economic and Monetary Affairs
EMTAP	The Economic Management Technical Assistance Program
EU	The European Union
FASB	The Financial Accounting Standards Board
FBCCI	The Federation of Bangladesh Chambers of Commerce and Industry
FDI	Foreign Direct Investment
FRA	Financial Reporting Act
FRC	The Financial Reporting Council
FSA	The Financial Services Authority
FSRP	The Financial Sector Reforms Programme
GAAP	Generally Accepted Accounting Principles
GCC	The Gulf Cooperation Council
GDP	Gross Domestic Product
GOB	The Government of Bangladesh
GPS	Global Player Segment
IAS	International Accounting Standards
IASB	The International Accounting Standards Board
IBA	Institute of Business Administration
ICAA	The Institute of Chartered Accountants in Australia
ICAB	The Institute of Chartered Accountants of Bangladesh
ICAEW	The Institute of Chartered Accountants in England and Wales
ICAI	The Institute of Chartered Accountants of India
ICAP	The Institute of Chartered Accountants of Pakistan
ICAS	The Institute of Chartered Accountants of Scotland
ICASL	The Institute of Chartered Accountants of Sri Lanka
ICMAB	The Institute of Cost and Management Accountants of Bangladesh
IDLC	Industrial Development Leasing Company of Bangladesh
IFAC	The International Federation of Accountants
IFAD	The International Fund for Agricultural Development
IFR	International Financing Review
IFRIC	The International Financial Reporting Interpretations Committee
IFRS	International Financial Reporting Standards
IMF	The International Monetary Fund
IO	Individual Organisation Level
IOSCO	The International Organization of Securities Commissions

IPO	Initial Public Offering
IPSAS	International Public Sector Accounting Standards
IRD	The Internal Resources Division
JICPA	The Japanese Institute of Certified Public Accountants
JMB	Jama'atul Mujahideen, Bangladesh
KSE	The Karachi Stock Exchange
MLA	Martial Law Administration
MNC	Multinational Companies
MOC	Ministry of Commerce
MOF	Ministry of Finance
MoU	Memorandum of Understanding
MP	Member of Parliament
NBR	The National Board of Revenue
NGO	Non-Governmental Organisation
NGWF	The National Garment Workers Federation
OECD	The Organisation for Economic Co-operation and Development
OF	Organisational Field Level
PO	President's Order
RJSC	The Registrar of Joint Stock Companies
ROSC	Reports on the Observance of Standards and Codes
RQ	Research Question
Rs.	Indian/Pakistani Rupee(s)
SAARC	The South Asian Association for Regional Cooperation
SAFA	South Asian Federation of Accountants
SEC	The Securities and Exchange Commission
SIC	The Standing Interpretations Committee
SME	Small and Medium Enterprises
SOE	State-Owned Enterprises
SRO	Self-Regulatory Organisations
TIB	Transparency International Bangladesh
Tk.	Bangladeshi Taka
TRC	Technical and Research Committee
UGC	The University Grants Commission of Bangladesh
US	The United States
UK	The United Kingdom
UN	The United Nations
UNCTAD	The United Nations Conference on Trade and Development
UNFPA	The United Nations Population Fund
USA	The United States of America
VAT	Value Added Tax
WTO	The World Trade Organization

About the author

Dr. Mohammad Nurunnabi FHEA FRSA FAIA (Acad) is an Associate Professor in Accounting and chair of the Department of Accounting at Prince Sultan University, Riyadh, Saudi Arabia. He holds a PhD in Accounting (International Financial Reporting Standards – IFRS) with an outright pass (no corrections) from the University of Edinburgh. Previously he was a senior lecturer in Accounting and research leader in the Accounting Group at the University of East London (UK). He also taught in the University of Bedfordshire and Edge Hill University (UK). He teaches Advanced Accounting, Accounting Theory, Auditing, and Management Accounting. He is a fellow of the Higher Education Academy (FHEA); an academic fellow of the Association of International Accountants, Academic FAIA (Acad); and a Fellow of the Royal Society of Arts (FRSA) (Royal Society for the Encouragement of Arts, Manufactures and Commerce), UK. He is an academic member of the Institute of Management Accountants (IMA), the European Accounting Association (EAA), the British Accounting and Finance Association (BAFA), the International Association for Accounting Education and Research (IAAER), and the American Accounting Association (AAA).

Dr. Nurunnabi's current research interests include IFRS; corruption and accounting development; politics, regulation and enforcement issues in IFRS; corporate governance; corporate social responsibility and religious values; Islamic accounting; and accounting education development. He is an editorial member of eight journals, including the *International Journal of Accounting, Journal of the Knowledge Economy* and *Journal of Islamic Accounting and Business Research*. He is the reviewer of 40 leading international accounting journals, including *Accounting Review, Corporate Governance: An International Review, Accounting Horizons* and *Journal of Business Ethics*.

Dr. Nurunnabi has received numerous prestigious research and teaching awards, including Outstanding Research Certificate from Prince Sultan University (2015); Certificate of Appreciation on Financial Leadership and Reporting from ACCA (2014); Recognition of Outstanding Service as an IMA Campus Advocate from the IMA (2014); and the Academic Excellence in Research and Teaching Award from Channel S, a UK-based TV channel (2013). In 2015, he was nominated as global advisor member of the Diversity Thought Leadership Pipeline (DTLP) Committee of the IMA (USA) and a country contributor on 'IFRS – Saudi Arabia' Wiley Insight IFRS, John Wiley & Sons Inc., USA.

Dr. Nurunnabi's article was ranked first in 2014 as the most downloaded published in the *Research in Accounting Regulation* journal. His research has appeared in a wide range of leading international journals, including: *Journal of Education for Business, Administration and Society; Business Ethics: A European Review; Environment, Development and Sustainability; Advances in Accounting, Incorporating Advances in International Accounting; Research in Accounting Regulation; International*

Journal of Critical Accounting; *Journal of Human Resource Costing and Accounting*; *International Journal of Health Care Quality Assurance*; *Journal of Asia Business Studies*; *International Journal of Managerial and Financial Accounting*; and the *Journal of Business Economics and Management*. He is currently working on a book titled *Intellectual Capital Reporting in Developing Countries*, which is due to be published in 2016. He has also presented papers at international conferences, including BAFA, Irish Accounting and Finance Association (IAFA), the Financial Reporting and Business Communication Conference, Scottish Doctoral Colloquium in Accounting and Finance, and the Institute of Chartered Accountants of Scotland (ICAS).

Preface

Based on extensive fieldwork and theoretical analysis, this book offers an important aspect that analyses the problems of International Financial Reporting Standards (IFRS) implementation from various perspectives. This book is an invaluable source for undergraduate final year accounting students (accounting theory course) and masters and PhD level students (MSc Accounting and Finance, MSc International Accounting, MRes Accounting) for postgraduate research courses. The book also aims to assist policy makers (at local, regional and international level), namely the IASB, World Bank, IMF, UNCTAD – practitioners and users with necessary insight about financial reporting environment and the role of the state's attitude towards accounting transparency in developing countries.

More than 138 countries have adopted IFRS throughout the world. However, the International Accounting Standards Board (IASB) did not provide any implementation index. Hence, financial reporting remains different by country, even within areas of the world that have apparently adopted IFRS. There is no book in the current market on IFRS implementation in developing countries. This book provides insightful information on how politics, accounting regulation and culture impact IFRS implementation in developing countries with reference to Bangladesh. This is also one of the very first books to provide a holistic view of IFRS implementation area of enquiry.

The book particularly examines what factors have been affecting the implementation of IFRS in developing countries, in particular Bangladesh. The study seeks to answer these specific research questions:

1. What is the relative impact of accounting regulatory frameworks and politico-institutional factors on the implementation of IFRS in developing countries such as Bangladesh?
2. How do cultural factors affect the implementation of IFRS?
3. How does a study of implementing IFRS help to build an understanding of a theory of the role of the state in accounting change in developing countries?

Adopting a mixed methodology (interviews, documentary analyses of IFRS-related enforcement documents and annual reports) the study finds that politico-institutional factors are stronger and more dominant factors than accounting regulatory frameworks for impeding IFRS implementation. The military-backed government was effective compared to the democratic government in terms of taking action against companies identified as being corrupt. Furthermore, deficiencies in training opportunities in the accounting profession and high levels of corruption are inhibiting IFRS implementation. Professional curricula contain limited content on IFRS, and there are limited training opportunities for accountants in the majority of companies. Looser enforcement of the laws is found during the periods of democratic government. However, the levels of corruption were lower during the military-backed government.

The book also finds that outcomes of accounting change in Bangladesh are observed from state and individual organisation levels. Extending Weber's argument on state-society, the study finds that for a state in an era of democratic government, politico-institutional factors and corruption (as an indication of societal values) may be more important and concentrated factors than for a state under a military-backed government in terms of impeding IFRS implementation and accounting transparency (Weber, (1958)[1904], (1968)[1922]).

This book addresses the implementing of IFRS issues to ensure that readers are aware of recent thinking and development of IFRS in developing countries, focusing on their relevance to application, with enough detail to explain the following areas: a review of literature (Chapter 2); theory (Chapter 3); the financial reporting environment in Bangladesh (Chapter 4); research methodology (Chapter 5); the relative impact of accounting regulatory frameworks and politico institutional factors (Chapter 6); the impact of training opportunities in the accounting profession, corruption and country-specific factors (Chapter 7); the theory of the role of the state in the implementation of IFRS (Chapter 8); and conclusions (Chapter 9).

I appreciate your taking time to read this note. I encourage your questions or comments or feedback. Please contact me at: mnurunnabi@psu.edu.sa or s_agor2001@yahoo.com.

Dr Mohammad Nurunnabi FHEA FRSA FAIA(Acad)
Associate Professor in Accounting
Chair, Department of Accounting
Prince Sultan University
Riyadh, Saudi Arabia

Acknowledgements

I wish to express my profound gratitude to the Almighty Allah (*subhanawataala*) for giving me the strength and ability to complete this project successfully. I would like to express my deepest gratitude to Professor Pauline Weetman, who has always been an inspiring role model and mentor to me. I also gratefully acknowledge the support from Dr Ahmed Yamani (Rector, Prince Sultan University), Dr. Saad Al-Rwaita (Vice-Rector, Administrative and Financial Affairs, Prince Sultan University), Dr. Abdelhafeez Feda (Vice-Rector, Academic Affairs and Research, Prince Sultan University), and Dr. Saad A. Almosa (Dean of the College of Business Administration, Prince Sultan University) for providing me essential support in this project. I owe sincere gratitude to several people whose comments and support were indispensable: Professors David Alexander, Mike Jones, Geoffrey Whittington, Christine Cooper, Christine Helliar, Falconer Mitchell, Irvine Lapsley, Ingrid Jeacle, Katherine Schipper, and Brian Singleton-Green (ICAEW); and Drs Iris Bosa and Simon Norton. I am grateful for the financial support from the University of Edinburgh and the Charles Wallace Trust, London. I must thank the various interviewees who provided vital information during the fieldwork of this project. I am also indebted to my family, my colleagues, and friends, all of whom have always been patient and understanding and have inspired me. Finally, I would like to thank the publishing team at Routledge for their continuous cooperation throughout this project.

Chapter 1

Introduction

The major emerging and transition economies of the world – Brazil, China, India, and Russia – are adopting or considering the adoption of IFRS, not US GAAP, in an effort to become integrated in the world's capital markets and attract the investment necessary to finance their development . . . There is clear momentum towards accepting IFRS as a common financial reporting language throughout the world . . . Investors are able to make comparisons of companies operating in different jurisdictions more easily.

(Tweedie, 2007, p. 2)[1]

[T]he most likely effect of local politics and local market realities on IFRS will be much less visible . . . I believe the primary effect of local political and market factors will lie under the surface, at the level of implementation, which is bound to be substantially inconsistent across nation.

(Ball, 2006, p. 16)

These two comments represent contrasting attitudes towards IFRS adoption and implementation. Although there are ample benefits in adopting IFRS as a common financial reporting language (Tweedie, 2007), an underlying question remains over the implementation issues because of political and market factors (Ball, 2006).

Debates persist around the justification for IFRS adoption. Two schools of thought exist, and the first is very supportive of the adoption of IFRS, arguing that the adoption of IFRS increases the transparency of financial information and the globalisation of capital markets, and attracts foreign direct investment (FDI) (Taylor and Turley, 1986; Wolk et al., 1989; Larson, 1993; Chamisa, 2000; Tyrrall et al., 2007). The second school of thought, however, is negative about the adoption of IFRS and argues that the Anglo-American nature of IFRS will not be beneficial for the developing countries because of various related factors, e.g. economic, social and, cultural differences (Nair, 1982; Hove, 1989; Perera, 1989; Wallace, 1988, 1993; McGee, 1999; Saudagaran and Diga, 2000; Abd-Elsalam and Weetman, 2003). Some researchers provide mixed opinions on IFRS adoption (Choi and Mueller, 1984; Chandler, 1992; Belkaoui, 2004; Ashraf and Ghani, 2005). Furthermore, financial scandals in the USA and Asia have focused attention on the regulatory bodies (Mitton, 2002; Baek et al., 2002; Tweedie, 2007; Trott, 2009; Bushman and Landsman, 2010). As the IASB possesses no powers of its own to enforce the adoption of its standards, it has to rely on persuading national jurisdictions or national regulators (Banerjee, 2002; Ball, 2006; Ahmed, 2010; Siddiqui, 2010). The relevant EU regulation[2] (1606/2002 of 19 July 2002) requires that all listed EU companies from 1 January 2005 onwards must prepare their consolidated accounts to conform to mandatory IFRS, representing considerable progress towards the goal of global adoption of the IASB's common financial reporting language (i.e. IFRS) (Hodgdon et al., 2009). This announcement has prompted developing countries to think about their position with regard to IFRS compliance (Tyrrall et al., 2007).

There is an increasing amount of literature on compliance with IFRS, in particular with regard to developed countries (Dumontier and Raffournier, 1998 [Switzerland]; Murphy, 1999 [Switzerland]; Street et al., 1999, 2000 [developed and developing countries]; Street and Bryant, 2000 [companies with and without the US listings]; Glaum and Street, 2003; Haller et al., 2009 [Germany]; Yeoh, 2005 [New Zealand]; Dunne et al., 2008 [UK, Italy and Ireland]; Tsalavoutas, 2009, 2011 [Greece]; Cascino and Gassen, 2010 [Germany and Italy]; Lama et al., 2011 [Spain and the UK]). Most previous studies have been concerned with settings where the use of IFRS is voluntary or not subject to national enforcement (Street et al., 1999; Tower, 1993). Following the widespread adoption of IFRS, attention has turned to the extent to which companies comply with IFRS in a mandatory setting (Schipper, 2005; Brown and Tarca, 2005).

However, little attention has been paid to developing countries. Only 11 studies have been conducted on mandatory IFRS compliance in developing countries (see Table 1.1). Table 1.1 shows that companies in these countries do not comply fully with IFRS disclosure requirements and that low compliance levels are common. There are various reasons for IFRS non-compliance: firstly, in terms of language familiarity, the levels of compliance with familiar aspects of IFRS disclosure requirements are significantly higher than the levels of compliance with relatively unfamiliar aspects of IFRS disclosure (Abd-Elsalam and Weetman, 2003 in Egypt). Secondly, from the view of regulatory aspects, significant changes are exhibited in the regulated environment (Al-Shiab, 2003 in Jordan; Abdelsalam and Weetman, 2007 in Egypt; Al-Shammari et al., 2008 in the Gulf Cooperation Council [GCC] member states) – for instance, corporate governance regulations are a very effective mechanism for the implementation of IFRS (Al-Akra et al., 2010 in Jordan). Thirdly, IFRS compliance may be difficult due to poor levels of enforcement – an example of this is that no action has been taken against managers, directors, or auditors for violating accounting rules and regulations in Jordan (Al-Shammari et al., 2008); Finally, in terms of cost-benefit analyses, big companies are inclined to comply with IFRS, whilst small companies tend to decide that the costs exceed the benefits (Fekete et al., 2008, in Hungary). Omar and Simon (2011, p. 184) suggest that 'Regulators should take into consideration the costs and the benefits associated with any plans to increase disclosure for firms which are small, not profitable, not listed in the first tier, in the services sector and not audited by the Big Four.'

It is also found in prior research that Bangladesh has the lowest level of disclosure in terms of IFRS mandatory disclosures (see Table 1.1). These mandatory studies did not reveal the reasons for non-compliance and have not yet reached any comprehensive conclusions, either in a comparative study or in a single country study. The findings provide solid grounds for concerns regarding the implementation of IFRS in a developing country such as Bangladesh where the level of disclosure is so low. It is therefore important to study the factors which are affecting the implementation of IFRS in Bangladesh, as an example of a developing country.

The next section describes the motivation of the study followed by the research questions. Then, I outline the research methods to be used in the study. The summary of findings and the structure of the book are presented next.

Table 1.1 Summary of the findings of mandatory studies on IFRS compliance in developing countries

Author(s)	Country	No. of Comp.	Average Disclosure	Sources
Ahmed and Nicholls (1994)	Bangladesh	63	51.33%	Appendix 3, p. 75
Abd-Elsalam and Weetman (2003)	Egypt	89	83%	Tables 8–9, pp. 78–9
Al-Shiab (2003)[a]	Jordan	50 (300 firm-years)	1998: 51%; 1999: 54%; 2000: 56%	Table 6.23, p. 338
Ali et al. (2004)	Bangladesh India Pakistan	Bangladesh 118; India 219; Pakistan 229	Bangladesh [78%]; India [79%]; Pakistan [81%] *Range: 78%–81%*	Tables 5–6, pp. 194–5
Akhtaruddin (2005)	Bangladesh	94	43.53% [Range: 17% –71.5%]	Table 10, p. 413
Abdelsalam and Weetman (2007)	Egypt	1991–92: 20 1995–96: 72	1991–92: 76% 1995–96: 84%	Tables 4–5, pp. 93–4
Hasan et al. (2008)	Bangladesh	86	Not mentioned	Table 1, p. 200
Al-Shammari et al. (2008)	GCC member countries	436	Bahrain [65%]; Kuwait [72%]; Oman [65%]; Saudi Arabia [75%]; Qatar [69%]; UAE [75%] *Range: 56–80%*	Table 8, p. 17
Fekete et al.(2008)	Hungary	18	62%	Table 4, p. 8
Al-Akra et al. (2010)	Jordan	80	1996: 54.7% 2004: 79%	Table 5, p. 182
Omar and Simon (2011)[b]	Jordan	121	83.12% *Range: 63.87–93.75%*	Tables 12–16, pp. 180–3

Notes:
a Between 1995 and 1997 IFRS were voluntary, therefore the disclosure levels from 1998–2000 are shown;
b the mandatory disclosure items are based on IFRS and the SEC law.

Motivations and rationale of the study

Bangladesh has received considerable attention from international investors following its adoption of an 'open door' economic policy aiming to encourage investment. The country's economy has been described as one of the fastest growing markets in emerging nations (World Bank, 2010). Over the past decade (2000–10), two reports on the observance of standards and codes (ROSC) have been published by the World Bank regarding accounting and auditing practices in Bangladesh. In the first report, the World Bank (2003, p. 1) states that: 'Accounting and auditing practices in Bangladesh suffer from institutional weaknesses in regulation, compliance, and enforcement of standards and rules.' The report also notes that Bangladesh lacks quality corporate financial reporting. After six years had passed, in the follow-up report, the World Bank (2009, p. 25) provided the same sentiments regarding low compliance with accounting standards. The World Bank (2009, p. 10) observed that;

> Efforts to implement IFRS for listed companies and other public interest entities should be accelerated. This will require either more frequent updating of BAS or simply adopting IFRS explicitly . . . Full implementation will also require that current donor assistance to ICAB be maintained, to allow for much needed professional development and expansion in the number of trained auditors and accountants.

The World Bank Newsletter (2009, p. 1) noted that 'With a population of 150 million, Bangladesh has only 750 Chartered Accountants; far too few to meet the needs of the growing economy.'

Bangladesh is one of the world's poorest countries, ranking third after India and China in the extent of its poverty levels (International Fund for Agricultural Development – IFAD, 2006). With an estimated population of over 150 million and per capita income of US$444, Bangladesh has the highest population density in the world (948 per sq km.). More than 63 million people live below the poverty line (United Nations Population Fund – UNFPA, 2008). Bangladesh faces the challenge of achieving accelerated economic growth and alleviating the massive poverty that afflicts nearly two-fifths of its people (UNFPA, 2008). Accordingly, the motivations of this book, on implementing IFRS in developing countries with special reference to Bangladesh, are given below.

Globalisation and the mobilisation of capital markets

Bangladesh as a country possesses distinct features which are relevant in consideration of harmonisation and global convergence issues, including the effects of globalisation and the mobilisation of capital markets. The concept of globalisation may be considered to represent the emergence of an international community where interests and needs can be shared from the developed world (Grieco and Holmes, 1999). Despite the challenges and obstacles of achieving targeted economic growth, Bangladesh made liberal market reforms in the mid-1980s, during the military-backed government (Ahmed, 2010). The aim was to move towards an open economic regime and integrate with the global economy. During the 1990s, notable progress was made in economic performance and, therefore, foreign aid dependency was significantly decreased. For instance, the annual economic growth rate (GDP %) increased during the democratic era: in the 1990s, it was 5.2%, compared to 1.6% during the military era in the mid-1980s (World Bank, 2011; see also Chapter 4).

The stock market in Bangladesh has existed for more than 55 years and has experienced rapid growth – e.g. the price indices have increased 104.42% compared to other stock markets in South Asia (see Table 1.2).[3] Significant growth in the numbers of listed companies and their volume of trading has been evident from 1998 to 2010 (see Figure 1.1). As of 30 June 2011, the Dhaka Stock Exchange (DSE) had 232 listed companies, with a market capitalisation

Table 1.2 Comparison of stock market performances in South Asia

Capital Market	Index	30 June 2008*	30 June 2009*	30 June 2010*	% Change 2009–10	Listed Companies 2011	Turnover (US$ m) 2011	Market Cap (US$ m) 2011	% of GDP 2011
Dhaka (Bangladesh)	DSE GEN	2,795.34	3,010.26	6,153.68	104.42	232	19,501.65	28,501.70	30.76
Colombo (Sri Lanka)	CSE All Share	1,631.34	2,721.64	4,612.46	69.47	277	4,946.20	17,627.41	29.91
Karachi (Pakistan)	KSE 100	5,865.01	7,177.64	9,721.91	35.45	613	9,221.73	37,362.69	18.39
Bombay (India)	SENSEX	9,647.31	14,493.84	17,700.90	22.13	5115	148,488.30	1,351,977.2	91.88

Source: World Federation of Exchanges and http://econstats.com (*accessed 12 February 2012*).

*The closing values of indices from 2008 to 2010 in South Asian stock markets.

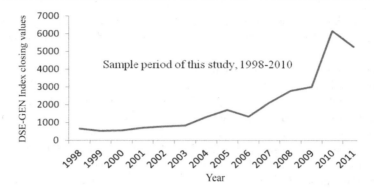

Figure 1.1 Performance of DSE-GEN Index, 1998–2011

of US$28,501.70 million, whereas the market capitalisation of 31 December 1998 was just US$1,034.00 million with around 150 listed companies.[4] While global stock markets have taken a beating, the DSE has performed reasonably well; it was the sixth best performing exchange in the world on a currency-adjusted basis and Asia's best performing benchmark after China's CSI 300 Index in 2008 (Bloomberg, 2008; Financial Express, 2008). Despite the fact that market capitalisation has been increasing significantly since 1998, the size of the country's capital markets remains low (World Bank, 2011).

The opportunity for FDI

Unlike in many other developing countries, FDI is not a major source of investment in Bangladesh. Indeed, FDI fell by 16% from 2006 to 2007 (UNCTAD, 2008). Net FDI turned negative in 2009 (US$110 million) (World Bank, 2011). This is possibly because of the adverse impact of various economic and political factors, including weak macroeconomic conditions, the predominance of public sector enterprises, a small domestic market, and political instability (Financial Express, 2011). Transparency International Bangladesh (TIB, 2005) noted that corruption is the main obstacle to attracting FDI into Bangladesh. Moreover, foreign investment has not increased since the 1970s (Financial Express, 2011). Foreign investors hold only 1% of shares on the DSE market (World Bank, 2011). In this regard, if companies in Bangladesh were to implement IFRS effectively, then this practice might attract foreign investors who rely on financial information provided according to international standards (i.e. IFRS).

Development towards a strengthened regulatory framework

A World Bank report (2009, p. 4) has stated that:

> [The] ICAB has incorporated a number of international standards, but not all have been adopted, and some that have not been updated. The CA [Companies Act] and other legislation also contain provisions that are not consistent with IFRS. Legally, these provisions are superseded by securities regulation, but in practice they still hinder IFRS implementation by companies. For example, many companies do not prepare consolidated accounts because of the general belief that it is not required under the CA.

At least eight major developments towards strengthening regulatory frameworks (directly or indirectly relevant to the corporate financial reporting issues in Bangladesh) are worth noting:

The Bangladesh Chartered Accountants Order, 1973 (P.O. No. 2 of 1973) came into force after independence, for the creation of better professional bodies in Bangladesh. The ICAB was established in 1972 under the Chartered Accountants Order, 1973.

Almost 16 years after independence, Bangladesh formulated its own Securities and Exchange Rules, in 1987. The Securities and Exchange Rules became effective in September that year. These superseded the Securities and Exchange Ordinance, 1969 and the Securities and Exchange Rules, 1971 (S.R.O. 92 (I)/71): In exercise of the powers conferred by section 33 of the Securities and Exchange Ordinance, 1969 (XVII of 1969), and the Ministry of Finance Notification No. S.R.O. 261(I)/79, dated 26 October, 1970. The Securities and Exchange Rules of 1987 emphasised maintaining books of audited accounts and other documents both by the stock exchange and its members (Rules 5, 7, and 8) and a requirement to submit annual and half-yearly reports by the issuers (Rules 12 and 13).

The Government of Bangladesh (GOB) enacted the Securities and Exchange Commission Act 1993 which took effect on 8 June 1993. The SEC is a statutory body and is attached to the Ministry of Finance, part of the government of Bangladesh. Its functions are intended to protect the interests of securities investors, and monitor securities markets.

The Companies Act was enacted in 1994 (Act XVIII) and came into force on 1 October 1995, replacing the old Companies Act of 1913. The Companies Act constitutes the main component of the financial reporting regulatory framework in Bangladesh. The Companies Act 1994 preserves the provisions of the 1913 Act with regard to a nine-month time limit within which companies are required to furnish their financial statements before their AGM. However, the new Act increases the penalty for non-compliance with relevant provision – Tk. 5,000 (Part IVA, Sec. 181, 192).[5]

The stock market crash in July and mid-November 1996 saw both the Dhaka and Chittagong stock exchanges experiencing an unprecedented boom and a subsequent collapse (Daily Star, 1996). During this period, market capitalisation increased by 265% and the average daily turnover increased by over 1,000%. There were about 192 securities listed in total in the two stock exchanges at the time. The share price index at the DSE increased by 281% and by 258% at the Chittagong Stock Exchange (CSE). Then share prices of both the stock exchanges dropped by 25% from the peak in mid-November (Daily Star, 1996). One of the reasons for this unusual rise and fall in securities prices was the artificial manipulation of securities prices carried out by a number of securities dealers and issuers in the absence of timely provision of reliable financial information in the market (Ahmed and Nicholls, 1994). After this market crash, the SEC insisted that the listed companies hold regular AGMs and publish annual reports complying with IFRS. Therefore, the SEC (SEC/Section-7/SER/03/132, dated 22 October 1997) amended the Securities and Exchange Rules of 1987 and required the listed companies to prepare financial statements in compliance with IFRS, as adopted by the ICAB.

The SEC requires that companies listed with any stock exchange in Bangladesh should be subject to certain further conditions, on a 'comply or explain' basis with regard to reasons for non-compliance, in order to improve corporate governance in the interest of investors and the capital market (SEC/CMRRCD/2006–158/Admin/02–06, dated 9 January 2006, Condition No. 5, section 2CC of the Securities and Exchange Ordinance, 1969 [XVII of 1969]). This was later amended by SEC order SEC/CMRRCD/2006–158/Admin/02–08, dated 20 February 2006.

To strengthen accounting and auditing practices in Bangladesh, the SEC – SEC order No: SEC/CMRRCD/2008–181/53/Admin/03/28), dated 4 June 2008, under section 2CC of the Securities and Exchange Ordinance, 1969 (XVII of 1969) – requires that issuer companies shall include the following statements/explanations in their yearly and periodical financial statements: (a) a clear and unambiguous statement of the reporting framework on which the accounting policies are based; (b) a clear statement of the company's accounting policies on all material accounting areas; (c) an explanation of where the accounting standards that underpin the policies can be found; (d) a statement confirming that the financial statements are in compliance with IFRS issued by the IASB, if this is the case; and (e) a statement explaining how the standards and reporting framework used differ from those of IFRS, as issued by the IASB, if this is the case.

The World Bank made initiatives aimed at improving financial reporting practices in Bangladesh under the Economic Management Technical Assistance Programme (EMTAP, called a 'Twinning Project') in 2006. Under this project, some professionals and academics from Bangladesh were sent to London for the ICAEW's IFRS certificate (ICAEW, 2008).[6] Further, the ICAB and Ministry of Finance signed a Memorandum of Understanding (MoU) with the ICAEW to develop a new syllabus in line with International Federation of Accountants (IFAC) requirements in 2009.[7]

Political regimes in Bangladesh (1971–present)

There have been two political patterns in Bangladesh, i.e. democratic and military eras. In 40 years of independence, the military-backed government ruled for 19 years and democratic government for the other 21.

To sum up, for the above significant reasons, Bangladesh is considered to be an ideal setting to study the implementation of IFRS. It is anticipated that an effective implementation of IFRS would allow the provision of transparent information, and may therefore attract FDI.

Research questions

Taking into consideration the above motivations for research, as well as the brief background provided here of the context of IFRS implementation in Bangladesh, this book addresses a 'motivating research question' to examine what factors have been affecting the implementation of IFRS in Bangladesh from 1998 to 2010. The definition of 'implementation' in the context of the present research is: the actual observed outcomes of introducing and monitoring the standards. These outcomes will include the actions of the government, the SEC, ICAB, ICMAB, DSE, and Bangladesh Bank. 'Effective implementation' means the positive outcomes of introducing and monitoring the standards.

In line with the motivating research question and the background of IFRS implementation in Bangladesh, this study will explore the following research questions (RQs):

RQ-1: What is the relative impact of accounting regulatory frameworks and politico-institutional factors on the implementation of IFRS in Bangladesh as an example of a developing country?

RQ-2(a): How do (i) training opportunities in the accounting profession and (ii) the state of corruption, as outcomes of culture in Bangladesh, affect the implementation of IFRS?

RQ-2(b): What other country-specific factors are affecting implementation of IFRS?

RQ-3: How does a study of implementing IFRS help to build an understanding of a theory of the role of the state in accounting change in a developing country such as Bangladesh?

The term 'accounting regulatory frameworks' means relevant regulations with respect to accounting (Companies Act 1994, SEC Rules 1987 and 1997, Banking Companies Act 1991, Dhaka Stock Exchange Listing Rules 1998, Listing Regulations of the Chittagong Stock Exchange, and Income Tax Ordinance 1984) for non-banking and banking sectors in Bangladesh. The term 'politico-institutional factors' in this study means politics and cooperation among state institutions and professional bodies impacting on the implementation of IFRS in Bangladesh.

In this study, the term 'state-society' means the relationship between external (i.e. the role of the state) and internal forces (i.e. individual organisations). This term has been used to explain how external and internal forces have influenced IFRS implementation, as an example of accounting change in Bangladesh.

Research methods: an overview

In terms of research design, a 'deductive approach' (Dubois and Gadde, 2002; Bryman, 2008) is employed in the present study, because the focus of the study is on testing the theory of the role of the state. The objective of this research is to explore the implementation of IFRS in a developing country, emphasising the impact of accounting regulatory frameworks, politico-institutional factors, cultural factors (e.g. training opportunities in the accounting profession, and corruption) and other country-specific factors. Given this consideration, the choice of research methods used in the present study has been informed by the research objectives and research questions.

Prior research argues that when theoretical expectations exist but the appropriate propositions need to be developed, mixed methods can be a useful tool for understanding and validating those theories (Colignon and Covaleski, 1991; Bennett and Braumoeller, 2006; Fuentes, 2008; Hesse-Biber, 2010). These mixed methods have been utilised for three reasons: firstly, a theoretical framework can be developed (Neuman, 2000); secondly, the complementary principle or the acceptability of mixed methods is better than a single method (Tarrow, 2004); thirdly, in terms of the generalisation of the conclusions, mixed methods are likely to contribute towards richer conclusions (Jick, 1979; Maxwell and Loomis, 2003); and finally, in relation to the philosophical views of the research, the present study uses 'critical realism' as a philosophical stance for choosing mixed methods. Critical realism supports mixed methods (Bhaskar, 1978; Archer, 2002; Sayer, 2004; Modell, 2010).

Two phases of data collection process are used to achieve the objectives of the study.

a.   Semi-structured interviews were conducted over a 12-week period, from June to August 2010, during a field trip. A total of 27 interviewees participated in the research. Miles and Huberman (1994) and Patton (2001) argue that six to eight interviews are enough to justify the results of a study. The length of most of the interviews here ranged from 60 minutes to 90 minutes. The interviewees were selected using a non-random stratified sampling method (Gibbs, 2008). The idea is to select interviewees purposively, identifying those who can help the researcher to understand the specific problem and the research question, in this case IFRS implementation issues in Bangladesh (Creswell, 2007, p. 178). This study therefore employed a broad spectrum of respondents, grouped into four defined groups for the interviews, as follows: (a) seven policy makers; (b) 12 accounts preparers and professionals; (c) six users; and (d) two academics/researchers.

The study also conducted a follow-up to the 1st round of interviews in order to investigate IFRS implementation issues in more depth. In particular, the aim was to discover the consistency of the interviewees' views, because the present democratic government was in its third year of power. Therefore, a gap of more than a year existed between conducting the two rounds of interviews (June 2010–September 2011). Although the researcher contacted 27 interviewees (i.e. the 1st-round interviewees), only 12 agreed to follow-ups: four policy makers; four accounts preparers and professionals; two users; and two academics/researchers. The follow-up interviews were conducted in September 2011. In general, follow-up interviews help researchers obtain detailed and in-depth data (Yin, 2003; Creswell, 2007). The questions for the 2nd round of interviews in this study were prepared based on the findings of the 1st round of interviews.

In the second stage of data collection, the study examines the enforcement notices (e.g. those that relate to violations of SEC rules and accounting regulations) issued by the SEC from the beginning of 1998 to the end of 2010. This period of study was selected because of the availability of data and because the SEC mandated IFRS from the beginning of 1998. The enforcement notices contain a very limited number of IFRS-related violations. After carefully reviewing the SEC announcements, I eliminate 57 observations that are repeated from an earlier press release; 24 are not accessible from the website, and so the final sample consists of 1,647 unique observations. However, only 42 of 1,647 enforcement notices are IFRS related. The data analysis in this study follows the procedure of prior research on enforcement notices (Bremser et al., 1991; Feroz et al., 1991; Campbell and Parker, 1992; Rollins and Bremser, 1997; Chen et al., 2005; Files, 2012).

Conclusion

Some studies have been conducted to examine the application of disclosure requirements in Bangladesh (e.g. Ahmed and Nicholls, 1994; Ali et al., 2004; Akhtaruddin, 2005; Hasan et al., 2008). However, there have been no studies on wider implementation issues in Bangladesh. Although this study is specific to Bangladesh, the research contained within it provides findings and conclusions which may be relevant to other developing countries. The results may be useful to other developing countries wishing to implement IFRS and to donor agencies supporting developing countries in implementing IFRS. Researchers can use the results from this study as guidelines for the implementation of IFRS in a developing country. The contributions arising from the three research questions in this study are given below.

RQ-1

In terms of RQ-1, this research discusses the relative impact of accounting regulatory frameworks and politico-institutional factors on the implementation of IFRS in a developing country. The contributions are: firstly, the study finds that politico-institutional factors are stronger and more dominant factors than accounting regulatory frameworks in impeding IFRS implementation in Bangladesh; secondly, a lack of cooperation among the institutional bodies has existed in both democratic and military-backed government eras. However, the military-backed government was more effective than the democratic government in terms of taking action against companies identified as being corrupt. Thirdly, there is evidence of a 'blaming culture' (Hood, 2007, 2009; O'Neill, 2002), with the state institutions and professional bodies blaming each other regarding the IFRS implementation process. This is possibly because 'the blame game' may be aimed at attempting to remove power and responsibility from other institutions in order to facilitate the legitimacy and increase the scope of government bureaucracy.

Finally, unlike prior researchers (e.g. La Porta et al., 1998; Kothari, 2000; Ball et al., 2000, 2003; Leuz et al., 2003) who argue that common-law origin is more transparent in terms of setting accounting standards, in this research, the country's common-law origin has little or no influence on implementing IFRS in Bangladesh. This is possibly because Bangladesh contains an unique environment which may be explained via training opportunities in the accounting profession; corruption; and other country-specific factors.

Some policymaking actions should be taken to facilitate an effective implementation process:

> Contradictions between local laws and the requirements of IFRS should be eliminated by incorporating IFRS in the Companies Act.
>
> Stakeholders should participate in the setting of standards and in publishing exposure drafts and consultation papers on standards at regular intervals.
>
> Tightened enforcement mechanisms (e.g. penalty criteria) should be introduced.
>
> Political lobbying and government intervention in the SEC and the ICAB should be minimised by establishing an independent supervisory board, e.g. a Financial Reporting Council.

RQ-2(a) and (b)

With respect to RQ-2(a) and (b), the contributions of this study are as follows: firstly, this study finds that deficiencies in the training opportunities in the accounting profession itself are impeding IFRS implementation. This finding differs from prior studies in developing countries (Parry and Groves, 1990; Abayo and Roberts, 1993; Ahmed and Nicholls, 1994; Haniffa and Cooke, 2002) that find that training opportunities in the accounting profession has no impact. According to the interviewees, the professional curricula contain limited content on IFRS, while the universities' curricula are without IFRS content at all. Further, the limited training facilities available to accountants are inhibiting IFRS implementation. With the exception of 'big four' and other large companies, the majority of companies are not providing training facilities for their company accountants. Secondly, high levels of corruption in Bangladesh have a negative influence in implementing IFRS. Given the fact that Bangladesh was top of the list of the most corrupt countries in the world for five consecutive years (2001–05), the present study's findings reveal that corruption is deeply rooted in Bangladesh society. Similar to Hofstede et al.'s index of Bangladesh (2010), the World Bank's Governance Indicators Data (2010) and La Porta et al. (1998)'s data (see also Leuz et al., 2003; Han et al., 2012), this study reveals lower rates of enforcement in Bangladesh compared with India and Pakistan. This is due to higher levels of corruption, a factor which weakens enforcement of laws and is marked by a secretive culture. In South Asia, Bangladesh and Pakistan have experienced political instability due to military intervention, and both of these countries have worse than average secrecy and enforcement scores. However, interestingly, corruption was measured as being lower in both countries during periods of military-backed government.

Some policymaking issues can be noted:

- Professional and university curricula should be updated in line with IFRS.
- The salary structure of CAs in Bangladesh should be made much more competitive, similar to India, Pakistan, or Sri Lanka.
- The current democratic government should introduce a culture of transparency in the public and private sector through a depoliticised anti-corruption bureau, to stop widespread corruption.
- The SEC and the ICAB should pressure company management to comply with IFRS.

- The copying of extracts from the notes to the financial statements (e.g. accounting policies) of big companies' financial statements should be subject to higher penalties as imposed by the ICAB.
- State-owned enterprises should not be given the privilege of optional non-compliance with IFRS.
- The SEC should follow stringent enforcement of the laws.

While most listed companies in Bangladesh are family-led businesses and are politically connected, the SEC should make sure that politicians and their associates are not extending their powers in order to violate the SEC rules; the SEC and the ICAB should emphasise the cost-benefit issues for small companies; and shareholders' activism and demand regarding the quality of annual reports available to them should be prioritised by the companies.

RQ-3

In relation to RQ-3, the contributions are as follows: firstly, this study contributes to IFRS implementation as an example of accounting change in a developing country by applying the Weberian view of the theory of the role of the state. Secondly, unlike prior research which did not consider the state–society relationship (i.e. external and internal forces) in accounting change in both developed and developing countries, in this study the adoption of the concept of institutional dynamics (Dillard et al., 2004) allowed me to provide broader understanding of the theory of the state and to overcome some of the limitations of previous studies by considering accounting change on two levels (e.g. external and internal forces). In particular, the outcomes of accounting change in Bangladesh are observed from the state and individual organisation levels. However, the influence of the organisational field level is unknown in this research. Extending Weber's argument on state-society (1958)[1904], 1968)[1922]), the study finds that for a state in an era of democratic government, politico-institutional factors and corruption (as indications of societal values) may be more important and concentrated factors than for a state under a military-backed government in terms of impeding IFRS implementation. The study reveals that all roles of the state have negative influences on accounting change. However, interviewees' initial concerns about the roles of donor agencies are transformed into concerns about the democratic government's failure to implement IFRS. Lastly, since the role(s) of the state are vague in prior accounting research, this study discusses roles of the state (i.e. the state approves experts to write rules; it consults with various stakeholders; it enforces outcomes; it is accountable to its citizens; and it engages with donor agencies) in a developing country's experience during the process of accounting change.

Structure of the book

This book is organised into nine chapters, informed by the research questions, as detailed below.

Chapter 2 presents some interesting areas in the existing literature, since there is no single theory explaining IFRS implementation in developing countries, and most of the studies on adoption and implementation issues are based on developed economies. In particular, theories of the role of the state (RQ-3) identify various key factors: for instance, accounting regulatory frameworks, politico-institutional factors, cultural factors (e.g. training opportunities in the accounting profession and corruption; and other country-specific factors). These factors are discussed to develop some interesting questions around implementing IFRS in developing countries.

Chapter 3 discusses 15 key papers on theories of the role of the state (in particular the Weberian view of the state) in relation to accounting change. The chapter helps develop a theoretical framework (RQ-3) from which to examine RQ-1 and RQ-2(a). More specifically, the role of the state and institutional dynamics are discussed in order to understand the links between the state and individual organisations. Based on the drivers of accounting change, i.e. the most discussed issues in the literature – accounting regulatory frameworks, politico-institutional factors, and cultural factors (e.g. training opportunities in the accounting profession and corruption) – three propositions were developed in Chapter 2. The theory of the role of the state helps to plan the investigation of the three propositions.

Chapter 4 provides some background information on Bangladesh. The chapter describes the political regime in Bangladesh; accounting regulatory frameworks for financial and non-financial companies; the accounting standard setting process, including the status of the adopted accounting standards in Bangladesh; and South Asian regional efforts to implement IFRS. Cultural factors (e.g. accounting profession and corruption issues) in Bangladesh are also outlined and analysed.

Chapter 5 describes the research methodology and methods employed in this book. A discussion of research methods is also provided in this chapter.

Chapter 6 presents the results for RQ-1 (the relative impact of accounting regulatory frameworks and politico-institutional factors). Based on the interview findings and documentary evidence, two propositions (as developed in Chapter 2) are discussed in this chapter. The first proposition relates to the effectiveness of accounting regulatory frameworks, and the second relates to politico-institutional factors in relation to IFRS implementation in Bangladesh.

Chapter 7 presents the results for RQ-2(a) (training opportunities in the accounting profession and corruption) and RQ-2(b) (other country-specific factors). Drawing on the interviews as well as on documentary analyses, the chapter answers proposition three and analyses issues around other country-specific factors. The third proposition was developed in Chapter 2.

Chapter 8 presents the results of RQ-3 (the theory of the role of the state in accounting change). Based on the interviews and enforcement documents, the chapter discusses insights which provide a broader view of the theory of the role of the state and institutional dynamics in explaining the implementation issues for a developing country such as Bangladesh. In particular, the chapter provides theoretical implications in order to gain an understanding of the role of the state and individual organisations, or between external and internal forces (i.e. the state–society relationship).

Chapter 9 provides a summary of the key findings and the contributions of this book. The chapter also highlights limitations and suggestions for further research

Notes

1 Sir David Tweedie, former chairman of the International Accounting Standards Board (IASB), addresses the Economic and Monetary Affairs Committee of the European Parliament, on 10 April 2007.
2 The IFRS Regulation (EC) 1606/2002 concerning the application of international accounting standards was adopted on 19 July 2002 by the European Parliament and the Council. The IFRS Regulation places an obligation on European companies whose securities are admitted to trading on a regulated market in the EU to prepare their consolidated accounts, as of 1 January 2005, in conformity with IFRS and SIC/IFRIC issued by the IASB and endorsed by the EU. Available at: http://ec.europa.eu/internal_market/accounting/docs/ias/com-2008–0215_en.pdf (accessed 12 February 2012).
3 After India, the stock market of Bangladesh is second in the South Asia in terms of turnover (US$ m), market capitalisation (US$ m) and parentage of GDP in 2011 (see Table 1.2).

4 Source: http://www.dsebd.org (accessed 12 February 2012).
5 The values given are in the Bangladeshi currency, the Taka (Tk.). The exchange rate on 31 March 2012 was Tk. 1 = £0.0083 or £1 = Tk. 119.815; source: http://www.hmrc.gov.uk/exrate/ bangladesh.htm.
6 See http://www.icaew.com/en/about-icaew/newsroom/accountancy/features/bangladesh-capacity-building-and-fighting-poverty-162054 (accessed 12 February 2012).
7 Source: http://www.icaew.com (accessed 12 February 2012).

Chapter 2

Review of literature

Introduction

The central aim of this chapter is to discuss the research questions (RQs). More specifically, the chapter seeks to achieve two goals. Firstly, the chapter will help identify unexplored areas in the existing literature, since there is no single theory explaining IFRS implementation in developing countries. Secondly, as most of the studies on adoption and implementation issues so far have been based on developed economies, the present study therefore considers some interesting questions around implementing IFRS in developing countries. In terms of the sequence of the sections, theories of the role of the state (RQ-3) precede RQ-1 and RQ-2 because RQ-3 helps identify various key factors, e.g. accounting regulatory frameworks as well as politico-institutional factors, cultural factors, and other country-specific factors. Further, RQ-3 will help test a theoretical framework through RQ-1 and RQ-2.

The chapter is organised into seven sections. Firstly, the next section evaluates the application of theories of the role of the state to a study of IFRS in developing countries. Then I review the impact of accounting regulatory frameworks and politico-institutional factors on IFRS implementation respectively: cultural factors (e.g. training opportunities in the accounting profession and corruption); and other country-specific factors that may have an impact on IFRS implementation. The final section summarises the chapter.

Theories of the role of the state in relation to accounting

This section aims to explore the role of the state and to examine factors causing accounting change.[1] The section also seeks to understand the underlying problems of IFRS implementation. The literature on the role of the state and accounting change is enormous. In this study, I have undertaken a survey of the prior literature, mainly emphasising accounting journals using version 4 of the Association of Business School Academic Journal Quality Guide, UK.[2] The 45 journals (see Appendix 2.1 for ABS ranking accounting journals) from the ABS ranking and two journals[3] – including *Research in Accounting Regulation* and *Research in Third World Accounting* (retitled *Research in Accounting in Emerging Economies* in 1995) – have been used to locate the relevant articles on the role of the state in relation to accounting change. The focus then turns to the e-journals available in the university integrated database (see Appendices 2.2 and 2.3).[4] Further, the present study employed Google Scholar, using the 'role of the state in relation to accounting change' as a key phrase.[5] The initial electronic trawl through the literature revealed 1,540,000 published 'works' by early 2012, a count that includes editorials, some newspaper articles, conference papers, works with no named authors, and duplicates. To simplify this complexity, I have used the following criteria to exclude papers from the analyses:

a. published working papers which lack author(s) name(s);
b. duplicate articles (e.g. articles that have already been selected from ABS b. ranking accounting journals);
c. editorials and newspaper articles; and
d. articles whose main focus is other than accounting.

Therefore, this study concentrates on articles, book chapters and conference papers. From a survey of Google Scholar, I found 23 papers including 11 articles from other journals, six working papers, five book chapters and one research report (see Table 2.1).

From both of these surveys (56 papers are from the ABS and 23 are from Google Scholar), I find that a range of disciplines have contributed to the literature on the role of the state and accounting change (see Appendix 2.4a and b). I found that 49 papers dealt with theoretical explanations, from a total of 79 papers. More specifically, only 15 out of 49 papers are in relation to the theory of the role of the state and accounting change (see Table 2.2). Three papers have solely focused on developing countries. Finally, the investigation is confined to frequently discussed issues that are covered in the literature rather than delving into other areas of enquiry.[6]

Table 2.1 Articles, papers, book chapters and research reports on the role of the state in relation to accounting, gathered using Google Scholar

Author(s)	Cited (times)
Watts (1977)	3,770
Hoogvelt and Tinker (1978)	35
Solomons (1978)	155
Streeck and Schmitter (1985)	1,274
Rose and Miller (1992)[2010]*	1,855
Walker (1992)	*2*
Napier and Noke (1992)	*33*
Stiglitz (1993)	*1,028*
Zeff (1993)	65
Walker and Robinson (1993)	66
Miller (1994)	*309*
Saudagaran and Diga (1998)	*24*
Klumpes (1998)	*2*
Faccio (2002)	*26*
Ordelheide (2004)	*19*
Leuz and Oberholzer-Gee (2006)	148
Zeff (2006)	*59*
Perry and Nölke (2006)	64
Leuz and Wysocki (2008)	*187*
Nobes and Zeff (2008)	7
Alexander and Servalli (2010)	3
Königsgruber (2010)	10
Zülch and Hoffmann (2010)	0

Notes: The author(s) and citations in italics indicate papers from book chapters, working papers and research reports.
* The article also appeared in 2010 in *The British Journal of Sociology*, 61(s1): 271–303 (special issue: The BJS: Shaping Sociology over 60 years).

Table 2.2 Key papers in relation to the theory of the role of the state and accounting change

Author(s)	Cited (times)	Source ABS journal/ Google Scholar	Country/Not Applicable (N/)A*
Hoogvelt and Tinker (1978)	35	Google	*Sierra Leone*
Tinker (1984)	105	ABS	N/A
Streeck and Schmitter (1985)	1,274	Google	N/A
Miller (1990)	176	ABS	France
Jonsson (1991)	30	ABS	Sweden
Rose and Miller (1992)[2010]	1,855	Google	UK
Krzywda et al. (1995)	28	*ABS*	*Poland*
Caramanis (2002)	54	ABS	Greece
Constable and Kuasirikun (2007)	6	*ABS*	*Thailand*
Moran (2010)	2	ABS	USA and UK
Alexander and Servalli (2010)	3	Google	EU and IASB
Kurunmaki et al. (2011)	2	ABS	N/A
Liguori and Steccolini (2012)	0	ABS	Italy
Norton (2012)	0	ABS	UK and USA
Oehr and Zimmermann (2012)	0	ABS	Germany, Canada and UK

Notes: Italics indicate articles based on developing countries. Not applicable (N/A) means that these articles are purely theory based.

Overview of the state

The concept of the state is very puzzling and difficult to explain (Alexander and Servalli, 2010). Mann (1986, p. 112) argues that 'state is undeniably a messy concept'.[7] It is frequently observed that the concept of the state is confused with government, with a nation-state or country, and with a given type of political regime. In particular, the state is often viewed as a synonym of government in the Anglo-Saxon tradition (Miliband, 1969). Government is regarded as the political elite that occupies the top positions of power in the state (Poulantzas, 1975, 1978). Cassese (1986) indicates that the state has at least 145 different meanings.[8] The evolutionary concept of the 'state' emerged in the sixteenth century and developed through to the nineteenth century (Chabod, 1964).[9]

The debate around the concept of the state has been quite lively (Miliband, 1969; Poulantzas, 1975; Taylor, 1975; Mann, 1986). Hegel, in his work *Philosophy of Right*, provides the broader view, that '[State] is the culmination of the appearance of freedom and reason in the relationships which man always has with those who surround him.'[10] Hegel distinguishes between three levels of social interaction: the family, civil society, and the state (Avineri, 1972, p. 80). However, Lewin et al. (2010, p. 5) argue that the concept of the state is not sufficiently defined in Hegel's writings. The critique of Hegel by Marx is that 'the state becomes the private property of officials in their struggle for self advancement' (Jessop, 1977, p. 354) and this predates the development of a class theory of the state. According to Marx, the state is part of the superstructure and reflects of the economic base (Mann, 1986). Dusza (1989, p. 71) argues that:

> the term 'state' lived on in Marxism, but the class of objects that it denoted was not identified exactly; it was used only as a catchword for the designation of the 'political superstructure . . . Recent works by the so-called neo-Marxists have not gotten farther than attributing to the state a greater degree of 'autonomy' than was proposed by Marx and Engels.

Marx completely rejected the cultural dimension of the state (Tilly, 1973). Tinker (1984, p. 61) also criticises Marx's view, and argues that the conceptual categories of the political economy of Marxism are specific to capitalism and thus neglect the social essence. Both groups start from what Poulantzas (1975) calls the 'relative autonomy' of the state, and both naturally reject liberal theories of the state as a neutral political agent (Carnoy, 1984; Hoffman, 1995; Hay, 1996).

Max Weber's (1968)[1922] concept of the state predominantly focuses on institutions. For Weber, 'the state can be defined in terms of what it looks like, institutionally and that the state is also inclusive of functional institutions within the market and civil society' (Mann, 1986, p. 112). A neo-Marxist like Jessop (1977) agrees that Weber acknowledges the positive effects of strengthening markets (e.g. institutions). Skocpol (1985) strongly argues that the state should be taken seriously as a macrostructure and should be differentiated from liberal and Marxist approaches (i.e. Marxism is fundamentally based on legitimate authority). Focusing on social norms and social conflict (in a 'Tocquevillian' sense, after the French thinker), Skocpol (1985) argues that social norms change over time and culture is seen as a primary determinant of the state. More precisely, the spirit of the Weberian perspective is reflected by Williamson (1985), who argues that to mix state and society represents 'new institutionalist' assertions.[11] From this point of view, the state is a combination of the macro–micro structure of a country.

Using a Weberian view (1968)[1922]) on state-society, Mann (1986, p. 112) argues that the state contains four elements:

(a) A differentiated set of institutions and personnel, embodying; (b) centrality, in the sense that political relations radiate outwards from a centre to cover a; (c) territorially demarcated area, over which it exercises; (d) a monopoly of authoritative binding rule-making, backed up by a monopoly of the means of physical violence.

The state must have a monopoly on the use of force; must be considered to be legitimated by the civil society; and must have the capacity to run a country (Mann, 1986). Explaining the basic functions of a state, Tinker (1984, p. 67) argues that:

The 'function' of the state is 'contract enforcement' in this view; politics is 'the struggle over the law' and over the state's prerogative over legal compulsion (or 'the monopoly of the legitimate use of physical force' to use Weber's famous phrase).

However, debates on power[12] still remain within Weber's concept of the state (Dusza, 1989). The socio-cultural or extra-societal allegiances[13] can tighten the relationship between 'state' and 'society' within social relationships (Robertson, 1990, p. 19). The World Bank (1997, p. 20) in a world development report, *The State in a Changing World*, provides practitioners' views of the Weberian concept:

State in its wider sense, refers to a set of institutions that possess the means of legitimate coercion, exercised over a defined territory and its population, referred to as society. The state monopolizes rule making within its territory through the medium of an organized government.

In accounting literature, the meaning of the state is ambiguous (Jonsson, 1991; Rose and Miller, 1992[2010]; Moran, 2010; Kurunmaki et al., 2011; Norton, 2012; Alexander and Servalli, 2010; Liguori and Steccolini, 2012), and most of the literature (Hoogvelt and Tinker, 1978; Krzywda et al., 1995; Caramanis, 2002; Constable and Kuasirikun, 2007; Oehr and

Zimmermann, 2012) ignores any exploration of the meaning of the state. A few studies – like Tinker (1984), Streeck and Schmitter (1985) and Miller (1990) – argue that the meaning and application of the state depend on the context of the study.

Definition of the state for this study

The state in this study means a set of institutions and roles (rules and actions over a territory or society) in the processes of accounting change (i.e. the actual observed outcomes of introducing and monitoring the standards). There are different meanings of institutions. Institutions are governance structures based on rules, norms, values, and systems of cultural meaning (North, 1990). Institutions are defined by Ostrom (1990, p. 51) as;

> the set of working rules that are used to determine who is eligible to make decisions in some arenas, what actions are allowed or constrained, what aggregation rules will be used, what procedures must be followed, what information must or must not be provided, and what payoffs will be assigned to individuals dependent on their actions.

Jepperson (1991), on the other hand, defines institutions as any social pattern characterised by standard sequences of interactions. In economics, institutions serve to minimise market transaction costs (North, 1990). In sociology, institutions are social structures which come to be sanctioned by norms and values, facilitate political cooperation, and reduce uncertainties (Hopwood, 1990, 1999). In this study, I focus on state institutions and professional bodies (i.e. the government, ministerial bodies, accountancy professional bodies, the stock exchange, the Securities and Exchange Commission and the central bank). Based on the concept of this section, the next section will discuss the role of the state in accounting change.

Role of the state and accounting change

I have used a particular definition of the state for this study (as mentioned in the previous section) because this particular meaning signifies the role of the state and accounting change within a society. Since the accounting literature suggests different meanings of the state, and the meanings depend on the purpose of the study, I follow the definition for three reasons: (a) the state is linked with the market and society (Weber, 1968[1922]); (b) it helps us to understand the role of the state (World Bank, 1997); and (c) the concept can inform policymakers and practitioners as to why some states are more effective than others (World Bank, 1997). One implicit caution is that this study focuses on the role of the state, but not to find out the meaning of the state.

In terms of accounting change, Napier (2006, p. 445) states that: 'Accounting has changed, is changing, and is likely to change in the future.' This statement might almost be regarded as a truism (Constable and Kuasirikun, 2007). Accounting methods, techniques, ideas, and practices differed in 2005 from those which were prevalent in 1975 or earlier (Napier, 2006). The state's role regarding accounting change has been largely ignored by historians, accountants and social scientists (Constable and Kuasirikun, 2007, p. 574). In a recent study, Liguori and Steccolini (2012, p. 28) argue that accounting is recognised as playing a fundamental role in organisational change. They demonstrate different outcomes of accounting change in the presence of similar environmental pressures. Accounting researchers are devoting greater attention to the social, political, and economic forces influencing accounting change (Parkinson, 1984; Pushkin and Pariser, 1991; Napier, 2006; Liguori and Steccolini, 2012).

Prior studies have established some links between the role of the state and accounting change (e.g. Tinker, 1984; Streeck and Schmitter, 1985; Miller, 1990; Moran, 2010; Alexander and Servalli, 2010). Roles of the state include:

a. approving experts (e.g. professional bodies) to write rules (Tinker, 1984; Jonsson, 1991; Alexander and Servalli, 2010; Moran, 2010; Norton, 2012);
b. consulting with various stakeholders (e.g. investors, professionals and researchers) for the validation of rules (Streeck and Schmitter, 1985; Rose and Miller, 1992 [2010]; Kurunmaki et al., 2011; Oehr and Zimmermann, 2012);
c. enforcing outcomes (Hoogvelt and Tinker, 1978; Krzywda et al., 1995); and
d. initiating change because the state is accountable to its citizens (Miller, 1990; Constable and Kuasirikun, 2007).

In order to explore the role of the state and accounting change, I have used articles from several sources – in particular the ABS and Google Scholar – and focused on the most frequently discussed issues in the literature (the process of selecting articles is described earlier in this chapter). However, only 15 key papers are identified in relation to the theory of the role of the state and accounting change. The most frequently debated issues (drivers of accounting change) from 79 papers – namely accounting regulatory frameworks, politico-institutional factors, and cultural factors – are discussed later in this chapter.[14]

This section has provided a generic discussion of the theories of the role of the state in relation to accounting change. As discussed in the previous section, 'the state' has many meanings and these can depend on the purpose of a study. Further, theories of the role of the state have been employed in relatively limited areas of accounting research; and, therefore, the theoretical literature implies that there is a gap in the application of the theories in relation to IFRS implementation. In the present study, I follow the Weberian concept of state (which will also be discussed in Chapter 3, relating to the theoretical framework).

As indicated, I have identified the three most frequently discussed issues in the literature in terms of the role of the state in relation to accounting change (i.e. accounting regulatory frameworks, politico-institutional factors, and cultural factors). These three issues will be discussed in later sections. More specifically, theories of the role of the state will be discussed in Chapter 3, in order to develop the theoretical framework for the present study.

Accounting regulatory frameworks

As mentioned in Chapter 1, 'accounting regulatory frameworks' in this study means relevant regulations with respect to accounting (Companies Act 1994; SEC Rules 1987, 1997; Banking Companies Act 1991; Dhaka Stock Exchange Listing Rules 1998; Listing Regulations of the Chittagong Stock Exchange; and the Income Tax Ordinance 1984) for non-banking and banking sectors in Bangladesh. The classification of accounting systems may differ because of various factors: legal, political, institutional, and cultural (see Chapter 1). This section provides the extant literature on 'accounting regulation',[15] with specific focus on the regulatory process, the standard setting process and its implementation, and the 'enforcement' mechanism of regulation into practice. The literature on accounting regulation is vast, and prior research focuses on different dimensions of regulation. However, the questions of particular interest to this section are: How does the regulatory process and standard setting process emerge? and With regard to its impact on IFRS implementation, what actions may be taken to ensure compliance with the standards as 'enforcement mechanisms?

Accounting regulatory process

Studies of the regulatory process have highlighted the changing relationships and tensions between the state and the profession, and how these vary according to national contexts (see Appendix 2.4a). From a historical point of view, researchers show that the state in Anglo-American countries (excluding the UK) has had a longstanding involvement with the development of accounting rules.[16] The state agencies help to create a demand for general financial management services, particularly within regulated firms (Jones, 1981). But this political involvement raises questions around the existence of a transparent regulatory process (Zeff, 2007).

Various empirical studies have employed the legal framework of La Porta et al. (1998) to examine the impact of the legal environment on the properties and quality of financial reporting. Most studies confirm the usefulness of such legal frameworks. Some of them, particularly, employ a legal system dichotomy, code-law versus common-law, to examine the association of legal systems with financial disclosure (Solomons, 1978; Bloom et al., 1998; Ball et al., 2000; Jaggi and Low, 2000; Naciri and Hoarau, 2001). Kothari (2000) presents a 'demand-supply argument'. Kothari (2000, p. 91) argues that 'a demand, and therefore supply, of quality financial information will be high in a common-law legal system'. As Alexander and Archer (2000, p. 550) put it: 'common law tradition coupled with private sector standard setting leads to a more flexible and responsive system for accounting regulation'. Ball et al. (2003) provide an 'irregularities argument' with respect to four East Asian common-law countries. In terms of 'irregularities argument' (i.e. a common-law vs. code-law approach), Ball et al. (2003, p. 235) argue that the IASB's standards derive from common-law sources (UK, US and IFRS) which are widely viewed as being of a higher quality – e.g. 'common-law approach of IFRS is transparent'(Ball et al., 2000, p. 47) – than code-law standards. Ball et al. (2003) find that a common-law legal system has a very detailed, prescriptive set of accounting standards that have little to do with the nature of the legal system.

By contrast, a codified law system made by the statute law to promulgate accounting rules leaves considerable scope for flexibility (Parker and Nobes, 1994). The common-law tradition tends to protect investors more than code-law (La Porta et al., 1998, 1999). Inchausti (1997) argues that it may not be possible to leave disclosure to the market alone, and it may be necessary to regulate accounting in order to ensure that firms satisfy the information needs of different users in Spain.

The prior literature provides contradictory views regarding the impact of government involvement in the accounting regulatory process. Firstly, government involvement can be seen as positively influential towards the regulatory process (Carpenter, 1991). For example, Masel (1983) feels that government authority is usually the only acceptable form of coercion in a standard setting process. Saudagaran and Diga (1997) find that in all five ASEAN countries, both government agencies and professional accounting bodies are well represented and actively involved in the formulating and enforcing of accounting regulations. Taplin et al. (2002) examine the extent of IFRS compliance in six Asia-Pacific countries[17] and find that companies in the four countries with British colonial links (Australia, Hong Kong, Malaysia and Singapore) have higher levels of disclosure. They call for more direct government intervention in achieving *de facto* harmonisation (Taplin et al., 2002, p. 172).

Secondly, research into the 'politics'[18] of the accounting regulatory process reflects not just social and economic developments but also the view of national power (Moran, 2010). National accounting has been characterised as closely linked to the exercise of national power (Miller, 1986). Consequently, the interrelations between accounting and the state have been viewed as central to the understanding of accounting change (Miller, 1990). In this context,

Puxty et al. (1987) highlight the point that the institutions and processes of accounting regulation in different nation-states cannot be understood independently of the historical and politico-economic contexts of their emergence within these respective states. So, it is a strange irony that while accounting in the former socialist countries is developing in the context of moving from a command economy, accounting in the advanced capitalist countries is increasingly being influenced by state regulation (Puxty et al., 1987). Cooke and Wallace (1990) conclude that the level of corporate financial disclosure regulation in many developed countries is more likely to be determined by internal factors, and that most developed countries are highly regulated, whereas regulation in many developing countries is more likely to be determined by external factors. Willmott et al. (1992) examine four capitalist countries[19] and find that accounting regulation in those countries is shaped by the disciplinary effects of hierarchical control (social order organised through bureaucratic agencies). Alexander and Micallef (2011, p. 19) argue that:

> the clarity of the applicable financial reporting regulatory framework, and the practical application of it, are of utmost importance. This is because a clear regulatory framework is needed to act as a central source of reference of the accounting principles requiring adherence to, and for a system of enforcement of, those principles. Consequently, greater specification and precision is required when amending an existing regulatory framework.

To overcome the structural weaknesses in developing countries, Banerjee (2002) proposes that direct government intervention is necessary to reform accounting regulations. In a Hungarian study, Boross et al. (1995) conclude that, while the impact of the move to the market economy is a visible factor both in the drafting of the law and in the perceptions of the likely users of the financial statements, the influence of state regulation still remains. Zeff (1995) suggests collaboration between a private sector standard setting body and a government regulatory body. Whilst the importance of accounting regulations in the internationalisation of policy regimes is now seen almost as a cliché (Jessop, 1990), many studies at the international level tend to focus on one particular 'international' institution or standard: much less attention is given the polycentric, network, or coordinated character of 'regulation work' and the complexity of relations between national agencies (Caramanis, 2002).

The standard setting process and its implementation

States have been taking an increased interest in accounting standards, seeing them as an important element of their financial policies (Cooper and Robson, 2006; Laughlin, 2007). Whittington (2005, p. 151) argues that 'Implementation of standards is of critical importance to the success of international standards . . . if this is not achieved, international standards will not command respect, however good their intrinsic quality.' The need to understand the process of accounting standard setting and its implementation in different countries is widely recognised (Choi and Mueller 1978). It is essential to consider the influence of the nation-specific environment on that process in each case (Previts, 1975; Nair and Frank, 1980). Miller and Redding (1988, p. xi) note that 'By its very nature, standards setting is very much a matter of politics.' Alexander and Archer (2000, p. 555) argue that 'The future of accounting standard setting at the national level may be in question.' The inevitably political nature of standard setting has been considered over many years by researchers across various jurisdictions.

The political nature of accounting standards setting has long been recognised (Moonitz, 1974; Fogarty, 1992) and there has been continued debate on the subject. Over the years, the accounting profession has sought to control the regulatory process as part of maintaining its authority within the traditional boundaries of its discipline; but at the same time, other interested parties and professions have seen opportunities therein to expand their spheres of influence (Perry and Nölke, 2006). In particular, governments have found wider benefits by granting, in the name of consensus, privileged access to the policymaking process to certain interest groups (Lehmbruck and Schmitter, 1982), which raises questions around the government's role in standard setting. However, the issues underpin the government's influence and position on the adopted standards in line with the terms of local national standards handling (Saudagaran and Diga, 2000). Walton (2009, p. 4) strongly criticises politicians' involvement in the standard setting process and argues that 'accounting standard-setting achieves nothing when politicians take it over. You wouldn't ask politicians to design a car for you, because they do not have the necessary knowledge and experience. Why would they be competent to write standards?'

It has been recognised that accounting information affects behaviour (Zeff, 1978). Watts (1977, 1980) argues that financial statements are products both of markets and of political processes (the interactions between individuals and interested groups). This implies that accounting standards are not 'neutral' with respect to political, economic and cultural factors (Leuz et al., 2004). The politics of setting standards is a principal concern in a developing country such as Armenia (Bloom et al., 1998). Stoddart (2000) finds evidence of lobbying actions by standard-setting bodies which are part of a much wider political process in Australia. He argues that the structure of setting accounting standards in Australia has substantially shifted in terms of power from the two professional accounting bodies (the ICAA and the ASCPA) to the government. Despite the existence of governmental influence on accounting standard setting in Australia, Miller (1996) claims that accounting standard setting in Australia is open, neutral, and independent because all stakeholders have a chance to make submissions on accounting issues within the 'due process' so that an equilibrium outcome is achieved. Similar findings are reported by Naciri and Hoarau (2001), who argue that the French standard-setting system is 'political'.

In China, Ezzamel et al. (2007) have analysed the relationship between political-economic factors and accounting standards setting during the transition from a state-controlled economy under Mao to a 'socialistic market economy' under Deng, and they find that in both eras accounting is construed as a malleable object shaped by the force of the dominant political discourse. Peng and Bewley (2009) also find evidence that Chinese standard setting is controlled, directly or indirectly, by powerful interests and the state, e.g. the Ministry of Finance. On the EU experience, Whittington (2005, p. 143) documents that:

> President Chirac of France wrote a much publicised letter to President Prodi of the EU expressing anxiety that the IASB standards were not sensitive enough to European interests and that, in particular, volatility resulting from application of the standards would be damaging to the European economy.

Zülch and Hoffmann (2010) illustrate evidence of linkages between parliamentarians and interest groups in the course of accounting standard setting in Germany.

In a similar vein, Königsgruber (2010) argues that if the relevant standard setters wish to achieve a harmonisation of accounting standards between the EU and the US, European companies have more lobbying leverage than their American counterparts because there are more political lobbying groups in the EU. Similar findings are reported by Chiapello and Medjad (2009). Mixed evidence exists within the USA. Whilst Naciri and Hoarau (2001) argue that accounting standards are based on a structure of 'coordinated concepts' in the USA, Zeff (2002) finds that political influence occurs because three actors are involved in the accounting legislative process (i.e. the Senate, the House of Representatives, and the president). In a cross-country study, Ball et al. (2000) conclude that in code-law countries, the comparatively strong political influence on accounting occurs at national and firm levels because the government establishes and enforces national accounting standards, typically with representation from major political groups. By contrast, the demand for accounting income under code-law is influenced more by payout preferences and less by a demand for public disclosure. However, the classification of Ball et al. (2000) contradicts an earlier study by Nobes (1998).[20]

Setting standards which are inconsistent with users' expectations could undermine the viability of a new regulatory system in a developing country (Bloom et al., 1998). To implement standards, accounting standards must fit the social, economic, and political climate of their countries (Naciri and Hoarau, 2001). Prior research offers a way to establish effective accounting standards-setting bodies (Jonsson, 1991; Laughlin, 2007; Christensen et al., 2010). For instance, Jonsson (1991) calls for an extended form of consultation before legal texts (e.g. accounting regulations) are formulated. This process of formulating regulations will then become public and the state may be said to have earned this legitimacy. Laughlin (2007, p. 277) argues that 'accounting, and, by implication, accounting regulation, needs to serve the accounting information needs of all stakeholders and not just shareholders and other finance providers'. He further emphasises that 'freedom guaranteeing' (i.e. amenable to substantive justification) mechanisms should always be viewed as the ideal model to aspire to in formulating regulations, rather than 'freedom reducing' ones (i.e. those which are 'legitimised only through procedure'). In a recent study, Kvaal and Nobes (2012, p. 367) report that the persistence of national patterns of policy choices makes it likely that there is persistence of international difference on IFRS topics. Zeff (2012, p. 833) argues that 'There is a great deal of variability in the effectiveness of regulator performance even within the EU . . . especially in emerging economies and developing countries.'

Enforcement mechanism of regulation

Hail et al. (2010, p. 575) argue that 'The implementation and enforcement aspects of global accounting convergence are largely missing from the IFRS debate, which we view as a serious shortcoming.' Christensen et al. (2010) point out that the effects of accounting regulation depend, crucially, on implementation and enforcement. To understand the 'enforcement mechanism', Foucault (1977, p. 23) offers a theory of power (the 'panopticon'),[21] which is laid out in the introductory section of the book *Discipline and Punish*. Foucault (1977, p. 47) draws down the principle of Bentham, that power should be visible and unverifiable.[22] Zimmerman (1998) argues that the panopticon idea becomes more powerful because power becomes more efficient through the mechanisms of observation available in modern society. A possible criticism of the idea of panopticon is that 'it is at once too little, for what matters is that he knows himself to be observed; and too much, because he has no need in fact of being so'(Butler, 1997, p. 35).

In terms of accounting regulation, the panopticon metaphor sheds light on and aims at identifying and preventing irregularities. Consequently, law enforcement mechanisms control all sorts of irregularities (Anechiarico and Jacobs, 1995, p. 362). Without enforcement 'the production of accounting rules will be nothing more than symbolic behaviour' (Walker, 1985, p. 12). Parker (1986) suggests that the enforcement stage should be given to the entity equipped with the power to enforce, i.e. the government. Zeff (1988, p. 20) supports this view that the government agency is in a much better position to enforce compliance with accounting standards. Walker (1990, p. 543) strongly argues that 'A serious weakness encountered by any private standard-setting agency may be the lack of true authority to enforce accounting standards.' Watts and Zimmerman (1986) earlier pointed out that market failures can be reduced by government regulation. The government therefore needs to play a more direct role in the design and enforcement of accounting standards (Watts and Zimmerman, 1990; Tower, 1993).

The prior studies have employed broad measures of legal enforcement, such as the efficiency of the judicial system (Hope, 2003; Leuz et al., 2003; Norton, 2012; Zeff, 2012). Jaggi and Low (2011) suggest that strict securities regulations in weak investor-protection countries play an important role in audit pricing because of higher effort and risk being involved in audits. Zeff (2012, p. 833) points out that 'A commitment by a country that its listed companies are required to use IFRS lacks credibility if it is not backed up by a vigilant and proactive regulator, whether in the private or public sector.' In a recent study, Houqe et al. (2012) highlight the importance of investor protection for financial reporting quality.

However, Coffee (2007, p. 80) observes that 'The United States employs an inefficient regulatory model, by allocating disproportionately high resources to enforcement of the law and punishment of securities fraud after it has occurred and been detected.' Later, Ball (2009, p. 316) confirms that there is a considerably lower frequency of reporting fraud in the UK, where the FSA regulates securities markets in a more consultative fashion and with less emphasis on enforcement after the fact; and there is a noticeable comparative success for the US system in detecting and correcting financial reporting fraud, but not in deterring it in the first instance. Nevertheless, reporting and disclosure would be very likely to be less adequate in developing countries because of the political nature of the enforcement (Belkaoui, 1983).

Researchers like Wagenhofer (2011), Leuz (2010), and Rahman (2000) argue that more regulation increases reporting quality. Wagenhofer (2011, p. 230) argues that regulators should delegate standards setting to an independent standards board. The standard setters then receive more weight of public trust than political trust. Ernstberger et al. (2010) report that regulatory reforms in enforcement have increased the degree of enforcement in Germany. Similarly, Hitz et al. (2012, p. 276) find that the two-tier enforcement systems (Deutsche Prüfstelle für Rechnungslegung [DPR] and Bundesanstalt für Finanzdienstleistungsaufsicht [BaFin]) have been working closely towards strong enforcement in Germany since 2005. The quality of accounting information is a function of both the quality of accounting standards and the enforcement of those standards, and therefore high-quality accounting standards with wide acceptance and effective enforcement mechanisms are necessary to create a transparent environment for investors (Rahman, 2000; World Bank, 2000; ADB, 2001).

Accounting standards on their own are ineffective mechanisms of regulation (Kothari, 2000). Kothari (2000, p. 90) argues that 'Demand, and therefore supply, of quality financial information will be high if corporations are best described as owned by widely dispersed, individually atomistic shareholders. High-quality investor protection laws, good enforcement of these laws, and a common-law legal system collectively are conducive to diffusely owned corporations.' This argument is important in terms of distinguishing between the quality of laws and effective implementation of the laws. For example, infrastructural arrangements for implementing and enforcing standards are important in giving accounting standards the capability to make accounting information relevant for capital markets (Hail et al., 2010). Saudagaran and Diga (2000) classify enforcement mechanisms into preventive and punitive enforcement mechanisms (preventive arrangements encourage and facilitate compliance, and punitive arrangements force compliance or lead to penalties for non-compliance). Thus, effective punitive enforcement will increase the confidence of investors in the credibility of financial reports, since any violation of standards would be punished (Rollins and Bremser, 1997). Saudagaran (2009) suggests that the government regulatory bodies and the accounting profession in developing countries suffer from structural weaknesses and often take a lenient attitude that results in inevitable non-compliance with standards, and calls for stronger enforcement mechanisms. For example, Karampinis and Hevas (2011) argue that in unfavourable economies like Greece with inadequate institutional infrastructures (e.g. a code-law tradition, bank orientation, concentrated corporate ownership, poor shareholder protection, and low regulatory quality), the implementation of mandatory IFRS is not effective. In contrast, in favourable economies like the USA, the findings of Files' study (2012, p. 371) suggest that 'firms are rewarded for co-operative behaviour, although the reward is manifested through lower penalties rather than a reduction in sanctions'. The result implies that the SEC's criteria for leniency following a law violation in the USA means that even the market reacts negatively to news of an SEC enforcement action or investigation (Feroz et al., 1991).

In order to have a sound financial system, high-quality, generally acceptable accounting standards and an effective enforcement mechanism have to be presented concurrently (Zeff, 1988; Ball, 2001). Since the goal of uniform enforcement raises particular challenges, including coordination of enforcement activities and sanctions in the EU (Brown and Tarca, 2005, p. 204), the study by Berger (2010, p. 18) recommends delegation of authoritative power to the Committee of European Securities Regulators (CESR) in the EU to ensure that effective enforcement is being implemented. Otherwise, the motivation of global IFRS will not be achievable. Holthausen (2009,p. 457) therefore argues that: 'As such, the "standards" themselves will become less uniform over time . . . which will lead to further differences in financial reporting over time, unless the underlying economic and institutional forces across countries become more similar.' To mitigate uniformity problems in global enforcement, Leuz (2010, p. 252) recommends that:

> [The] key message is that there are substantial enforcement differences around the world. . . . Thus, I propose . . . to create a GPS, in which firms play by the same reporting rules (i.e. IFRS), face the same enforcement, and are likely to have similar incentives for transparent reporting. The GPS could be created and operated by IOSCO or other supranational institutions . . . it would provide comparable enforcement across participating firms.

By contrast, Ball (2006, p. 15) argues that 'Despite increased globalization, most political and economic influences on financial reporting practice remain local . . . [a] toothless body of international enforcement agencies [is] currently in place.' Christensen et al. (2010) find that the same forces that have limited the effectiveness of securities regulation in the past are playing significant roles when new rules are introduced. This has important implications for the expected outcomes of regulatory reforms across countries in the EU.

Proposition I

In summary, the prior research suggests contradictory results with respect to accounting regulatory frameworks. The literature suggests that government involvement positively/negatively influences the regulatory process. However, power struggles and conflicts of interest exist in the regulatory process. Researchers such as Boross et al. (1995), Zeff (1995) and Banerjee (2002) call for a collaboration between a private sector standard-setting body and the government regulatory body in order to create effective regulation. Further, the standard-setting process has been evidenced as being political in nature, in both developed and developing countries. Without proper enforcement of the standards, the quality of accounting standards alone will not increase transparency. In developing countries, government regulatory bodies often take a lenient attitude towards creating effective enforcement mechanisms. The following questions still remain: firstly, do the regulatory and standard setting processes positively/negatively influence IFRS implementation in a developing country?; secondly, what effective enforcement mechanism(s) have been used by developing countries to implement IFRS, and are the enforcement mechanism(s) (un)even in their implementation of IFRS?

The prior research provides the reasons for positive/negative influence being exerted on accounting change, including: (a) the legal origins of the country (common-law/code-law); (b) high/low-quality investor protection laws; (c) stakeholders' participation/non-participation in the standard setting process; and (d) stringent/looser enforcement of the laws (i.e. the efficiency of the judicial system and punitive penalties/fines, and vice versa). This section leads to the first research proposition (P_I) of this study:

P_I: Accounting regulatory frameworks will have a positive influence on implementation of IFRS under the conditions of (a) common-law origin; (b) high-quality investor protection laws; (c) stakeholders' participation in the standard setting process; and (d) stringent enforcement of the laws.[23]

or

Accounting regulatory frameworks will have a negative influence[24] on implementation of IFRS under the conditions of (a) code-law origin; (b) low-quality investor protection laws; (c) stakeholders' non-participation in the standard setting process; and (d) looser enforcement of the laws.

Politico-institutional factors

As indicated in Chapter 1, 'politico-institutional factors' in this study means politics and co-operation among state institutions and professional bodies on the implementation of IFRS. With respect to politico-institutional factors, in this section I discuss how government intervention and political lobbying will likely play an important role in the implementation of IFRS.

Government intervention[25]

> Accounting is a big house that has accommodated many political regimes during the several hundred years of its existence without losing its identity . . . the politics of accounting unquestionably played an important role.
>
> (Ordelheide, 2004, p. 270)

Government interventions are complex and varied (McKinnon, 1984). The socio-political and socio-economic dimensions of accounting policy determination have emanated largely from Anglo-American nations, in particular the USA. Bushman and Piotroski (2006, p. 115) ask: 'Why would politicians care about accounting numbers? Accounting information is not the sole source of information of a company.' Explaining the different ways in which government intervention in the economy may emerge, the literature has been classified into two sets: *public choice* (Mueller, 1967) and *theories of economic regulation* (Posner, 1974). Buchanan (1962) argues that welfare economics and the public choice tradition can be powerful tools for explaining government intervention. Watts and Zimmerman (1978) explain that certain groups of voters have an incentive to lobby for a regulatory process. This idea that politicians seek to intrude into the affairs of corporations and redistribute wealth away from them comes from the earlier work of Stigler (1971), Peltzman (1976) and Jensen and Meckling (1976). Further, politicians create crises and then come to the rescue with simple legislative solutions. For example, a crisis in which unions and monopolies are creating inflation requires price controls (Peltzman,

1976). These 'solutions' almost invariably increase the resources controlled by government, and hence the resources controlled by the elected representatives who constitute the government (Meckling, 1976, p. 21). To counter such pressure from politicians, Watts and Zimmerman (1978, p. 115) suggest that:

> corporations employ a number of devices, such as social responsibility campaigns in the media, government lobbying and selection of accounting procedures to minimize reported earnings . . . management can reduce the likelihood of adverse political actions and, thereby, reduce its expected costs. The magnitude of the political costs is highly dependent on firm size.

Cooper (1995, p. 179) argues that the state creates political and economic compromises and that these compromises are universal interests.

In terms of political influence and accounting changes, prior studies suggest that politics are negatively associated with the development of accounting systems and accounting change. In a study of Japan, Reischauer (1977, p. 139) argues that the cultural attribute of Japanese society derives from the precept, from Confucius, of the natural existence of 'the ruler' (bureaucracy) and 'the ruled' (the people). The role of the government in policy determination operates through a heavy reliance on bureaucracy (Fukui, 1981, p. 186). McKinnon (1984, p. 318) provides several factors that contribute to the intensification of government involvement in accounting policy determination in Japan: first, administration of corporate financial disclosure under the SEC law is the direct responsibility of the Ministry of Finance; second, accounting standards in Japan are formulated by the Business Accounting Deliberation Council (BADC), but standards are issued and enforced as Ministry of Finance ordinances; and third, the Ministry of Finance, through its administration of the CPA law, controls registration and deregistration and oversees the activities of the Japanese Institute of Certified Public Accountants (JICPA). Consequently, 'blame' for perceived 'crises' of inadequate financial disclosure at both national and international level in Japan is channelled directly to the Ministry of Finance. In most Anglo-American nations, by contrast, this 'blame', where necessary, is typically spread more broadly across the accounting profession and independent or quasi-governmental regulatory authorities.

Xiao et al. (2004) is one of the very first studies providing evidence of political influence on IFRS implementation in China. They conclude that the government of China is in part self-motivated, and in part under external pressure to develop IFRS for accounting harmonisation purposes. They claim that 'Chinese people have political sensitivity regarding foreign accounting theory and practice' (Xiao et al., 2004, p. 214). Political factors, in particular the direct involvement of the government in accounting regulation, have weakened the demand for, and supply of, accounting standards, making it difficult to adopt IFRS. Chen et al. (2011) find that government intervention distorts firms' investment behaviour and leads to investment inefficiency in China. This is because the majority of appointments of state-owned enterprise (SOE) managers are political, and their motive is political rather than for profit maximisation (Wu et al., 2012). The study by Leuz and Oberholzer-Gee (2006) can be viewed as claiming a greater influence of politics in developing countries like Indonesia. Their findings are consistent with an earlier study in East Asia by Knowles and Garces (2000), who reported that high-level government intervention resulted in government-owned firms which were less efficient.

In terms of political institutions, Bushman and Piotroski (2006, p. 141) find that firms in common-law based countries facing high state involvement in their economy tend to speed up recognition of good news. In contrast, in civil law based countries, high state involvement leads firms to speed up recognition of bad news. In a similar study, Ball et al. (2003) earlier document that only the institutional characteristic (i.e. common or civil law legal origin) is directly incorporated in accounting practices in four East Asian economies. In a recent study, Oehr and Zimmermann (2012) find that the state's involvement in accounting is much deeper in Germany (which has a civil law origin), and the regulative process is not only an outcome of the political process but is also consistent with national societal motives and values. Despite the legal classification, Bushman and Landsman (2010) strongly argue that political forces affect the regulation of firm-level information and accounting standard setting, in particular when accounting information is perceived to potentially affect the stability of the financial markets.

Three studies find that government intervention has little or no influence in accounting disclosure. For instance, Giroux (1989) examines the disclosure quality relationships based on the political and economic incentives of the groups who are actively involved in governmental processes. The result suggests that each group in possession of political power has only a limited influence on the disclosure quality. Similarly, Nobes (1998, p. 176) notes that political factors do not have major explanatory power to discuss the accounting systems in the developed western countries. Later, Laughlin (2007, p. 280) argues that government interventions are not an essential factor, as, for example: 'when there is no intervention it can be assumed that government is still watching but they are content that the current regulatory activities are working in their perception of the public interest'.

By contrast, some studies strongly emphasise that government intervention is essential. For example, Jaggi (1975, p. 84) argues that:

> Interference by governments may be essential to ensure higher reliability (which is vital for the expression of industries in these countries), for creating public confidence and trust in corporations, for creating an atmosphere where industrialization can progress, and for making economic and social decisions.

Belkaoui (1983, p. 210) notes that the higher the level of government intervention, the more adequate reporting and disclosure are likely to be. He explains that government is assumed to be accountable to the people, and that therefore, intervention may be favourable to the development of an accounting profession and a disclosure tradition. He further offers that: 'The role of governments in developing accounting principles and providing legal authority is assumed to result in a higher reliability of financial disclosures in the developing countries' (Belkaoui, 1983, p. 211). Carpenter (1991) finds that political competitions (e.g. interest groups, electoral and parliamentary competition) are positively related to state governments' decisions to adopt generally accepted accounting principles in the USA. He observes that the legislative branch is effective because its primary responsibilities towards monitoring the activities are transparent.

Political lobbying

Ordelheide (2004, p. 270) argues that 'The usual model of interaction between politics and accounting is that the political process changes accounting practices.' Accounting has been seen as the outcome of complex interactions among parties interested in or affected by accounting standards (Kelly-Newton, 1980; Oehr and Zimmermann, 2012). Therefore, Watts and Zimmerman (1978, p. 115) note that 'politicians have the power to effect upon corporations wealth re-distributions by way of corporate taxes, regulations etc.' There have been ample studies of political lobbying in accounting literature (see Appendix 2.4a).[26] Political lobbying helps companies gain access to legislators and regulators to discuss their positions on proposed legislation, in an attempt to influence policy outcomes (Sunder, 1988; Ryan et al.,

1999). According to Smith (2000, p. 39), political access 'means that during deliberations leading to relevant legislative decisions . . . Corporations giving political contributions . . . gain a valuable opportunity to present their perspectives.'

The prior studies examine the interactions between companies, business interest groups, and legislators as participants in a political market. It has been found that the participants in the lobbying process are viewed as actors motivated by self-interest where they intend to legislate on those issues which are beneficial to them (Cohen and Hamman, 2003). For example, Sutton (1984) demonstrates earlier evidence from the USA in which the CEO of Cisco, John Chambers, met with the SEC chairman, Arthur Levitt, about the accounting for business combinations and 'made it plain that if Levitt went ahead with his plans, he would have to contend with the substantial lobbying weight of Cisco and every other tech company' (Beresford, 2001, p. 79). Beresford finds that congressional (parliamentary) hearings in the USA are only arranged when companies or industry associations have lobbied Congress, claiming that an accounting standard will cause economic harm. Ramanna (2008) similarly finds that firms which have incentives to lobby against the elimination of pooling as an acceptable accounting method for business combinations can be linked via political contributions to Congress representatives who then become involved against the FASB proposal. Georgiou (2004, p. 233) gives some justification for a company's overall lobbying posture, and argues that 'more lobbying may go on "behind the scenes" and [it] provides monetary contributions to politicians as a proxy for political lobbying'. In Germany, the industry lobby group representing preparers exerts the greatest influence on the decisions of the German legislature, but the relative power of preparers is seen to be far lower (Leuz et al., 2004). In a study of Japan, McKinnon and Harrison (1985) find that corporate lobbying there takes the form of a unified voice in Keidanren (the Japan Business Federation) in which Keidanren provides a powerful link between the corporations and the government ministries. In Indonesia, the adoption of IFRS has changed a little image to protect the foreign investors' right owing to the presence of high political ties (Rosser, 2003).

The convergence process has been characterised by a 'very skilful orchestration of the world-wide lobbying pressures', particularly by multinational enterprises and international accounting firms (Hopwood, 1994, p. 245). Caramanis (2002) argues that multinational accounting firms, through their economic influence and brand power, have the authority to control accounting agendas, the primary aim of which is to enhance self-interest. In addition to multinational enterprises, the EU may influence accounting change. Whittington (2005, p. 143) therefore argues that accounting has become an explicitly political issue: 'It is, of course, a matter for the EU to choose what standards it wishes to adopt, and . . . whether they are designed to meet the perceived interests of the EU economy or particular groups within it.' With potential for the diminution of state sovereignty under the conditions of globalisation, Risse (2004) questions the ability of states to make the best decisions for their citizens. Similarly, Chua and Taylor (2008, p. 462)argue that outsourcing the manufacture of accounting standards to a single private agency appears to be a lower-cost option; however, such outsourcing must be perceived to be legitimate because it possesses potential impact on powerful interest groups/regulators and internationality.

The prior literature evidences that political lobbying is not only limited to the standard settings. Firms with political ties and lobbying power often receive cheap loans from state-owned banks so that they do not need to tap into foreign capital markets; they are likely to pay fewer taxes and have larger market shares (Faccio, 2002, 2010; Chaney et al., 2011). For example, Leuz and Oberholzer-Gee (2006) find that Indonesia has low levels of mandatory disclosure, suggesting that the firms which are close to the Suharto regime are reluctant to follow regulations. It has been found that Asian firms with foreign securities maintained higher-quality disclosure and transparency during the Asian financial crisis (Doidge et al., 2004). In a cross-sectional study, Braun and Raddatz (2010, p. 234) show that the highest rank of political connectivity (e.g. politician–banker connections) is in countries such as Myanmar, China, Bangladesh, India, and Mexico. They note that this high level of political connectivity is strongly negatively related to economic development.

The prior research offers some policy prescriptions to reduce the complexity of political lobbying. Belkaoui (1983, p. 209) suggests that the political freedom (i.e. democracy) of a country is important to the development of accounting: 'When people cannot choose the members of government or influence government policies, they are less likely to be able to create an accounting profession based on the principle of full and fair disclosure.' The OECD (2001, p. 18) recommends that the principal ways for governments to engage with their citizens on policymaking to reduce lobbying are 'an advanced two-way relation between government and citizens based on the principle of partnership'. So, participation rights are crucial to a healthy democracy (Frey and Stutzer, 2001). Western economies follow a discursive democracy,[27] whereas developing countries move in the opposite direction (Risse, 2004). Similarly, some studies point out that institutional cooperation[28] is essential to implement IFRS effectively (Wallace and Briston, 1993; Mir and Rahaman, 2005; Zeghal and Mhedhbi, 2006). These studies argue that institutional co-operation will reduce the uncertainty of implementing IFRS under the democratic government in which stakeholders' rights are ensured. In a recent study, Hail et al. (2010, p. 575) argue that political independence is an important guiding principle in institutionalising a standard-setting body that is responsive to the needs of investors and capital markets. Equally important is the role of an effective securities regulator that monitors the development, implementation, and enforcement of the national accounting standards (Leuz and Wysocki, 2008). Zeff (2007, p. 300) raises questions regarding the seriousness of lobbying by asking:

> Will the political lobbying which emanates from special interests within the EU be congruent, or clash, with the special interests of important companies and countries based elsewhere in the world?. . . If a powerful company or group of companies do not like a draft standard, they will have an incentive to engage in politicking of the standard-setting body.

Proposition II

In summary, the prior research suggests conflicting results with respect to politico-institutional factors. This section shows that the literature provides contradictory views of government intervention: one group suggests that politics is negatively associated with the development of accounting systems and accounting change, while the other group suggests that politics has little or no influence. Some researchers even make strong calls for government intervention, seeing it as essential in developing countries. In terms of political lobbying, most researchers agree that the participants in the lobbying process and levels of political connectivity are viewed as grounded in self-interest and that, therefore, political independence or freedom (i.e. discursive democracy) is essential to reduce lobbying. There has been relatively little research on political influence in relation to IFRS implementation in developing countries. Most notably, Xiao et al. (2004) and Chen et al. (2011) in China, and Ball et al. (2003) in Thailand report that the government is politically motivated in introducing accounting standards. The following questions still remain: firstly, does politics (e.g. government intervention, lobbying activities) positively/negatively influence the implementation of IFRS in a developing country?; and, secondly, to what extent is co-operation among institutions supportive or unhelpful in the implementation of IFRS?

Prior studies suggest that politics may have a positive/negative influence on accounting change because of several different factors: e.g. (a) the legal origin of the country (common-law/code-law); (b) a lower/higher level of government intervention; and (c) a lower/higher level of political lobbying. Researchers agree that institutional co-operation may help the effective implementation of IFRS. The impact of institutional co-operation on IFRS implementation depends largely on (a) the democratic government/undemocratic government and (b) the participatory/non-participatory rights of the stakeholders. This section in relation to politico-institutional factors leads to the second proposition (P_{II}):

P_{II}: Politico-institutional factors will have a positive/negative influence on implementation of IFRS.

P_{IIA}: Politics will have a positive influence on implementation of IFRS under the conditions of (a) common-law origin; (b) a lower level of government intervention; and (c) a lower level of political lobbying.

or

Politics will have a negative influence on implementation of IFRS under the conditions of (a) code-law origin; (b) a higher level of government intervention; and (c) a higher level of political lobbying.

P_{IIB}: Co-operation among institutions will have a positive influence on implementation of IFRS under the conditions of (a) democratic government and (b) ensuring the participatory rights of the stakeholders.

or

Lack of co-operation among institutions will have a negative influence on implementation of IFRS under the conditions of (a) undemocratic government and (b) an absence of participatory rights for the stakeholders.

Cultural factors

[T]he technical and/or political dimensions of the debate, although essential, are not the only issues involved. Opposition to IFRS is not driven exclusively by contractual motives or a claimed technical superiority but also by diversity in cultural factors.

(Ding et al., 2005, p. 343)

Research addressing the wider social and political influences on accounting has been scarce (Hopwood, 1976, p. 3). Hopwood (1999, p. 378) provides specific national and cultural contexts of accounting: namely political dominance, religious dominance, class structures, or education systems which drive national differences. This may then lead to identifying why and how accounting is undertaken in a nation. According to Hofstede (2001, p. 1), 'Culture is defined as collective programming of the mind; it manifests itself not only in values, but in more superficial ways: in symbols, heroes, and rituals.' Societal or national culture is shared among the groups within a social system and across social systems within a given society (Hofstede, 2001, p. 15).

Prior research suggests that the accounting practices of a country are highly influenced by cultural forces (Burchell et al., 1980; Lowe et al., 1983). Accounting is a product of its environment and a particular environment is unique to its time and locality (Perera, 1989). It receives its inputs from the environment and produces outputs for the consumption of the environment (Radebaugh, 1975). The importance of culture in influencing the process of accounting policy formulation in any nation, and in explaining the diversity of accounting policy across nations, is well documented (Jaggi, 1975; Zeghal and Mhedhbi, 2006). For example, using a change framework (source, diffusion, and reaction phases of each change),[29] Harrison and McKinnon (1986) analyse the process of corporate reporting regulation change in Japan. They conclude that different phases of change indicate how culture influences the system of corporate reporting regulation in a specific nation. Later, Gray (1988, p.1) argues that 'There have been claims that national systems are determined by environmental factors. In this context, cultural factors have not been fully considered.' Although he does not empirically test the hypotheses, he proposes a theory of cultural influence in accounting change. Based on Hofstede's (1980) country-based indices (i.e. power distance, individualism, masculinity, and uncertainty avoidance), Gray (1988) hypothesises that financial disclosures will be negatively influenced by the cultural dimensions of uncertainty avoidance (UAI) and power distance (PDI), and positively by individualism (IDV) and masculinity (MAS). Gray (1988, p. 14) suggests that 'in interpreting the results of empirical research relating to culture, the influence of any change factors will also need to be taken into account'. However, Lee (1997, p. 20) argues that Gray ignores other factors, such as political systems and legal systems, which have significant power in shaping accounting systems. Wickramasinghe and Hopper (2005) argue that how and why cultural and political factors are relevant to accounting change in a developing country like Sri Lanka. They point out that 'accounting change cannot be explained by culture alone and outcomes were contingent' (p. 503). They further call for research on accounting, and culture would benefit by adopting a cultural political economy to understand accounting practices.

Some studies have also been carried out to examine IFRS practices and cultural influences.[30] For example, Sudarwan and Fogarty (1996) find that an empirical relation exists between the change in cultural factors and the change in accounting values in Indonesia. They suggest that the conflicting influences of extensive government involvement in the economy and market competition are a possible explanation of the results. Dahawy et al. (2002) argue that socio-economic factors affect the implementation of IFRS in Egypt, and that the inclination for secrecy that is embedded in Egyptian culture overrides the IFRS requirements. Therefore, disclosure reports by the sample companies are decreasing considerably. Choi (2002) concludes that corporate financial disclosures are deeply imbedded in cultural norms in Korea and, for that reason, change in accounting practices may take a long time to fully implement. Abdelsalam and Weetman (2007) similarly note that the economic changes of 1991–92 can be contrasted with the previous era of central planning in Egypt where accounting was characterised by conservatism, secrecy, and a relatively weak profession; and, subsequently, the move to IFRS therefore requires a change of culture as well as a change of law. Ding et al. (2005, p. 325) suggest that 'IAS is not exclusively driven by contractual motive . . . but also by diversity in cultural factors'. Dima and Cristea (2009) propose that culture is relevant to the national characteristics of IFRS implementation. In a recent study, Samuel and Manassian (2011, p. 622) argue that 'culture could be an impediment to development of accounting'. In the case of developing countries, accounting information is seen as both passive and active: passive in the sense that financial reporting practices may be explained by a country's particular cultural history or stage of development (Mueller, 1967; Bloom et al., 1998; Naciri and Hoarau, 2001; Wu et al., 2012), and active in that a nation's choice of financial reporting practices shapes its economic development (Enthoven, 1965). In another recent study, using the Hofstede–Gray framework, Perera et al. (2012) have found that there is a link between cultural values and accounting professionalism in Samoa and New Zealand. They conclude that their study may have implications for the application of IFRS and the analysis of differences in the judgements of professional accountants on measurement, disclosure, and ethical issues.

Researchers suggest that increasing 'democratic or sectarian cultural biases' in western-type societies since the 1960s have created more pressure to blame those who are at the top of powerful institutions and organisations for the harm they are perceived to do to the powerless (Douglas, 1982). Watts (1977, p. 66) points out the blaming culture by politicians in the USA and argues that:

> Many crises which led to corporate regulation and, in particular, to regulation of corporate financial statements were blamed by political entrepreneurs on the lack of adequate corporate disclosure or misleading corporate disclosure . . . [the] US politicians claimed that inadequate corporate disclosure was partially to blame for the stock market crash of 1929.

Hood et al. (1999) similarly argue that an 'audit society' is developing, in which declining popular trust in formerly respected professionals and institutions produces increasing support for formal audit, inspection, and oversight systems to replace an older pattern of self-regulation by mutuality (Power, 1997; O'Neill, 2002). Later, Hood (2004) documents that public management reform takes place in a social and political context due to falling levels of trust in government and institutions, highlighting an increased negativity bias.[31] The negativity bias is the commonly observed tendency to pay more attention to negative than to positive information (Hood, 2007). The causes of negativity bias are debated in politics and government, and in most cases outcomes are higher levels of dissatisfaction. Hood therefore claims that the pervasive prescription of transparency as a key to good governance meets the widely observed behavioural tendency of blame avoidance in politics and public administration. He concludes that: 'the tension between the pursuit of transparency and the avoidance of blame is at the heart of some commonly observed problems . . . something other than the "bureaucratic" strain of transparency may be called for when those problems are serious' (Hood, 2007, p. 191).

Studies such as Larson (1993), Larson and Kenny (1995) and Perera (1989) strongly point out that the complete implementation of IFRS in developing countries is near impossible because the IASB mainly focuses on developed nations' cultures (especially the USA and the UK) when they promulgate standards. Nobes (1984, 1998) identifies that no cultural influences exist. Jaggi and Low (2000) argue that cultural values have an insignificant impact on financial disclosures by firms in common-law countries. Although researchers such as Hofstede (1980, 1987) and Gray (1988) provide a good foundation for incorporating culture as one of the explanatory variables in determining accounting system differences and the recognition of its importance (Ding et al., 2005), the key problem is that the research in this area fails to explore cultural factors (Haniffa and Cooke, 2002). Haniffa and Cooke (2002, p. 317) conclude that 'There have been calls for research to look at the peculiar cultural characteristics inherent in a country.'

Prior research provides various proxies for choosing the relevant cultural factors in accounting research. In this study, training opportunities in the accounting profession (Perera, 1989; Ahmed and Nicholls, 1994; Haniffa and Cooke, 2002; Zeghal and Mhedhbi, 2006; Perera et al., 2012) and corruption (Rock and Bonnett, 2004; Wu, 2005, 2009; Wu et al., 2012) have been used as proxies for cultural factors. In the next section, I outline the prior research on the accounting profession and corruption.

Training opportunities in the accounting profession

Accounting education is the pillar for modern, complex accounting systems (Zeghal and Mhedhbi, 2006, p. 377) because 'an increase in the level of education in a country may increase political awareness and demand for corporate accountability' (Cooke and Wallace, 1990, p. 84).

The prior research finds that education can be an important cultural determinant of disclosure practice (Zarzeski, 1996; Bloom et al., 1998; Haniffa and Cooke, 2002). Belkaoui (1983, p. 208) strongly argues that 'A well-developed accounting profession and system for accounting education in a given country lead to a tradition and/or effort of providing adequate reporting and disclosure.' Similarly, Perera (1989, pp. 151–2) says that 'the deficiencies in accounting education and training in developing countries are fairly well known'; it cannot therefore be expected that accountants will always exercise appropriate judgements if the level of accounting education is low. He further emphasises that a country with a shortage of skilled accounting personnel should adopt a mandatory IFRS system, and this uniformity system will help them to improve the overall usefulness of accounting information. Gray (1988) earlier identifies education as one of the institutional consequences affecting accounting values and practices.

It has been argued that not only education but also the professional status of accountants is important in explaining accounting systems. Perera (1989, p. 152) argues that 'If, in a society, accounting is not regarded as a profession of high public esteem, and accountants are not trusted for their honesty and integrity, then accounting uniformity may seem to be a better alternative for the protection of that society.' This proposition has been supported by some researchers: for instance Radebaugh (1975), who finds that accounting is not recognised as a profession, and even has a low status in Peru; Var (1976) reports that the profession in Turkey is faced with a credibility problem; and Choi (1979) finds that the accounting profession in Thailand with respect to the proliferation of accounting standards is very weak. Therefore, Cooper and Robson (2006, p. 431) argue that the proliferation of both non-governmental organisations (NGOs) – such as the IASB, IFAC, ASB, FASB, IOSCO, UN, EU, and WTO – and government networks has had profound effects upon the co-ordination of accounting policies, in particular accounting education developments in developing countries. Neu et al. (2006) demonstrate that accounting education has been central in recent years and that is why the World Bank has made attempts to reform educational practices and systems all over the world.

There is mixed evidence of the relationship between accounting education and corporate disclosure practices. One group finds that a positive relationship exists. For example, Gernon et al. (1987) find that there is a positive relationship between the education level and the competence of professional accountants. Grace et al. (1995) propose that if the board of directors of a firm have an academic background in accounting, then they may choose to disclose more information (Hambrick and Mason, 1984). It may be argued that a western influence in education in developing countries will lead to a 'homogeneous effect' and result in higher corporate disclosure (Merchant et al., 1995). Adoption and implementation depend on the high level of education, competence, and expertise required to be able to understand and interpret accounting information (Doupnik and Salter, 1995). Dahawy et al. (2002) support Hofstede and Gray's hypotheses, and find inadequate disclosure practices in Egypt because of Egypt's secretive culture. Later, Zeghal and Mhedhbi (2006) find that the countries with the highest education levels proceed with the adoption of IFRS. Lower levels of education lead to lower expertise and real barriers to the adoption of IFRS (Bloom et al., 1998); and therefore Abdelsalam and Weetman (2007, p. 96) suggest that 'Achieving education and training success is likely to be more problematic in developing countries where there are limitations on financial and technical resources.' In a recent study, Chand et al. (2012, p. 153) show that national culture has a significant effect on the judgements of accounting students when interpreting and applying selected IFRS containing uncertainty expressions. They conclude that Chinese students exhibit greater conservatism and secrecy compared to Australian students. They suggest that global accounting education systems may influence implementing IFRS.

Another group finds that accounting education is less useful (Nobes, 1998), and even that a negative association exists between accounting education and corporate disclosure. Nobes (1998, p. 168) opines that 'In particular . . . level of education and stage of economic development are not necessary.' He notes that '[these factors] may be a result of accounting differences rather than their cause' (p. 168). Moreover, the findings of Ahmed and Nicholls (1994) and Parry and Groves (1990) suggest that there is no impact on the quality of financial reporting through having qualified accountants. Similarly, Abayo and Roberts (1993) find that accounting education and qualifications alone are not the solution to problems faced by developing countries, at least with respect to Tanzania and inadequate accounting disclosure practices there. Similar findings come from Haniffa and Cooke (2002), who show that disclosure behaviour in Malaysia is not affected by culture. Their findings are contrary to the Hofstede and Gray hypotheses because Hofstede and Gray propose that societal values (meaning that they best describe the accounting value of being highly secretive in terms of the accounting practice known as disclosure) of the bumiputra/Malay are in congruence with the level of secrecy in disclosure.

Corruption

Defining corruption as a cultural norm, Sandholtz and Koetzle (2000, pp. 33–4) argue that '[The] definition of corruption that is portable across cultures. . . . Corrupt acts are, in every definition, improper or illegitimate.' The region-specific and country-case literature suggests that politics and corruption affect accounting (Whitehead, 1989, 2000; Rock and Bonnett, 2004). The reasons for high-level political corruption arise from substantial government intervention in the economy (Weyland, 1998). Some studies have argued that high-level corruption can be explained through analysis of double transitions: (a) from authoritarianism to democracy; and (b) from interventionist to market-oriented economic policies, which have commonly been accompanied by even higher levels of political corruption (Geddes and Ribeiro-Neto, 1999). Cooke and Wallace (1990, p. 84) argue that 'In societies where a strong oral tradition exists or where corruption is endemic, the development of accounting may be impeded.' In an African study, Sandbrook argues that Africa's post-colonial governments have often emerged under extremely inauspicious circumstances. He criticises that 'Given the deep mistrust among Africans of markets, trade, and foreign investment, it is not surprising that both market-oriented and socialist-oriented governments adopted highly interventionist (policies) . . . these strategies ultimately failed' (Sandbrook, 1993, p. 22). However, there is little evidence that such high-level corruption increases either investment or growth (Lopez, 1998; Schneider, 2002). In Latin America, the role of hyper-presidentialism is very costly high-level political corruption. Whitehead (1989, p. 783) observes that 'the whole apparatus of the state (is geared) to the task of their personal enrichment'. High-level political corruption has been seen in Mexico and Brazil (Geddes and Ribeiro-Neto, 1999; Manzetti, 2000). In an Eastern European study, Bloom et al. (1998) argue that corruption is widespread and that secrecy has long been a tradition in Armenia. Accounting is cash based and oriented to the stewardship needs of the government, and the non-compliance of standards reflects its culture.

In an Asian study, Rock and Bonnett (2004) demonstrate the comparative politics of corruption on accounting in the East Asian Paradox, and find that corruption slows growth and/ or reduces investment in most developing countries. Wu (2005) confirms the corporate sector as the main source of corruption problems in Asia, and argues that 'high quality accounting standard(s) alone will not automatically bring down the level of bribery in Asian firms' (p. 57). Wu (2009) further reports that Bangladesh is one of the most corrupt countries in Asia, where

'96% of firms report that they regularly bribe public officials' (p. 82). In a study of China, Wu et al. (2012) conclude that politically connected managers of firms can help their firms obtain tax benefits. In a comparative study (covering both developed and developing countries), Sandholtz and Koetzle (2000) argue that corruption poses fundamental challenges both to democratic governance and to market economies, and find that there is a significant relationship between corruption and accounting quality.[32]

Besides government intervention, Lessmann and Markwardt (2010) argue that corruption crucially depends on the effectiveness of the monitoring bureaucrats' behaviour. They argue that the benefits of decentralisation only occur if there is a supervisory body; this is often lacking in a substantial number of developing countries. Similarly, Arikan (2004) concludes that levels of corruption are lower in decentralised countries. These results are supported in studies by Enikolopov and Zhuravskaya (2007) and Lederman et al. (2005). In contrast, in line with Shleifer and Vishny (1993), Fan et al. (2009) find a negative impact of decentralisation (in terms of vertical government tiers) on corruption. They conclude that a lack of co-ordination of government institutes increases with the complexity of government structures.

Proposition III

In summarising the literature on cultural factors' influences on accounting change (specifically IFRS implementation), the empirical evidence suggests that cultural characteristics change over time, and that the cultural factors rely on a particular country's environment. Most of the studies support a statistical association between culture and corporate reporting requirements, yet they also acknowledge an inability to explain the nature of that association. It is observed from the literature that very few studies have measured cultural factors in implementing IFRS, yet negativity bias and blame cultures are ignored by the researchers in interpreting the relationship between culture and IFRS implementation. Because conflicting evidence exists both in country-specific and cross-sectional studies, the question arises as to whether training opportunities in the accounting profession and corruption have positive or negative associations with IFRS implementation.

The prior research provides some suggestions for inconclusive evidence (i.e. positive/ negative influence on accounting change): for example, (a) an effective/ineffective development of training opportunities in the accounting profession; and (b) low/high levels of corruption. Researchers suggest that effective/ineffective development of training opportunities in the accounting profession depend on higher/lower standards of education, effective/ ineffective accounting education policy, and high/low professional status in society, whilst low/ high levels of corruption depend on a culture of transparency/secrecy. This section leads to the final proposition.

P_{IIIA}: Effective development of training opportunities in the accounting profession will have a positive influence on implementation of IFRS.

or

Ineffective development of training opportunities in the accounting profession will have a negative influence on implementation of IFRS.

P_{IIIB}: Low levels of corruption will have a positive influence on implementation of IFRS.

or

High levels of corruption will have a negative influence on implementation of IFRS.

Other influences: country-specific factors[33]

Despite a large amount of literature on accounting regulatory frameworks, politico-institutional factors, and cultural factors, the prior research suggests that some other country-specific factors exert influences on financial reporting practices (see Appendix 2.4a). In this section, I outline various factors highlighted by the prior research, namely colonial power, multinationals, transfers of technology and foreign aids, and public sector dominance – all of which may influence financial reporting practices.

Colonial power

Most developing countries have a common feature of past colonial rule, and their level of political institutions and culture are largely influenced by the socio-political traditions and culture of the previous colonial power (Verma and Gray, 2009; Al-Akra et al., 2009). When the colonial powers acquired their colonies, there were no formal accounting systems in most of these countries, and thus the prevailing accounting vacuum was typically filled by accounting systems introduced by the colonial masters (Briston, 1990; Saudagaran and Diga, 1998). Examples of such introduction may be found in the promulgation of the Indian Companies Act 1913, drafted in accordance with the English Companies Act 1908;[34] the modelling of Moroccan and Algerian financial reporting systems on the French standardised accounting system (Hagigi and Williams, 1993); and the predominant influence of the Dutch accounting system in Indonesia (Briston and Hadori, 1993). During the British colonial period, for example, British accounting traditions spread to many countries, so that British rule could be employed in managing British business interests (Perera, 1975). In a study on the colonial experience in Fiji, Davie (2007) claims that Fijian experience of accounting practices is very much historical in nature because they are still following the British rule. Al-Akra et al. (2009) argue that the reasons for Jordan's attitude towards full adoption of IFRS are grounded in their strong colonial experiences.

Saudagaran and Diga (1998, p.1) suggest that the early evidence of accounting practices in the ASEAN countries (Indonesia, Malaysia, Singapore, and Thailand) is heavily influenced by colonial experiences, but the post-independence history of the dominance of banks and financial institutions is conducive to adopting a macro-user oriented accounting system dominated by the needs of government users.[35] Similarly, Wijewardena and Yapa (1998) conclude that after 50 years of independence, Sri Lanka is still following the colonial system to produce its accounts, whereas Singapore moved away from the colonial system within four years of independence. In South Asia, Banerjee and Iyer (2005) point out that Bangladesh, India, and Pakistan were under British colonial rule for around 200 years. British rule in India (i.e. in the central part of the former colony) extended from 1757 to 1947.[36] After independence, India, Pakistan, and Bangladesh established different accounting systems, mixing the UK GAAP, US GAAP and IAS/IFRS. For example, India adopted mandatory IAS/IFRS in 2012,[37] Bangladesh did so in 1998,[38] and Pakistan in 1997.[39] Banerjee and Iyer (2005) raise the question of the colonial impact on accounting systems.

Studies like Bloom et al. (1998) and Naciri and Hoarau (2001) believe that the historical and social background of a country influences its accounting practices. For example, Bloom et al. (1998, p. 641) point out that:

> No accounting system can be judged superior to any other without considering how the system serves society in a specific country. Given the totalitarian history of Armenia and its linkage to the former Soviet Union, it is not surprising that Armenia clings to a Soviet

chart of accounts. The government has long dominated and controlled the Armenian economy, and thus has been the 'user' of accounts.

Naciri and Hoarau (2001, p. 235) show that American and French philosophies of financial reporting diverge from each other. While the American system is influenced by the very positive financial and economic environment of the nineteenth century, the French system is impacted by political and wartime considerations from the twentieth century.

Multinationals, transfers of technology and foreign aid

Multinational companies (MNCs) have been one of the most powerful channels of technology transfer, including accounting technology, for host countries (Wilkinson, 1965; Chandler and Holzer, 1984). Seidler (1969, pp. 36–7) explains that 'The strongest vehicle for the current international dissemination of accounting information is the Multinational Corporation and its associated activities.' The main concern of MNCs, though, is to make money, and they have little regard for the domestic requirements of the host countries because they see the elimination of dissimilarities in local practices purely as a means to facilitate their operations (Needles, 1976; Nair and Frank, 1981). Wallace and Briston (1993, p. 215) express reservations that:

> [T]he media of transfer may not always have similar effects on recipient countries, because of the differences in economic conditions, levels of preparation, willingness to account, skills, behaviour and culture of the people, training methods adopted and complexities of accounting legacies inherited. Some countries may be successful in the transfer of accounting technology; others may not.

Perera (1975) attempts to portray the complex links between the various channels used to transfer accounting technology in Sri Lanka. He concludes that almost all the joint stock companies are owned by British investors and accountants who have come from the UK. Therefore, even though these firms are actually located in Sri Lanka, they are managed as though they are based in Britain. Despite this, no attempts are made to develop the accounting systems so that they are more suitable for local conditions.

In the same way, the professional accounting bodies[40] have played a significant role in the process of transferring accounting technology to the developing countries, particularly to the former British colonies. British accountants emigrated to the colonies and formed the nucleus of the establishment of the professional bodies in the developing countries (Hove, 1986). Although these professional bodies in the developing countries were granted autonomy, the British accountancy bodies continue to exert considerable influence in both the general administration of professional bodies in developing countries and in the style of their examining processes (Saudagaran and Diga, 1998). Neu et al. (2006) document that the World Bank increases its legitimacy with other potential borrower countries on accounting/financial practices, and in this way it ensures its continuing influence.

Further, foreign aid plays a vital role in the process of developing accounting systems and transferring technology from the developed donor countries to the developing countries (Perera, 1985; Rahaman, 1997). The World Bank, the IMF and other donor agencies require financial statements explaining the ways in which aid has been utilised by recipient countries (Mir and Rahaman, 2005). Hoarau (1995) argues that 'Imperialist institutions such as the World Bank and International Monetary Fund have become major active agents responsible for the proliferation of IAS in developing countries.' The financial statements have to be prepared on the basis of the procedures followed by the donor agencies (Mir and Rahaman, 2005). Although Wilkinson (1965, p. 11) argues that 'the accounting principles and practices of Western capitalist countries were never "sold" to developing countries on the basis of convincing arguments in support of their superior quality in terms of local needs', Points and Cunningham (1998) observe that foreign donor agencies (e.g. the World Bank and the IMF) are continuously trying to impose the IASB standards instead of assisting real accounting reforms within the developing countries.

Discussing the donor agencies' attempts to assist the development of accounting systems in developing countries, Wallace and Briston (1993, pp. 216–17) argue that 'Donor agencies should collaborate more closely with the recipient country to ensure that their assistance is delivered only in accordance with national accounting development plans.' Problems with the transfer of accounting practices from developed countries to developing countries are manifold. First, no attention is given to ascertaining the needs of domestic users, resulting in an inappropriate accounting practice with limited usefulness (Mir and Rahaman, 2005). Second, the developing countries cannot modify their accounting practices in response to the changing needs of the corporate environments (Points and Cunningham, 1998). Third, it is very difficult to implement micro- and macroeconomic goals on the basis of reported financial statements; and it must be kept in mind that every society contains unique features in terms of its social, cultural, economic, and political aspects (Belkaoui, 1983, 1985). Finally, international lending agencies have become a major influence upon government policies (Uddin and Hopper, 2003). For example, the World Bank's enhanced authority has emerged from the economic dependence and political weakness of Bangladesh, in particular because 'Military leaders in Bangladesh turned to Western ideologies, especially Thatcherism and Reaganism, to legitimise their undemocratic actions' (Uddin and Hopper, 2003, p. 741). Despite the widespread corruption of the Colombian government, the World Bank provides financial support for accounting education and does not question the state's ability to implement the programmes (Neu et al., 2006).

Public sector dominance

The prior research finds that modern accounting concepts and principles are not being implemented adequately in most developing countries, in part at least because of the dominant public sector.[41] In Egypt, the government controls approximately 80% of economic resources (Amer, 1969); in East Central Europe,[42] the state controls over 85% of production (Dobosiewicz, 1992). Perera (1975) reports that Sri Lankan companies are more interested in preparing tax returns than accounting reports. Abu-Nassar and Rutherford (1995) find that users of annual accounting reports in Jordan doubt their reliability and credibility. It has been argued that governments of developing countries review and redefine the role of accounting under the new order in ways which are more supportive to their public sectors (Briston, 1978; Samuels and Oliga, 1982). Accounting transparency becomes irrelevant in state-owned enterprises (SOEs) because political influence over decisions outweighs formal accountability within the systems (Jones and Sefiane, 1992).

Increasingly, attention has been paid to raising accounting standards in developing countries where it is considered to be a prerequisite of granting FDI. This raises the question of the role of financial reporting in developing countries – is the dominant public sector supportive of the implementation of IFRS? This is because some researchers find that public sector firms (e.g. SOEs) are not transparent. For example, Wang et al. (2008) find that, compared with non-state-owned firms, Chinese state-owned enterprises are controlled by province, city, and county governments (local SOEs) which are more likely to hire small auditors within the same region (small local auditors) because the tendency is to hide information. Similar findings are also observed in Armenia (Bloom et al., 1998). Despite the Armenian privatisation movement, adopted in 1997, the country's public sector is reluctant to disclose information (Bloom et al., 1998).

There are already many developing countries with dominant private sectors, reported by Cairns (1990) and Gernon et al. (1990) who find that some countries adopt the IFRS as national standards. Bennell (1997, p. 1801) argues that:

> The World Bank, IMF, and most of the major aid agencies are significantly increasing the pressure on governments to privatize, and wherever possible sell, most SOEs . . . consequently, meeting privatization targets is becoming an increasingly central feature of the performance.

Although the public sector controlled about 350 SOEs (92%) in 1974 in Bangladesh, Uddin and Hopper (2003) provide evidence of a trend of highly concentrated family ownership patterns during the 1980s. Ahmed and Nicholls (1994) find significant evidence of non-compliance by Bangladeshi listed companies within the dominant private sector, and only 63 company reports are available out of a sample of 95 companies for the fiscal year 1987–88. Similar findings are reported by Farooque et al. (2007) and Khan et al. (2011) in Bangladesh; Ghazali and Weetman (2006) in Malaysia; and Abd-Elsalam and Weetman (2003) in Egypt. In India, Narayanaswamy (1996) reports that the quality of financial reporting disclosure remains low, despite widespread regulatory reforms aiming to internationalise and liberalise business. These arguments contradict the findings of Bennell (1997), who reports that privatisation improves the fiscal situation in developing countries and improves their efficiency. Therefore, Siddiqui (2010, p. 260) argues that public sector dominance and private sector dominance can be explained by ownership structures, and views that: 'Like many other developing countries, most companies in Bangladesh are either family owned or controlled by substantial shareholders (corporate groups or government).'

In summary, the prior literature provides diverse evidence on colonial power, multinationals, the transfer of technology and foreign aid, and the public sector. This section shows that the prior research provides inconclusive evidence regarding accounting practices and colonial influence. For instance, some countries' accounting practices are (heavily) influenced by colonial experience, whilst others are not. This section also shows that prior research argues that multinational companies' efforts to transfer accounting technology in developing countries are complex processes. Prior studies raise questions around foreign professional bodies and donor agencies' influence in transferring accounting technology and, in particular, accounting practices in developing countries. Prior researchers suggest that the IFRS are not being effectively implemented in most developing countries, at least in part because of their dominant public sectors. They raise questions around the privatisation programmes and the issue of the effective implementation of IFRS. However, little attention has yet been given to the work of other country-specific factors in the implementation of IFRS; nor has much research attempted to examine these factors. Therefore it will be interesting to examine the impact of other country-specific factors on the implementation of IFRS in a developing country.

Conclusion

The overall discussion of this chapter leads towards the consideration of some research gaps which exist in the literature on IFRS implementation. As discussed in earlier sections of this chapter, there has been relatively limited research into theories of the role of the state in relation to accounting change (e.g. implementation of IFRS) in accounting literature. Additionally, the notion of 'the state' has many meanings, which can themselves depend on the purpose of the study. I have chosen to employ a Weberian concept of the state in the present study. The analysis of the literature identifies that the most frequently discussed issues in terms of the role of the state and accounting change are accounting regulatory frameworks, politico-institutional factors, and cultural factors. Answers regarding the theory of the role of the state's application in a developing country still remain elusive, and the question therefore remains: How does a study of implementing IFRS help to build an understanding of a theory of the role of the state in accounting change in a developing country?

In considering the relative impact on accounting regulatory frameworks and politico-institutional factors (RQ-1), it is observed by prior research that government involvement is not conducive to creating effective accounting regulatory frameworks. It has been argued that collaboration or co-operation between the private sector standard-setting body and the government regulatory body is essential in creating effective regulatory frameworks. Further, most researchers agree that standard setting is political in both developed and developing countries; but they raise the question of how best to create effective enforcement mechanisms in developing countries. Therefore, the researchers suggest that accounting regulatory frameworks may either help or hinder accounting change. In terms of accounting regulatory frameworks the following questions still remain: (a) do the regulatory and standard-setting processes positively/negatively influence IFRS implementation in a developing country?; (b) what enforcement mechanism(s) have been used by developing countries to implement IFRS?; and (c) are the enforcement mechanism(s) (un)even in implementing IFRS? The first proposition (P_I) of the present study was developed in that section.

Regarding RQ-1, prior research shows that opinions vary regarding politics because some researchers find that politics has a negative impact on accounting change, while others find that politics does not have any notable influence. In particular, opinions vary regarding government intervention because one group finds that government intervention is negatively associated with the development of accounting systems and accounting change, while the other group argues that intervention has little or no influence. Some researchers call for government intervention in developing countries. Most agree that participants in the lobbying process and those with political connectivity are (viewed as being) self-interested and, therefore, guarantees on political independence and freedom are essential to reduce lobbying. Because of the existence of mixed evidence in the literature on politico-institutional factors, the literature identifies the following questions: firstly, do politics (e.g. government intervention, lobbying activities) positively/negatively influence the implementation of IFRS in a developing country?; and, secondly, to what extent is co-operation among institutions supportive or unhelpful in relation to the implementation of IFRS? Then, based on the prior literature, the second proposition (P_{II}) of the present study was developed in that section.

In terms of RQ-2(a), researchers are divided on the impact of cultural influences on accounting change because one group finds a positive association between cultures and accounting change, while the other group finds no significant relationship. One possible explanation for this is that cultural characteristics change over time and depend on a particular country's environmental characteristics. Most of the studies are, as yet, unable to explain the nature of a positive association – or, alternatively, the lack of association. In this study, training opportunities in the accounting profession and corruption have been used as proxies for cultural factors. Because conflicting evidence exists both in nation-specific and cross-sectional studies, the following question still remains: Do training opportunities in the accounting profession and corruption positively/negatively influence the implementation of IFRS? Based on the prior literature, the final proposition (P_{III}) of the present study was developed.

Regarding RQ-2(b), it is suggested that not only do accounting regulatory frameworks, politico-institutional factors, and cultural factors influence accounting change, but that other country-specific factors – such as past colonial power, multinationals, transfer of technology, and foreign aid and public sector dominance – also have impacts on financial reporting in developing countries. Prior studies report mixed findings. Therefore, it will be interesting to examine the impact of these other country-specific factors and their influence on the implementation of IFRS in a developing country.

This research attempts to fill the gaps by adding to the existing body of knowledge concerning the problems of implementing IFRS from a developing country's perspective. Keeping these key research gaps in mind, the study's theoretical framework will be discussed in the next chapter.

Notes

1 Accounting change means the outcome of IFRS implementation.
2 Source: http://www.the-abs.org.uk/files//Combined%20Journal%20Guide.pdf, 17 November 2010 (accessed 12 February 2012).
3 The two journals are not included in the ABS Ranking.
4 University of Edinburgh Database, http://small.lib.ed.ac.uk (accessed 12 February 2012).
5 http://scholar.google.co.uk (accessed 10 February 2012).
6 I use the term 'frequently discussed issues' as drivers of accounting change.
7 Graf (1995, p. 140) argues that: 'If the mainstream development literature of the 1960s and 1970s presupposed a "modernising" or "developmental" state and the Marxist approaches of the same period invoked the "strong", "overdeveloped" and (relatively) "autonomous" postcolonial state; and if the eighties produced rather more ambiguous concepts such as the "rentier state", the "peripheral state" or the "bureaucratic-authoritarian state"; then in the nineties the imagery has turned relentlessly negative as expressed in such coinages as "vassal state", "predator state", "vampire state", "receiver state", "prostrate state" and even "fictitious state", "show of state" or "collapsed state".' Beyme (1986, p. 115) also observes that 'American scholars have sometimes argued that the state is either a legal or a Marxist term'.
8 Cassese (1986, p.120) offers the view that 'Since 1931, when 145 usages of it were found, the word 'state', like all terms with too many meanings, has ceased to distinguish any concept useful for purposes of study.'
9 Chabod (1967, p. 605; cited in Cassese, 1986) studies different meanings of state, such as dominion, institution and political lordship in the sixteenth century.
10 Cited in Avineri (1972, p. 80).
11 Although the Williamsonian perspective has acknowledged macro and micro institution, his works are limited to analyses of the relations of micro institutions (Evans and Rauch, 1999, p. 749).
12 Weber (1968, p. 152, cited in Uphoff, 1989, p. 295) defines power as '*Herrschaftist, wiegleichzuerortern, ein Sonderfall von Macht* (Authority is, as will be discussed, a special kind of power)'. Mann (1986) believes that four sources of power (ideological, economic, military and political) underpin the development of the state.
13 According to Mann (1986), this process, termed 'diffused power', e.g. social norms, is a subtler, more normalised power where individuals follow social norms either because they are natural, moral or arise from self interest.
14 The most-argued issues will also be discussed in later sections in order to develop three propositions.
15 The definition of regulation is: 'The intentional restriction of a subject's choice of activity, by an entity not directly party to or involved in the activity' (Mitnick, 1980, p. 5). The definition of accounting regulation is: 'the imposition of constraints upon the preparation, content and form of external financial reports by bodies other than the preparers of the reports, or the organisations and individuals for which the reports are prepared' (Taylor and Turley, 1986, p. 1). The definition of

accounting regulatory frameworks is: 'a mandatory call for information that the preparer may have not voluntarily provided' (Taylor and Turley, 1986, p. 7).

16 See Zeff (1972), Loft (1994), Miranti (1986), and Previts and Merino (1998).

17 Australia, Hong Kong, Malaysia, the Philippines, Singapore and Thailand.

18 Watts and Zimmerman (1978), Hussein and Ketz (1980), Newman (1981), Hope and Gray (1982), Lowe et al. (1983), McKee et al. (1991), and Walker and Robinson (1993).

19 Sweden, the UK, the USA and Germany.

20 Nobes (1998) proposes a general model of the reasons for international differences, based on culturally self-sufficient (CS) and culturally dominated (CD) countries.

21 The panopticon is a type of prison building designed by the English philosopher and social theorist Jeremy Bentham in 1785. The concept of the design is to allow an observer to observe (*opticon*) all (*pan*) prisoners without the prisoners being able to tell whether they are being watched, thereby conveying what one architect has called the 'sentiment of an invisible omniscience' (Matthieson, 1997).

22 *Visible:* the inmate will constantly have before his eyes the tall outline of the central tower from which he is spied upon; and *unverifiable:* the inmate must never know whether he is being looked at any one moment, but he must be sure that he may always be so, and the presence or absence of the inspector should be unverifiable so that the prisoners, in their cells, cannot even see a shadow (Foucault, 1977).

23 In this study, stringent enforcement means the efficiency of the judicial system, and punitive penalty/fine.

24 In this study, 'negative influence' is equivalent to an impediment to accounting change.

25 The term 'government intervention' refers to the actions on the part of government that affect economic activity, resource allocation and, especially, the voluntary decisions made through normal market exchanges (available at: www. encyclopedia2.thefreedictionary.com).

26 Using Downs' (1957) model of voting, Sutton (1984) identifies the conditions under which rational lobbying will occur. Given a choice between two alternative proposals, lobbying is predicted in those circumstances where the differential wealth effect associated with the two proposals, discounted by the perceived probability of influencing the outcome, exceeds the cost of lobbying. Hence, the propensity for lobbying is hypothesised to increase in both (i) the magnitude of the perceived wealth effect and (ii) the expectation of influencing the final decision.

27 Discursive democracy 'is ultimately about involving the stake-holders, i.e., those concerned by a particular social rule, in a deliberative process of mutual persuasion about the normative validity of a particular rule' (Risse, 2004, p. 310). The basic legitimacy of a discursive political community is founded on its members' general rights to exercise equal liberties, along with membership rights and guaranteed legal remedies (Habermas, 1988).

28 In this study, institutional co-operation means collaboration among various state institutions and professional bodies to implement IFRS.

29 The framework allows examination of the system's norms and values; the nature of its interdependencies both internally and with other social systems; the factors to which the system is especially sensitive; and the way in which culture influences the form and functioning of the system's elements (Harrison and McKinnon, 1986, p. 233).

30 Sudarwan and Fogarty, 1996; Choi, 2002; Dahawy et al., 2002; Ding et al., 2005; Abdelsalam and Weetman, 2007; Dima and Cristea, 2009.

31 Negativity bias denotes a commonly observed cognitive tendency for more attention to be paid to negative than to positive information, and for losses to be valued more highly than gains which are of an equivalent amount (Hood, 2009).

32 They hypothesise that levels of corruption are higher: (1) the lower the average income level; (2) the greater the extent of state control of the economy; (3) the weaker the democratic norms and institutions; (4) the lower the degree of integration in the world economy; and (5) the lower the share of the population with a Protestant religious affiliation.

33 'Other country-specific factors' is a term I use in this study to explain any other factors outside accounting regulatory frameworks, politico-institutional and cultural factors (i.e. training opportunities in the accounting profession and corruption) which may have an influence on IFRS implementation.

34 The early history of company law in India was laid down in the British Companies Act 1844 on the basis of which the Joint Stock Companies Act 1850, the first company law for the sub-continent, was formulated. This act was based on 'unlimited liability'. Through a major amendment in the Joint Stock Companies Act 1850 in 1857, the provision of unlimited liability was replaced by 'limited liability' and the act was renamed as the Companies Act 1857. With the expansion of trade and commerce, the Companies Act 1857 was amended in 1860, 1866, 1882, 1887, 1891, 1895, 1900 and 1908. The Indian Companies Act of 1913 was actually the amended and reformed version of the English Companies Act of 1908 (available at: http://www.legalserviceindia.com/articles/eocindia.htm).

35 For example, accounting regulations in Thailand traditionally prefer a more conservative, creditor-oriented and tax-driven accounting system, similar to Germany and Japan (Yunus, 1988).

36 Bangladesh, India and Pakistan were ruled through the same central administration until the independence period, with Bangladesh and Pakistan breaking from India in the late 1940s and Bangladesh eventually splitting from Pakistan in the early 1970s (Lange, 2004).

37 Source: http://www.iasplus.com/en/jurisdictions/asia/country9 (accessed 12 February 2012).

38 Source: The Securities and Exchange Commission Rules 1987.

39 Source: Section 234 of the Companies Ordinance 1984, http://www.secp.gov.pk/corporatelaws/pdf/CompaniesOrdinance984-17-03-2011.pdf (accessed 12 February 2012).

40 The Institute of Chartered Accountants in England and Wales (ICAEW), the Institute of Chartered Accountants of Scotland (ICAS), the Association of Chartered Certified Accountants (ACCA) and the Chartered Institute of Public Finance and Accountancy (CIPFA).

41 For example, Ghafur (1976) and Ahmad (1976) in Bangladesh; Briston (1978) in Indonesia, Sri Lanka and Tanzania; Samuels and Oliga (1982) in Egypt; and Perera (1985) in Sri Lanka.

42 Albania, Czechoslovakia, Hungary, Poland and Yugoslavia.

Chapter 3

Theory

Introduction

This chapter will help develop the theoretical framework consistent with RQ-3: How does a study of implementing IFRS help build an understanding of a theory of the role of the state in accounting change in a developing country such as Bangladesh? As mentioned in Chapter 2, there is no single theory which explains accounting change in a developing country in a broader context; therefore, a review of theories of the role of the state is offered in order to predict accounting changes (i.e. the implementation of IFRS).

In Chapter 2, the propositions of this study were developed. The drivers of accounting change were selected by employing a systematic review of literature on the role of the state and accounting change. It has been shown that three frequently discussed issues in the literature are accounting regulatory frameworks, politico-institutional factors, and cultural factors (with specific selection for this book of training opportunities in the accounting profession and the presence of systematic corruption). Based on the drivers of accounting change, three propositions were then developed.

Chapter 3 is organised as follows: The next section will provide key papers on theories of the role of the state in relation to accounting change. In particular, I will discuss the role of the state and institutional dynamics in order to understand a link between the state and individual organisations and gain an in-depth understanding of IFRS implementation issues in a developing country. This section will also discuss the fact that the state is not solely responsible for accounting change, as lobbying groups and individual companies are also responsible. The final section will contain a summary of the chapter.

Key papers on theories of the role of the state in relation to accounting

The process of choosing 15 key papers in relation to the theory of the role of the state and accounting change has been described in Chapter 2. In particular, of the 15 papers, nine focus on developed countries, three are purely theory centred, and a further three are based on developing countries. The theoretical framework of this study has been developed based primarily on these 15 papers (see Table 2.2).

The role of the state (external forces)

Prior research has identified that a state framework is based upon external forces. For example, Miller (1990) criticises Marxist views of the state and stresses the importance of a socio-historical approach to accounting change. Miller uses a state theoretical framework by following two basic approaches, 'functional' and 'external factors'. The implicit assumption of Miller's framework is that external factors can explain broader changes in accounting. Liguori and Steccolini (2012) argue that the prior research on the role of the state has primarily focused on external forces; but change is not a simple matter of adjustment to external pressures. Researchers like Tinker propose that theories of the role of the state may be applied to more specific accounting questions and may have greater implications in research on accounting and public policy. Tinker (1984, p. 71) identifies some questions and argues that neoclassical thought excludes such questions as, for example:

> What underlies major shifts in the regulatory practices of the state and how much importance should accountants attribute to these changes? What determines the state's level of autonomy vis-à-vis advantaged and disadvantaged groups and, in this regard, how much credence may be attached to the views of writers, such as Benston [1976], that disclosure regulations are captive of vested interest? Does the degree of state autonomy vary across regulatory spheres of interests? What stance should the accounting profession take in relation to the 'contested terrain' of state regulation? Who are the sides in the struggle for control over the state's regulatory apparatus, and how should accountants choose a side to support?

Although the outcomes of accounting change can be investigated at different levels of analysis, most studies explicitly employ external or macro-level analysis. Hence, I will explore how the state behaves and its role in accounting change emphasising external forces. As derived from Chapter 2, the roles of the state are outlined below.

The state approves experts to write rules

The state approves experts (e.g. professional bodies) to write rules (Tinker, 1984; Jonsson, 1991; Alexander and Servalli, 2010; Moran, 2010; Norton, 2012). Prior research argues that state intervention in regulatory processes means a questioning of the state's role. Jonsson (1991) proposes that state intervention should be avoided or minimised in order to formulate independent accounting rules and norms. Accounting finds a role through regulation. He further points out that 'The state may grow stronger by not intervening' (Jonsson, 1991, p. 521).

Alexanderand Servalli (2010) examine the extent to which, and in what ways, the state should be involved in the regulation of financial accounting and reporting, using historical and conceptual analyses of 'the state' and 'accounting'. They further explore accounting regulation in the Anglo-Saxon (common-law) and continental (Roman law) traditions, considering political polemics relating to the roles and interrelationships of the IASB and investor/creditor/fiscal/legal/prudential regulation stakeholders. They conclude that:

> [S]elf-interested interference is endemic, is actively facilitated by 'due process', and that, crucially, a necessary (but not sufficient) condition of effectively dealing with this problem is to ensure that 'the State', whilst maintaining an essential overall monitoring role on the fundamental effectiveness of the process, is allowed, whether in the guise of elected representatives or otherwise, zero influence in the details and operational content of financial accounting and reporting regulations for market-based resource-allocation-focussed information.
>
> (Alexanderand Servalli, 2010, p. 2)

The theoretical underpinnings of their findings are 'conceptually distinct, but a connection exists in that state involvement may, or may not, be conducive to more effective achievement of the purposes of financial reporting' (Alexander and Servalli, 2010, p. 35). Moran (2010, p. 274) argues that:

> Making sense of the political economy of regulation involves making sense of national patterns of regulation . . . . the application of these social technologies is inevitably a political matter, and is therefore shaped by the political setting – institutional and cultural – in which it operates accounting practice is a critical arena where politics and economics meet – and is therefore critical to the political economy of the market system.

He differentiates between the US (which is the single most important national system of capitalist democracy) and the EU regulatory systems using the political economy of accounting analyses. The US capitalist democracy has been distinctive not only in its scale and global influence but also as it has established a special kind of state–business relationship, and this American regulatory state has a number of distinctive features. Since the Reagan revolution of the 1980s, these contradictory aspects of the state have struggled for supremacy (Moran, 2002, 2010). Moran suggests that the state is a manager of the market system, but a manager that intervenes only to return it to a point of equilibrium. The political leadership, the language of the 'pilot' of society in the democratic arena, can also mean that '[one of] the authoritarian governing systems of the 20th century, (China) celebrated the leadership of the "Great Helmsman", Mao Zedong – one of the most savage tyrants in a century of savage tyrants' (Moran, 2010, p. 216). This argument questions the political economy of regulatory aspects within authoritarian (i.e. military) and democratic regimes respectively. In a theory-based paper, Tinker (1984, p. 56) criticises Stigler's (1971) view[1] of the role of the state by arguing that: 'There is no mention of the supply mechanisms that generate regulations (that is, little consideration is given to the various pressure groups, institutions, incentives, and other forces that combine to bring regulations into being).' However, he does not explore this view by providing empirical evidence. Theorising about minimising state intervention in the accounting regulatory process, Norton (2012, p. 119), using a Hegelian perspective, suggests that 'separation of functions between the executive branch of government and the judiciary is an essential prerequisite to the legitimacy of the state's claim to the wealth and income of the individual and the use of coercion when that claim is resisted'.

Prior studies provide 'mixed evidence' of state intervention in the accounting regulatory process (as indicated in Figure 3.1). For instance, the first group finds that state intervention should be minimised or even avoided (Jonsson, 1991; Norton, 2012), while the second group finds that state intervention may or may not be helpful in having an effective regulatory process (Alexanderand Servalli, 2010); and the third group finds that political economy may influence the regulatory process, depending on whether a regime is authoritarian or democratic (Tinker, 1984; Moran, 2010).

The state consults with various stakeholders

The state consults with various stakeholders (e.g. investors, professionals, and researchers) on the validation of rules (Streeck and Schmitter, 1985; Rose and Miller, 1992)[2010]; Kurunmaki et al., 2011; Oehrand Zimmermann, 2012). Streeck and Schmitter (1985, p. 120) argue that 'a state without some kind of spontaneous solidarity among its citizens is no more than a bureaucratic or military conspiracy, and modern communities without a state would always be in danger of losing their identity and independence'. They suggest that a state may increase its effectiveness by involving the market and the community, whilst state intervention may distort markets. By distinguishing between two types of welfare state – residual (e.g. the UK, the US, and Canada)[2] and institutional (e.g. Germany, France, and Japan)[3] – Oehr and Zimmermann

(2012) find that state involvement in the standard-setting process is a political process in institutional welfare states.

By contrast, Rose and Miller (1992, p. 173)[2010, p. 271] investigate problems of government, and demonstrate welfarism as a mode of 'social' government. They criticise the rhetoric of the welfare state because the welfare state depends on bureaucracy and is subject to constant pressure from bureaucrats wishing to expand their own empires. They point out that 'the welfare state has a morally damaging effect upon citizens, producing "a culture of dependency" based on expectations that government will do what in reality only individuals can' (p. 198 [296]). In terms of a neo-liberal state, they argue that:

> One of the central mechanisms of neo-liberalism is the proliferation of strategies to create and sustain a 'market', to reshape the forms of economic exchange on the basis of contractual exchange. The privatization programmes of the new politics have formed perhaps the most visible strand of such strategies, and one most aligned with the political ideals of markets versus state.
>
> (p. 198 [297])

Kurunmaki et al. (2011, p. 1) emphasise that 'Much is missed if we neglect the interaction between these [accounting and the state] twin poles.'

These studies imply that accounting operates both within and beyond the state. Accounting involves calculative practices; but it should be noted that the ways in which these are mobilised depend on the nature of the state within which they are operating. The above studies provide 'mixed evidence' (as indicated in Figure 3.1). For instance, one group finds that the state (e.g. a residual and neo-liberal state) consults with various stakeholders (Streeck and Schmitter, 1985; Rose and Miller, 1992[2010]; Oehr and Zimmermann, 2012), while the other group finds that the state (especially welfare states and, in particular, institutional welfare states) usually does not consult stakeholders, because of the complex political process and bureaucracy (Oehr and Zimmermann, 2012).

The state enforces outcomes

The state enforces outcomes (Hoogvelt and Tinker, 1978; Krzywda et al., 1995). The prior literature identified a lack of regulatory enforcement in developing countries. For instance, Hoogvelt and Tinker assess the changing role of the state in Sierra Leone. They find that the 'post-colonial period is characterised by a further recursion in the relations of exploitation: this time, a decline in returns to the state and an increase in allocations' (Hoogvelt and Tinker, 1978, p. 67). Through a periodisation analysis, they find that the government lacks regulatory enforcement. According to Hoogvelt and Tinker (1978, p. 69):

> Political sovereignty, however, permits the state to demand an increasingly higher price for its 'comprador role':[4] when this finally outweighs the attractions of low wage costs and ground rents, a company will pack up and cease their activities.

They argue that historical and political influences may help or hold back regulatory enforcement (p. 75).

In a Polish case study, Krzywda et al. find that the existence of Soviet-era traditions prevents the functioning of fully transparent accounting systems; hence, this influence may inhibit enforcement activities. The Soviet-era traditions include 'the continuing influence of the Ministry of Finance in accounting regulation and the continuation of state authorisation of accountants as members of the Chamber of Auditors and as the foundation of the audit profession' (Krzywda et al., 1995, p. 651). Further, a lower rate of privatisation and a higher rate of subsidisation of state-owned enterprises undermine the emergence of transparent accounting practices (Krzywda et al., 1995, p. 652). One limitation is that this study will not implicitly examine whether the state is accountable to its citizens in Bangladesh.

The state is accountable to its citizens

The state initiates change because it is accountable to its citizens (Miller, 1990; Constable and Kuasirikun, 2007). Miller argues that political machineries provide the mechanisms whereby government, the state, or businesses can be held accountable to society. He further emphasises that: 'Accounting can be understood through such a model by reference to the role it plays in assisting corporate accountability, installing monitoring systems within firms, contributing to the overall maximization of welfare in society, or even obviating the need for politico-regulatory mechanisms' (Miller, 1990, p. 319). Constable and Kuasirikun argue that power and dominance play a critical role in political identity and nation-state formation in a developing country like Thailand.

The two studies outlined above suggest that the state's accountability to its citizens depends on the nature of the country, and therefore the evidence is 'mixed' (as indicated in Figure 3.1). For example, in developed countries, the state is accountable to society, given that the state dispenses justice and protects equality, usually within an established tradition (Miller, 1990); whereas in developing countries, due to the power and dominance of the state, its accountability to its citizens may not be so guaranteed (Constable and Kuasirikun, 2007).

The role of donor agencies

Prior research has identified that the presence of donor agencies' assistance and collaboration with the state may help in producing better outcomes of accounting change. For instance, Krzywda et al. (1995, p. 652) call for future research into donor agencies' roles in accounting change in a developing country. Irvine (2008, p. 128) argues that there has been an increase in interaction between states and donor agencies such as the World Bank, the IMF, and the Asian Development Bank (ADB). She finds that the adoption of IFRS was mediated through the World Bank in the UAE. She further raises the question of the donor agencies' 'pushed down' effort for IFRS adoption in developing countries. Researchers such as Points and Cunningham (1998), Mir and Rahaman (2005), and Uddin and Hopper (2003) were critical about donor agencies' efforts in reforming financial reporting regimes in developing countries. Wallace and Briston (1993) propose collaboration between the state and donor agencies as the best way to move towards effective reforms of accounting. Since prior research provides mixed evidence (as indicated in Figure 3.1) regarding donor agencies' efforts in reforming accounting in developing countries, in this study I will explore the donor agencies' influences on accounting change. I therefore wish to modify Proposition II (P_{IIA}), which was initially developed in Chapter 2:

> P_{IIA}: Politics will have a positive influence on implementation of IFRS under the conditions of (a) common-law origin; (b) a lower level of government intervention; (c) a lower level of donor agencies' pressure; and (d) a lower level of political lobbying.
>
> *or*
>
> Politics will have a negative influence on implementation of IFRS under the conditions of (a) code-law origin; (b) a higher level of government intervention; (c) a higher level of donor agencies' pressure; and (d) a higher level of political lobbying.

The proposed initial theoretical model

The prior research called for future research into the interrelation between accounting and the state, because an examination of this relationship may offer the possibility of identifying the key factors which define the nature of accounting change.

The proposed initial theoretical model of the role of the state and accounting change can be expressed diagrammatically to show how the state is accountable for the outcome of accounting change (Figure 3.1). In this process, the one-directional dotted line represents donor agencies that indirectly assist the government in making active decisions for the protection of stakeholders' interests. In terms of the 'drivers of accounting change', as I have already demonstrated in Chapter 2, accounting change can be explained through accounting regulatory frameworks, political-institutional factors, and cultural factors (exemplified in this study through training opportunities in the accounting profession and through the presence of systematic corruption). The prior studies suggest that the drivers of accounting change may either help or impede the outcome of accounting change (see the propositions development set out in Chapter 2). In Figure 3.1, the donor agencies, the state and drivers of accounting change in relation to the outcomes of accounting changes are indicated by 'E' (i.e. external forces). The one-directional arrow shows how the state is directly influencing accounting change through drivers of accounting change.

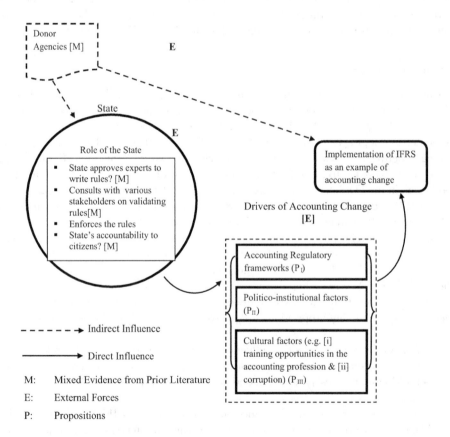

Figure 3.1 Proposed initial theoretical framework (role of the state and accounting change)

The Weberian view of state-society

Figure 3.1 expresses a general model of accounting change. Internal forces are missing in the model, since they were not indicated by the prior research. It is therefore important to pay attention to the Weberian view of state, in which Weber (1968)[1922] clearly demonstrates the relationship between the state and society (i.e. involving external and internal forces). A view of culture in relation to the role of the state can be derived from Weber (1958)[1904] and Weber (1968)[1922]. In terms of the state-society argument, Weber (1968, p. 156)[1922] stresses that the role of the state through parliamentary process and democracy is intended to deliver power to all citizens through the creation of meaning in everyday life, and that power is ultimately social. Skocpol (1985, p. 7) points out the need for 'a fundamental rethinking of the role of states in relation to economies and societies'. For Weber, 'human beings are motivated by ideal and material interests . . . social systems exist to realize their core values, and values explain why different actors make different choices even in similar situations' (Swidler, 1986, p. 274). Weber (1958)[1904] acknowledges that cultural values are not immutable, as 'they will change as the environment facing the society changes' (Richardson, 1987, p. 344), and 'culture should have enduring effects on economic action' (Swidler, 1986, p. 278). The Weberian view of the state-society will be discussed in Chapter 8.

The next section addresses the linkages between the roles of the state and society (i.e. between external and internal forces).

Institutional dynamics (link between the role of the state and individual organisations): external vs. internal forces[5]

> [The] regulation of any domain of economic life is a political affair. And since it is a political affair at its heart lies a set of relationships between business interests and the state. Disentangling those relationships – making sense of that grand phrase 'the political economy of regulation' – involves close attention to territorial patterns of regulation, since states inhabit a world of territory.
>
> (Moran, 2010, p. 224)

A link between the theory of the role of state and institutional dynamics can be derived from Moran's (2010) argument on the relationships between business interests (i.e. internal forces) and the state (i.e. external forces). He views accounting as being shaped by the political setting (institutional) in which it operates. He further argues that 'Accounting practice is a critical arena where politics and economics meet – and is therefore critical to the political economy of the market system' (Moran, 2010, p. 224). However, he did not implicitly explore business interests in the study, and calls for further research. In a recent study, Liguori and Steccolini argue that external forces fail to fully explain the final outcome of accounting change and, hence, internal forces (i.e. micro-processes or individual organisation and organisational field level of institutional dynamics) are seen to be important in driving accounting change in Italy. They argue that the internal forces occurring within organisations are significant in determining 'how the environment is interpreted and how organisations respond' (Liguori and Steccolini, 2012, p. 30).

Although these two studies (Moran, 2010; Liguori and Steccolini, 2012) analyse the role of state and individual organisations, neither provides any explicit model (i.e. the relationship between the state and society or between external and internal forces) to support their arguments. Therefore, to explore the relationship between the external and internal forces, I rely on Dillard et al.'s (2004) institutional dynamics model.[6] Drawing upon Weber (1958[1904],

1961[1927] and 1968[1922]), Dillard et al. propose an articulation of institutional dynamics indicating how criteria and practices are linked over three levels of social systems. Their model postulates that 'action is changed but constrained by structure to develop a recursive institutionalisation model that prioritises processes over outcomes' (Dillard et al., 2004, pp. 512–13). The institutionalisation, transposition, and de-institutionalisation of practices (P) are continual and dynamic, and involve actors' power and interests (Dillard et al., 2004, p. 513). The overarching political and economic level (PE) or state level establishes general, widely taken for granted norms (C_{PE}). These norms are disseminated to society and the organisational field level (OF), which translates into the individual organisation level (IO) (Hopper and Major, 2007). Different actors influence proceedings at different levels; for example, government officials, regulators, and legislators do so at the PE/state level; industry leaders and trade unions at the OF level; and managers and workers at the IO level (Irvine, 2008). Considering institutional dynamics, the prior literature discusses two issues – actors and their interests, and politics and power.

Firstly, actors and their interests constitute an imperative issue in institutional dynamics (Burns and Scapens, 2000). Scapens (1994, p. 147) identifies the state and the professions as the primary modern shapers of institutional forms. Burns (1996, p. 28) argues that rules constitute a power resource and that social agents act in their own interests. Therefore, it should not be assumed that the nation-state and the professions will share the same interests (Scott, 1987). State officials are more likely to create bureaucratic arrangements that centralise discretion at the top of the structure (Simon, 1983). By contrast, professional bodies will generally prefer more decentralised administration (Friedland and Alford, 1991). Subsequently, state actors are more likely to employ coercion in pursuing their ends, whilst the professions attempt to create cultural forms and beliefs (Moran, 2010). DiMaggio (1988, pp. 4–5) emphasises (1) norms or taken for granted assumptions 'that make actors unlikely to recognize or to act upon their interests'; and (2) behavioural constraints or cognitive limitations 'that cause actors who do recognize and try to act upon their interests to be unable to do so effectively'. Taking a contrary view, Scott (1987) identifies the missing point of the 'common utilitarian position' as being that actors attempt to pursue their interests. Extending the work of Friedland and Alford (1991), Scott (1987, p. 508) argues that: 'Institutional factors determine that actors in one type of setting, called firms, pursue profits; that actors in another setting, called agencies, seek larger budgets; that actors in a third setting, called political parties, seek votes.' In terms of changing accounting practice, Carpenter and Feroz (2001) identify the factors that may lead to initial resistance to the adoption of GAAP and argue that, if accounting bureaucrats are not active in professional associations, then powerful interest groups may impede GAAP. Therefore, Coad and Herbert (2009, p. 190) offer the view that individual organisational actors and their interests are regarded as having a mutually constitutive nature of structure and agency.

Secondly, politics and power play a central role in institutional dynamics,[7] where complex processes of change exist through time (Dawson, 1994). The politics can take place at various hierarchical institutional levels, and the power refers to the means through which powerful individuals' desires are exerted on others (Buchanan and Badham, 1999, p. 11). In essence, power and politics are interconnected in an institutional analysis (Pfeffer, 1981). Power is intended 'to produce intended effects' in line with perceived interests (Pettigrew and McNulty, 1995), whereas politics is 'the practical domain of power in action' (Buchanan and Badham, 1999, p. 11). Pfeffer (1981,p. 7) states that 'politics involves those activities or behaviours through which power is developed'. However, power in itself is not necessarily sufficient to achieve intended outcomes; it is important that individuals act (Mintzberg, 1983). Analyses of power and politics have been utilised by various researchers in the accounting domain. For example, Covaleski and Dirsmith (1988, p. 562) show that the process of institutionalisation appears to be infused with *power and self-interest*. Fogarty (1992, p. 348) and Mezias (1990, p. 455) argue that the structure of the FASB reflects the extensiveness of institutionalised involvement. Similarly, Bealing et al. (1996, p. 318) conclude that the SEC is a political institution because of its efforts and lack of success in terms of preserving the status quo in power relations among the business and political communities. Later, Hardy (1996, p. 11) develops a power mobilisation framework with regard to the processes of accounting change, but raises questions around the three forms of power's roles as facilitators /barriers in accounting change.[8]

As previously mentioned, Weber emphasises the state's role in politico-cultural terms in shaping a particular form of society. Colignon and Covaleski (1991, pp. 154–5) hint that:

> Theoretically, Weber's framework provides a critical and political basis for evaluating accounting . . . Weber's use of accounting indicates that although accounting calculation may be considered neutral in its execution, accounting is not neutral in its consequences, which raises the issue of the social impact of accounting practices on organizations, industries, and society. On the other hand, this tension suggests accounting practices and procedures are mechanisms of domination and objects of struggle among social groups.

It has also been argued that the Weberian framework provides 'a more specific and heterogeneous view of the socio-historical context of accounting and the contingent relations of accounting to organizations and society' (Colignon and Covaleski, 1991, p. 155).

The proposed new theoretical model

Most studies have utilised Weber's works in gaining a perspective of developed countries. More specifically, only three studies (Hoogvelt and Tinker, 1978; Krzywda et al., 1995; Constable and Kuasirikun, 2007) have focused on developing countries' experiences. None of these studies focused on the state–society relationship (i.e. between external and internal forces). Therefore, in the present study, I use Weber's framework to provide a broader understanding of the role of the state and the relationship between the state and society in accounting change. In doing so, I want to explore whether there is a link between the state's role and that of individual organisations in the process of accounting change.

Drawing upon Dillard et al. (2004)'s study of institutional dynamics (i.e. the relationships between the state, the organisational field level, and the individual organisation level), I have developed a proposed new theoretical framework, which is shown as Figure 3.2. This is the extended form of the proposed initial theoretical framework, Figure 3.1. Figure 3.2 contains three levels: firstly, the state level includes government, ministerial bodies, regulatory bodies and donor agencies; secondly, the organisational field level includes trade unions and industry leaders; and, finally, the individual organisation level includes individual organisations/companies listed in stock exchanges. In this model, the organisational field level and the individual organisation level are defined as internal forces (as indicated by 'I' in Figure 3.2), whilst state and donor agencies are defined as external forces (as indicated by 'E'). The one-directional dotted lines (black for donor agencies and grey for lobbying groups/organisational field levels) represent indirect influences on accounting change. The one-directional straight line indicates that state and individual organisations directly influence the outcome of accounting change through the drivers of accounting change. As mentioned in above, the drivers of accounting change are depicted as discussed in Chapter 2.

The role of the state is to make rules and enforce those rules (E), but lobbying groups or bureaucrats and individual organisations (I) may influence these processes. Specifically, at the organisational field level, 'the bureaucracy is a means of domination whose use and direction

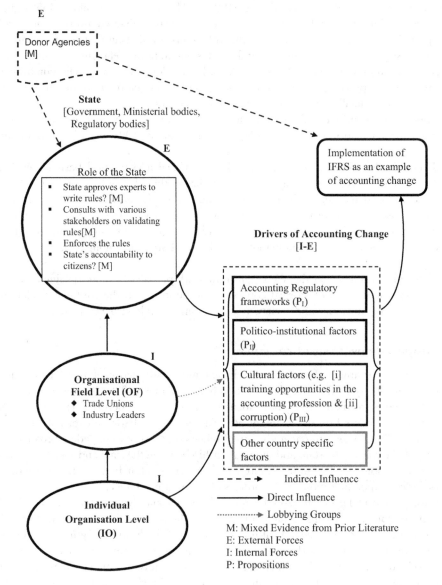

Figure 3.2 Proposed new theoretical framework (linking the state and individual organisations through institutional dynamics)

is distinct and whose consequences for social action are . . . accounting practices are key elements of the bureaucratic means of domination' (Colignon and Covaleski, 1991, p. 150; Dillard et al., 2004). It will be interesting to investigate, via this framework, whether state actors are pursuing individual interests, bureaucratic interests, and/or political power in shaping accounting change. At the individual organisation level, I will investigate whether individual organisations/companies are following social norms or regulations imposed by the state. This framework will be discussed in Chapter 8.

Conclusion

In summary, this chapter has developed a generic theoretical framework of the role of the state in relation to accounting change. The relatively limited previous research has been conducted employing theories of the role of the state in accounting change. This chapter then described key papers with reference to their theories of the role of the state in accounting change, and further described the external forces characteristics of the state, based on 15 selected papers, as mentioned in Chapter 2.

The majority of papers call for further research to broaden understanding of the Weberian view of the state and, in particular, the link between the state and society. Therefore, this chapter illustrates institutional dynamics, drawing upon Dillard et al. (2004)'s framework. I have discussed the relationship between the state and individual organisations in order to develop a proposed modified theoretical framework. This chapter also shows that the state alone is not responsible for accounting change; the outcome of change can also be explained by (1) actors and interests, and (2) politics and power. It is assumed that the theory of the role of the state may explain the different forces that have a bearing on individuals acting within social organisations. The prior literature provides different opinions; for example, one group argues that actors are acting in their own interests, while the other group suggests that actors are unlikely to act primarily in their own interests. Most researchers agree that power and politics hinder accounting change. The proposed theoretical model in the present study will be used to justify the research methods set out in Chapter 5. The framework will also be employed in the findings section in Chapter 8.

Notes

1   According to Stigler (1971, p. 3), 'The central tasks of the theory of economic regulation are to explain who will receive the benefits or burdens of regulation, what form regulation will take, and the effects of regulation on the allocation of resources.'
2   In the residual welfare state, 'accounting is designed to maintain the efficiency of markets' (Oehr and Zimmermann, 2012, p. 139).
3   In the institutional welfare state, 'the rules and standard setting at large will generally be state organised, state involvement in accounting runs much deeper, and this is in line with the societal motives and values' (Oehr and Zimmermann, 2012, p. 139).
4   Early colonial (1930–47), late colonial (1948–61) and post-colonial (1962–75). Each of these periods reflects the underlying socio-political realities in Sierra Leone (Hoogvelt and Tinker, 1978, p. 75).
5   In this study, 'internal forces' means micro processes of accounting change (i.e. individual organisation and organisational field levels of institutional dynamics).
6   Moran (2010) did not use Dillard et al.'s (2004) model. He emphasises the political economy of the market system. Dillard et al. provide a model to discuss the practice of accounting in organisations.
7   Over the last few decades, research into the dimensions of politics and power has blossomed within institutional dynamics analysis (Pettigrew, 1973, 1990; Pfeffer, 1981; Mintzberg, 1983; Burns and Scapens, 2000; Perry and Nölke, 2006). I use the terms politics and power in an analysis of the state level (PE), the organisational field level (OF) and the individual organisation level (IO).
8   (1) *Power over resources* refers to instances where actors deploy (or restrict) key resources to modify the behaviour of others; (2) *power over decision making* refers to an exerting of influence over subordinates' participation in decision making processes; (3) *power over meaning* means influencing actors' perceptions and/or preferences so that they accept the status quo.

Chapter 4

The financial reporting environment in Bangladesh

Introduction

The purpose of this chapter is to provide, evaluate, and contextualise background information on Bangladesh – including its political regime, accounting regulatory frameworks, cultural factors and corruption problems. The information discussed in this chapter can help when analysing findings and answering the following research questions:

> RQ-1: What is the relative impact of accounting regulatory frameworks and politico-institutional factors on the implementation of IFRS in Bangladesh as an example of a developing country?
>
> RQ-2(a): How do training opportunities in the accounting profession and the state of corruption, as outcomes of culture in Bangladesh, affect the implementation of IFRS?
>
> RQ-2(b): What other country-specific factors are affecting implementation of IFRS?
>
> RQ-3: How does a study of implementing IFRS help to build an understanding of a theory of the role of the state in accounting change in a developing country such as Bangladesh?

In this chapter I will discuss the political regime in Bangladesh; the accounting regulatory frameworks for financial and non-financial companies; the accounting standard-setting process, including the status of the adopted accounting standards in Bangladesh and South Asian regional efforts to implement IFRS; cultural factors; and a summary of the chapter.

Political regimes in Bangladesh: 1971–present

Bengal was absorbed into the Mughul (or Mughal) Empire in the sixteenth century, and Dhaka, the seat of the nawab (the representative of the emperor), gained some importance as a provincial centre (Ghafur, 1976). Portuguese, Dutch, and French traders were the first westerners to reach Bengal in the latter part of the fifteenth century. In 1859, the British Crown directly took the place of the East India Company, extending British dominion from Bengal, which became a region of India (Jahan, 2003; Ahmad, 1976). After the partition of British India in 1947, the independent states of India and Pakistan were created. It is argued that the government of West Pakistan contributed very little to the development of East Pakistan (Khan and Husain, 1996). Ahmad (1950, p. 194) argues that 'Industrialization of East Bengal [East Pakistan] . . . showed signs of an initial unbalanced development'. In 1948, Sheikh Mujibur Rahman formed a students' organisation, the 'Chhatra League', to protest against inequality and injustice in comparison with West Pakistan (Jahan, 2005). In 1966, Sheikh Rahman became President of the Awami League (AL) and emerged as leader of the Bengali autonomy movement (Ahmad, 1976). On 26 March 1971, following a bloody attack by the Pakistani army, Bengali nationalists declared an independent 'People's Republic of Bangladesh'. There were an estimated 3 million people killed during the fight between the army and the Bengali Mukti Bahini freedom fighters. On 16 December 1971, Pakistani forces surrendered, and Bangladesh – meaning 'Bengal country' – emerged as an independent state. The new country became a parliamentary democracy under a 1972 constitution (Jahan, 2003). The first government of the new nation of Bangladesh was formed in Dhaka, with Justice Abu Sayeed Choudhury as President and Mujibur Rahman as Prime Minister (Jahan, 2005). The successive political regimes in Bangladesh are described below and listed in Figure 4.1.

Sheikh Mujibur Rahman (1972–75): Sheikh Mujibur Rahman came to office with massive personal popularity levels, and he created a new constitution on a modified Westminster model which came into force in December 1972 (Ghafur, 1976). In March 1973, the first parliamentary elections were held under the 1972 constitution, and the Awami League won with a massive majority. No other political party in Bangladesh's early years was able to challenge the Awami League's popularity (Ahmad, 1976). In December 1974, Sheikh Mujibur Rahman decided to establish a one-party system, the Bangladesh Krishak Sramik Awami League (BAKSAL) (Ahmed, 1998). In August 1975, Sheikh Mujibur Rahman and most of his family were assassinated by army officers (Ahmad, 1976).

Ziaur Rahman (1975–81): Successive military coups resulted in the emergence of Army Chief of Staff General Ziaur Rahman as a strongman leader (Halim, 2005). He used Martial Law Administration (MLA) and banned political parties (Jalal, 1995). In November 1976, he became Chief Martial Law Administrator (Jalal, 1995). In elections in June 1978, he won a five-year term with a 76% majority (Ahmed, 2003). In May 1981, Ziaur Rahman was assassinated in Chittagong by the military (Khan and Husain, 1996). In accordance with the constitution, Vice President Justice Abdus Sattar became the President, and the army stepped in once again (Jalal, 1995).

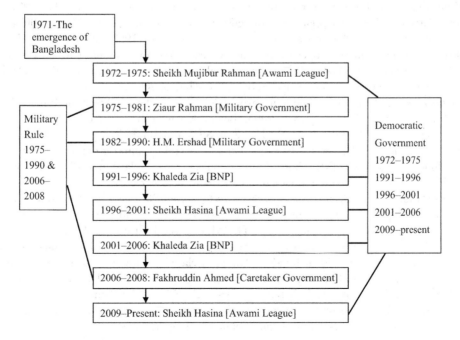

Figure 4.1 Time frames of Bangladesh governments, 1971–present

H.M. Ershad (1982–90): Army chief Lt. General Hussain Muhammad Ershad assumed power in a bloodless coup in March 1982 (Ahmed, 1998). He suspended the constitution and declared martial law (Jahan, 2003). He sought public support for his regime in a national referendum on his leadership in March 1985, and after winning overwhelmingly he founded a new party named the Jatiya Party (Zafarullah, 1999). In 1986 elections, he won a majority of the 300 parliamentary seats, and in July 1987 the government began to arrest scores of opposition activists under the Special Powers Act of 1974 (Jahan, 2005). He then dissolved Parliament and scheduled fresh elections for March 1988 (Jalal, 1995). On 6 December 1990, Ershad offered his resignation, and on 27 February 1991, an interim government, headed by Acting President Chief Justice Shahabuddin Ahmed, conducted the country's most free and fair parliament elections to date (Ahmed, 2003).

Khaleda Zia (1991–96): The Bangladesh Nationalist Party (BNP) won a majority of seats and formed a government with support from the Islamic party Jamaat-I-Islami. The BNP leader, Begum Khaleda Zia (widow of President Ziaur Rahman), became Prime Minister. The former President, General Ershad, served out a prison sentence on corruption charges (Bangladesh Observer, 1991). In October 1991, MPs elected a new head of state, President Abdur Rahman Biswas, and recreated a parliamentary system. They also bestowed power on the office of the Prime Minister similar to that of Bangladesh's original 1972 constitution (Zafarullah and Akhter, 2000; Daily Inquilab, 1991). In March 1996, following escalating political turmoil, the sitting Parliament enacted a constitutional amendment to allow a neutral caretaker government (Chief Justice Mohammad Habibur Rahman was Chief Adviser, a position equivalent to Prime Minister) in order to conduct new parliamentary elections (Halim, 2005).

Sheikh Hasina (1996–2001): Under the caretaker government, new parliamentary elections were held in June 1996. The Awami League (AL) won a majority and formed a government with support from the Jatiya Party, led by former President Ershad (Jahan, 2003). The AL party leader, Sheikh Hasina (daughter of Sheikh Mujibur Rahman), became Prime Minister and formed a 'government of national consensus'. In September 1997, the Jatiya Party withdrew its support from the government (Zafarullah and Akhter, 2000) and a four-party opposition alliance was formed at the beginning of 1999 (Ahmed, 2003). In July 2001, the AL government stepped down to allow a caretaker government to preside over fresh parliamentary elections (Halim, 2005). The caretaker government was successful in holding a parliamentary general election on 1 October 2001 (Ahmed, 2003).

Khaleda Zia (2001–06): The four-party alliance led by the BNP won more than a two-thirds majority in parliament (Jahan, 2005). Begum Khaleda Zia became Prime Minister for the second time (the first was in 1991). However, Sheikh Hasina rejected the results and boycotted Parliament (Halim, 2005). During 2005, an extremist Islamist group named Jama'atul Mujahideen Bangladesh (JMB) claimed responsibility for bomb blasts in 63 districts. In February 2006, the AL returned to parliament and demanded early elections.

Caretaker (military-backed) government (2006–08): The 13th Amendment to the constitution required the President to offer the position of Chief Adviser to the last Chief Justice of the Supreme Court (Knox, 2009). The AL opposed Justice K.M. Hasan and claimed that he became the Chief Adviser in order to help the BNP win the parliamentary elections. On 11 January 2007, President Iajuddin Ahmed declared a state of emergency, resigned as Chief Adviser and indefinitely postponed parliamentary elections (Alamgir, 2009). On 12 January 2007, former Bangladesh Bank governor Dr Fakhruddin Ahmed became the new Chief Adviser. Under emergency provisions, the government suspended certain fundamental rights guaranteed by the constitution and detained a large number of politicians and others on suspicion of involvement in corruption and other crimes (Alamgir, 2009). The government arrested former Prime Ministers Sheikh Hasina and Khaleda Zia on charges of corruption;

and, after western pressure, the government eventually decided to step down, and the Election Commission then declared that parliamentary elections would take place (Ahmed, 2010).

Sheikh Hasina (2009–Present): On 29 December 2008, parliamentary elections were held and the AL leader, Sheikh Hasina, became Prime Minister for the second time (the first had been in 1996). As Bangladesh is one of the most vulnerable countries in terms of climate change, Sheikh Hasina has been a vocal advocate for mitigation and adaptation, aligning with the Copenhagen Accord in January 2010 (Daily Star, 2010). During her term, in February 2009, there was a mutiny by the Bangladesh Rifles (BDR)[1] in which more than 50 army officers were killed (Guardian, 2009).

How do political regimes and the country's political history interact with business?

During the first democratic era (1972–75), Bangladesh followed a socialist economic model by nationalising all industries. The government took various positive steps regarding the capital markets: Firstly, the government established the Institute of Chartered Accountants of Bangladesh (ICAB); the Institute of Cost and Management Accountants of Bangladesh (ICMAB), the National Board of Revenue (NBR), and Bangladesh Bank. Secondly, in order to ensure stability in all legal spheres in the newly independent country, the Laws Continuance Order 1971, Presidential Order No. 5 of 1972, Presidential Order No. 91 of 1972, and the 1972 Constitution of Bangladesh were introduced (Chowdhury, 2002).

In the second democratic era (1991–2006), the major regulatory reforms of the early 1990s were aimed particularly at moving towards an open economy. Examples include the announcement of a flexible market-oriented interest rate policy in January 1990 by Bangladesh Bank; the Financial Sector Reforms Programme (FSRP) in 1990; the establishment of the Securities and Exchange Commission (SEC) in 1993; the Privatisation Board in 1993; the Privatisation Commission in 2000; the SEC Act 1993; the Companies Act of 1994 replacing the older Companies Act of 1913; the Money Loan Court Act 1990; the Bank Companies Act 1991; the Financial Institutions Act 1993;the Bankruptcy Act 1997; the Banking Reform Committee (BRC) in 1996; and the Securities and Exchange Rules in 1997 requiring the mandatory compliance of IAS. A major scam in the share market then took place, in 1996. Those who were involved in the scam were bailed by the High Court through political connections (Economist, 1997). According to the ADB (2005, p. 7), 'The share scam cases lodged by the SEC after the 1996 market manipulation remain unresolved.'

During the first military regime (1975–90), socialist concepts were abandoned. Some positive contributions were made by the government during this regime. Firstly, institutions like the Bangladesh Garment Manufacturers and Exporters Association (BGMEA), the Law Committee, and the Board of Investment (BOI) were established. The ICAB became a member of the International Accounting Standards Board (IASB) and started working on the adoption of IAS in 1983. Secondly, the financial and capital market liberalisation trends of the 1980s brought increasing volatility into global financial markets and increased the need for information as a means to ensure financial stability (Chowdhury, 2002). More specifically, a privatisation programme was started in 1982, with the privatisation of two nationalised commercial banks, and the country entered into the IMF/World Bank adjustment programmes. The financial sector's reform agenda was launched in 1984. Finally, development of the legal system took place with, for example: the Ombudsman Act 1980 (Act XV of 1980); the Administrative Tribunals Act 1980 (Act VII of 1981); the Income Tax Ordinance 1984 (Ordinance XXV of 1984); the Land Reforms Ordinance 1984 (Ordinance X of 1984); the Family Courts Ordinance 1985 (Ordinance XVIII of 1985); and the Law Reform Ordinance 1978. During the

Table 4.1 World Bank Governance Indicators for Bangladesh (1996–2010)[2]

Political Regimes	Democratic Government					Military Government		Democratic Government
Governance Indicators	1996	1998	2000	2002	2004	2006	2008	2010
Political Stability and Absence of Violence/ Terrorism	24.52	**29.81**	23.56	17.31	9.13	8.65	9.62	9.91
Government Effectiveness	24.88	**39.02**	32.20	26.83	19.51	24.88	27.67	21.53
Regulatory Quality	16.18	17.65	18.63	18.14	13.24	18.14	18.93	**21.53**
Rule of Law	16.75	19.62	22.01	22.01	16.27	21.05	**26.92**	26.54
Control of Corruption	27.32	**38.54**	12.68	5.37	2.44	3.90	14.56	16.27
Voice and Accountability	46.63	**41.83**	39.42	37.02	26.92	32.697	33.17	38.39

Sources: http://info.worldbank.org/governance/wgi/pdf/wgidataset.xls (accessed 12 February 2012); Kaufmann et al. (2010).

second military era (2006–08), the corporate governance codes (comply or explain) ordinance was introduced (in 2006). The government proposed the Financial Reporting Ordinance 2008 in order to implement IFRS (Hasan et al., 2008).

Additionally, economic development in terms of the Annual Growth Rate of GDP (%) from 1972 to 1975 was-0.35; in 1975–90: 3.39; in 1991–2006: 5.01; in 2006–08: 6.41 and in 2009–10: 5.9 (World Bank, 2011). These figures indicate that the highest GDP was during the second era of military government (2006–08). Surprisingly, Pakistan also experienced its highest growth rates (6.7%) during military rule (Khan, 2011). According to World Bank Governance Indicators, Bangladesh experienced significant deterioration in political stability (see Table 4.1). Deterioration continued in terms of government effectiveness, control of corruption, and voice and accountability. The regulatory quality and the rule of the law improved slightly. During the military government in 2008, the implementation of law was better than it was under the democratic government. It is observed that comparing years in the period 2000–08, government effectiveness and control of corruption were better in the military government period. However, Barkat et al. (2004) argue that the military-led government can be denoted as vulnerable to attracting foreign capital inflows, whilst mis-governance and a legitimised civil system of military rule are the de facto situation in Bangladesh. This evidence questions the overwhelming significance of democracy in Bangladesh.

Accounting regulatory frameworks

Accounting regulatory frameworks for non-financial companies

According to the World Bank (2009,p. 19):

> Bangladesh is a common law country and has been influenced by British, and to a lesser extent, Indian and Pakistani law and legal tradition. The Companies Act (CA) and other legislation are based on dated UK equivalents. The Securities and Exchange Commission (SEC) have used their regulatory authority to compensate for this dated legal structure; however, key gaps remain in the current framework.

The accounting regulatory frameworks for non-financial companies in Bangladesh can be found in the following sources: the Companies Act 1994[3] (for all companies, except public enterprises); the Securities and Exchange Rules 1987 (for listed companies on the Dhaka Stock Exchange (DSE) and the Chittagong Stock Exchange (CSE)); Dhaka Stock Exchange Listing Rules 1998 (for companies listed on the DSE); Listing Regulations of the Chittagong Stock Exchange (for companies listed with the CSE);[4] and Income Tax Ordinance 1984 (for all companies). For financial companies, the regulatory frameworks are the Bank Companies Act 1991 (for banking companies) and the Insurance Act 1938 (for insurance companies). The accounting rules and guidelines governing Bangladesh have been inherited from the period of British rule, and exhibit a pattern similar to those in the UK (Ahmed, 2006). Bangladesh's progress regarding corporate disclosure has been comparatively very slow due to inconsistencies between the regulatory frameworks (Ahmed, 2010; World Bank, 2003, 2009; Solaiman, 2006; Azizuddin, 2006).

The Companies Act 1994 provides basic requirements for financial reporting by all listed companies in Bangladesh. Yet, the Companies Act 1994 is silent about Bangladesh Financial Reporting Standards (BFRS)/IFRS (World Bank, 2009).[5] The Companies Act 1994 lacks clarity with regard to statutory requirements on disclosures in the financial statements (World Bank, 2009). Moreover, some accounting requirements prescribed by the Companies Act 1994 are incompatible with IFRS. Several examples can be given. Firstly, contrary to IAS 21 (The Effects of Changes in Foreign Exchange Rates), the Companies Act 1994 (Sec. 185, Schedule XI, Part I) requires that capitalisation of gains and losses arising from changes in foreign exchange rates will be adjusted in balance sheets (see, for example, X Limited,[6] which is an 'A Category' company in the DSE[7] and which complied with the Companies Act 1994 instead of IFRS in 2010).

Secondly, the Companies Act 1994 does not require consolidated statements for a group (Sec. 186),[8] but this is required under the IFRS. According to Section 186, the Act requires that a set of financial statements for each subsidiary, together with some additional statements, be annexed to the holding company's balance sheet. The World Bank (2003, p. 3) mentions that 'Companies Act provisions are not fully in line with IAS requirements on preparing consolidated financial statements.' Thirdly, Sections 210(3a, b and c) and 211 of the Companies Act 1994 support the long-term employment of an auditor. In accordance with the Act, if the company auditor is appointed through a resolution passed at the AGM, the auditor will be guaranteed for an unlimited period unless the auditor is proven to be dishonest or unqualified, or they resign.

Fourthly, a cash flow statement is not mandatory under the Companies Act 1994. Section 183(4) provides that the financial year of a company may be more or less than a calendar year but shall not exceed 15 months. It may, however, be extended to 18 months with a Special Resolution/Extraordinary Resolution of the Registrar of Joint Stock Companies (Form VII of RJSC). Section 185 (Schedule XI, Part I) recommends the format and the content of the balance sheet, but not the format of the profit and loss account (Schedule XI, Part II). The provisions of this section, however, shall not apply to banks, insurance companies, or electricity companies because forms of balance sheets have been specified elsewhere, in the respective laws governing such companies.

The Securities and Exchange Commission Rules 1987 require compliance with IFRS as adapted by the ICAB in Bangladesh; these are known as Bangladesh Financial Reporting Standards or BFRS (see also section below for the accounting standard-setting process in Bangladesh). The rules which are relevant to the preparation of financial statements are: 'All listed companies' financial statements shall be prepared in accordance with the requirements laid down in the Schedule and the IFRS as adopted by the ICAB' (Amended SEC/Sec-7/ SER-1987/03/132, dated 22 October 1997). In this sub-rule, IFRS refers to the accounting standards issued by the International Accounting Standards Board. However, the SEC Rules of 1987 suffer from a few shortcomings – e.g. that no disclosure of significant accounting policies is required, and a statement of changes in financial position is not required (IAS 1).

Inconsistencies are also found between the Income Tax Ordinance 1984 and IFRS. For example, provisions are not allowed under the Income Tax Ordinance, and therefore provisions are not tax deductible; but, according to IAS 37, provisions are mandatory. Some expenditures, for instance, amortisation and entertainment expenses, are handled differently (tax ordinance requires the limit of the expenses but, according to IFRS, an actual amount should be presented) (Section 30, Ordinance No. XXXVI of 1984). The tax authority also believes that the company should have a predetermined rate of gross margin, which is quite unusual and is contradictory to IFRS (Section 53DD, Ordinance No. XXXVI of 1984) (Azizuddin, 2006).

Despite the comments of various researchers (Ahmed, 2010; Solaiman, 2006; Azizuddin, 2006) and World Bank reports (World Bank, 2003, 2009) regarding inconsistencies in accounting regulatory frameworks, no real change has taken place. The former President of the ICAB, A.B.M. Azizuddin (2006, p. 3) states that:

> Though the requirements of mandatory rules and non-mandatory guidelines need to be improved to attract foreign investors, the main problem is the implementation and compliance of the rules and guidelines . . . the real problem lies regarding avoidance of laws and the annual reports, particularly the financial statements, are no exception.

He strongly recommends that the Companies Act 1994 and the Securities and Exchange Commission Rules 1987 should be modified.

Accounting regulatory frameworks for banks

The Bangladesh Bank Order 1972 states that:

> [The] Central Bank in Bangladesh [is] to regulate the issue of currency and the keeping of reserves and manage the monetary and credit system in Bangladesh with a view to stabilizing domestic monetary value; preserving the par value of the Bangladesh Taka; promoting and maintaining a high level of production, employment and real income in Bangladesh; and fostering growth and development of the country's productive resources in the best national interest.
>
> (Government of Bangladesh 1972, President's Order No. 127, p. 4)

The Bangladesh Bank Order 1972 and the Bank Companies Act 1991[9] empower the Bangladesh Bank to regulate and supervise the banking sector of Bangladesh (World Bank, 2003, 2009). As mentioned earlier, the Securities and Exchange Commission Rules 1987 and the Companies Act 1994 listing requirements of the DSE and the CSE and adopted accounting standards by the ICAB are the main basis of financial reporting practices for banking companies in Bangladesh. However, complexities in banking regulations exist in Bangladesh (World Bank, 2009; Sobhan and Werner, 2003); see Table 4.2 for various regulations in relation to banking companies. Therefore, disclosure of information for the banking sector in Bangladesh has not increased over the last two decades (Ahmed, 2010). The regulatory frameworks set minimum legal requirements as to the disclosure of accounting information in corporate annual reports, and are likely therefore to produce statements which are confined only to concepts of 'minimum disclosure' (Ahmed, 2006).

Table 4.2 Relevant regulations for the banking industry in Bangladesh

- Bangladesh Bank Order No. 127, 1972
- Bangladesh Bank (Amendment) Act, 2003
- Banking Companies Act No. 14, 1991
- Bank Company (Amendment) Act No. 13, 1993
- Banking Companies (Amendment) Act No. 25, 1995
- Banking Companies (Amendment) Act, 2003
- Companies Act No. 18, 1994
- Money Laundering Prevention Act No. 7, 2002
- Bangladesh Bank Framework for Internal Control Systems in Banking Organisations
- Bangladesh Bank Guidelines for Merger/Amalgamation of Banks/Financial Institutions
- Bangladesh Bank Prudential Regulations for Banks, 2007
- Bangladesh Bank Guidance Notes on Prevention of Money Laundering (Act No. 8 of 2009)
- Banking Regulation and Policy Department Circular No. 5, 2006
- Banking Regulation and Policy Department Circular No. 14, 2007

The Companies Act 1994 does not contain any provision for mandatory observance of the adopted IFRS and ISAs in practice (Siddiqui, 2010). For insurance companies, the Insurance Act 1938 does not mandate compliance with BFRS/IFRS. For other unlisted companies, neither the law nor the by-laws of the ICAB mandates compliance with BAS (Ahmed, 2006). This shows that different companies (in different sectors) are using different accounting policies and procedures in the preparation and presentation of their financial statements within annual reports (ADB, 2007). As a result of the diversified use of accounting practices, meaningful comparison of financial position as well as performance among the companies becomes difficult to interpret on the part of the users of accounting information for their decision-making purposes (Siddiqui, 2010). To ensure more transparency in financial institutions in Bangladesh, the central bank (i.e. Bangladesh Bank) issued Banking Regulation and Policy Department (BRPD) Circular No.14,[10] dated 25 June 2003, for the mandatory adoption of IAS 30 (Bangladesh Bank, 2006–07).[11]

Major institutions involved in accounting regulatory frameworks

The Securities and Exchange Commission (SEC)

The Commission was established in 1993 under the provisions of the Securities and Exchange Ordinance 1969. The functions of the Commission as laid down in the SEC Act 1993 are to ensure proper issuance of securities; to protect the interests of investors in securities; and to promote the development of, and regulate, the capital and securities market (Akhtaruddin, 2005). The SEC issued Corporate Governance (CG) guidelines (to comply or explain) in 2006 during the caretaker (military-backed)government; it has not issued any guidelines or taken any steps so far toward the implementation of IFRS. Siddiqui (2010) argues that, although similar to many other developing nations, Bangladesh has also adopted the Anglo-American shareholder model of corporate governance, and such adoption may be prompted by exposure to legitimacy threats rather than being for valid efficiency reasons. There are some contradictory issues between the SEC rules and the Companies Act 1994. For example, the Companies Act 1994 (Section 210) allows both sole practitioners and partnership firms to act as auditors. However, according to the SEC Rules 1987, only partnership firms with seven years' experience in professional practice are allowed to audit listed companies (World Bank,

2009). The SEC also requires that auditor rotation takes place once every three years, except where the company declares dividends at a rate prescribed by the SEC, in which case the same auditor can continue in office (Azizuddin, 2006). The practice of linking auditor rotation with the company's dividend declaration is highly unusual, and it is not clear what purpose it serves or is intended to serve (World Bank, 2003). World Bank (2003, p. 2) also points out that:

> The SEC claims that its February 2000 rule on audit reports has mandated full compliance with IFRS, although this requirement does not appear to have the force of law. To ensure compliance and clarify its position, the SEC should issue a rule for mandatory observance of IFRS in preparing statutory financial statements.

The Institute of Chartered Accountants of Bangladesh (ICAB)

The ICAB is the national professional accounting body of Bangladesh. The institute was established in 1973 and given its legal status by the Bangladesh Chartered Accountants Order 1973 (Presidential Order No. 2 of 1973). The ICAB is an active member of various international and regional accounting bodies – such as the International Federation of Accountants (IFAC), the International Accounting Standards Board (IASB), the Confederation of Asian and Pacific Accountants (CAPA), and the South Asian Federation of Accountants (SAFA). The institute circulates all IFAC releases in relation to IFRS to its members. The problem, though, is that the institute cannot enforce the accounting standards unless the standards are incorporated in the Companies Act 1994 or the institute is given legal power to do so by the SEC (Hasan et al., 2008). Until this happens the institute is limited to an advisory role rather than an enforcing role. Nevertheless, in the absence of an accounting standards board in Bangladesh, the ICAB acts as the standard-setting body in most cases where there is a need for standards (Akhtaruddin, 2005). There are some major problems, including a shortage of Chartered Accountants (CAs), and the audit fees structure may impede the ICAB's objective to implement IFRS.

Firstly, with regard to the shortage of CAs, the ICAB was founded with only 80 members (Siddiqui, 2010). The institute had 610 members in 1992 and 700 in 2000 (Ahmed, 2006). Of these 700 members, 565 were resident in Bangladesh and 135 were resident abroad; 274 were practising as public accountants and the rest were serving in various sectors (Azizuddin, 2006). In 2009, the institute had a total of 914 members, of which 662 were fellow members and 252 were associate members. In 2010, the number had grown up to 1,200, of which 300 are in practice and the remainder are serving the government, public enterprises, NGOs, donor organisations, and different corporate sectors (Siddiqui, 2011). According to Ahmed (2010), Pakistan had over 3,000 Chartered Accountants, Sri Lanka had over 2,700, and Nepal had around 270, while Bangladesh had around 1,200 CAs. This indicates the shortage of CAs in Bangladesh. Since the economy of Bangladesh is expanding rapidly, it is estimated that the actual number of qualified accountants needed is more than 12,000 (Siddiqui, 2011). In 2010, among the four nationalised commercial banks in Bangladesh, two of them did not have any CAs; around 90 banks and insurance companies had only 15 CAs; 14 out of 52 state-owned enterprises (SOEs) had CAs; and 35 out of 250 listed companies had CAs (Ahmed, 2010). The government of Bangladesh does not employ any professional accountants in managing its budget of over Tk. 1,150 billion (Siddiqui, 2011). Therefore, transparency in both the public and private sectors is questionable (Daily Star, 2011).

To increase the number of CAs in Bangladesh, the World Bank and the ICAEW are working together with the ICAB. For example, the ICAEW was awarded a contract under the Economic Management Technical Assistance Programme (EMTAP) called a 'Twinning Project', funded by the World Bank, to strengthen accounting and auditing standards practices in Bangladesh (ICAEW, 2008). In 2009, the ICAB signed a Memorandum of Understanding (MoU) with the ICAEW to develop a new syllabus in line with IFAC requirements, and the new syllabus has been drawn up to increase the pass rate of candidates, meeting local and international demand for accounting professionals (Siddiqui, 2010).

Secondly, with regard to the audit fees structure, audit fees of public sector enterprises were fixed during the Pakistani era and have continued in this way with only slight/nominal increases (Siddiqui, 2011). Audit fees in Bangladesh are very low compared to those in India and Pakistan. The audit fees of the Central Bank of Pakistan are Rs. 3,500,000,[12] those of the Reserve Bank of India are Rs. 4,500,000; and in Bangladesh they are Tk. 7,200,000. In Bangladesh, the audit fees of state-owned commercial banks are less than Tk. 1 million for portfolios of more than Tk. 100–200 billion, and other SOEs are no exception.[13] Even the audit fees of private sector foreign banks are much lower compared with India, Pakistan, and Sri Lanka (Siddiqui, 2011). Therefore, overall, the audit fees of India and Pakistan are substantially higher than those of Bangladesh.

The Institute of Cost and Management Accountants of Bangladesh (ICMAB)

The ICMAB was established in 1973 under the Cost and Management Accountants Ordinance (1977) and is attached to the Ministry of Commerce (MOC). The primary objective of the institute is to develop and train cost and management accountants. Fellows qualifying from the ICMAB are not required to go through practical accounting and auditing training with a professional accounting firm (Solaiman, 2006). The ICMAB's capacity is constrained by the shortage of well-trained instructors and resources – i.e. a lack of high-quality training programmes on the practical application of IFRS (Hasan et al., 2008). The institute has no auditing power, and hence does not play any role regarding financial accounting standards (Akhtaruddin, 2005).

The Dhaka Stock Exchange (DSE)

The DSE is registered as a public limited company and its activities are regulated by its Articles of Association rules and regulations and by-laws along with the Securities and Exchange Ordinance 1969, the Companies Act 1994, and the Securities and Exchange Commission Act 1993.[14] The volume of transactions and the number of quoted companies on the DSE have increased significantly (Siddiqui, 2010). There are 250 companies quoted on the Dhaka Stock Exchange.[15] While accounting is of little use to individual investors, it is widely used by institutional investors (Mir and Rahaman, 2005). For instance, there is no professional advisory service by financial analysts in the market, but institutional investors have their own financial analysts (Imam and Malik, 2007). The DSE mainly requires the submission of past financial statements, but does not call for a financial disclosure checklist (disclosure requirements are covered by the Securities and Exchange Rules 1987, the Companies Act 1994, and IFRS) (Hasan et al., 2008). Consequently, the stock exchange does not regard monitoring the quality of published accounts to be part of its function (Ahmed, 2010).

The Registrar of Joint Stock Companies (RJSC)

The function of the Registrar is to grant registration to new incumbents (Hasan et al., 2008). The Companies Act 1994 requires that every joint stock company obtains a registration from the Registrar and files a copy of their annual report, including audited accounts, with the

Registrar (Ahmed and Nicholls, 1994). However, the Registrar's role is reduced to one of routine licensing of companies, in exchange for a specified fee, and housing the files of companies' accounts (World Bank, 2009; Ali et al., 2004). Parry (1989, p. 65) earlier opined about the RJSC's physical environment, mentioning 'the shabby conditions of the office'. In addition, bribery has become a must for all applicants obtaining registration within a reasonable time, and without bribery it may take months or even years to obtain registration (Ahmed, 1996). The Registrar admitted that hundreds of companies have not filed annual accounts for years, and no action other than sending reminders has so far been taken against companies failing to file accounts with the Registrar (Hasan et al., 2008). The World Bank (2003, p. 3) questions the activities of the RJSC by stating that:

> The directors of limited companies both private and public are responsible for filing annual audited financial statements with the Registrar of Joint Stock Companies within 30 days of the annual general meeting. An annual general meeting should be held within 15 months of the previous annual general meeting. However, it is possible to get permission from the Registrar for a three-month extension.

The National Board of Revenue (NBR)

The NBR was established by President's Order No. 76 of 1972, under the Internal Resources Division (IRD) of the Ministry of Finance. The NBR is the central authority for tax administration in Bangladesh, and is responsible for the formulation and continuous reappraisal of tax policies and tax laws; negotiating tax treaties with foreign governments; and participating in inter-ministerial deliberations on economic issues which have a bearing on fiscal policies and tax administration (Ahmed, 2006). The main task of the NBR is to collect domestic revenue for the government (primarily import duties and taxes, VAT and income tax).[16] However, the World Bank (2003, p. 2) criticises its operation by saying that:

> Taxation authorities do not accept some IFRS-compatible accounting treatments for determining taxable profit, for example, recognizing finance leases, prior period adjustments, and expensing of pre-operation costs. Although there is no legal requirement on observance of tax accounting rules in external financial reporting, those who prepare and audit financial statements generally ensure that the accounting treatments that are acceptable to the taxation authorities are used not only for tax reporting purposes but also for preparing the general-purpose financial statements.

The accounting standard-setting process

The accounting standards, and particularly disclosure standards, in Bangladesh originate from a combination of legal, institutional, and professional bodies providing rules and guidelines (Parry, 1989; Ahmed and Nicholls, 1994; Hasan et al., 2008). The professional responsibilities and conduct of Chartered Accountants are governed by the Bangladesh Chartered Accountants Bye-laws 1973 (Solaiman, 2006). These bye-laws have not been amended to require mandatory compliance with the adopted standards by ICAB members (Farooque et al., 2007). International Accounting Standards (BAS) and IFRS (BFRS) are developed by the ICAB and based specifically on the original versions of IFRS (Solaiman, 2006).[17] Since the updated version is not mentioned in the SEC Rules of 1987 or 1997, a company is allowed to use the original version. Figure 4.2 shows that the Technical and Research Committee (TRC) of the ICAB proposes the standards.[18]

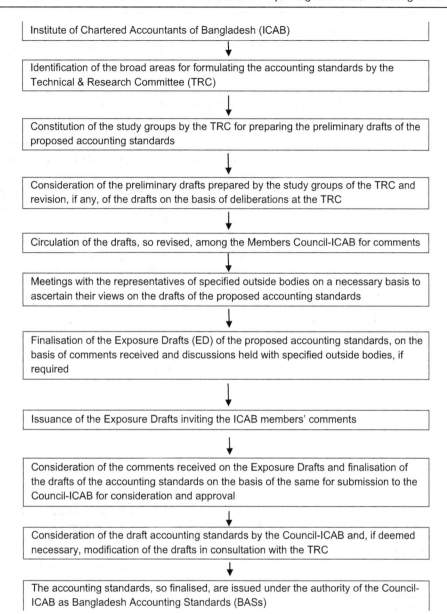

| Institute of Chartered Accountants of Bangladesh (ICAB) |

↓

| Identification of the broad areas for formulating the accounting standards by the Technical & Research Committee (TRC) |

↓

| Constitution of the study groups by the TRC for preparing the preliminary drafts of the proposed accounting standards |

↓

| Consideration of the preliminary drafts prepared by the study groups of the TRC and revision, if any, of the drafts on the basis of deliberations at the TRC |

↓

| Circulation of the drafts, so revised, among the Members Council-ICAB for comments |

↓

| Meetings with the representatives of specified outside bodies on a necessary basis to ascertain their views on the drafts of the proposed accounting standards |

↓

| Finalisation of the Exposure Drafts (ED) of the proposed accounting standards, on the basis of comments received and discussions held with specified outside bodies, if required |

↓

| Issuance of the Exposure Drafts inviting the ICAB members' comments |

↓

| Consideration of the comments received on the Exposure Drafts and finalisation of the drafts of the accounting standards on the basis of the same for submission to the Council-ICAB for consideration and approval |

↓

| Consideration of the draft accounting standards by the Council-ICAB and, if deemed necessary, modification of the drafts in consultation with the TRC |

↓

| The accounting standards, so finalised, are issued under the authority of the Council-ICAB as Bangladesh Accounting Standards (BASs) |

Figure 4.2 Accounting standard-setting process in Bangladesh

The adoption of standards requires the approval of the ICAB Council, and adopted BAS/ BFRS are legally enforceable for the listed companies (ICAB, 2010–11; Deloitte and Touche Tohmatsu, 2007). However, these standards are not mandatory or enforceable through the ICAB bye-laws 1973 (Siddiqui, 2011). The question may arise of whether there are significant departures from the requirements of IAS/IFRS while formulating the accounting standard, i.e. whether the TRC of the ICAB Council considers IFRS compatibility with local laws, conditions, and practices (Hasan et al., 2008). Unlike as in Pakistan and Sri Lanka, implementation of the adopted standards are neither backed by law nor professionally mandatory (Ahmed, 2010). Hence, the auditor's report and basis of presentation notes only refer to conformity with IFRS instead of full compliance with IFRS in Bangladesh (Hasan et al., 2008).

Status of adopted accounting standards in Bangladesh

The Securities and Exchange Commission (SEC), through its Gazette Notification of December 1997, amended the Securities and Exchange Rules 1987 whereby all listed companies in Bangladesh are required to comply with the requirements of all applicable IAS, as adopted by the ICAB, in the preparation and presentation of their financial statements (Rule 12(2)). The SEC, in its Gazette Notification of February 2000, then further amended the statutory rules to require conformity with all applicable IFRS – deleting the ICAB adoption reference (Hasan et al., 2008). The ICAB Council decided to amend its bye-laws in 2001 to mandate the 'professional enforceability' of adopted IFRS and IAS among its members (Solaiman, 2006). This step is a positive one towards full implementation of IFRS and audit practices in Bangladesh. However, there are no separate standards for small and medium-sized entities (SMEs) (Imam and Malik, 2007).

Bangladesh has adopted the original version of 28 out of 29 International Accounting Standards (see Table 4.3). The reason for non-adoption of the one remaining standard is that IAS 29 (Financial Reporting in Hyperinflationary Economies) is not applicable in the context of Bangladesh (Ahmed, 2010). In addition, eight IFRS were adopted in 2008, and these became effective from January 2010. However, no amendments to IAS/IFRS have been made since

Table 4.3(a) Status of Bangladesh accounting standards (BAS), 2009–2010

BAS No.	BAS/IAS Title	Version of IAS	Effective Date	Remarks/Adoption Status
1	Presentation of Financial Statements	1987	01.07.98	Adopted original version, revised in 2003, as amended in 2005
2	Inventories	1992	01.01.95	Adopted original version, revised in 1993
7	Cash Flow Statement	1992	01.01.94	Adopted original version Subsequently amended
8	Accounting Policies, Changes in Accounting Estimates and Errors	1993	01.01.95	Adopted original version
10	Events after the Reporting Period	1999	01.01.99	Adopted original version, revised in 1999
11	Construction Contracts	1993	01.01.95	Adopted original version
12	Income Taxes	2000	01.01.00	Adopted original version Subsequently amended
16	Property, Plant and Equipment	1997	01.01.95	Adopted original version, revised in 1998[a]
17	Leases	1998	01.12.98	Adopted original version, revised in 1997
18	Revenue	1993	01.01.95	Adopted original version Subsequently amended
19	Employee Benefits	1998	01.01.99	Adopted original version, approved in 1998

BAS No.	BAS/IAS Title	Version of IAS	Effective Date	Remarks/Adoption Status
20	Accounting for Government Grants and Disclosure of Government Assistance	1983	01.01.95	Adopted original version
21	The Effects of Changes in Foreign Exchange Rates	1993	01.01.95	Adopted original version, revised in 1993[b]
23	Borrowing Costs	1993	01.01.95	Adopted original version, revised in 1993
24	Related Party Disclosures	1994	01.01.95	Adopted original version, revised in 1994
26	Accounting and Reporting by Retirement Benefit Plans	1987	01.01.95	Adopted original version
27	Consolidated and Separate Financial Statements	1998	01.01.98	Adopted original version, revised in 2003
28	Investments in Associates	1998	01.01.98	Adopted original version, revised in 2000[c]
29	Financial Reporting in Hyperinflationary Economics	Not yet Adopted	Not applicable	Not applicable
31	Interest in Joint Ventures	1999	01.01.99	Adopted original version, revised in 2000
32	Financial Instruments: Presentation	1995	01.01.96	Adopted original version, revised in 2000[d]
33	Earnings per Share	1997	01.01.99	Adopted original version, Revised n 1997[e]
34	Interim Financial Reporting	1998	01.01.99	Adopted original version
36	Impairment of Assets	1998	01.07.99	Adopted original version
37	Provisions, Contingent Liabilities and Contingent Assets	1998	01.07.99	Adopted original version
38	Intangible Assets	1998	01.07.99	Adopted original version
39	Financial Instruments: Recognition and Measurement	2000	01.01.01	Adopted original version
40	Investment Property	2000	01.01.03	Adopted original version
41	Agriculture	2003	05.07.06	Adopted original version

Source: http://www.icab.org.bd/bas.php (accessed 12 February 2012).

Notes:
a   SIC-6 Cost of Modifying Existing Software; SIC-14 Property, Plant and Equipment – Compensation for the Impairment or Loss of Items; SIC-23 Property, Plant and Equipment – Major Inspection or Overhaul Costs.
b   SIC-11 Foreign Exchange – Capitalisation of Loss Resulting from Severe Currency Devaluations; SIC-19 Reporting Currency – Measurement and Presentation of Financial Statements under IAS 21 and IAS 29; SIC-30 Reporting Currency – Translation from Measurement Currency to Presentation Currency.
c   SIC-3 Elimination of Unrealised Profits and Losses on Transitions with Associates; SIC-20 Equity Accounting Method-Reconnection of Losses; SIC-33 Consolidation and Equity Method – Potential Voting Rights and Allocation of Ownership Interests.
d   SIC-5 Classification of Financial Instruments – Contingent Settlement Provisions; SIC-16 Share Capital Required Own Equity Instruments (Treasury Shares); SIC-17 Equity – Costs of Equity Transition.
e   SIC-24 Earnings Per Share – Financial Instruments and Other Contracts that may be settled in Shares.
*BAS no. 30 is not listed as it is not in the regulation.

Table 4.3(b) Status of Bangladesh accounting standards (BFRS), 2009–2010

BFRS No.	Title	BFRS Effective Date	Adoption Status of ICAB
1	First-time adoption of International financial Reporting Standards	01.01.2010	Adopted as BFRS on 21 April 2008
2	Share-based Payment	01.01.2010	Adopted as BFRS on 05 July 2006
3	Business Combinations	01.01.2010	Adopted as BFRS on 15 December 2005
4	Insurance Contracts	01.01.2010	Adopted as BFRS on 23 October 2008
5	Non-current Assets Held for Sale and Discontinued Operations	01.01.2010	Adopted as BFRS on 15 December 2005
6	Exploration for and Evaluation of Mineral Resources	01.01.2010	Adopted as BFRS on 05 July 2006
7	Financial Instruments: Disclosures	01.01.2010	Adopted as BFRS on 27 July 2008
8	Operating Segments	01.01.2010	Adopted as BFRS on 21 April 2008

Source: http://www.icab.org.bd/bas.php (accessed 12 February 2012).

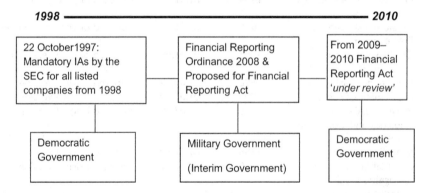

Figure 4.3 IAS/IFRS time frames in Bangladesh, 1998–2010

the ICAB adopted the original version of the standards. After the SEC Gazette Notification in 1997, the caretaker government proposed a Financial Reporting Ordinance in 2008 and urged the future democratic government to pass a Financial Reporting Act and establish a Financial Reporting Council (FRC) in order to implement IFRS effectively (Hasan et al., 2008). Hasan et al. (2008) argue that the establishment of the FRC is essential to implement IFRS because of the need for stakeholder engagement and an effective monitoring policy. The present democratic government is still considering the proposal (see Figure 4.3 for IAS/IFRS time-frames under different political regimes).

South Asian regional efforts to implement IFRS

The Institutes of Chartered Accountants in Bangladesh (ICAB), Pakistan (ICAP), India (ICAI), and Sri Lanka (ICASL) are engaged in the adoption and implementation of IFRS in their respective countries (Ahmed, 2010). Pakistan has incorporated the standards that are relevant in its particular environment into its laws for listed companies; India recently adopted IFRS as the major component of its financial reporting standards. In Sri Lanka, accounting standards are formulated by the ICASL, but their statutory compliance is laid down by the Sri Lanka Accounting and Auditing Standards Act. The South Asian Federation of Accountants (SAFA) announced the establishment of a technical directorate to ensure and monitor IFRS with regard to requirements, contents, and consistent application in the region.[19] The process of adopting and issuing accounting and auditing standards in four of the eight South Asian Association for Regional Cooperation (SAARC) countries[20] are substantially similar (Siddiqui, 2010). The relevant council committee from SAFA critically scrutinises the IFRS in line with local laws and regulations, and recommends them to their councils for adoption, with or without modification (Ahmed, 2010).

A significant aspect of progress in the direction of implementation is reflected by the Best Presented Published Accounts Competition organised in Bangladesh, Pakistan, India, and Sri Lanka (Ahmed, 2010). This competition was launched by SAFA in 1997 as a regional competition and has since generated substantial interest among leading companies in the region in the presentation of audited published financial statements in the financial and non-financial sectors (Imam and Malik, 2007). In 1995, a regional World Trade Organization (WTO) sub-committee was formed in the SAFA regions to ensure standardisation in professional accountancy qualifications, experience and ethics aimed at presenting a united regional and cross-border practice of accountancy (Hossain, 1999).

Cultural factors

Hofstede's model, Gray's model, World Bank governance indicators data and La Porta et al.'s data

The initial study by Hofstede (1980) did not include Bangladesh, although two neighbours, India and Pakistan, were included in his study.[21] Bangladeshi culture is quite similar to Indian and Pakistani culture, due to historical and religious ties between the people of these three countries (Abdullah et al., 2011). Observations of commonalities between these countries have been made in the experiences of researchers through their personal interactions with citizens of the countries and field observations. Commonalities can be explained through a number of historical facts. Bangladesh was once part of the undivided Indian subcontinent and also, for a time, part of Pakistan (1947–71). Pakistan, a predominantly Muslim country (about 90% of the population are Muslim), has many common practices with Bangladeshi Muslims in terms of societal practices (CIA, 2008). As India has large representations of both Islam and Hinduism, it too possesses cultural similarities with Bangladesh (Hossain, 1999). Cultural values for the three countries, based on Hofstede's model (1980) and Gray's model (1988), are shown in Table 4.4, while Table 4.5 shows their cultural scores according to Hofstede et al.'s model (2010).

As mentioned, Hofstede et al. (2010) include Bangladesh to explain cultural dimensions (see Table 4.5). In the case of Bangladesh, the high Power Distance Index (PDI) score indicates a high level of inequality of power and wealth within the society. The high Uncertainty Avoidance Index (UAI) indicates the society's low level of tolerance for uncertainty and that the society does not readily accept change – i.e. a society may be more/less open to unstructured ideas and situations (Sudarwan and Fogarty, 1996). The combination of these two high scores (UAI and PDI) create a society that is highly rule-oriented, with laws, rules, regulations, and controls in place to reduce the amount of uncertainty, while inequalities of power and wealth have been allowed to grow within the society (Abdullah et al., 2011, p. 198). The culture in

Table 4.4 Cultural values based on Hofstede's model (1980) and Gray's model (1988) in Bangladesh, India and Pakistan

	Dimensions	Bangladesh	India	Pakistan
Hofstede's Model (1980)	Individualism (IDV)	Collectivism	Collectivism	Collectivism
	Power Distance Index (PDI)	Large power distance	Large power distance	Large power distance
	Uncertainty Avoidance Index (UAI)	Strong uncertainty avoidance	Weak uncertainty avoidance	Strong uncertainty avoidance
	Masculinity (MAS)	Masculinity	Masculinity	Masculinity
Gray's Model (1988)	Professionalism vs. Statutory control	Statutory control	Statutory control	Statutory control
	Secrecy vs. Transparency	Secrecy	Secrecy	Secrecy
	Uniformity vs. Flexibility	Uniformity	Uniformity	Uniformity
	Conservatism vs. Optimism	Conservatism	Conservatism	Conservatism

Source: Author, based on Hofstede (1980) and Gray (1988); emphasis added for Bangladesh.

Table 4.5 Cultural scores based on the Hofstede et al. (2010) model

	Bangladesh	India	Pakistan
Power Distance Index (PDI)	80	77	55
Individualism (IDV)	20	48	14
Masculinity (MAS)	55	56	50
Uncertainty Avoidance Index (UAI)	60	40	70
Long-Term Orientation (LTO)	47	51	50
Indulgence versus Restraint (IVR)	20	26	0*

Source: http://www.geerthofstede.com/media/651/6%20dimensions%20for%20website.xls (accessed 12 February 2012); Hofstede et al. (2010).

Note: The score was 0 because of the influence of fundamentalist religious views.

Bangladesh is more likely to follow a caste system (e.g. the ruling-class social group) that does not allow significant upward mobility for its citizens (Uddin and Hopper, 2001). This could be due to a combination of these two dimensions creating a situation where leaders have virtually ultimate power and authority, and the rules, laws, and regulations developed by those in power reinforce their own leadership and control (Dahawy et al., 2002). This condition does not necessarily subvert the population, but rather it is accepted by the population as a cultural norm.

Bangladesh's Long-Term Orientation (LTO) score is 47. It is argued that a higher LTO score can be indicative of a culture that is parsimonious, in which society is ready to adapt to change (Hofstede et al., 2010). With respect to masculinity (MAS), India's score is 56, which is the third highest ranking in Hofstede's dimension, with the world average slightly lower at 51. A similar picture is found in Bangladesh. The higher the country ranks in this dimension, the greater the gap between the score of men and women. In terms of individualism (IDV), Bangladesh is on the collectivist side, meaning that people are integrated into strong, cohesive in-groups from birth; these are often extended families (Abdullah et al., 2011). The word collectivism in this sense has no political meaning: it refers to the group, not to the state. Again, the issue addressed by this dimension is an extremely fundamental one, relatable to all societies in the world. Finally, the lower score for Indulgence versus Restraint (IVR) indicates that

Bangladesh's society suppresses its gratification of needs, and instead regulates it by means of strict social norms. In particular, natural human drives in relation to enjoying life and having fun are missing in a restrained society (Hofstede et al., 2010).

As mentioned, Bangladesh is a Muslim-dominated country and therefore it is not surprising that low scores for IVR and LTO are found.[22] It is important to mention that the cultural scores have not changed from 1980 to 2010 in comparison with the Hofstede (1980) and Hofstede et al. (2010) studies. Based on Hofstede's (1980) data, Han et al. (2012, p. 38) find that 'Pakistan is one of the most secretive countries'.[23] They argue that firms in more secretive countries tend to disclose less. Further, investor protection in Pakistan is weaker than it is in India. To explore the secrecy culture of Bangladesh, I use Hofstede's scores from 1980 and 2010. The comparison of India, Pakistan and Bangladesh is shown in Table 4.6. Unsurprisingly, the scores for Bangladesh and Pakistan are almost the same in 2010. This means that Bangladesh and Pakistan have more secretive cultures, while India follows weak uncertainty avoidance and hence has a more transparent culture.

Comparing the enforcement data, the present study finds that a lower rate of enforcement is seen in Pakistan and Bangladesh compared with India (see Table 4.7). This is because both Bangladesh and Pakistan have higher levels of corruption, a factor which weakens enforcement mechanisms. According to Leuz et al. (2003, p. 516), 'Legal Enforcement is measured as the mean score across three legal variables used in La Porta et al. (1998): (1) the efficiency of the judicial system, (2) an assessment of rule of law, and (3) the corruption index.' Han et al. (2012) and Leuz et al. (2003) use the data presented by La Porta et al. (1998, p. 1142). In this research, I use the World Bank's Worldwide Governance Indicators data (2010), which ranges from 0 to 100, while La Porta et al.'s data ranges from 0 to 10.

Focusing on corporate culture, Uddin and Hopper (2003, p. 767) reveal that privatised companies in Bangladesh are reluctant to disclose financial information, due to a tax avoidance

Table 4.6 Secrecy culture in India, Pakistan and Bangladesh

Secrecy Culture (PDI+UAI-IDV)	1980	2010
Bangladesh	N/A	120
India	77	69
Pakistan	123	111

Source: http://www.geerthofstede.com/media/651/6%20dimensions%20for%20website.xls (accessed 12 February 2012).

Table 4.7 Enforcement in India, Pakistan and Bangladesh

	World Bank Governance Indicators (2010)								La Porta et al. (1998)			
	1998				2010				1998			
	J	R	C	Avg.	J	R	C	Avg.	J	R	C	Avg.
Bangladesh	17.65	19.62	38.54	**25.27**	21.53	26.54	16.27	**21.45**	N/A[24]	N/A	N/A	N/A
India	34.80	61.72	43.41	46.65	39.23	54.50	35.89	43.21	8	4.17	4.58	5.6
Pakistan	27.94	26.79	15.61	**23.45**	30.14	25.59	11.96	**22.57**	5	3.03	2.98	3.7

Source: http://info.worldbank.org/governance/wgi/pdf/wgidataset.xls (accessed 12 February 2012).

Notes: J = efficiency of the judicial system/regulatory quality; R = rule of law; C = control of corruption; Avg. = average of judicial system, rule of law and control of corruption, N/A = not applicable.

culture and the weakness of regulatory frameworks and lack of enforcement culture. They raise questions around the veracity of financial data disclosed and the difficulties of using it. Donor agencies like the World Bank have made great efforts to create an 'enabling environment' for privatisation in Bangladesh by financing but paying little attention to regulatory frameworks and enforcement issues that facilitate transparent capital markets (Uddin and Hopper, 2001; Uddin and Choudhury, 2008). Akhtaruddin (2005, p. 402) supports the view that 'Cultural value is no less important a determinant of disclosure or transparency'. For example, Bangladesh has a high sense of secrecy in its culture and, therefore, management is less likely to pursue a high level of disclosure. He concludes that 'The lacklustre disclosure performance by Bangladeshi firms can be attributed to organizational culture, poor monitoring, and lapses in enforcement by the regulatory body . . . Disclosure decisions are culture-driven' (p. 415). Mir and Rahaman (2005, p. 832) also note that 'India, next door to Bangladesh, which has cultural and economic similarities with Bangladesh, did not go for the wholesale adoption of IFRS.' However, the corporate sectors in India are more transparent compared to Bangladesh (Banerjee, 2002). One reason for this might be weak professionalism, for instance, classifying those countries which fall behind in terms of professionalism and rely on statutory controls. Askary (2006) finds that Bangladesh has a tendency towards statutory control and the least professionalism among 12 Muslim developing countries.

Corruption

Corruption is perceived as most rampant in Bangladesh, which is one of the poorest countries in the world (Knox, 2009; Riaz, 2006).[25] Therefore, corruption remains a major obstacle to fully addressing developmental issues. For five consecutive years (2001–05), Bangladesh topped the list of the most corrupt nations in the world on the Corruption Perception Index (Transparency International Bangladesh/TIB, 2005). Huque (2010) explains that corruption has taken many forms in the public sector, and has rendered the framework of accountability very weak. Corruption has progressively intensified since the gaining of independence in 1971. Some of the key agencies of government such as the police, customs, taxation, and the central secretariat are among the most corrupt departments (Riaz, 2006). Key politicians, including the former and current Prime Minister, have been charged with corruption (Knox, 2009). The political parties in power initiate cases of corruption against those in opposition (Huque, 2010). Choudhury (2008) argues that the MPs/legislators are corrupt and encourage corrupt people to be involved in politics. For example, Article 66 of the Constitution of Bangladesh states that:

> A person shall be disqualified for election as, or for being, a member of Parliament, who has been convicted for a criminal offence involving moral turpitude, or sentenced to imprisonment for a term of not less than two years, unless a period of five years has elapsed since his release.

These ideas appear to be based on unreasonable assumptions and might encourage corrupt personalities to run for membership of the legislature (Knox, 2009). Ministers and public officials become partners in corrupt deals, and avoid practices that would potentially make the country's administrative systems more transparent (Riaz, 2006; Daily Star, 2009; Banglanews24.com, 2012). Decisions are made by people in authority without consulting stakeholders, and the network of corruption protects its members from being exposed or prosecuted (Ahmad, 2002; New Age, 2012). Consequently, accountability suffers, as the existing channels and frameworks are never put to use (IMF, 2005, 2010).

In terms of accountability and transparency, Mir and Rahaman (2005, p. 832) find that some companies have taken it for granted that their auditors will fulfil the directors' wishes, and there is a large amount of malpractice in the corporate sectors including (and linked to) insider trading and unacceptable profit manipulations. However, the auditors have provided qualified audit opinions. Malpractice has been overlooked by the SEC. They warn that 'Corruption is becoming endemic in the Bangladeshi culture and should be the main focus, if accountability is required. Without eradicating the culture which enhances corruption, accountability would continue to be seen as rhetoric' (pp. 832–3). The IMF (2010, p. 20) suggests that 'Bangladesh Bank banking supervision needs to implement a model anti-corruption program for its staff, both protecting staff from corruptive incentives and making known the high integrity of its personnel.'

To tackle the widespread corruption, the government of Bangladesh has established institutions and laws over the years. The key initiatives have been the Prevention of Corruption Act 1947; the Anti-Corruption Act 1957; the Criminal Law Amendments Act 1958; and the Anti-Corruption Tribunal Ordinance 1960. However, TIB (2005) criticises the transparency of the Anti-Corruption Bureau, since the bureau was established within the Prime Minister's department. On 26 April 2010 the democratic government amended the relevant legislation to require the commission to seek the government's approval before initiating a case against any government official (Daily Star, 2010). Therefore, the Anti-Corruption Bureau needs to make such an institution clearly independent of the executive. While the necessary laws and institutions seem to be in place, their effectiveness in curbing corruption is limited in practice, in part because of the widespread prevalence of non-transparent practices in the public and private sectors (Huque, 2010).

Conclusion

This chapter has described the political regimes, accounting regulatory frameworks, accounting standard-setting process, and cultural factors in Bangladesh. In summary, firstly, with regard to the political regimes in Bangladesh, there are two political patterns – i.e. democratic and military eras. In 40 years of independence, the military-backed government ruled for 19 years and democratic government for the other 21. During both the democratic and the military eras, many initiatives have been introduced, including the Companies Act 1994, the adoption of IFRS, the proposed Financial Reporting Act, and development of the private sector. Questions still remain about the implementation of these paper-based laws because of the scarce application of their rules and regulations in different political eras in practice – in particular from 1998–2010 (RQ-1, Proposition P_I and P_{IIA}). The political regimes were not covered by the interview questions, and the interviewees mentioned that the nature of the two different regimes may have an impact on the implementation of IFRS in Bangladesh.

Secondly, in relation to accounting regulatory frameworks, the Companies Act 1994 provides the basic requirements for financial reporting by all listed companies; and the Securities and Exchange Commission Rules of 1987 and 1997 require that financial statements shall be prepared in accordance with the ICAB-adopted IFRS. However, some contradictions exist between the Companies Act 1994 and IFRS. The inconsistencies are observed in the SEC Act 1993, the SEC Rules 1987 and 1997, the Income Tax Ordinance 1984, and the Banking Companies Act 1991. The World Bank (2003, 2009) has criticised the current regulatory frameworks. Major institutions like the SEC, ICAB, ICMAB, the DSE, the RJSC and the NBR are involved in the accounting regulatory process in Bangladesh. ICAB is responsible for adopting IFRS, but the standard-setting process is not cooperative or fully engaged with the stakeholders. This study therefore investigates how the slow pace of the accounting regulatory reforms and the standard-setting process influences the implementation of IFRS (RQ-1, Proposition P_I).

Finally, with respect to cultural factors in Bangladesh, the chapter discussed Hofstede's model, Gray's model,[26] the World Bank's Governance Indicators and La Porta et al.'s data. As has been mentioned in this chapter, cultural scores for Bangladesh have not significantly changed over the last 30 years (comparing Hofstede's 1980 and Hofstede et al.'s 2010 models). It has also been argued that negative aspects of the corporate sector – e.g. a secrecy culture, low levels of professionalism, and a lack of consistent enforcement – remain common in Bangladesh; corruption spreads to every corner of society and hinders the country's economic development. Legislators, the major political parties, and auditors are involved in corrupt activities to some extent (i.e. at least some members of each are involved). Unfortunately, the Anti-Corruption Bureau is acting as no more than a political institution. As mentioned in Chapter 2, the present study concentrates on [i] training opportunities in the accounting profession, and [ii] corruption in relation to cultural factors in Bangladesh. The question remains as to how training opportunities in the accounting profession and corruption in Bangladesh can affect the implementation of IFRS (RQ-2a, Proposition P_{IIIA} and P_{IIIB}). These issues will be used to discuss the findings in Chapters 7 and 8.

Notes

1 The Bangladesh Rifles (BDR) were renamed Border Guards Bangladesh (BGB) in 2010.
2 'The six aggregate indicators are: *Voice and Accountability*, which reflects perceptions of the extent to which a country's citizens are able to participate in selecting their government, as well as freedom of expression, freedom of association, and a free media; *Political Stability and Absence of Violence/Terrorism*, which reflects perceptions of the likelihood that the government will be destabilised or overthrown by unconstitutional or violent means, including politically-motivated violence and terrorism; *Government Effectiveness*, which reflects perceptions of the quality of public services, the quality of the civil service and the degree of its independence from political pressures, the quality of policy formulation and implementation, and the credibility of the government's commitment to such policies; *Regulatory Quality*, which reflects perceptions of the ability of the government to formulate and implement sound policies and regulations that permit and promote private sector development; *Rule of Law*, which reflects perceptions of the extent to which agents have confidence in, and abide by the rules of, society, and in particular the quality of contract enforcement, property rights, the police, and the courts, as well as the likelihood of crime and violence; and finally, *Control of Corruption*, which reflects perceptions of the extent to which public power is exercised for private gain, including both petty and grand forms of corruption, as well as "capture" of the state by elites and private interests' (World Bank, 2010). The rankings range from 0 (lowest) to 100 (highest). Data are only available from 1996.
3 The Act was originally formulated by the British authorities in India on 27 March 1913 and came into force on 1 April 1914. The Act has been amended on a number of occasions, once quite extensively, in 1936, in order to bring it into line with the British Companies Act of 1929. This Act was eventually adopted in Pakistan in 1949 and in Bangladesh in 1972 after these two countries became independent in 1947 and 1971 respectively. Finally, the Companies Act 1913 was extensively amended in 1994 and enacted as a new Act, the Bangladesh Companies Act 1994. Since Bangladesh is a former British colony and its legal system is influenced by the British legal system, Bangladesh is a common-law country (Hasan et al., 2008).
4 The year of listing regulations is unknown (i.e. the year is not indicated in CSE or SEC publications or websites); see http://www.cse.com.bd/listing-regulation.php (accessed 12 February 2012).
5 The Companies Act 1994 does not contain any provision for mandatory IFRS.
6 http://www.summitpower.org/update%20info/Audited%20Financial%20Statements%20-%20 2010.pdf (accessed 12 February 2012).

7   The DSE introduced 'A' Category Companies from 2 July 2000. The category was introduced based on a company's financial strength and performance (i.e. holding annual general meetings regularly and declaring dividends at the rate of 10%or more in a calendar year) to give clear information to investors (DSE, 2009–10).

8   The Companies Act 1994 requires separate financial statements for each company.

9   The amendment of the Banking Ordinance 1961 was replaced by the Banking Companies Act 1991.

10 http://www.microfinancegateway.org/gm/document-1.9.25611/38073_file_BRPD_Circular_No_14.pdf (accessed 12 February 2012).

11 IAS 30 (BAS30) was superseded by IFRS 7 (BFRS 7) Financial Instruments: Disclosures effective from 1 January 2010.

12 The Bangladeshi currency is the Taka (Tk.), the Indian currency is the Indian Rupee (Rs.) and the Pakistani currency is the Pakistani Rupee (Rs.). The exchange rate on 31 March 2012 was £1 = Bangladeshi Tk. 119.815; £1 = Indian Rs. 75.634; and £1 = Pakistani Rs. = 138.963]. Source: http://www.hmrc.gov.uk/exrate/bangladesh.htm.

13 For example, the audit fee for the Power Development Board is less than Tk. 7,500,000 to audit a balance sheet of more than Tk. 260 billion; for the T&T Board it is Tk. 170,000 for a balance sheet of Tk. 50 billion and BTCL (formerly BTTB) has discontinued their private sector audit since 1997 and no financial statements have been prepared or audited (Ahmed, 2010).

14 The DSE was incorporated in 1954 (East Pakistan) and formal trading started in 1956 at Narayanganj, Bangladesh.

15 Source: http://www.dsebd.org (accessed 12 February 2012).

16 Source: http://www.nbr-bd.org (accessed 12 February 2012).

17 The accounting standard-setting process is very vague and no information is provided on the ICAB websites or in any of their publications. Therefore, I conducted an interview with the Technical and Research Committee (TRC) of the ICAB on 25 August 2010.

18 The TRC consists of a Vice President and not more than five other members of the council. The council may co-opt such number of members of the institute as it sees fit. The TRC performs various functions, including research in accounting, auditing, and framing recommendations on technical and professional matters for the ICAB members and Articled students; reviewing the latest national and international pronouncements of accounting standards on a regular basis; and carrying out technical reviews for the adoptability and acceptability of these in the country's context. They arrange at least four technical CPE seminars in a calendar year for members. However, the council shall always have the power to review any decision/recommendation of the TRC, in exercising its aforesaid functions.

19 The SAFA was established in 1984 and its motivations are: (i) improvement in the regional comparability of financial statements by narrowing areas of difference in accounting and audit practices; (ii) improvement in the principles and conceptual approach to financial reporting and audit practices, and influencing future professional developments in the region; and (iii) contribution to enactment of new laws and regulations concerning accounting and auditing practices aimed at regional harmonisation.

20 Bangladesh, Pakistan, India and Sri Lanka.

21 Hofstede et al. (2010) include Bangladesh (see Table 4.5).

22 Hofstede et al. (2010) argue that the lower score of LTO and IVR are found in Muslim world.

23 Han et al. (2012, p. 37) defined a secrecy culture score as UAI + PDI – IDV. UAI, PDI and IDV scores derived from Hofstede (1980).

24 La Porta et al. (1998) did not include Bangladesh.

25 Almost half the population lives on less than 1 dollar per day (Oxford Economics, 2008).

26 In line with Hofstede's (1980) and Hofstede et al.'s (2010) cultural perspectives, Bangladesh's culture is based on: collectivism, Large power distance, Strong uncertainty avoidance, Masculinity, Short-term oriented and Restraint. According to Gray's model (1988), Bangladesh's culture is based on Statutory control, Secrecy, Uniformity and Conservatism.

Chapter 5

Research methodology

Introduction

The objective of this chapter is to discuss the research methodology and methods used to achieve the research objectives set out in Chapter 1. It attempts to provide a comprehensive description of the mixed methods employed (interviews and documentary analyses) and the philosophical justification of using these methods in the present study. Firstly, qualitative methods using primary data sources are suitable for answering research questions, and interviews have therefore been used to gather the information necessary to study the implementation of IFRS in Bangladesh. Secondly, documentary analyses (e.g. of enforcement data) are used to justify the regulator's role in the compliance of IFRS in a developing country.

The remainder of this chapter is organised as follows: research design, mixed methods, qualitative interviews, documentary analyses (e.g. enforcement actions by the SEC), and a summary of the chapter.

Research design

According to De Vaus (2001, p. 9), 'The function of a research design is to ensure that the evidence obtained enables us to answer the initial question as unambiguously as possible.' It has also been argued that a research design should minimise any incorrect causal relation between a theory and research question (Bryman and Bell, 2007). There are two types of research approach to research design: deductive and inductive. The deductive approach is a method employed by researchers who are concerned with developing hypotheses in a form which is testable in the real world (Bryman, 2008).[1] With inductive approaches,[2] on the other hand, researchers 'begin with detailed observations of the world and move toward more abstract generalisations and ideas' (Neuman, 2000, p. 49). Unlike a (positivist) deductive approach, the theory is inductively derived from the observations/findings of the inductive approach.

In the present study, the focus is on testing the theory of the role of the state. Given this consideration, the choice of research methods to be used is informed by the research objectives and research questions. The objective of this research is to explore the implementation of IFRS in a developing country, emphasising accounting regulatory frameworks; politico-institutional factors; cultural factors (e.g. training opportunities in the accounting profession and corruption); and other country-specific factors. This objective can be achieved through qualitative research. Because the present study is explorative in nature, a deductive approach fits, as a theory is to be tested rather than generated. The initial phase of the research, as set out in Chapter 2, helps identify various issues in relation to IFRS implementation, and Chapter 3 (containing the theoretical framework) creates a general theoretical framework. In the second phase of the research, the 1st and 2nd round of interviews and documentary analyses will help in testing the theory of the role of the state. The theoretical framework in the present study informs the paradigm of research design, and in particular the use of mixed methods. The Weberian notion of the state suggests that 'the development of accounting is not an evolutionary or holistic process, but emergent, open-ended and contingent' (Mommsen, 1987, p. 35). It therefore provides a methodological strategy for analysing the relations between state and society (Colignon and Covaleski, 1991).[3]

Mixed methods

The strengths of one method can be balanced by the weaknesses of the other method (Bennett and Braumoeller, 2006). Fuentes (2008, p. 1592) argues that mixed methods provide 'richer detail than either method can generate alone'. The prior literature illustrates some of the advantages of mixed methods in their studies. Firstly, when some theoretical expectations exist but appropriate propositions need to be developed, a mixed method can be a useful tool for understanding and validating those theories (Hesse-Biber, 2010). Secondly, the complementary principle or the acceptability of mixed methods is better than a single method.[4] Finally, in terms of the generalisation of the conclusions, mixed methods provide evidence which contributes towards richer conclusions and a wider set of plausible explanations (Maxwell and Loomis, 2003). In terms of 'philosophical issues' (with regard to mixed methods), the traditional view of ontological and epistemological approaches to social sciences is as a differentiation between two schools of thought. A critical debate exists when choosing paradigms (ontology and epistemology) and evaluating their validity and ability to generate an understanding of the social system (Bhaskar, 1978; Sayer, 2004). Watts and Zimmerman (1990, p. 149) argue that '.debating methodology is a "no win" situation because each side argues from a different paradigm with different rules and no common ground'. Therefore, 'critical realism' as a philosophical stance can explain the reasons for choosing mixed methods (Archer, 2002; Llewellyn, 2007). This view is also supported by Modell (2010, p. 125), who argues for 'critical realism as a more appealing foundation for mixed methods research providing some paradigmatic "middle ground" entailing clearly articulated analytical procedures'.

It has been stated in Chapter 1 that the methods employed in this research are determined by the research questions and objectives (see Table 5.1). One of the purposes of this research

Table 5.1 Research questions (RQs) and how to investigate them (mixed methods)

RQs	How to Investigate
RQ-1: What is the relative impact of accounting regulatory frameworks and politico-institutional factors on the implementation of IFRS in Bangladesh, as an example of a developing country?	Interviews and documentary analysis (the SEC Ordinance, Company Act, Stock Exchange Regulations, DSE SEC and ICAB library)
RQ-2a: How do training opportunities in the accounting profession and the state of corruption, as outcomes of culture in Bangladesh, affect the implementation of IFRS? *RQ-2b:* What other country-specific factors are affecting implementation of IFRS?;	Interviews and documentary analysis (newspapers, comments, DSE, SEC and ICAB library)
RQ-3: How does a study of implementing IFRS help build an understanding of a theory of the role of the state in accounting change in a developing country such as Bangladesh?	Literature review, interviews and documentary analysis

is to explore the problems experienced in IFRS implementation in a developing country such as Bangladesh. This aim can be achieved using interviews because constructing a social reality is a characteristic of this area of research. Another specific objective of the present research is to explore the evidence of the regulator's role in IFRS compliance over a period of time, and the documentary analyses will help in achieving this objective. It may be argued that a survey questionnaire and disclosure studies could be used as alternative methods in this research. However, these will overlap with the findings because prior research already informs of the poor level of IFRS compliance in Bangladesh.

Qualitative interviews

Semi-structured interviews: 1st round

A total of 27 semi-structured interviews were conducted over a 12-week period from 3 June to 30 August 2010 during a field trip. Communication with all interviewees was through email regarding the date of the interview. A letter of introduction and interview questions was sent in advance before the interview (see Appendix 5.1). The researcher's initial motivation was to record all interviews. However, 13 of the interviewees (four policymakers, seven account preparers and professionals, and two users) were not convinced about recording the interview. Therefore, extensive notes were taken during the interviews. The length of most of the interviews ranged from 60 to 90 minutes. In addition, notes were taken on the major issues raised by respondents, not only for back-up purposes but also as a quick reference during subsequent interviews. Then, the interviews were transcribed through coding, and respondent anonymity was guaranteed based on the interviewees' permission.

The study uses a non-random stratified sampling method, often used in qualitative research, to select the interviewees (Gibbs, 2008). The idea behind the qualitative research is to purposively select interviewees who can help the researcher understand the specific problem and the research question (Creswell, 2007, p. 178). Qualitative research does not necessarily suggest a large number of participants, as are found in quantitative research (Patton, 2001). Therefore, Miles and Huberman (1994) suggest that six to eight interviews are enough to justify the results. Similarly, the present study considers 27 interviews consisting of four groups. Street (2002, p. 218) argues that:

> Yet, this final [implementation of IFRS] step will represent a long process and significant progress will require a joint effort in each country by the government, stock market regulators, preparers, users and standard setters, and the accounting profession. Achieving the Vision is dependent on various parties, including accounting educators, contributing their resources and expertise to this important effort.

Consistent with this comment, in the present study a broad spectrum of respondents, grouped into four defined groups – (a) policymakers; (b) accounts preparers and professionals; (c) users; and (d) academics and researchers – were selected for the interviews (see Table 5.2 for the summary of the interviewees and Appendix 5.2 for the detailed summary of the interviewees). These interviewees were chosen because they play important roles in the implementation of IFRS in Bangladesh. The selection criteria for the four groups were as follows:

a.   The policymakers included ICAB, ICMAB and SEC officials, World Bank liaison personnel, a Bangladesh Bank official, and a Ministry of Finance official. These were selected because they were directly and closely involved in the decision-making processes of the

adoption and implementation of Bangladesh Accounting Standards (BAS) and IAS/
IFRS. These interviewees were responsible for standard-setting and for monitoring compliance with the standards.

b.   Accounts preparers and professionals (e.g. auditors and company accountants) were chosen because they were responsible for following/complying with the mandated standards
in the financial statements. This group includes 12interviewees, selected based on their
experience (at least five years) of preparing accounts and auditing.

c.   Users (e.g. bank managers, credit rating agency officials and stockbrokers) were chosen
because they could voice their opinions on the adoption and the implementation process.[5]
In this study, I have used a bank manager, a credit rating agency official, and a stockbroker
as proxies of users because some users in developing countries like Bangladesh would have
no direct knowledge of IFRS. I selected six interviewees based on their experience (of at
least five years) in banks, credit rating agencies, and stock broking houses.

d.   The academics and researchers were selected because they have been researching the
adoption and implementation of IFRS issues in Bangladesh and have formed opinions on
this issue. Two interviewees were chosen based on their experiences (of at least 10 years)
in researching accounting standards issues in Bangladesh.

Table 5.2 Summary of the interviewees

	Code	Company/Organisation	Work Exp.(yrs)
Policymakers (7)	PM1	Institute of Chartered Accountants of Bangladesh (ICAB)	26
	PM2	ICAB	10
	PM3	ICMAB	30
	PM4	Securities and Exchange Commission of Bangladesh (SEC)	11
	PM5	World Bank	14
	PM6	Bangladesh Bank	40
	PM7	Ministry of Finance	16
Preparers and professionals (12)	AP1	Big four accountancy firm in Bangladesh	32
	AP2	Pharmaceutical company	24
	AP3	Big four accountancy firm in Bangladesh	9
	AP4	Small accountancy firm	10
	AP5	Bank	10
	AP6	Engineering company	8
	AP7	Bank	15
	AP8	Small accountancy firm	5
	AP9	Small accountancy firm	20
	AP10	Multinational company	11
	AP11	Pharmaceutical company	7
	AP12	Big four accountancy firm in Bangladesh	15
Users (6)	US1	Bank	10
	US2	Stockbroker and Central Depository Bangladesh Limited (CDBL)	9
	US3	Financial institution and (CDBL)	8
	US4	Bank	10
	US5	Credit Rating Agency of Bangladesh (CRAB)	5
	US6	Bank	18
Academics (2)	AR1	Private university, Bangladesh	21
	AR2	Public university, Bangladesh	10

In addition to the planned interviews, informal discussions with senior executives and directors of government departments provided initial briefings for this study. These included personnel from the Ministry of Finance, Bangladesh; the Technical and Research Committee of the ICAB; the Credit Rating Agency of Bangladesh (CRAB); senior officials from Bangladesh Bank; the Securities and Exchange Commission of Bangladesh; and various university academics in Bangladesh.

All the interview questions were open-ended and semi-structured in order to allow respondents to provide their views through a 'free-flowing' discussion. Cottle (1977, p. 27) argues that 'Without allowing people to speak freely we will never know what their real intentions are, and what the true meaning of their words might be.' In order to prepare the interview questions, Wengraf (2006, p. 75) suggests that the interview questions should follow sequences starting from the theory research question, research propositions, and follow-up questions (reflections) (Kvale, 1996). This approach is also discussed by Easterby-Smith et al. (2002), who argue that the interview questions should include open/commenting questions that allow the interviewees opportunities to remark on the particular issues they feel important (Healey, 1991; Jankowicz, 2005). In the present study, I used Wengraf's (2006) sequential pyramid model to prepare the interview questions (see Figure 5.1). However, Beardsworth and Keil (1992, pp. 261–2) expressed the view regarding the sequential approach, that:

> The semi-structured interviews programme should not be based upon a set of relatively rigid pre-determined questions and prompts. Rather, the open ended, discursive nature of the interviews permitted an iterative process of refinement, whereby lines of thought identified by the earlier interviewees could be taken up and presented to latter interviewees.

The interview questions (IQ) in the present study are prepared based on the prior research on the role of the state and accounting, propositions development, and the theoretical

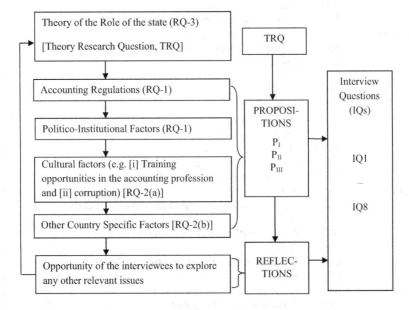

Figure 5.1 Sequential pyramid models to prepare the interview questions in the study

framework. IQ1 and IQ2 are related to accounting regulatory frameworks (Proposition I). IQ3 and IQ4 are related to politico-institutional frameworks (Proposition II). IQ5, IQ6, and IQ7 concern [i] training opportunities in the accounting profession and [ii] corruption (Proposition III). IQ8 refers to other country-specific factors, while IQ9 concerns interviewees' further comments regarding IFRS implementation. Figure 5.2 provides a link between the 1st round interview questions and the present study's theoretical framework.

The general interview guides for the study are shown in Appendix 5.3.[6] these guides are modified because the study includes four different groups (i.e. policymakers, preparers and professionals, users, and academics and researchers).

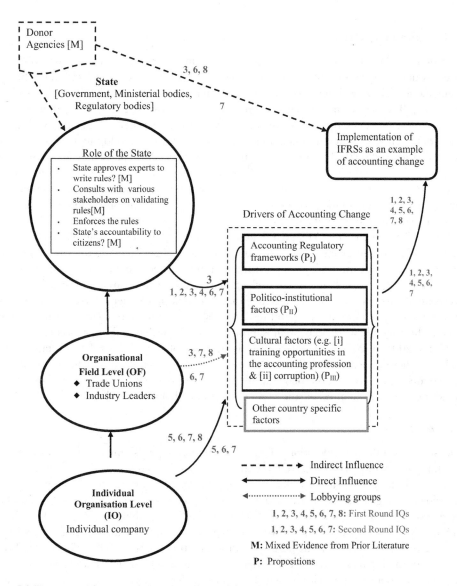

Figure 5.2 Theoretical framework based on Figure 3.2 and interview questions

Table 5.3 12 interviews from the existing pool of 27 interviewees (2nd round)

Two Phases of Interviews	Year	PM	AP	US	AR	Total	
2nd round	2011	4 [PM1, PM2, PM4, PM5]	4 [AP5, AP6, AP10, AP12]	2 [US4, US5]	2 [AR1, AR2]	12	
1st round	2010	7	12	6	2	27	
2nd round interviews to 1st round interviews (%)		57% [4/7]	33% [4/12]	33% [2/6]	100% [2/2]	12/27	44%

2nd-Round interviews

I decided to follow up the 1st round of interviews in order to investigate IFRS implementation issues in more depth; 27 interviewees (i.e. 1st round interviewees) were therefore contacted for follow-up interviews via email and telephone, but only 12 of them agreed (see Table 5.3). The follow-up interviews were conducted between 2 and 27 September 2011. Creswell (2007) argues that follow-up interviews help researchers obtain detailed and in-depth data. They also provide some useful information for the development of an analytical framework (Yin, 2003). The interview questions for the 2nd round interviews were prepared based on the findings of the 1st round interviews (see Appendix 5.4 and Figure 5.2). Figure 5.2 provides a link between the 2nd round interview questions and the theoretical framework. This systematic process has been used to validate the propositions and theoretical framework of the present study.

   Table 5.3 shows that the AP and US groups represent 33% of the sample when comparing the 2nd round interviews to the 1st round interviews. The follow-up rate was below 50%, but selection bias was minimised by ensuring that interviewees from all the groups were seen. Wrate et al. (1985, p. 622) argue that well-standardised measures can minimise selection bias. Myers and Newman (2007, p. 22) also note that representing a variety of voices can overcome various biases (e.g. selection bias), and researcher(s) should therefore include a variety of subjects in their sample at various organisational levels if possible and appropriate. Hayes and Walsham (2001, p. 265) view that, 'Given the number of interviewees (33 in total) it is most likely that there were a variety of voices represented'. However, no articles in financial reporting research have reported on follow-up interview selection bias.[7] The findings from the 2nd round interviews in the present study are discussed in Chapters 6 and 7.

Ethical Issues

The study includes consideration of the human participants' involvement (in the semi-structured interviews). With regard to research questions 1, 2 and 3 (see Table 5.1), *confidentiality* (Elliot and Judy, 1997) and *informed consent* (Esterberg, 2002) are rigorously maintained. The participants are guaranteed that their involvement in the study will not be disclosed and that their *anonymity* will be preserved as well (Henslin, 1995). In addition, *debriefing* (Lincoln and Guba, 1989) means that the interviewees involved in the study are assured that they will have a 100% right to withdraw from participation at any time (Kvale, 1996). The study also follows the research ethics guidelines. The data that the researcher collects are kept confidential. Information about the participants which has been collected during the research is put away and access restricted so that no one but the researcher is able to consult it. Any information about the participants has a code number instead of the participant's name and/or their organisation's name.

The data are managed on the researcher's personal laptop, with password protection and a firewall system installed. Only the researcher has access to the laptop. File-sharing services have not been used by the researcher, since sharing services such as Google Docs or Dropbox may not be completely secure. So, the data are not shared with, or given to, anyone. The data are not sent via email or by any other file transfer means without encryption. It is also assured that no names will be identified or kept by the researcher, and that the data will be destroyed after 10 years.

Coding and analysing

Three main methods for developing themes and codes are the theory-driven approach, the prior research-driven approach, and the data-driven approach (Boyatzis, 1998). For the purposes of this study, the main methods used are prior-driven and theory-driven approach. With regard to Chapter 2 (previous research) and Chapter 3 (theoretical papers), these are used to develop the theoretical framework to be used as coding schemes for the propositions. Three propositions (i.e. accounting regulatory frameworks, politico-institutional factors, and cultural factors) and other country-specific factors are used as the main themes in the coding. Data from the interviews are analysed using the coding, which constitutes 'two simultaneous activities: mechanical data reduction and analysis categorisation of data into themes' (Neuman, 2000, p. 421). In this research, the main aim is to summarise data and categorise it into information relating to different themes. Two types of coding are used in this research. The first type is open coding – policymakers (PMs); account preparers and professionals (AP); users (US); and academics and researchers (US) – which condenses the bulk of the data into manageable categories (Easterby-Smith et al., 2002).

In this research, the open codes consist of four themes: the three propositions and other country-specific factors. The second type of coding is axial coding (Jankowicz, 2005), which the researcher uses for the additional coding of sub-themes: quality of investor protection laws; stakeholder participation/non-participation in the standard-setting process; and stringent/looser enforcement of the laws are all sub-themes of accounting regulatory frameworks. With reference to coding bias, it is worth mentioning that non-coded texts have been excluded for consistency with the research questions. For instance, out of 27 interviewees, only one, a policymaker, mentions trade unions by stating:

> I think [that] there should be some kind of discussion and all that. But to implement or formulate IFRS, you cannot please everyone. So it is not like an open-ended participatory approach because trade bodies and business people will object to so many things, especially some of the regulatory laws.
>
> (PM6: Q)

Hence, this issue has been excluded from coding.

Creswell (2007, pp. 57, 185) states that qualitative interview data can be analysed using several generic processes. With regard to analysis, this research therefore employs coding schemes to analyse data from the interviews, using several generic processes (see Figures 5.3 and 5.4). In this study, the interviews are translated into English, as most of the interviewees responded in Bengali. The text data generated from the 1st round of 27 and the 2nd round of 12 interviews comprised 253 pages (in Bengali and English versions). The data are organised and highlighted. Thirdly, from the interview data, the four themes are classified into sub-themes.

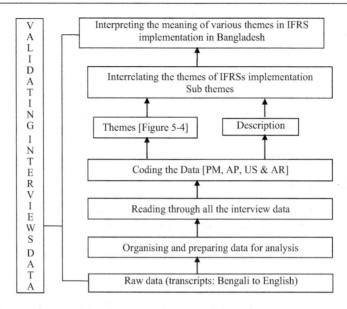

Figure 5.3 Data analysis procedures in the study

Fourthly, any information that would not fit within any of the four themes, such as opinions/ suggestions, is also highlighted. Lastly, the researcher re-read the transcript in order to ensure consistency and validity.

One limitation of this analysis is the fact that the interviews are time-consuming because all conversations required translation into English. Therefore, a computer-aided software program was not used to analyse data in the present study. Some researchers point out that software can make the analysing process faster and more efficient (Bryman and Bell, 2007). Wengraf (2006) suggests that a researcher may analyse qualitative information into a quantitative form. However, if the sample size is small, the researcher can use descriptive statistics to analyse the data (Boyatzis, 1998). Since the number of interviewees in the present study is only 27, and this does not represent a very large dataset, the data are therefore analysed manually.

Limitations of interviews

Some limitations arise from conducting the interviews in Bangladesh as an example of a developing country. Firstly, some of the interviewees cancel their appointments, and in some cases the waiting time is too long.[8] Some interviewees are attending to phone calls, having conversations with colleagues, and there is background noise during the interviews. Secondly, some interviewees answer 'yes/no' and/or 'no comment' and are reluctant to explain much. Thirdly, as most of the interviewees answer in Bengali, it is time-consuming to translate all the conversations into English. I rely on the behaviour, tone, and intentions of the interviewees and on extensive note-taking during the interviews. Finally, there are a number of technical difficulties observed when translating information from Bengali to English. Some words have the same meanings, a different meaning, or no equivalent meaning. For example, 'democracy' or 'democratic' has been used to explain 'cooperative' purposes, or 'gravity' to explain 'nature'; and there is no equivalent of the Bengali words *sailab* or *sairachar*, etc. in English. Grammatical and syntactical structures also vary. For example, the majority of interviewees' responses

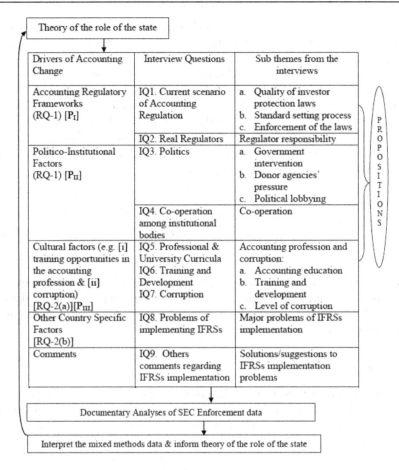

Drivers of Accounting Change	Interview Questions	Sub themes from the interviews	
Accounting Regulatory Frameworks (RQ-1) [P$_I$]	IQ1. Current scenario of Accounting Regulation	a. Quality of investor protection laws b. Standard setting process c. Enforcement of the laws	
	IQ2. Real Regulators	Regulator responsibility	
Politico-Institutional Factors (RQ-1) [P$_{II}$]	IQ3. Politics	a. Government intervention b. Donor agencies' pressure c. Political lobbying	
	IQ4. Co-operation among institutional bodies	Co-operation	
Cultural factors (e.g. [i] training opportunities in the accounting profession & [ii] corruption) [RQ-2(a)][P$_{III}$]	IQ5. Professional & University Curricula IQ6. Training and Development IQ7. Corruption	Accounting profession and corruption: a. Accounting education b. Training and development c. Level of corruption	
Other Country Specific Factors [RQ-2(b)]	IQ8. Problems of implementing IFRSs	Major problems of IFRSs implementation	
Comments	IQ9. Others comments regarding IFRSs implementation	Solutions/suggestions to IFRSs implementation problems	

Figure 5.4 Data analysis relationships: drivers of accounting change and interview questions from the theory and sub-themes from the interview data

are a mix of Bengali and English, and also often feature incomplete sentences, overlapping speech, and a lack of clear-cut endings in speech. This is understandable because the official language of the interviewees is Bengali and therefore they feel comfortable speaking Bengali. Allowing interviewees to respond in their primary language increases their comfort levels with the researcher (Edwards, 1998). Further, the researcher as translator/interpreter, and sharing the cultural background of the participants' country(ies), may minimise the problems with language barriers to some extent (Williamson, 2011, p. 391). This process helps the researcher obtain richer data from first-language responses (Esposito, 2001).

Reliability and validity

Neuman (2000, p. 170) defines reliability as 'dependability and consistency'. During the research process, some concerns may arise, such as errors and bias. Audiotape and videotape recording are important methods of recording information (Boyatzis, 1998). In this study, an audio recorder (digital stereo recorder) is used to record the interviews, together with manual note-taking during the interviews. During the interviews, cross-checked questions are helpful in ensuring reliability. For example, the researcher asks the same questions more than once. The consistency of the coding is thereby maintained.[9] The researcher checks the transcripts twice to make sure that no mistakes are made during the transcription.

Qualitative validity means that researchers check the accuracy of their findings by employing certain procedures (Gibbs, 2008). So, validity is based on determining whether the findings are accurate from the standpoint of the researcher, the participant, or the readers (Creswell and Miller, 2000). However, Neuman (2000) argues that qualitative researchers are more interested in authenticity than in validity.[10] In the present study, 12 second round/follow-up interviews (i.e. interviews from each category – PM, AP, AR and US) help the researcher gain confidence in the generalisability of the findings:

- internal validity – the selection of interviewees;
- external validity – generalisability of the conclusion; and
- construct validity – reflection of theory concepts (Jick, 1979; Miles and Huberman, 1994).

In addition, different data sources and comparisons of people with different points of view from each category (triangulation)[11] are used to build a coherent justification of themes (Ryan et al., 2002; Modell, 2005; Gibbs, 2008). The researcher uses SEC enforcement data to confirm information received from the interviews.

Documentary analyses

The study examines the enforcement notices issued by the SEC from the beginning of 1998 to the end of 2010 that relate to violations of accounting regulations. The period of study is selected because the SEC began taking a more proactive role in the monitoring of those involved in the disclosure process during this period because the SEC mandated IFRS compliance from 1998. In addition, this time period corresponds to a period of significant change which occurred within the market and the political regime, including comments from ICAB on the quality of annual reports; the SEC Corporate Governance Ordinance 2006; recommendations for Financial Reporting Act; the establishment of an independent oversight board; recommendations for education requirements for the accountancy profession; significant changes in the overall practice of accounting firms (e.g. quality control and the scope of services of audit firms); and different government systems (democratic and military-backed government).

The enforcement notices during this period are SEC releases which address a number of accounting, auditing, and reporting concerns. However, few of these releases involve SEC enforcement action on accounting standards. The researcher has hand-collected information from the SEC website.[12] Each SEC filing is carefully reviewed to ensure consistency (Rollins and Bremser, 1997; Chen et al., 2005). I carefully review SEC announcements and eliminate 57 observations that are repeated from an earlier press release; 24 are not accessible from the website.[13] The 1,647 enforcement actions are not equal to the number of releases because, as mentioned, some of the releases contain more than one enforcement action. Bremser et al. (1991), Feroz et al. (1991), Campbell and Parker (1992) and Files (2012) also address the fact that some releases repeat enforcement actions. The data analysis in this study is based upon the examination of these enforcement actions, as contained in the releases of SEC during the study period.[14] My final sample consists of 42 unique observations because these enforcement notices are related to specific violations of accounting regulations.

There are some limitations in terms of the data collection and analyses: first, some of the enforcement actions in Bengali and part of the notices are not readable. Second, the information given in some of the notices is not available on the website. The researcher contacted SEC by email and with a personal visit but was unable to collect the information. It can be understood that since SEC is a state institution, it is likely to be highly bureaucratic and its employees may be uncomfortable or even afraid to disclose information. Third, a few of the releases contain repeated information on the same enforcement actions. Fourth, manually retrieving press release announcements is time-consuming because the bandwidth of the website they are posted on is very low. For example, SEC does not maintain a fully computerised database for enforcement systems and still maintains a manual filing system. Fifth, no full record of enforcement documents was available; for instance, data related to 13 years prior was not available. Sixth, there was a lack of coordination among the staff. The researcher had to get signatures from all the staff in the Enforcement Department of the SEC. Seventh, there was a tendency to frequently cancel meetings with the researcher. Finally, the study follows a subjective analysis of the SEC enforcement releases. The material does not lend itself to quantitative analysis. Nevertheless, this limitation is mitigated by the fact that a substantial number of enforcement releases are analysed. Thus, subjective interpretations are reinforced throughout the study period in reviewing all the actions taken by the SEC. As a result of this analysis additional research avenues are identified, in particular regarding the role of the SEC in developing countries.

Conclusion

To recap, this chapter has focused on the research methods involved in the study. The deductive approach has been used in this research to achieve the closely related objectives set out in Chapter 1 (e.g. the specific objective of this research is to study the implementation of IFRS in Bangladesh). This research is designed as a combination of interviews and documentary analysis (i.e. mixed methods). The critical realism philosophy justifies the reasons for choosing the mixed methods. With regard to qualitative analyses, 27 semi-structured interviews (1st round) and 12 second round interviews are conducted. In order to analyse data from the interviews, coding schemes are developed using Creswell's (2007) generic approach. The limitations of conducting interviews are also reported. The reliability and validity issues involved in qualitative interviews are discussed. The results of the interviews are reported in Chapters 6–8.

The second method employed is documentary analysis. The study examines 42 IFRS-related enforcement notices issued by the SEC from the beginning of 1998 to the end of 2010, relating to violations of accounting regulations. In order to analyse the data, the study uses manual analysis.

Mixed methods employed in the study will help in discussing the findings of research questions in the next three chapters. Firstly, in Chapter 6(RQ-1), the main objective is to provide findings on the relative impact of accounting regulatory frameworks and politico-institutional factors on the implementation of IFRS. Secondly, in Chapter 7, the impact of training opportunities in the accounting profession and corruption – (RQ-2a), and other country-specific factors (RQ-2b) – in the implementation of IFRS will be discussed. Finally, in Chapter 8 (RQ-3), the theory of the role of the state in accounting change will be explored based on the findings from the interviews and the enforcement data. More specifically, this mixed methods approach will generally attempt to evaluate the three propositions and their theoretical application in terms of IFRS implementation in a developing country such as Bangladesh.

Notes

1   Theory————————→Observations/findings [Deductive].
2   Observations/findings————————————→ Theory [Inductive].

3   According to Colignon and Covaleski (1991, p. 154), 'Weber's advocacy of multiple methodologies, alternatively employing nomothetic institutional analysis with more ideographic historical and cultural features, provides the guidelines for bringing sociology and history together for the study of accounting'.

4   The weakness of single method usage will be overcome through mixed methods (the complementary principle) (Jick, 1979; Tarrow, 2004).

5   The author gratefully acknowledges Professor David Alexander and Brian Singleton-Green (ICAEW) for commenting on the selection of users in the study (BAFA Colloquium 2010, Cardiff).

6   This approach is suggested by Creswell (2007).

7   In financial reporting literature, although Illés et al. (1996, p. 531) comment on selection bias based on the 1st round interviews and opine that 'Respondents were generally very cooperative. Consequently respondent bias is not thought to be a problem in these particular cases. Crosschecking the overall attitudes to the specific responses on any accounting issues did not reveal any significant bias', they did not conduct 2nd round interviews or, therefore, encounter the risk of follow-up selection bias.

8   For example, the initial appointment time was 10:00 am, and on one occasion I waited until 3:00 pm to conduct the interview.

9   Miles and Huberman (1994) recommend that the consistency of the coding means at least 80% of the time for good qualitative reliability.

10 Authenticity means giving a fair, honest and balanced account of social life from the viewpoint of someone who lives it every day.

11 Campbell and Fiske's study (1959, p. 83) defines triangulation as 'use of multiple methods'. Later, Patton (1999, 2001) argues that issues of reliability and validity can be maintained by triangulation.

12 http://www.secbd.org/ (accessed 12 February 2012).

13 For example, Sl. No. 3, Date: 09/02/2010, Subject: Warning: Non-compliance of securities laws: Regarding inspection. RLtd.http://www.secbd.org/List%20of%20Enforcement%20Actions%20 for%20the%20month%20of%20February%202010.htm.

14 In the study, the data is analysed following the procedure of Campbell and Parker (1992) and Files (2012).

Chapter 6

The relative impact of accounting regulatory frameworks and politico-institutional factors

Introduction

This chapter presents the results of RQ-1: What is the relative impact of accounting regulatory frameworks and politico-institutional factors on the implementation of IFRS in Bangladesh as an example of a developing country? The principal objective is to ascertain interviewees' views regarding the implementation of IFRS. Based on a review of prior literature (see Chapter 2), I developed three propositions with regard to the discussion of IFRS implementation in Bangladesh. The interview questions are developed in Chapter 5. These questions cover the three propositions and request information about how the four groups of interviewees perceive the implementation of IFRS in Bangladesh. In this chapter, based on an analysis of the interview data,[1] I will emphasise the first two propositions (i.e. accounting regulatory frameworks and politico-institutional factors). A limitation of the interviews is that most of the interviewees gave their answers in Bengali. As mentioned Chapter 5, I rely on the tone of the interviewees and on extensive note-taking. In this study, italics in an interview quote indicate that the interviewee strongly emphasised the specific issue (i.e. I have tried to convey the interviewees' tone by the use of italics).

The first proposition relates to the effectiveness of accounting regulatory frameworks. Accounting regulation and its effect upon IFRS implementation is the central issue to be considered. The second proposition relates to politico-institutional factors, including government intervention in terms of IFRS implementation, and the degree of cooperation between other institutional bodies in ensuring effective implementation of IFRS. I used enforcement documents from 1998 to 2010 available from the SEC websites. Firstly, the documentary evidence will offer insights into trends in accounting standards-related violations in Bangladesh. Secondly, the issue of a lack of regulations to carry out the regulators activities is discussed. Thirdly, I ask: is there any political influence in monitoring violations of accounting rules, and is there any co-operation between different institutional bodies in support of the regulator's activities?

The next section reports the interview findings and the documentary evidence on accounting regulatory frameworks, followed by the findings on politico-institutional factors. Then, I will discuss reflections on the relative impact of accounting regulatory frameworks and politico-institutional factors, followed by summary of the chapter.

Accounting regulatory frameworks (Proposition I)

In this section, I will explore the following proposition:

P_I: Accounting regulatory frameworks will have a positive influence on implementation of IFRS under the conditions of (a) common-law origin; (b) high-quality investor protection laws; (c) stakeholders' participation in the standard-setting process; and (d) stringent enforcement of the laws.

or

> Accounting regulatory frameworks will have a negative influence on implementation of IFRS under the conditions of (a) code-law origin; (b) low-quality investor protection laws; (c) stakeholders' non-participation in the standard-setting process; and (d) looser enforcement of the laws.

In doing so, I will analyse whether Bangladesh's accounting regulatory frameworks will have a positive/negative influence on implementation of IFRS under four conditions. As mentioned in Chapter 4, Bangladesh has common-law origins. The following sections will discuss the conditions of (b), (c) and (d) to analyse Proposition I.

The interviewees were asked: How would you describe the accounting regulatory frameworks in relation to the existing laws for investor protection, the standard-setting process, and enforcement issues in Bangladesh? As shown in Table 6.1, out of 24 respondents who are negative, nine believe that solid regulations are essential because of low-quality 'investor protection laws'; four believe that the standard-setting process should be more participatory, democratic, engaging, and transparent rather than having a 'closed-door policy'; and 11 argue that enforcement is questionable because of apparent looser outcomes of the laws. Only three interviewees are convinced that the current regulations are satisfactory. The following sections will evaluate the accounting regulatory frameworks for implementing IFRS in Bangladesh in line with Proposition I.

Table 6.1 Perceptions of the current regulation scenario in Bangladesh (1st round interviews)

Non-satisfactory regulations (A)	PM	AP	US	AR	Total	%
Low-quality investor protection laws	4 [PM1, PM3, PM4, PM6]	2 [AP1, AP5]	3 [US1, US3, US4]	0	9/27	33
Stakeholders' non-participation in the standard-setting process	0	3 [AP3, AP6, AP10]	0	1 [AR1]	4/27	15
Looser enforcement of the laws	2 [PM2, PM5] [PM3]*	5 [AP4, AP7, AP8, AP11, AP12]	3 [US2, US5, US6]	1 [AR2]	11/27	41
Total (A)	6	10	6	2	24/27	89
Satisfactory regulations (B)	1 [PM7]	2 [AP2, AP9]	0	0	3/27	11
Total (B)	1	2	0	0	3/27	11
Subtotal (A+B)	7 [6+1]	12 [10+2]	6 [6+0]	2 [2+0]	27 [24+3]	100

Notes: Interviewee codes for this and subsequent tables – PM: policymakers; AP: preparers and professionals; US: users; AR: academics and researchers.
*The interviewee mentions more than one issue. The less discussed issue = '0', otherwise '1'.

Quality of investor protection laws

Regarding 1st round of interviews, nine interviewees – four policymakers (PM), two account preparers (AP), and three users (US) – are sceptical about the corporate motives behind the need for regulations (see Table 6.1). In their opinions, the regulations are not satisfactory and there is a need to establish efficient regulations for improving the transparency of corporate reporting to gain the public trust. They question the intentions and motivations behind creating an effective regulatory system. According to the interviewees, effective regulations are a prerequisite of the implementation of solutions for any accounting issues: effective regulatory mechanisms will ensure transparency of information provided by companies. The following comment is representative of those made by the interviewees regarding the need for regulation:

> *I think that many international investors really require transparent information in financial reporting*, and corporate sectors recently realised that unless they produce good financial standards with all disclosures and compliance with the IFRS, they will not be able to please the investors [or] make them happy. So, *the motivations are to make sound regulatory systems for providing transparent and detailed information.*
>
> (PM1)

The users and account preparers are also sceptical about the current state of regulations. They argue that the inconsistencies between local laws and IFRS are overlooked by the regulatory bodies and need much more attention to make the regulatory systems effective. One account preparer expressed the following view:

> *Well, I would say it's not very satisfactory because there is lack of consistency between the Companies Act 1994 and IFRS. This inconsistency has not yet been resolved by the ICAB or the SEC for the last 13 years.* To be honest, the accounting profession and sectors like the ICAB, SEC, DSE, and CSE [Chittagong Stock Exchange] do not care to resolve this matter.
>
> (AP5)

To make effective regulations, the policymakers (four interviewees) believe that the most effective way to improve corporate accountability is through public pressure exerted by domestic and international organisations. The following comment represents the sentiments of these interviewees:

> Yes, the government has already made a commitment to international authorities such as the World Bank, the ADB, and other donor agencies, that they will take steps to implement IFRS. *That's why the interim government has already enacted one provision under the Financial Reporting Ordinance which is supposed to supervise the implementation of status of IFRS.*
>
> (PM3)

The interviewees from the AP group see the recent move by the ICAB and SAFA (i.e. best published annual reports award in Bangladesh and South Asia) as encouraging and an excellent way of potentially improving the quality of financial reporting. The motivating factors for companies to make competitive reports include greater initiatives taken by the ICAB and SAFA. Two interviewees from the AP group supported the ICAB:

> I think [that] introducing best published accounts [by the] ICAB really motivates companies to follow IFRS. I also think [that] the more you make it competitive, the more [there will be] compliance with IFRS. So, *the motivation is basically [as to] how to make this published accounts good to enhance the image of the company and the investors.*
>
> (AP1)

> Three years ago, the financial regulation situation in Bangladesh was not good. But in [the] last two to three years the scenario has changed. *The ICAB provides rewards to local companies for better compliance with accounting regulations. Companies who get reward[s] from the ICAB can qualify for a SAFA award.* So, it becomes very important for the competitive image of companies to comply with IFRS [*for example, Bangladeshi companies have received the best annual report practice award within the SAFA*].
>
> (AP5)

However, according to the interviewees, legal and corporate governance reforms that are beneficial to less powerful stakeholders may be difficult to implement because of relatively high levels of government corruption in Bangladesh. It is hard to anticipate whether or not accounting professionals will do their jobs in creating a transparent corporate environment. The interviewees feel that the fundamental problems lie in the fact that accountants are fulfilling the wishes of directors, and most privatised companies in Bangladesh are closely family-led businesses. Hence, those companies do not want to disclose confidential information. Questions are raised by three interviewees (two policymakers and one academic/researcher) about the professional ethics as well. One interviewee expressed this sentiment:

> I don't think it is very satisfactory, because CAs are paid fees for their audit services and they submit the reports to the companies and regulatory bodies. *The CA firms are obligated to the clients [companies].* They should give a completely impartial view but *I have seen, in my past experience as a governor, that many of the reports [by] companies, banks, or financial institutions [sent] to Bangladesh Bank and different regulatory agencies only reflect their [company director's] wishes. . .* So, *there is no impartiality or professionalism in preparing the reports . . .* there is a large scope for improvement of accounting regulations of Bangladesh.
>
> (PM6)

The evidence from the 1st round interviews suggests the importance of high-quality investor protection regulations which can play a positive role in the development of financial reporting in Bangladesh, especially regarding the implementation of IFRS. However, in order to effect meaningful change, the interviewees suggest that reforms to existing corporate laws and corporate governance structures are necessary.

Regarding the 2nd round of interviews, the interviewees were asked: 1(a). How would you describe the accounting regulatory process in Bangladesh? Eleven interviewees (92%) feel that there is a need for regulations in order to implement IFRS because of the existing low-quality investor protection laws. The only interviewee from the SEC believes that there are enough regulations already (see Table 6.2). This is an understandable view of Bangladesh because the SEC official is linked with the Ministry of Finance. Two out of the 11 interviewees also feel that some contradictory regulations exist between Bangladesh Bank and IFRS 7 (BFRS 7), explained as follows:

> There are some contradictory issues between the BRPD Circular No.14 and IFRS 7 . . . *if the company follows BRPD Circular No. 14, the true profit (held for maturity) of the company will not be shown.* (PM5)

Table 6.2 Perceptions of the quality of investor protection laws in Bangladesh (2nd round interviews)

	PM	AP	US	AR	Total	%
Low-quality investor protection laws	3 [PM1, PM2, PM5]	4 [AP5, AP6, AP10, AP12]	2 [US4, US5]	2 [AR1, AR2]	11/12	92
High-quality investor protection laws	1 [PM4]	0	0	0	1/12	8

> BRPD Circular No. 14 contradicts the financial instrument valuation . . . this *means that fair value accounting is not applicable in Bangladesh.*
>
> (AP5)

Stakeholder participation/non-participation in the standard-setting process

Regarding the 1st round of interviews, four interviewees (three account preparers and one academic/researcher) express disappointment regarding the accounting standard-setting process in Bangladesh (see Table 6.1). They state that the standard-setting process should be more transparent (e.g. stakeholder participation in the process) than it is at present. The current practice of standard-setting in Bangladesh is viewed as far from satisfactory and does not promote the desired levels of transparency and accountability. One interviewee states this clearly:

> It is very important that a form of the Bangladesh Accounting Standard Board (BASB) be established under the statute by virtue of the Securities Commission Act. *The accounting professions (the ICAB and the ICMAB), the regulatory agencies (for example, SEC), stock exchanges, chamber of commerce, and major users of corporate annual reports should participate [in] reviewing accounting standards.* The standard-setting should be broad-based, with legal backing and punitive measures in respect of non-compliance.
>
> (AR1)

In line with accountability and transparency, accounts preparers are also supportive of creating a Financial Reporting Council (FRC) and enforcing it through a Financial Reporting Act (FRA). However, this is a political process, since the caretaker government made the encouraging step of the Financial Reporting Ordinance of 2008; the present democratic government is reluctant to make this ordinance an Act. The key advantages of making an FRC and FRA are engagement and an effective monitoring policy, rather than having too many key actors in the regulatory process. One interviewee expressed this sentiment:

> I suggest that if the MOC can really asks professional bodies to fully comply with IFRS as to what needs to be done and how we can get the task done . . . then we should work out together towards an action plan so that *full compliance and monitoring responsibilities can be given to the proposed Financial Reporting Council (FRC). Once the FRC is in place [then] they can monitor. So, one step is to establish the FRC and another is to make the FRC fully effective and functional . . . Therefore, the MOC should include the preparers and accountants in the standard-setting process in order to accommodate the problems we are facing in practice.*
>
> (AP10)

Table 6.3 Perceptions of the real regulators of accounting issues in Bangladesh

	PM	AP	US	AR	Total	%
ICAB	7/27	12/27	5/27	2/27	26/27	96
SEC	4	3	2	2	11	41
BB	2	2	0	0	4	15
ICMAB	2	1	1	0	4	15
MOF	1	0	0	0	1	4
MOC	1	0	0	0	1	4
DSE	0	1	0	0	1	4

The interviewees in the study also reveal that the standard-setting process in Bangladesh is highly political in nature.[2] The interviewees criticised the standard-setting process, seeing it as 'political' for various reasons, including the fact that there is no exposure draft and that the members of the standard-setting committee change when a new democratic government comes into power.

The interviewees are asked: Who really regulates accounting issues in the country [Bangladesh] today? It is found that 26 of the 27 respondents perceive the ICAB to be the regulator of accounting issues in Bangladesh (see Table 6.3). The majority of interviewees strongly believe that the ICAB is the key regulatory body.[3] In reality, there are other regulatory bodies – e.g. the SEC, Bangladesh Bank (BB), the ICMAB, MOC, MOF and DSE/CSE) – which are also involved in the accounting regulatory process. The interview findings reveal that the ICAB is restricted to supervising different accounting issues rather than having any overall enforcement power enabling it to take action against companies violating accounting rules. If the ICAB is the real regulatory body, its activities and powers should fundamentally shape organisational behaviour to gain legitimacy. But, does the ICAB (as a real regulator) cover major accounting issues? This sentiment is captured in the following quote given by one of the policymakers:

> There are three accounting regulatory institutions: the SEC, the ICAB, and the BB. The SEC is a regulating authority for listed companies. Rule 12 states that only financial statements should be prepared on the basis of IFRS and IFRS which are adopted by the ICAB. The ICAB only gives licences to the CA firms [which have] authority to do statutory audit jobs, and Bangladesh Bank monitors the banking sector. The ICAB is indeed the regulatory body of accounting issues in Bangladesh.
>
> (PM2)

Hence, the comment represents the narrow scope of the ICAB's activities. One of the users extends the policymaker's views:

> There are two accounting regulatory bodies: the ICAB and ICMAB. *The accounting regulations are basically published in the first instance by the ICAB. They are the real authority which regulates the accounting profession in Bangladesh . . . either by adoption of IFRS or in advising the SEC to issue circulars or guidelines with regard to the IFRS.*
>
> (US1)

Five interviewees (three policymakers and two academics/researchers) demonstrate the centrality of regulators in the implementation of IFRS. They also feel that the need for 'regulators' is exacerbated especially because of the lack of engagement with the companies listed

Table 6.4 Perceptions of the stakeholders' participation/non-participation in the standard-setting process in Bangladesh (2nd round interviews)

	PM	AP	US	AR	Total	%
Stakeholders' non-participation in the standard-setting process	2 [PM4, PM5]	4 [AP5, AP6, AP10, AP12]	2 [US4, US5]	2 [AR1, AR2]	10/12	83
Stakeholders' participation in the standard-setting process	2 [PM1, PM2]	0	0	0	2/12	17

on the DSE and CSE, lack of enforcement, and particularly following the lack of initiative in making sure that companies are following rules and regulations including IFRS. The following opinion demonstrates the emerging realisation of the need for real regulators. One of the policymakers is very critical about the 'regulators':

> Strictly speaking, *there is no 'real' regulatory body as such to oversee [the] implementation of accounting regulations.* What happens is [that] the regulatory bodies like Bangladesh Bank and SEC require some kind of financial statements formats which are mandatory. Companies must submit their quality report to the respective regulatory bodies. However, *IFRS are not strictly being examined by any particular body* . . . . As you know [that] no particular body cares much . . . . *ICAB should give orientation and guidelines. ICAB is supposed to really look into this matter. But I don't think [that] ICAB is competent or that they have the mandate to do that.*
>
> (PM6)

This interviewee, from a policymaking group, thus enthusiastically acknowledges the need for real regulators. However, my interpretation is that most of the interviewees (i.e. 20 of 27) from the other interviewee groups are reluctant to express their views regarding real regulators because of the perceived 'threat and fear' to a company's reputation.

Regarding the 2nd round of interviews, the interviewees were asked: How would you describe the accounting standard-setting process in Bangladesh? Ten interviewees (83%) feel that the standard-setting process is not transparent and is non-participatory (see Table 6.4). An account preparer commented that:

> *Nobody knows what the standard setting committee is. It is awful that this committee has not produced any consultation paper(s) on any standards as yet.*
>
> (AP12)

On the other hand, two of the policymakers (17%) from the ICAB think that the standard-setting process is a very authentic and democratic process in which stakeholders actively participate (see Table 6.4). In the 1st round of interviews, only four interviewees (15%) commented on the standard=setting process (see Table 6.1).

Stringent/looser enforcement of the laws

As explained in Chapter 4, the sharing of responsibility by a number of government agencies (e.g. ICAB, DSE, SEC, RJSC, MOC and MOF) complicates the enforceability of corporate regulations and reduces overall effectiveness. The SEC is to be the main institution for enforcement issues. Interviewees explained that enforcement mechanisms that encourage and facilitate compliance, and 'punitive arrangements' that force compliance, are, to a great extent, absent in Bangladesh. To make enforcement mechanisms more effective, interviewees hinted that the SEC and other regulatory bodies might be 'stricter'. The only AR is very sceptical about the SEC's enforcement role:

> *The enforcement issue is indeed frustrating.* Companies are not following mandatory IFRS . . . The adoption of the accounting standards did not bring any remarkable changes in the financial reporting practices of Bangladesh. *What is the role of the SEC? The SEC did not constitute a separate Financial Reporting Council or take any punitive measures against the directors of the respective companies in order to revise financial statements (those who do not follow IFRS in the preparation of their Financial Reports). Again, disciplinary action is simply not taken if any accountant fails to comply with IFRS or audit ethics (for example, a fine or expulsion from the respective professional bodies).* That is why Bangladesh has had to wait a long time to achieve the target of compliance with IFRS – because regulations and enforcement are not linked as they should be in the requirements.
>
> (AR2)

The interviewees feel that that tightening the enforcement culture will create *high-quality financial reporting* that will also ensure investors' faith and trust in a firm's fundamental soundness. All three users who respond are very critical about the current scenario of enforcement. One of the users observes that:

> *The regulation and accounting standards are there but there is no enforcement* . . . . You will be amazed to hear that the authority doesn't care enough to make it enforceable. My question is: *What benefit do they [the monitoring bodies] gain from not enforcing the rules?*
>
> (US2)

Although the SEC's enforcement role in the context of IFRS implementation is unclear, there are some infrastructure problems which are not supportive of the SEC's functions. As mentioned in Chapter 4, there are no qualified accountants in the SEC commission and salary structures are not competitive. The SEC lacks sufficiently trained staff to conduct detailed analyses to monitor compliance with accounting and financial reporting requirements. There are mixed opinions of the SEC's role in implementing IFRS among accounts preparers. Two interviewees feel that the SEC's infrastructure problems are key problems in monitoring compliance issues:

> The SEC has no qualified accountants to oversee IFRS disclosures. So, the enforcement solely relies upon other aspects [for example] AGMs, Interim Reporting etc.
>
> (AP4)

Why does the government not recruit qualified accountants into the SEC? The answer is that the salary is only Tk. 15,000 [£150] to 20,000 [£200] monthly. Do you think any qualified accountant would be interested in joining the SEC with this salary structure? Obviously, the answer is 'no way'. So, the government should appoint qualified accountants otherwise 'dreams of implementing IFRS will never come true'!

> (AP12)

Two interviewees comment that the SEC is more active now in comparison with prior years:

Before 2003, the regulatory systems were less strict. Nowadays, it is strictly regulated. However, I feel [that] this trend should be further improved soon. What is the benefit of those regulations if there is no enforcement?

(AP7)

To an extent, the SEC is working on enforcement and monitoring whether full compliance exists in disclosures [or not].

(AP11)

One policymaker from the ICAB tried to push the full burden onto the SEC and believed that the SEC should take the responsibility of all blame not assumed by the ICAB. This represents a perspective that conflicting interests exist between the regulatory bodies in Bangladesh. The majority of the interviewees agreed that the ICAB had not made an effective effort to review the practices of the auditors and audit firms and to evaluate the existing degree of compliance with the auditing requirements. Such efforts will require the unhealthy rivalry between the members of ICAB and SEC to be set aside in the interests of accounting development in the country. The policymaker emphasises that:

> *The current situation of accounting is a controversial issue.* How can I answer? *ICAB is trying to regulate but I don't know to what extent the SEC is contributing. So, the SEC is fully responsible for this controversy around regulatory aspects.*

(PM2)

The reason for blaming the SEC is so that the ICAB takes the power and responsibility to monitor the compliance with IFRS. A policymaker phrases this in the following way:

> The accounting regulations are obligatory for listed companies, not others [non-listed companies]. *If any listed company doesn't prepare accounts according to guidelines [the] ICAB provides, then the ICAB can't take any legal action against them. The SEC and the Bangladesh government have no guidelines for IFRS and therefore they should delegate the ICAB to monitor the implementation issues. The preparation of financial statements according to IFRS is the task of the company; the CA firm can't do this if the company does not want it to be done.*

(PM5)

Interviewees from the AP and US groups also stress the usefulness of regulating professional bodies to improve the current enforcement mechanisms. These interviewees express concerns about the professional bodies and their role as regulators, often viewing conflicting roles among different institutions and political pressures as the most likely causes of difficulties in implementing IFRS. One AP comments that:

> *Professional bodies are not regulated enough in Bangladesh.* If you look at the ACCA and the ICAEW in the UK, they have disciplinary committees, whereas in Bangladesh this sort of disciplinary practice is very rare and minimal. *There is no compliance watchdog committee to oversee professionals.*

(AP8)

In order to make enforcement activities more proactive, the interviewees from the US group focus on the need for a depoliticised regulatory body. This sentiment is critical since the regulatory body needs to be stable rather than making radical changes at frequent intervals. This culture (i.e. frequent changes of regulatory body) fundamentally weakens effective enforcement in Bangladesh. One user said that:

> To be honest *the regulatory body is not stable. If the government changes, the regulatory staff will change. Even [if] any company violates the regulatory requirements and is linked with the political party in govern-ment, the authority won't take any action against them. The government is aware of this fact but chooses to ignore it.*

> (US6)

According to two policymakers, the culture of changing regulatory body can be resolved through concerted efforts by the government, the accounting profession, and the Chamber of Commerce in Bangladesh (see Table 6.1). A policymaker (PM3) strongly adds that the gov-ernment, the SEC, and the ICAB are not involved as much as they should be, and that their involvement is essential to reform the regulation. He commented that:

> *The main problem is the lack of enactment of the appropriate legislation* because it has not been made compulsory to follow the same principles in preparing the accounting statements and *there is no clear central regulatory body in Bangladesh to supervise or oversee the implementation of IFRS* and that's why ICMAB is always advocating the establishment of one supervisory oversight board in Bangladesh.

> (PM3)

For unlisted companies, the financial reporting formats and disclosure requirements set out by the Companies Act 1994 are mandatory, but these requirements are not consistent with IFRS. For listed companies, the SEC requires full compliance with IFRS. Only one interviewee (AR2) points out that there are some contradictions between the Companies Act 1994 and IFRS:

> *This is the right time for Bangladesh [to] modify the Companies Act 1994, Securities Exchange Regula-tions and Ordinances* . . . including standards-setting and implementation guidelines

> (AR2)

In the 2nd round interviews, the interviewees were asked: How effective is the enforcement mechanism in implementing IFRS? Most of the interviewees (i.e. 11 out of 12) believe that enforcement is not effective in Bangladesh (see Table 6.5). Only one interviewee from the SEC chooses not to make any comment on enforcement issues (see Table 6.5). This quite possibly means that the SEC official does not wish to take any blame for their enforcement activi-ties. However, interviewees from all groups feel that the SEC should be responsible for non-compliance of IFRS. The SEC is lenient in taking action against nationalised organisations. The following comment is representative of the interviewees' sentiments:

> The SEC cannot identify corrupt CA firms for non-compliance with IFRS, because the SEC itself does not have qualified accountants. For example, in 2009, Janata Bank pro-vided 'miscellaneous earnings' which were equivalent to 80% of their total income, but there is no explanation of these miscellaneous earnings. . .in their cash flow statement, they provided 15 billion interest received and in their income statement 14.8 billion as interest income. How can they recover 105%? It is shocking that *the SEC did not take any appropriate action against the nationalised bank.* You see [that] *where we live regarding IFRS implementation.*

> (PM2)

Table 6.5 Perceptions of stringent/looser enforcement of the laws (2nd round interviews)

	PM	AP	US	AR	Total	%
Looser enforcement of the laws	3 [PM1, PM2, PM5]	4 [AP5, AP6, AP10, AP12]	2 [US4, US5]	2 [AR1, AR2]	11/12	92
No comment on enforcement of the laws	1 [PM4]	0	0	0	1/12	8

Regarding documentary analysis, I will emphasise enforcement in relation to violations of accounting standards.

The distribution of regulatory enforcement actions by year is shown in Figure 6.1. The number of enforcement actions peaked in 2006 and 2007. The number of enforcement actions in 2006 and 2007 totalled about four times those taken in 1999 and 2000. During the period 1998–2010, there were 1,647 market enforcement actions, and of these documents 42 are related to IFRS (see Appendix 6.1). The accounting standards were not addressed in the enforcement documents; hence, in reading all enforcement documents, I found only 42 enforcement notices which were IFRS related. In relation to enforcement actions based on IFRS, 42 actions started from the year 2006, representing 2.6% (42/1,647) of the total of enforcement actions, which is a very low proportion (see Appendix 6.1). Appendix 6.1 shows that the enforcement notices are based on 15 accounting standards, namely, IAS 1 (30 times),[4] IAS 2 (11 times), IFRS 7 (three times), IAS 12 (four times), IAS 16 (nine times), IAS 17 (once), IAS 19 (once), IAS 23 (once), IAS 24 (once), IAS 34 (four times), IAS 36 (once), IAS 37 (twice), IAS 38 (once), IAS 39 (twice), and IAS 41 (once). It is clear that the most of the violations are based on IAS 1, IAS 2, IAS 12, IAS 16, IAS 34 and IFRS 7.

In my opinion, one possible explanation for the SEC's lack of identifying violations regarding IFRS compliance is a lack of personnel. As mentioned in Chapter 4, they have no qualified accountants. This means that the enforcement department of the SEC relies heavily on basic accounting requirements like inventory amounts or methods; the formats of the balance

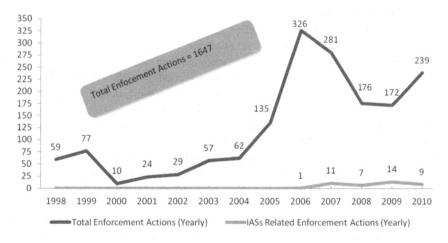

Figure 6.1 Comparison of total enforcement actions vs. IFRS-related enforcement actions (yearly), 1998–2010

sheets, income statements, and cash flow statements; depreciation methods; and disclosures of true and fair view.

The level of penalty also varied. For example, the minimum issued was a warning and a fine of Tk. 0.10 million, the maximum was Tk. 15 million, and the average was Tk. 1.61 million; 25 of the 42 enforcement notices imposed a penalty of less than Tk.1 million. Further, the lack of regulatory frameworks regarding penalty criteria possibly encourages companies not to comply with the SEC regulations (or at least, nothing exists to discourage them). For instance, Appendices 6.2 and 6.3 show that penalty amounts for violating regulations (in particular, the Companies Act 1994 and the SEC Act 1993) and even for providing false information in statements are not more than Tk. 200 (or less than £2). Therefore, the lack of regulation regarding stringent enforcement mechanisms (e.g. punitive fines/penalties) may impede the implementation of IFRS in Bangladesh.

Reflecting on accounting regulatory frameworks

The results show that in Bangladesh, accounting regulatory frameworks have a negative influence on implementation of IFRS under conditions of (b) low-quality investor protection laws; (c) stakeholders' non-participation in the standard-setting process; and (d) looser enforcement of the laws. This section brings together the arguments of interviewees that effective regulations for investor protection, stakeholders' participation in the standard-setting process, and stringent enforcement of the laws are prerequisites for the effective implementation of IFRS.

In relation to the quality of investor protection laws (condition b), negative perceptions are observed with regard to the current regulations. The interview findings reveal that there are contradictions between the local laws and IFRS. For instance, the Companies Act 1994 does not require mandatory IFRS compliance or compliance with BRPD Circular No. 14 and IFRS 7. Although the ICAB encourages companies to follow IFRS fully, in reality accountants are fulfilling directors' wishes (i.e. usually not to follow IFRS). The interviewees mention that most companies are closely family led and their cultural instinct remains one of hiding information in Bangladesh. The majority of interviewees in the 2nd round interviews also question the quality of investor protection laws.

In terms of stakeholders' participation/non-participation in the standard-setting process (condition c), the findings reveal that the standard-setting process is not transparent. According to some interviewees, the ICAB has a standard-setting committee but this committee does not consult with stakeholders to make effective decisions regarding IFRS implementation. The interviewees also feel that the ICAB is developing and making comments on IFRS/BFRS in Bangladesh and, therefore, the ICAB are the real regulators in Bangladesh. In particular, the policymakers strongly perceive a necessity for real regulators in Bangladesh. However, the findings suggest that the ICAB has not published any exposure drafts, consultation papers, or even the standard-setting committee's reports. The interviewees argue that the military-backed government's proposals to set up an independent supervisory body (i.e. the FRC) and the Financial Reporting Act 2009 have been slowed or even stopped completely by the present democratic government. This raises questions around the democratic government's intentions towards the full and effective implementation of IFRS. There is a consistency between the perceptions revealed in the 1st and 2nd rounds of interviews. For instance, in the 2nd round interviews, most of the interviewees argue that the regulations should be updated and that stakeholders should participate in the standard-setting process to implement IFRS effectively.

With respect to enforcement of the laws (condition d), the findings reveal that effective enforcement mechanisms are vital in effectively implementing IFRS. The majority of the interviewees are negative about the SEC's role regarding enforcement actions. This is possibly because the enforcement mechanisms themselves are not tight enough to deal with the viola-tors (i.e. those companies who are not complying with IFRS). In the 2nd round of interviews, the findings also question the current enforcement mechanisms. They add that these enforce-ment mechanisms are very unclear and lack strict penalties/fines. In addition to the 1st round of interviews, the interviewees in the 2nd round generally feel that the political lobbying and government intervention in the SEC are impeding the enforcement process. The SEC should therefore be depoliticised, and the SEC should take action against nationalised organisations. The interviewees (the AR and US groups) suggest that the SEC is itself a government institu-tion and not inclined to take action against nationalised organisations' violations. The only interviewee in the PM group who has an affiliation with the SEC denies any wrongdoing. The documentary analyses offer evidence that a lack of regulations may hinder the stringent enforcement of laws in Bangladesh. It is found that a very limited number of IFRS-related enforcements (i.e. 2.6%) from 1998–2010 raises questions as to the effective implementation of IFRS.

Politico-institutional factors (proposition II)

This section will explore the following proposition: Politico-institutional factors will have a positive/negative influence on implementation of IFRS.

P_{IIA}: Politics will have a positive influence on implementation of IFRS under the condi-tions of (a) common-law origin; (b) a lower level of government intervention; (c) a lower level of donor agencies' pressure; and (d) a lower level of political lobbying.

or

Politics will have a negative influence on implementation of IFRS under the conditions of (a) code-law origin; (b) a higher level of government intervention; (c) a higher level of donor agencies' pressure; and (d) a higher level of political lobbying.

P_{IIB}: Cooperation among institutions will have a positive influence on implementation of IFRS under the conditions of (a) democratic government and (b) ensuring the partici-patory rights of the stakeholders.

or

Lack of cooperation among institutions will have a negative influence on implementation of IFRS under the conditions of (a) undemocratic government and (b) an absence of participatory rights for the stakeholders.

In examining the above proposition, I will discuss findings concerning political pressure and co-operation among institutional bodies with regard to IFRS implementation in Bangla-desh. In relation to P_{IIA} (political influence), the conditions of the legal origin of the country (common-law/code-law) were mentioned in Chapter 4 (i.e. Bangladesh is a common-law country), and therefore the analysis of P_{IIA} in this section is done under the conditions of (b) a higher/lower level of government intervention; (c) a higher/lower level of donor agen-cies' pressure; and (d) a higher/lower level of political lobbying.

With respect to P_{IIB} (co-operation among institutional bodies),condition (b) – the participa-tory/non-participatory rights of the stakeholders – was discussed in an earlier section of this chapter, where the findings derived from the interviewees' responses suggest that the stakeholders have no participatory rights in accounting regulatory and standard-setting processes in Bangladesh. The analysis in this section will be carried out under condition (a) – democratic government or undemocratic government. In particular, co-operation/lack of co-operation among institutional bodies in implementing IFRS will be discussed.

Political influences

In terms of political influences, the interviewees were asked: Is there any higher/lower level of political pressure (e.g. government intervention, donor agencies' pressure and political lobbying) to implement or not implement IFRS?A total of 27 interviewees express their sentiments on politics in ways which can be classified into five categories: (a) relating to a higher level of government intervention; (b) a higher level of donor agencies' pressure (i.e. pressure from the World Bank, the IMF, and the ADB); (c) a higher level of political lobbying; (d) no government intervention; and (e) no comment on politics (see Table 6.6). Of the 27 interviewees, two are critical of the government's intervention; five feel that donor agencies' efforts towards implementing IFRS are political pressure; and seven believe that a higher level of political lobbying are significant contributing factors in impeding the implementation of IFRS (see Table 6.6). However, 12 interviewees provided no comment at all on politics, and only interviewee thinks that there is no government intervention in IFRS implementation. My interpretation of this is that the main reason for avoiding comment on politics, especially by the accounts preparers and by members of the professional group, is that the interviewees feel that doing so would pose a risk to their job security.

Table 6.6 Views on political influences to implement or not implement IFRS (1st round interviews)

	PM	AP	US	AR	Total	%
A higher level of government intervention	1 [PM6]	0 [AP1]*	1 [US5]	0	2/27	7%
A higher level of donor agencies' pressure	2 [PM1, PM7]	2 [AP1,AP2]	0	1 [AR1]	5/27	19%
A higher level of political lobbying	3 [PM2, PM3, PM5]	2 [AP5,AP12] [AP1,AP2]*	2 [US2, US3]	0	7/27	26
Total (A)	*6*	*4*	*3*	*1*	*14/27*	*52*
No government intervention	1 [PM4] [PM7]	0	0	0	1/27	4
Total (B)	*1*	*0*	*0*	*0*	*1/27*	*4*
No comment on politics	0	8 [AP3,AP4, AP6,AP7, AP8,AP9, AP10,AP11]	3 [US1, US4, US6]	1 [AR2]	12/27	44
Total (C)	*0*	*8*	*3*	*1*	*12/27*	*44*
Subtotal (A+B+C)	7	12	6	2	27/27	100

* The interviewee mentions more than one issue; the less discussed issue = '0', otherwise '1'.

Higher/lower level of government intervention

In terms of the 1st round of interviews, the respondents believe that 'government intervention' is one of the major problems in impeding IFRS implementation in Bangladesh. They think that the government is 'not sincere' about establishing an independent board, and instead simply wants to keep bureaucratic control over the determination of accounting standards and monitoring processes in the country. No progress has been made towards the development of an independent board since then. Therefore, the bureaucracy of the government ministry has seemingly been deeply influenced by Bangladeshi culture's reliance on secrecy (see Chapter 4). One AP is highly sceptical in this regard:

> Two to three years ago, there was a Financial Accounting Ordinance . . . I would not say it had gone through a proper political process as such . . . Bureaucrats wanted to prevent the making of the Ordinance into an Act . . . when the bureaucrats [e.g. government ministry] took an interest, they did not understand the standards, but they thought they could impose an Act of this nature and would exercise a controlling authority over the accounting professionals. *Bureaucracy, you see, is a never ending process in Bangladesh, and they want to extend their influence everywhere.*
>
> (AP1)

The different government systems help explain the issues with regard to high/low levels of government intervention. The only PM feels that a higher level of government intervention has existed under the democratic government in comparison to the military-backed government. A military-backed government earlier took the initiative on the FRA, and finally it seems that full commitment will depend on a democratic government. He said that:

> I really appreciate the initiative that the caretaker government [i.e. the military-backed government] took in producing the Financial Reporting Ordinance of 2008, but it has not been effectively enacted. I think this was initiated during the BNP government when Mr Saifur Rahman, the ex-Finance Minister, being a chartered accountant, also felt the necessity for such an Act. But he was also *influenced by political pressure not to run very fast* . . . When the caretaker government came to power . . . after taking the comments of the chartered accountants, business people and the trade bodies. . . they passed the principles but could not implement them . . . when the Awami League government came into power, they found it to be a very *sensitive* [in terms of being transparent] and loaded Act because lots of people in their party possibly did not really want to go ahead with it.
>
> (PM6)

The two respondents from the policymaking group deny that the existence of government intervention as such is responsible for implementing IFRS. This is not surprising given the fact that some policymaking interviewees represent government institutions or ministerial bodies. For instance, the SEC Executive Director (under the Ministry of Finance) and the Deputy Secretary (of the Ministry of Finance) are directly involved with the government. The interviewees do not really drill down to the question of differences in the comments between some groups' feelings about the importance of political pressure and some groups' denials of the same. In fact, they focus on explaining non-political approaches. Only two interviewees (both policymakers) believe that politicians are unconcerned about accounting issues in Bangladesh:

Table 6.7 Perceptions of higher/lower levels of government intervention (2nd round interviews)

	PM	AP	US	AR	Total	%
A higher level of government intervention	4 [PM1, PM2, PM4, PM5]	0	2 [US4, US5]	2 [AR1, AR2]	8/12	67

I have not felt any political pressure by the government to implement it . . . You know [that] there are two groups of the government: one of them is demanding implementation of IFRS while the other group is not. There is political competition among the government officials as to who will be the chairman of the SEC/DSE.

(PM4)

I don't think government intervention is impeding the implementation process. I am doubtful as to whether the politicians know what IFRS is and what the implications of IFRS are . . . *Government intervention is immaterial. It is only the ICAB's intention whether they will implement it or not (which matters).*

(PM7)

In the 2nd round of interviews, the interviewees were asked to comment on the existence of political pressure to implement or not implement IFRS in Bangladesh. Nine out of the 12 interviewees were of the opinion that politics within the government is responsible for intervening in implementing IFRS (see Table 6.7). Consistent with the 1st round interviews, all the interviewees from the PM group agree that higher levels of government intervention impede the implementation process. They point out that auditors' qualified opinions do not matter and carry no value for the regulators, and that even government departments are not following International Public Sector Accounting Standards (IPSAS). One PM stresses that:

The auditors provide *emphasis of matter* as qualified audit opinion. The presentation of financial statements by non-financial companies is not up to proper international market standards because the Board is in somebody's control (for example, due to politics and/or family ties) and often tries to hide the true picture of the company.

(PM1)

Higher/lower level of donor agencies' pressure

As mentioned in Chapter 3, donor agencies play a key role behind the scenes in adopting IFRS, including during the implementation phase in developing countries. Developing economies like Bangladesh, which are in great need of external funds, have been forced to open up their economies as part of the donor agencies' sponsored globalisation processes.[5] These donor agencies have encouraged the adoption of internationally accepted accounting and corporate governance practices as a prerequisite for obtaining loans, and the interviewees express their concerns about the roles of the donor agencies in terms of their influence on the development of accounting practices in Bangladesh. One interviewee sums up the IFRS as a form of global political pressure:

For IFRS there is international pressure from donor agencies. I think it is like, *'you are asking somebody to sing but he/she can't'*. ICAB already adopted some policies of IFRS but they converted those IFRS standards to Bangladeshi standards. However, IFRS in fact were not implemented.

(PM7)

The interviewees point out that there is an absence of private sector rule-making bodies in Bangladesh, something which creates a gap for the donor agencies to exploit by intervening with pressure to implement their policymaking decisions through private sector think-tanks. Thus, decisions in favour of wholesale adoption and implementation of IFRS have been prompted by exposure to threats to legitimacy, rather than by efficiency perspectives. The interviewees in the present study tend to believe that the whole process is very political and that the engagement of local professionals and corporate employees is being ignored in terms of decision making while the 'donor agencies' wishes are transformed through the government without considering local cultures. One of the policymakers strongly argues that:

> *It is an injustice to the developing countries to implement the requirements of IFRS, because they are not logistically prepared.* Making it compulsory for everybody without any adequate training and support does not make sense to us. *The IFAC and IASB are dominated by accounting firms based in developed industrialised countries [who] dominate these issues and even the development of any IFRS.* But in the cases of developing countries, they have their own problems . . . *the developing countries' unique characteristics are being ignored in reality.* The IASB should consider the development of IFRS in developing countries by engaging their (local) accountants and policymakers.
>
> (PM1)

Three interviewees (two PM and one AP) feel that the political nature of the World Bank's relationship with Bangladesh and the degree of aid dependence have been excessive, and that these factors have therefore seriously distorted accounting development patterns. They recommend that donors take a long-term view of their aid commitments to Bangladesh and that aid funding should not involve any government intervention. Interviewees think that donor agencies are aware that the funds are not utilised efficiently, but they have been careless. It is argued that the aid provided by donor agencies to implement IFRS in Bangladesh, without considering the basic problems of accounting infrastructure and institutions, may produce negative outcomes in the near future:

> We need technical assistance from [say] the ICAEW or AICPA [American Institute of Certified Public Accountants]or EAA [European Accounting Association] for a project like this to teach us, not only for the qualified members but also for the SEC. We had a lecturer from Greenwich University, UK, under the World Bank-Twinning Programme . . . we enjoyed his visit very much and learned a lot from his lecture here. So, this should be a continuous process . . . *But the problem here is that the World Bank [and] ICAEW are heavily linked with the government, so they want to spend money to make the government's bank balance healthier, not the country's direct benefit.* As you know, funds are transferred from them [World Bank] to the government and then the government tries not to spend them for the purposive issues.
>
> (AP1)

Another interviewee from AP extended this issue that the World Bank is one of the key donor agencies for financing the diffusion of accounting practices in Bangladesh, but that the actual usage of its funds is often questionable. Despite the World Bank's role in encouraging the adoption of IFRS in Bangladesh, the interviewee criticises the way in which the Bank's lending activities are taking place:

The World Bank is pressuring for regulating as per westernised countries' IFRS . . . . although International Accounting Standards have been introduced – *there's no implementation guideline from the World Bank.* They need implementation but there's no help for it. They are very careless about providing resources and help. . . *giving foreign aid to implement it, but they do not care much where those funds are used and how effectively they are used.*

(AP2)

The findings reveal that the behaviour desired by the World Bank becomes somewhat political in the context of Bangladesh. Arguably, these lending/donor agencies must have an interest in the exercise, and similar fashions are still practised now. Therefore, the influence of donor agencies in implementing IFRS (in terms of the political and economic level of a country) varies, and is mixed in Bangladesh. For example, the only researcher (AR1) put it this way:

The ICAB received a grant totalling *US$200,000 from the World Bank to facilitate the adoption process; however, this process is much more political than the establishment of legitimacy. The SEC also received technical as well as financial assistance from the ADB to support a number of projects for ensuring a smooth transition to the use of IFRS, but the real motivations for those projects are unclear.*

In the 2nd round of interviews, the interviewees did not provide any comments on the donor agencies' political pressure. This is possibly because the present democratic government has so far failed to introduce the Financial Reporting Act of 2009, to tackle the stock market crash, or to establish an independent supervisory board like the Financial Reporting Council.

Higher/lower level of political lobbying

Seven interviewees criticise the political lobbying involved in implementing IFRS in Bangladesh (see Table 6.6). They provide different opinions as to how a higher level of political lobbying is negatively associated with the most needed goals, of transparency and the implementation of IFRS.

Firstly, they express concerns that some politicians do not actually want transparency in financial reporting. They hint that transparency (e.g. creating global standards) is a threat to politicians in continuing to receive corrupt money. An example is:

I am sure about the existence of political pressure . . . there are some problems which lie with politicians and they fear that if it is implemented the true picture of the companies will be mirrored in the public sphere and they might have fewer options to make corrupt money.

(US5)

An account preparer and professional (AP2) provides an interesting example of the political lobbying taking place around IFRS implementation:

You know [that] the *World Bank and ICAEW provided around £180,000 to support Bangladesh for implementing IFRS* . . . in August 2008, the Ministry of Finance sent 35 people from different sectors to London to study for the ICAEW's IFRS certificate. On their return, the people planned to train others around the country. But the political process is dominant in selecting those people . . . [which] is shocking . . . *the ministry selected 35 people from the Ministry of Health, the Ministry of Environment, the Ministry of Science and Technology and some tutors from college level who have no knowledge of accountancy whatsoever, but they are politically involved in the government . . . ultimately the government spent £180,000 for nothing* and the country did not gain any benefit from this project.

Secondly, it is argued that the parliamentary process of passing or approving accounting-related laws is political in nature in Bangladesh, since some MPs simply do not want to pass a Financial Reporting Act. The interviewees express a belief that the government is delaying the process because of political lobbying. The following two interviewees comment on this issue:

> Political lobbying is one of the biggest obstacles to implementing IFRS . . . there are some interested groups in the parliament who are directly involved in the corruption taking place, as they are directors of many companies. In addition, a majority of professionals (doctors, engineers, and solicitors etc.) exists in the parliamentary committee. So, they don't want to pass the FR Act 2009. The ICMAB is trying to amend the Income Tax Act, but because of those parliamentary members, it is delayed quite often.
>
> (PM3)

> As far as I know, there is a bit of political pressure, although the terms are technical and only related professionals know about it. The interesting part is that the politics of imple-mentation *are a political process* because *some parts of the government and MPs do not want the IFRS . . . therefore, the government is not more focused on this issue.*
>
> (US3)

Thirdly, the government has a set of predetermined beliefs and a political manifesto which excludes accounting-related issues, and it prefers that the banking sector is the main driving force in improving the economy; and the government feels the banking sector should be more regulated than the non-banking sectors. The non-banking sectors are mostly run by politicians (see Chapter 4). One user sums this up in the following way:

> *Under the same domain, the government is very conscious of the financial sector, where they think [that] the banks should follow strict laws and regulations, but it is careless about the non-financial sector. . .* [this] is the government's pre-determined concept or how things should be. However, the non-financial sectors constitute half of the economy. *The government thinks that losses in the non-financial sector are losses for shareholders, not for the economy. So, if you are only concerned about 50% of the economy, there will be scope for corruption and a non-disclosure tendency.* That's exactly what is happening in the non-financial sector. But, I think [you see] *the garments sector, and jute, are doing really well and are potential industries for investment by foreign investors.* If those industries do not represent the true picture by following IFRS, then Bangladesh is losing opportuni-ties . . . *the governmental body should come out from the predetermined concepts and look more broadly than the current, narrow focuses allow.*
>
> (US2)

Although the 12 interviewees (i.e. eight AP, three US and one AR) are silent about the existence or otherwise of political pressure (see Table 6.6), three interviewees (from the AP group) viewed political influences by the government – in particular, government intervention and political lobbying – as indirect factors in implementing IFRS. These three interviewees, who appeared most in favour of opposing direct political influence by the government, pro-vide evidence about why political pressure is not important. The following two quotations are representative of this issue:

Table 6.8 Perceptions of higher/lower levels of political lobbying (2nd round interviews)

	PM	AP	US	AR	Total	%
A higher level of political lobbying	4 [PM1, PM2, PM4, PM5]	1 [AP5]	2 [US4, US5]	2 [AR1, AR2]	9/12	75
No comment on politics		3 [AP6, AP10, AP12]			3/12	25

> There is *no direct political pressure. The issue of pressure comes when any company is involved with forgery.* For instance, when any bank is involved with forgery then the Central Bank and the Ministry of Finance try to control the situation . . . politically connected Banks do not get any punishment or fine.
>
> (AP1)

> *I don't see, or I have no idea, about political pressure* because our politicians are mostly unconcerned about what is happening in the accounting world.
>
> (AP12)

In the 2nd round of interviews, only one of the four APs thinks that political lobbying is a key problem, but the other three APs are silent on the issue (see Table 6.8). This evidence is similar to the findings of the 1st round of interviews.[6] Only AP5 argues that:

> *We follow IFRS to satisfy only the SEC and the tax authority, and not shareholders.* You know, only 10% of companies provide actual information in Bangladesh. The rest of them are heavily politically connected and they can easily satisfy the SEC and the tax authority.

All academics and users were critical regarding political lobbying. The views given by the following two interviewees represent the political problem:

> You see [that] the recent stock market crash (i.e. 2011) occurred due to political connections.
>
> (AR1)

> I think [that] many companies are politically connected and therefore they do not feel scared of violating regulations.
>
> (US4)

Nine interviewees had emerging expectations of action from the present democratic government regarding the effective implementation of IFRS. One of the policymakers commented that:

> Actually, within one year, no such improvement has happened. You see, *political connectedness is a major problem in Bangladesh in implementing IFRS.* Because of political connectedness, the basic requirements, like trial balances and books of accounts, are not being properly followed. *If the basic requirements are not followed, how can we expect compliance with IFRS?* To me it is like a dream.
>
> (PM5)

Co-operation/lack of co-operation among institutional bodies

In Bangladesh, the levels of co-operation among the major institutional bodies that are involved in accounting regulatory frameworks, the standards-setting process, and in monitoring the capital market are atrocious, according to respondents. All the interviewees agreed that implementation could be successful in Bangladesh through a huge improvement in co-operation among the major actors (see Table 6.9). The respondents suggest that all the actors (i.e. institutions) involved tend to blame one another in trying to maintain their individual positions. So, the implementation process seems to be focused on individual actors' efforts, rather than the necessary team-working and co-ordinated efforts. The majority of respondents perceive that the whole exercise is flawed because of the undemocratic nature of the accounting standard-setting, regulating and monitoring processes which presently exist in Bangladesh.

The policymaking group (all seven interviewees) are critical of the current co-ordination of decision making, consultation and monitoring issues regarding IFRS implementation. One PM sums it up this way:

> There is really *no drive*. A good mind-set among the professional bodies and a sufficient human resource base for making the system popular are essential. We have to have someone to deliver the reforms. *I don't know why the Ministry of Commerce is not in a position to lead professional bodies and there is really no one who can lead this agenda in the professional bodies.* Basically there's a lack of change agents in the institutions. There are of course many problems. *We have a lack of institutional transparency and a lack of capacity to implement, and even when you accept new standards, there are lots to be adopted, and resource constraints exist.* So, all of these issues need to be addressed.
>
> (PM7)

The existence of a 'blame culture' is something which is also strongly expressed by the respondents. The interviewees think that the two major institutions (i.e. the ICAB and the SEC) appear to be uncritically supportive of efforts by the World Bank and other donor agencies in the implementation of IFRS in Bangladesh, without reflecting on the long-term implications of such proposals. As previously pointed out in this chapter, these interviewees are undivided in their opinions when it comes to blaming one another. They are in favour of their own institutional activities, and criticise other institutions' activities. To co-operate with each other, this culture needs to end – and achieving this might be a panacea for co-operation among them.

Table 6.9 Perceptions of co-operation/lack of co-operation among institutional bodies (1st round interviews)

Need for co-operation	PM	AP	US	AR	Total	%
Agree, 'with explanation'	7 [PM1, PM2, PM3, PM4, PM5, PM6, PM7]	2 [AP1, AP2]	0	1 [AR2]	10/27	37
Agree, but 'no explanation'	0	10 [AP3, AP4, AP5, AP6, AP7, AP8, AP9, AP10, AP11, AP12]	6 [US1, US2, US3, US4, US5, US6]	1 [AR1]	17/27	63
Total	7 [7+0]	12 [2+10]	6 [0+6]	2 [1+1]	27/27 [10+17]	100

The following comments from different institutions' policymakers represent the frustrating scenarios which exist regarding non co-operation:

> Yes co-ordination is needed. We are basically working with SEC, MOF, and professional bodies on how you can create a congenial environment that allows the corporate sector to adopt and implement IFRS. I believe [that] once the Financial Reporting Act (FRA) is implemented then it will, perhaps, create a big change in our corporate culture. So, *we strongly encourage the Ministry of Finance to pursue IFRS so that it can be enacted in the parliament.*
>
> (PM5)

> We developed a corporate governance code, in 2005–06, which is mandatory. We also carried out an assessment in 2005 that brought out lots of issues facing the corporate sector in terms of compliance with IFRS. *The main findings concerned the lack of government support, and the professional bodies – the SEC and the MOF which are responsible for enacting laws governing financial reporting standards.* However in practice, *government provides very little (or no) support to the corporate sector to strengthen audit and quality assurance projects.* Therefore, the institutional bodies and the government should work together to come up with a solution.
>
> (PM2)

> *Our department has no role, as the role is reserved by the ICAB and the corporate world.* However, with some World Bank finance project initiatives, we are trying to create a separate authority by enacting a new law, [the] Financial Reporting Act. This is largely in line with the UK system in creating a separate independent council or FRC to issue, to implement, and to oversee the accounting standards. In that reporting Act, we will keep a provision which is in the line with international accounting standards. So, IFRS will be included.
>
> (PM4)

Accounts preparers and professionals/researchers expressed many of the same sentiments. They strongly believe in a need for co-operation among institutions like the ICAB, the ICMAB, the SEC, and the Ministry of Commerce. The following two comments represent this issue:

> *[T]hey are trying but I must say that there is still scope for institutional bodies like the ICAB and the ICMAB to be more rigorous* and careful about the adoption and implementation of IFRS, through active and continuous monitoring systems.
>
> (AP1)

Ten interviewees also explained what they felt were the reasons for non-cooperation among institutional bodies (see Table 6.9). They believe that the major actors could work together, but that problems tended to occur owing to their conflicting interests. One policymaker views the problem in this way:

> Obviously, the institutional and professional bodies can work together to better implement IFRS. But the real scenario is complicated. The two professional bodies (the ICAB and the ICMAB) are very much conflicted. In recent times, to pass the Financial Reporting Ordinance 2008, the ICAB disputed the making of an Act. The professional bodies only care about their own interests, not the greater good of companies, or the country, or the stakeholders. This is a cultural problem in our country, because we can't accept that some companies are doing well and we are jealous about it.
>
> (PM3)

The policymakers think that transparency among institutional bodies and a consultation process like the exposure draft in the UK or the USA should be conducted, which would engage corporate people. But actions are more important than discussion, otherwise the implementation process would be a 'political manifesto agenda' rather than a real agenda. One of the policymakers states that:

> I think there should be some kind of discussions. But in implementing IFRS, you would not please everyone. So, *it is not like an open-ended participatory approach, because trade bodies and business people will have objections to too many things, especially in the cases of some of the regulatory laws. So, I think [that] if possible the ICAB, ICMAB, SEC, Bangladesh Bank, listed companies, and the government should take a lead in the implementation of IFRS.* They can take opinion from business people but I am doubtful about whether these could be implemented, because these people will give so many comments and you would not be able to implement them all. My comment would be that they can make a comprehensive report based on the comments received and, later on, they can incorporate and adjust. At the last stage, they can discuss with stakeholders and the discussion report can be passed to the cabinet. But what happens is that *the more you discuss the matter, the less you will be able to implement it.*
>
> (PM6)

In the 2nd round of interviews, all the interviewees agree that co-operation among institutional bodies is essential in implementing IFRS. In the 1st round of interviews, all the AP and US interviewees (making a total of 18) agreed on co-operation, but only two from the AP group provided any explanation of their views. In the 2nd round of interviews, all of them agreed and provided explanations (see Table 6.10).

Firstly, multiple regulators create problems because there is no unified and co-ordinated appreciation of the application of IFRS between them. These multiple regulators fail to consult with the professionals, and therefore a communication gap (i.e. lack of co-operation) appears among different institutional bodies:

> In the Companies Act 1994, IFRS are not mandatory . . . *there are multiple regulators* like the SEC and Bangladesh Bank and *they are not knowledgeable* enough regarding the IFRS. In my experience, *if we follow IFRS then Bangladesh Bank, the SEC, and the NBR will create many problems.*
>
> (US4)

> There is no co-ordination among the policymakers. Most importantly, the ministry does not consult with the professionals and even they do not understand the standards. Whatever they think is the final decision.
>
> (AP5)

Table 6.10 Perceptions of politico-institutional factors in relation to IFRS implementation (2nd round interviews)

	PM	AP	US	AR	Total	%
Lack of co-operation among institutional bodies	4 [PM1, PM2, PM4, PM5]	4 [AP5, AP6, AP10, AP12]	2 [US4, US5]	2 [AR1, AR2]	12/12	100

Secondly, blame culture is another key aspect of non-cooperation. For instance, the Credit Rating Agency of Bangladesh (CRAB) thinks that auditors should take the responsibility for non-implementation of IFRS. Meanwhile, the SEC thinks that the DSE should be more accountable in overseeing implementation issues; and the ICAB is not co-operative because it (i.e. the ICAB) is reluctant to take action against its members (i.e. people who qualified through the ICAB). The following comment is representative of this issue:

> Our (SEC) officials and the stock exchange in Bangladesh are working together to implement IFRS. We believe [that] there should be a separate FRC, as in the UK, to oversee IFRS implementation issues. I think [that] the Dhaka Stock Exchange should take responsibility for non-compliance with standards. *Listed companies are the stock exchange's children and therefore the DSE should take care of them. . . . It is not our responsibility to identify who are following or not.* In addition, *the ICAB is not co-operating. For example, if we identify any mistakes in annual reports and violations against CA firms, then we seek comments from the ICAB. But they don't bother replying within six months, even after reminder(s) are sent.* The ICAB is like a clubhouse in which the ICAB is very reluctant to take action against their club members.
>
> (PM4)

Based on the documentary analysis, I will discuss the enforcement actions taken under different political regimes in Bangladesh.

With respect to these different political regimes, Table 6.11 shows that, in the democratic era, there have been 864 enforcement actions (representing 52% of the total of enforcement actions), while the military era saw 783 enforcement actions (representing 48% of the total of enforcement actions) (see Figure 6.2). This is surprising given that the military government ruled for only three years while the democratic government ruled for more than 10 years. This fact raises questions around the efficiency of the democratic government. The relative failure of the democratic government may well be due to the partisan political landscape and the tendency to politicise each and every sector when a new government comes to power. For example, the normal practice of appointing the SEC chairman is that the chairman has political ties to the government.

Table 6.12 shows that different chairmen were appointed under different government regimes, meaning that each of the chairmen has been appointed by each successive government. This political connectedness may well slow down the enforcement activities of the SEC. One SEC chairman has stated that:

> The chairman and the members shall be appointed from amongst the persons of capability and standing who have shown capacity in dealing with problems relating to company matters, securities markets or have special knowledge and experience of law, finance, economics, accountancy and such other disciplines as, in the opinion of the Government, shall be useful to the Commission. According to the securities law, the Commission ensures proper issuance of securities and registers, supervises and regulates the stock exchanges,

Table 6.11 Enforcement actions by political regime

Period	Total Enforcement Actions	Political Government Type
2006–08	783	Military
1998–2005, 2009–10	864	Democratic

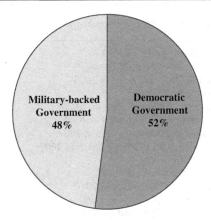

Figure 6.2 Enforcement actions by political regime, 1998–2010

Table 6.12 Securities and Exchange Commission (SEC) chairmen under different political regimes

Sl.	Period	Government Type
1.	1997–98	Awami League
2.	1999–June 2003	Awami League and BNP
3.	July 2003–Oct. 2003	BNP
4.	2003 Nov–Feb. 2006	BNP
5.	March 2006–April 2009	Military
6.	May 2009–May 2011	Awami League
7.	June 2011–Present	Awami League

Note: The Awami League and the Bangladesh Nationalist Party (BNP) are democratic governments.

broker/dealers, merchant bankers, portfolio managers, mutual funds, asset management companies, trustees', custodians, depository company and all other intermediaries, persons or institutions related with the capital market. The expenses of the Commission are met out of the fund contributed by the government as grants and money received from other sources viz. consent fees for raising capital, registration fees etc.

(SEC, 2004–05, p. 5)

This quotation emphasises that the role of the SEC is to efficiently monitor the market; in reality, the scenario is different. To illustrate this point, I find that 13 of 42 IFRS-related violations are cases in which 13 companies have continuously violated regulations (see Table 6.13). Most notably, J Ltd and N Ltd violated six times in 2007, whilst C Ltd did so three times and L Ltd four times in 2007. It is found that the SEC has not taken significant action against any of them. This is possibly because of political connections between these violators and the SEC. This state of affairs may slow the implementation of IFRS.

Reflecting on politico-institutional factors

The findings of Proposition II (P_{II}) show that politico-institutional factors have a negative influence on implementation of IFRS in Bangladesh.

Table 6.13 Companies with repeated violations regarding IFRS compliance, 1998–2010

✓ A Ltd. (Textile): Once in 2008 and twice in 2009
✓ B Ltd. (Textile): Once in 2009 and once in 2010
✓ C Ltd. (Textile): Three times in 2007 and once in 2009
✓ D Ltd. (Food and Allied): Twice in 2008
✓ E Ltd (Food and Allied): Once in 2009 and once in 2010
✓ F Ltd. (Food and Allied): Once in 2007 and once in 2008
✓ G Ltd. (Food and Allied): Once in 2006 and twice in 2007
✓ H Ltd. and I Ltd. (Food and Allied) [H-I Group]: Twice in 2007
✓ J Ltd. (Tannery): Six times in 2007
✓ K Ltd. (Tannery): Once in 2008 and once in 2009
✓ L Ltd. (Cement): Four times in 2007 and once in 2010
✓ M Ltd. (Miscellaneous): Twice in 2007
✓ N Ltd. (Miscellaneous): Six times in 2007 and once in 2009

Note: Company names have been anonymised. Detailed information is available on request from the author.

With respect to political influences (P_{IIA}), the findings reveal that politics have a negative influence on the implementation of IFRS in Bangladesh, under three conditions. This political pressure emerges from a higher level of government intervention (condition b); a higher level of donor agencies' pressure (condition c); and a higher level of political lobbying (condition d). This study finds that higher levels of government intervention and political lobbying have negative influences on the effective implementation of IFRS in Bangladesh. The findings suggest that the government's role is negatively associated with the potential for achievement of the most urgently needed goals of transparency in Bangladesh. The parliamentary process of approving accounting-related laws is also political in nature. Hence, regulatory efforts often struggle in Bangladesh because business elites utilise their political connectedness in order to influence any progress. The 2nd round of interviews confirms that companies are repeatedly violating SEC regulations and that in doing so they are protected from punishment by their political connections.

The study finds that the donor agencies' efforts regarding IFRS adoption and implementation in Bangladesh are transformed through government intervention without considering local culture. Since IFRS implementation in Bangladesh depends highly on donor agencies' funding, the country is exposed to diverse international pressures. The donor agencies' funding processes towards the development of the financial reporting environment in Bangladesh are marked by a lack of consultation and transparency. However, the interviewees in the 2nd round of interviews did not mention political pressure by donor agencies. This is possibly because they may have an interest in, or expectations of, the current democratic government. As the year ended (i.e. 2010–11), no significant improvements had emerged and, therefore, they felt frustration with the government's role in IFRS implementation.

In relation to co-operation/non-cooperation among institutional bodies (P_{II}) the findings reveal that the absence of co-operation among institutional bodies – including state institutions and professional bodies (e.g. the ICAB, ICMAB, SEC, MOC and MOF) – impedes the implementation process in Bangladesh. The policymakers, who represent different institutions, were sceptical about non-cooperation in implementing IFRS. The reason for non-cooperation among institutional bodies was seen as being that major actors are working in their own self-interests. For example, the ICAB disputed the creation of the Financial Reporting Act. A lack of transparency among institutional bodies is also observed. In Bangladesh, the ICAB's standard-setting body does not produce any exposure drafts or consultation papers whatsoever. Hence, the implementation process seems to come down to individual actors' efforts rather than co-ordinated team-working efforts. An absence of co-ordination is observed during the adoption process,[7] which immediately results in dissension, confusion, and in the communication problems that stakeholders experience in Bangladesh. It is important to add that all the interviewees in both the 1st and 2nd round of interviews agreed that, in order to implement IFRS effectively, co-operation among institutional bodies needs to be established – this is a vital prerequisite for success. The findings reveal that the institutional bodies are eager to blame one another for the difficulties encountered so far in implementing IFRS. The documentary analyses reveal that the military-backed government is surprisingly efficient in terms of stringent enforcement, while a lack of co-operation among institutional bodies is found under both the democratic and military-backed government eras. Ultimately, politicised government institutions are impeding the implementation of IFRS in Bangladesh.

Relative impact of accounting regulatory frameworks and politico-institutional factors

To illustrate the relative impact of accounting regulatory frameworks and politico-institutional factors, after reading and reflecting on the transcripts, I summarised the 1st and 2nd round interviewees' attitudes to IFRS implementation and set this information alongside each interviewee's work experience and qualifications (see Appendices 6.4 and 6.5). I also developed ordinal categories for their responses regarding the main topics and questions that were asked. The view of each interviewee on a given topic is represented by one answer (see Q1 to Q4 in Appendices 6.4 and 6.5). This approach requires making a judgement about the interviewee's primary opinion about a topic if he/she expresses positive/negative/no comment. This allowed me to detect any relationship between the four groups of interviewees' perceptions on IFRS implementation. In addition, this comparison helps to establish whether the interviewees' background characteristics, such as their work experience and qualifications, are related to or influence their attitudes. However, there is relatively little opportunity to obtain cell sizes sufficiently large for a chi-square test, and therefore the analysis concentrates on descriptions of the extent and cause of IFRS implementation. The conclusions seek to draw out general factors influencing IFRS implementation, but specific comments by the respondents are presented to give the reader an indication of the breadth of reasons for poor implementation of IFRS in Bangladesh.

Interview Questions 1 and 3 of Appendix 6.4 are examples of areas of IFRS implementation in which interviewees' perceptions differ. Q1 is relevant to accounting regulations and Q3 is relevant to politico-institutional factors. From the responses to Questions 1 and 3, it is found that there is a relationship between interviewees' perceptions of accounting regulatory frameworks and political influence. The majority of interviewees who are disappointed with the accounting regulatory frameworks feel that there is a political influence in the implementation of IFRS. However, some dissimilarities are observed. Firstly, two policymakers' (PM4 and PM7) views are different on political issues and accounting regulation. For example, PM4 (an SEC executive director) is unhappy with current regulations, but at the same time sees no political influence. This is understandable given that the interviewee's position is closely related to the government's Ministry of Finance. PM7 (Deputy Secretary, Ministry of Finance) is pleased with the accounting regulations, but commented on politics. It is not surprising that this interviewee commented on donor agencies' political influence rather than the government's political influence. This is possibly because of his appointment in the current democratic government (i.e. the Ministry of Finance), which is a 'political appointment'. Therefore, this policymaker is cautious of talking about any possible negative role of the government.

Table 6.14 Quantification of perceptions of interviewees (1st round interviews, n = 27)

Code	Accounting Regulation	Politico-Institutional	
	Q1	Q3	Q4
PM1	0	0	1
PM2	0	0	1
PM3	0	0	1
PM4	0	1	1
PM5	0	0	1
PM6	0	0	1
PM7	1	0	1
AP1	0	0	1
AP2	1	0	1
AP3	0	9	1
AP4	0	9	1
AP5	0	0	1
AP6	0	9	1
AP7	0	9	1
AP8	0	9	1
AP9	1	9	1
AP10	0	9	1
AP11	0	9	1
AP12	0	0	1
US1	0	9	1
US2	0	0	1
US3	0	0	1
US4	0	9	1
US5	0	0	1
US6	0	9	1
AR1	0	0	1
AR2	0	9	1
Positive perceptions	11% [3/27]	4% [1/27]	100% [27/27]
Negative perceptions	89% [24/27]	52% [14/27]	0%
No comment	0%	44% [12/27]	0%
Total	**100%**	**100%**	**100%**

Notes:'0' = negative perceptions,'1' = positive perceptions,'9' = no comment.
Q1:'0' = negative (non-satisfactory) perceptions,'1' = positive perceptions on accounting regula-
tion; Q3:'0' = political pressure,'1' = no political pressure,'9' = no comment on political pressure;
Q4:'0' = no need for co-operation,'1' = need for co-operation among institutional bodies;
Q2: Regulators cannot be quantified due to the nature of the questions and perceptions of the
interviewees.

Secondly, while 52% of respondents were negative about political influence, 44% interviewees (12 out of 27) provided no comment on politics (see Table 6.14). In particular, the majority of the account preparers (nine out of 12) were hesitant to discuss politics. This could be due to feelings of insecurity towards their jobs.

As mentioned in Chapters 1 and 5, the purpose of the 2nd round of interviews was to test the reaction of the interviewees, as the 2nd round of interviews took place a year after the first.

The 1st round of interviews was conducted when the present democratic government was in its second year (2010), while the 2nd round was conducted in its third year (2011). I assumed that the interviewees might change their attitudes because of the maturity of the democratic government (i.e. the democratic government had been in power for a longer period) and the interviewees are of course free to comment. In the 2nd round interviews, the attitudes of the interviewees were not very different from previous responses (see Appendix 6.5 and Table 6.15). In line with accounting regulatory frameworks, the majority of interviewees provide negative sentiments on accounting regulation, the standard-setting process, and enforcement issues.

With respect to politico-institutional factors, 75% of interviewees feel that political pressure by the government is impeding implementation of IFRS, whilst 100% of respondents say that institutional co-operation is also needed. Some similarities in the interviewees' perceptions are observed; for example, 100% of interviewees in both the 1st and 2nd round of interviews feel that co-operation among institutional bodies is needed. Some differences in the interviewees' perceptions are observed: firstly, the 2nd interviewees were more critical, in particular, of the possibility of political pressure by the government (75% compared to 52%). Secondly, the lower level of 'no comment' (25% compared to 44%) on political influence adds some confirmation to the greater critical sentiments of the 2nd round respondents. This is possibly because the interviewees are more open to talking about politics in the 2nd round interviews. Thirdly, the 2nd round interviewees only mention political pressure by the government, whilst

Table 6.15 Quantification of perceptions of interviewees (2nd round interviews, n=12)

	Accounting Regulation			Politico-Institutional	
1st Round IQs	Q1			Q3	Q4
2nd Round IQs	Q1(a)	Q1(b)	Q2	Q3	Q4
PM1	0	1	0	0	1
PM2	0	1	0	0	1
PM4	1	0	1	0	1
PM5	0	0	0	0	1
AP5	0	0	0	0	1
AP6	0	0	0	9	1
AP10	0	0	0	9	1
AP12	0	0	0	9	1
US4	0	0	0	0	1
US5	0	0	0	0	1
AR1	0	0	0	0	1
AR2	0	0	0	0	1
Positive perceptions	8% [1/12]	17% [2/12]	8% [1/12]	0%	100% [12/12]
Negative perceptions	92% [11/12]	83% [10/12]	92% [11/12]	75% [9/12]	0%
No comment	0%	0%	0%	25% [3/12]	0%
Total	100%	100%	100%	100%	100%

Notes: '0' = negative perception, '1' = positive perceptions, '9' = no comment.
Q1(a): '0' = negative perception and '1' = positive perception of accounting regulation; Q1(b): '0' = negative perception and '1' = positive perception of standard setting process; Q2: '0' = negative perception and '1' = positive perception of enforcement; Q3: '0' = political pressure; '1' = no political pressure and '9' = no comment on political pressure; Q4: '0' = no need for co-operation and '1' = need for co-operation among institutional bodies.

in the 1st round the interviewees mentioned political pressure from other sources (e.g. donor agencies). PM1, PM2 and PM4 provided negative comments on accounting regulatory frameworks in the 1st round of interviews. Surprisingly, in the 2nd round of interviews, PM1 and PM2 both said that the standard-setting process is already becoming more co-operative, and PM4 is happy with current accounting regulations and the SEC's enforcement actions. This is possibly due to the fact that PM1 and PM2 are officials of the ICAB (under the MOC) and PM4 is an official of the SEC (under the MOF), and they want to legitimise and justify their government's position.

A further observation from Appendices 6.4 and 6.5 is that there is no association between the interviewees' work experience/qualifications and their attitudes. For example, based on similar work experience (years), seven interviewees have 20 years and above, 13 have 10–20 years, and seven have five–nine years' experience. However, variations are observed in their perceptions. Similarly, based on the qualifications, 11 are qualified accountants, two are part-qualified CAs, three have PhDs and 11 are postgraduates (e.g. MBA/MSc/MCom/MA in Accounting).

The findings on the interviewees' attitudes indicate that politico-institutional factors are stronger and more dominant factors than accounting regulatory frameworks. The findings reveal that political connectedness in the regulatory process and looser enforcement of the laws are hindering the effective implementation of IFRS during the democratic government era, while the military government era is depoliticised and effective in terms of its stringent enforcement of the law. However, stakeholders' non-participation in policymaking is evident in both the democratic and military government eras. Comparing the 1st and 2nd round of interviews, nothing significant has changed in the interviewees' attitudes. The 2nd round interviewees were more negative about the current democratic government's initiative regarding IFRS implementation in Bangladesh. According to the majority of the interviewees, political pressure by the government is impeding IFRS implementation, with the exception of the views of the policymaking group. This is possibly because these policymakers are politically appointed by the present democratic government.

Conclusion

The aim of this chapter has been to reflect upon the evidence from the two rounds of interviews and on the available information regarding the enforcement actions in the implementation of IFRS in Bangladesh. Two propositions are discussed, involving accounting regulatory frameworks and politico-institutional factors. Proposition P_I on accounting regulatory frameworks is examined. The evidence suggests that the current accounting regulatory frameworks in Bangladesh have a negative influence on the implementation of IFRS.

In relation to the quality of investor protection laws (condition b), the findings confirm that low-quality investor protection laws in Bangladesh are impeding IFRS implementation. The contradictions between local laws and IFRS are delaying the implementation process, causing it to be less effective.[8] This implies that companies have some scope to decide not to comply fully with IFRS, and can do so because the legal systems in Bangladesh are flawed and thus highly unlikely to punish them.

In relation to stakeholders' participation/non-participation in the standard-setting process (condition c), the findings reveal that the ICAB does not engage stakeholders in the standard-setting process in Bangladesh. The ICAB, as the real regulator, is seen as being responsible for accounting standard-setting. The absence of any consultation with stakeholders and publishing exposure drafts calls into question the effectiveness of this institution. This is because a government ministry is involved with the ICAB, and the government is directly or indirectly intervening in appointing the chairman and the members of the standards-setting committee. In addition, the findings suggest that the present democratic government is not inclined to set up the FRC or FRA.

In relation to enforcement of the laws (condition c), the SEC, as the enforcer institution, is failing to perform effectively in Bangladesh. The evidence gained from interviews and documentary analysis suggests that the SEC is not tightening its enforcement mechanisms to make sure that companies are bound by regulation to comply with IFRS. This is likely to be due to political lobbying and government intervention in the SEC, which impedes the enforcement process. The SEC is unable to identify IFRS-related violations because there are no qualified accountants in the institution. Further, the penalty criteria for the violators are vague and insignificant.

This chapter also presents evidence on politico-institutional factors in relation to propositions P_{II}, P_{IIA} and P_{IIB}. The findings confirm that politico-institutional factors have a negative influence on implementation of IFRS in Bangladesh.

Taking first P_{IIA}, Bangladesh is a common-law country (condition a). In relation to the level of government intervention (condition b), the findings confirm that a higher level of government intervention in Bangladesh inhibits the implementation process. In relation to the level of donor agencies' pressure (condition c), interviewees mentioned a higher level of pressure in Bangladesh. The donor agencies are providing funding towards the successful implementation of IFRS, but the funding is not utilised in appropriate ways. The question has therefore been raised by the interviewees: if the donor agencies are aware of these corrupt activities, then why they are not taking action against the government?

In relation to condition (d), a lower/higher level of political lobbying, the findings suggest that higher levels of political lobbying in Bangladesh are hindering the effective implementation of IFRS. Respondents give strongly negative sentiments regarding the government's political influence. For example, the regulators (e.g. the SEC and the judiciary) are toothless in penalising companies which are politically well connected. Furthermore, the government has not legislated for new regulations, or even updated the existing accounting-related regulations, for the last 14 years.

With respect to co-operation/lack of co-operation among institutional bodies (P_{IIB}), it is found that a lack of co-operation among institutional bodies is slowing down the implementation process. In relation to ensuring the participatory rights/an absence of participatory rights for the stakeholders (condition a), the findings suggest that no participatory rights for stakeholders exist in Bangladesh. In terms of democratic/undemocratic government (condition b), the study finds that a lack of co-operation exists among the institutional bodies which are responsible for the implementation process, under both democratic and undemocratic governments. However, the military-backed government was more efficient in taking action against corrupt companies. This is possibly because the implementation of law is seemingly better in the military era, in comparison with the democratic era in Bangladesh. The institutions are blaming each other, and this 'blame culture' is not assisting the implementation process. In my opinion, blame is deployed as an attempt to remove power and responsibility from others in order to facilitate the legitimacy of, and increase the scope of, government bureaucracy.

The overall conclusion to be drawn in this chapter is that, despite the fact that Bangladesh is a common-law origin country[9] (condition a of each proposition), the findings of other conditions (in particular, b, c, and d) of both propositions (P_I and P_{II}) reveal that common-law origin has minor or no influence on implementation of IFRS in Bangladesh. This is possibly because Bangladesh contains an unique environment which may be explained via several factors – e.g. (a) training opportunities in the accounting profession, and corruption; and (b) other country-specific factors. This study raises a question as to why a common-law origin country has no influence on the implementation of IFRS or has moved toward code-law regarding the implementation of IFRS.

In relation to the relative impact of accounting regulatory frameworks and politico-institutional factors, a comparison of interviewees' perceptions and reflecting attitudes has been discussed. The findings suggest that politico-institutional factors are stronger and more dominant factors than accounting regulatory frameworks with regard to the effective implementation of IFRS in Bangladesh. It is observed that there is a link between the interviewees' views on accounting regulatory frameworks and political influences. However, the majority of interviewees are very concerned about the impact of the democratic government's political influence in implementing IFRS. The attitudes of the interviewees indicate that policymakers are keen to comment on donor agencies' political influence, while denying the existence of government intervention or political lobbying. As mentioned earlier, this is likely to be because the policymakers represent different government institutions. In the 1st round of interviews, account preparers and professionals seem hesitant to talk about politics. One interpretation is that these interviewee groups feel too insecure to comment, and believe that doing so may harm their livelihoods. But, in the 2nd round of interviews, the interviewees are more critical of the present democratic government's perceived attempts to apply political pressure. The persisting feeling expressed is that the interviewees are becoming more familiar with the present democratic government because the government is in its third year in power, so its methods are becoming clearer to observers. The interviews and documentary evidence collected in the study also reveal that, in addition to politicised government institutions, outdated accounting regulatory frameworks are impeding the implementation of IFRS in Bangladesh. This is an indication that accounting change has not taken place over the last decade. In particular, the accounting regulations are outdated even though the national political government has changed. This state of affairs also confirms the current democratic government's failure so far to play a major role in driving the effective implementation of IFRS in Bangladesh.

Notes

1   The details of the interview data analysis process are provided in Chapter 5.
2   The ICAB has a standard-setting committee that selects particular IFRS as the basis for drafting BAS. The BAS are prepared by adapting IFRS to reflect specific local requirements under Bangladeshi laws and regulations. The draft versions of the BAS are then submitted to the council of the ICAB for discussion, finalisation and adoption.
3   A majority simply means more than 50% of the interviewees' perceptions are in agreement.
4   Number of times indicates the number of violations which have occurred against each standard.
5   This is a specific concept which is being used in a generalised sense in the present study, because IFRS are a global idea.
6   AP5 is critical regarding political lobbying in the 1st round of interviews, and AP6 and AP10 are silent in the 1st round.
7   For example, in an attempt to resolve the stalemate between the ICAB and the ICMAB, the Ministry of Commerce (MOC), acting on behalf of the Government of Bangladesh, issued a memorandum in October 1999 which proposed the establishment of a Bangladesh Accounting and Auditing Standards Monitoring Board involving all interested parties; but this proposal was rejected by the ICAB, which perceives itself as 'the only competent legal authority in the country to adopt IAS' (ICAB,1998–99, p. 19;cited in Mir and Rahaman, 2005, p. 829).
8   The Companies Act 1994 has not been updated, despite the formation of a government committee to update regulations.
9   As explained in Chapter 4.

The impact of training opportunities in the accounting profession, corruption and country-specific factors

Introduction

The purpose of this chapter is to present the results of the second research question with reference to the implementation of IFRS in Bangladesh, as follows:

> RQ-2(a): How do training opportunities in the accounting profession and the state of corruption, as outcomes of culture in Bangladesh, affect the implementation of IFRS?
>
> RQ-2(b): What other country-specific factors are affecting implementation of IFRS?

In particular, the findings will answer Proposition III and analyse issues around other country-specific factors. As mentioned in Chapter 2, the most frequently discussed issues in the prior literature on the role of the state and accounting change are accounting regulatory frameworks, politico-institutional factors, and cultural factors (investigated here through training opportunities in the accounting profession and through corruption). In this chapter, drawing on the 27 1stand 12 2nd round interviews as well as documentary analyses, I will discuss the third proposition which was developed in Chapter 2 and other country-specific factors. The third proposition relates to training opportunities in the accounting profession and corruption as proxies for cultural factors.

As mentioned in Chapter 2, the present study does not explore cultural values or beliefs, as proposed by Hofstede (1980, 1987), Hofstede et al. (2010) and Gray (1988). Although Weber (1958/1904) argues that cultural changes played a critical role in the development of capitalism and its institutions, the Weberian view of the state is opposed to Hofstede's model (Baskerville, 2001; Wickramasinghe and Hopper, 2005). Hofstede's cultural dimensions model has been criticised in prior literature (Gernon and Wallace, 1995; Baskerville, 2001, 2003, 2005; Stulz and Williamson, 2003; Wickramasinghe and Hopper, 2005). This is because Hofstede's survey was limited to a single organisation and may not be applicable to other contexts (Gernon and Wallace, 1995). Baskerville (2001, p.3) also argues that 'the "dimensions of culture" provided by Hofstede (or Gray) allows accounting researchers to sample and survey behaviour, and apply cultural indices to isolate the impact of the social environment . . . [and] could be attributed to non-cultural causes, such as corporate practices and ethics'. Another possible criticism comes from Wickramasinghe and Hopper (2005, p. 478), who argue that the cultural practices associated with accounting practices are 'unlikely to be consistent within single national values (c.f. Hofstede, 1980) . . . culture, politics and the state, economics or accounting: they are intertwined and wax and wane according to contingencies'. An understanding of accounting practices cannot be obtained without reference to its cultural political economy, because culture will provide arguments that help to rationalise political arguments (Merryman, 1985; Rajan and Zingales, 2000).

The present study identifies some country-specific factors that are impeding the implementation of IFRS in Bangladesh, which are as follows: a lack of qualified accountants; a lack of interest in IFRS by managers of some companies; a culture of secrecy; a lack of research; public sector dominance; and a predominantly family-based private sector. Some of these factors are supported by prior research. The interview questions include references to training opportunities in the accounting profession and corruption, and other country-specific factors. Enforcement documents from 1998–2010 available from the SEC websites have also been used in this study. As mentioned in Chapter 4, Bangladesh's culture is strongly ingrained, meaning that corruption is rife (both in the private and public sectors).[1] Subsequently, the analyses will examine whether corruption is hindering the regulators' attempts to enforce the regulations.

The following section will discusses training opportunities in the accounting profession and corruption in relation to Proposition III. The influences of other country-specific factors in the implementation of IFRS in a developing country will then be discussed, followed by a summary of this chapter.

Training opportunities in the accounting profession, and corruption (proposition III)

In this section, I will explore the following proposition:

P_{IIIA}: Effective development of the training opportunities in the accounting profession will have a positive influence on implementation of IFRS.

or

Ineffective development of the training opportunities in the accounting profession will have a negative influence on implementation of IFRS.

P_{IIIB}: Low levels of corruption will have a positive influence on implementation of IFRS.

or

High levels of corruption will have a negative influence on implementation of IFRS.

I will analyse whether or not Bangladesh's training opportunities in the accounting profession and levels of corruption are impeding the implementation of IFRS.

Effective/ineffective development of training opportunities in the accounting profession

In terms of effective/ineffective development of training opportunities in the accounting profession in Bangladesh, the interviewees are asked:

Do you feel that the current professional accountancy qualification syllabus is suitable to implement IFRS effectively?
Will IFRS be included in the universities' curricula?

Eighteen of the 27 interviewees feel that the current professional exam syllabus is not suitable to better implement IFRS (see Table 7.1). All the interviewees agree that university curricula should include IFRS content.

The 1st round interviews

Professional and university curricula

There is mixed evidence regarding the suitability of the current professional syllabus for implementation of IFRS. Nine out of 27 interviewees felt that the current syllabus is at an equivalent level to international standards (see Table 7.1). This view is summed up by the following comment by PM1, the president of the ICAB:

> *Of course, recently we have initiated a combined project known as the Twinning Project in which we have tried to match international accounting education standards.* Further, members of the ICAB can be members of the ICAEW, and this is a milestone intended to encourage Bangladeshi students.[2]

The majority of the interviewees (18 out of 27) mention that the professional syllabus is not suitable to implement IFRS (see Table 7.1). According to the interviewees, the syllabus does not contain related examples and applications of IFRS, and the students gain inadequate knowledge of IFRS from the teaching which is offered by the ICAB.[3] Therefore, the quality of newly qualified auditors in Bangladesh still remains questionable. The following two comments summarise this view:

> *The syllabus of the professional bodies in Bangladesh does not include any courses on IFRS* that will help accountants in preparing annual reports which are based on mandatory accounting standards.
>
> (AR2)

> *I don't think the ICAB's syllabus is up to date enough to really implement IFRS and Basel II* . . . The ICAB should include IFRS in their syllabus and also engage students in arranging regular seminars and workshops on IFRS.
>
> (PM6)

All the interviewees comment that the universities' curricula should include IFRS content (see Table 7.1). The interviewees point out that none of the universities has an accountancy and

Table 7.1 Views on the suitability of accounting education (professional and university curricula) for IFRS implementation (1st round interviews)

Curricula	View	PM	AP	US	AR	Total	%
Professional	Current syllabus is *suitable* for implementing IFRS	3 [PM1, PM2, PM5]	4 [AP1, AP3, AP10, AP12]	2 [US1, US6]	0	9/27	33
	Not suitable for implementing IFRS	4 [PM3, PM4, PM6, PM7]	8 [AP2, AP4, AP5, AP6, AP7, AP8, AP9, AP11]	4 [US2, US3, US4, US5]	2 [AR1, AR2]	18/27	67
University	Should include IFRS content in universities' curricula	7 [PM1, PM2, PM3, PM4, PM5, PM6, PM7]	12 [AP1, AP2, AP3, AP4, AP5, AP6, AP7, AP8, AP9, AP10, AP11, AP12]	6 [US1, US2, US3, US4, US5, US6]	2 [AR1, AR2]	27/27	100

finance programme linked to the professional bodies. Therefore, the accountancy graduates who become company account preparers are unaware of IFRS. Consequently, they cannot prepare financial statements complying with IFRS. For instance, one interviewee argues that:

> *The IFRS content is missing in the universities' curricula in Bangladesh. The public universities are inclined to incorporate IFRS curricula. However, the private universities are reluctant to incorporate IFRS content at all.* More than 55% students are studying at private universities.
>
> (AP8)

However, the real problem of involving IFRS content in the university syllabus is the lack of qualified accountancy academics. There are about 82 universities with a total of 19,409 academics in Bangladesh.[4] According to interviewees there are about 200 accounting academics. Two interviewees mentioned:

> Yes, there is a global desire to include IFRS in the universities curricula. *However, there is a shortage of academics to teach the content.*
>
> (AP11)

> To be honest, there is a shortage of accounting academics. You know the method of teaching is different here because teachers only teach theoretical underpinnings, and ignore practical application.
>
> (PM7)

Training and development

The interviewees are asked: What kind of training and development are you offering them (the preparers and professionals) to cope with IFRS?[5] Two PMs from the ICAB respond that they are providing training to cope with IFRS (see Table 7.2). For instance, the ICAB arranges regular seminars on IFRS which teach preparation of financial statements in accordance with IFRS. In addition, they have included Continuing Professional Development (CPD) hours for an accountant to participate in IFRS seminars and discussions. However, the SEC, the ICMAB, the World Bank in Bangladesh, Bangladesh Bank and the Ministry of Finance have no training opportunities. One interviewee from the World Bank reflects on that issue:

> *In the World Bank [Bangladesh office], there is nothing mentioned about IFRS related training in Bangladesh.* In 2006, the UN General Assembly adopted the IPSAS which are followed by IFRS.
>
> (PM5)

Secondly, three out of 12APs say that they have attended IFRS-related training programmes (see Table 7.2). These three interviewees included two accountants from a 'big four' and one from a multinational company. This is a clear indication that multinationals and big four are aware of global standards. The training opportunities are also limited (e.g. IFRS seminars and disclosure requirements). Nine interviewees did not attend any training programme. Four CA firms do not offer any training to their accountants. This view is summed up concisely by an accountant preparer:

> I do not have any training at all. I am interested in attending the IFRS training programme. However, the company is not in favour of it. *The company doesn't care, so why should I?*
>
> (AP11)

Table 7.2 Views on training and development from four groups of interviewees (1st round interviews)

PM: Providing Training and Development to Cope with IFRS (n=7)

	PM1	PM2	PM3	PM4	PM5	PM6	PM7	Total	%
Provide training	√	√						2/7	29
Not providing training			√	√	√	√	√	5/7	71

AP: Attended Training to Cope with IFRS (n=12)

	AP1	AP2	AP3	AP4	AP5	AP6	AP7	AP8	AP9	AP10	AP11	AP12	Total	%
Yes	√									√		√	3/12	25
No		√	√*	√*	√	√	√	√*	√*		√		9/12	75

*AP3, AP4, AP8 and AP9 work in CA firms but have not attended any training on IFRS.

US and AR: Training and Development Are Essential to Cope with IFRS (n=8)

Training is essential	US1	US2	US3	US4	US5	US6	AR1	AR2	Total	%
	√	√	√	√	√	√	√	√	8/8	100%

Finally, all US and AR respondents feel that training is very much essential. All the interviewees express the cynical view that the current culture of providing limited training to account preparers and professionals by the companies and professional bodies would not benefit the effective implementation of IFRS at all. The following quotation from an AR, is illustrative of this point of view:

> I strongly believe [that] *there is a need to train the trainers/teachers to comply with IFRS.* The ICAB is not doing such a remarkable job. The preparers [and] professionals need extensive training regarding IFRS.
>
> (AR1)

The 2nd round interviews

The interviewees are asked: Q5. How effective are accounting education and the profession in implementing IFRS? Twelve interviewees agree that accounting education and the profession can be improved by including a syllabus of IFRS content in university and professional exams (see Table 7.3). In addition, they point out that syllabus should be more practically based rather than purely theoretically oriented.

In the 1st round of interviews, 67% of interviewees said they felt that the current syllabus of professional exams is not suitable, and all of them thought that the university syllabuses should include IFRS-related content (see Table 7.1). In the 2nd round of interviews, 100% of the interviewees were concerned about the current syllabuses – i.e. both the professional exams and the universities' curricula (see Table 7.3). It can be argued that PM1, PM2, PM5, AP10 and AP12 feel that the current syllabus is suitable for the implementation of IFRS, but in the 2nd round they raise questions around the current syllabus. It is understandable

Table 7.3 Perceptions of effective/ineffective development of training opportunities in the accounting profession in relation to IFRS implementation (2nd round interviews)

	PM	AP	US	AR	Total	%
Ineffective development of training opportunities in the accounting profession	4 [PM1, PM2, PM4, PM5]	4 [AP5, AP6, AP10, AP12]	2 [US4, US5]	2 [AR1, AR2]	12/12	100

that they changed their views (June 2010 to September 2011) because very little progress has been made, although the ICAB and the World Bank signed a memorandum in 2009 to reform the syllabus. The interviewees feel that professionalism is not being practised by accountants. The most striking point is that the preparers do not know the standards. Two interviewees from the AR and AP groups extensively commented along the following lines:

> There are no values of disclosure because it is not culturally accepted in Bangladesh. Companies are not following this because the preparers and even the auditors do not know the standards.
>
> (AR1)

> There are around 100 CA firms in Bangladesh. Apart from the big four, the others follow director's wishes. Some CA firms are like a one-man show, in which case quality assurance is not maintained at all. This is a deliberate negligence by the CA firms regarding IFRS implementation.
>
> (AP6)

Documentary analyses

In this section, I examine CA firms' violations from 1998 to 2010. Based on the analysis, approximately 36% of independent auditing firms (31 from a total of 86) have violated the SEC rules regarding IFRS.

Table 7.4 shows that enforcement notices were not released against the CA firms until 2002. The largest number of violations was identified during the years 2006 and 2009. The findings reveal that none of the firms were penalised for violating the SEC's rules, with the exception of two cases. This means that 36 violations were flagged – the SEC stated 'Failure to comply with securities related laws regarding financial statements of the issuers' [Warning] – and two of them were fined. In terms of the two exception cases, in 2008, the SEC stated 'Failure to submit qualified audit report of the issuer' [Penalty]; and in 2010 the SEC stated 'Failure to comply with securities related laws regarding financial statements of the issuers' [Penalty]. None of these firms paid a penalty.

Table 7.4 CA firms' violations (1998–2010)

2010		2009		2008		2007		2006		2005		2004		2003		2002		2001		2000		1999		1998		Total	
O	F	O	F	O	F	O	F	O	F	O	F	O	F	O	F	O	F	O	F	O	F	O	F	O	F	O	F
3	3	8	8	5	3	6	4	8	6	2	2	2	2	3	2	1	1	0	0	0	0	0	0	0	0	38	31

Notes: O = Number of occurrences (i.e. the term used for violations in this study); F = number of CA firms. Company names have been anonymised. Detailed information is available on request from the author.

Certain audit situations were very common in many of the independent CA firms' violations which were examined. For instance, some CA firms continually violated the SEC rules. For example, A & Co. were warned for non-compliance with securities-related laws in connection with the audited financial statements of Bangladesh X Ltd. for the years ended 30 June 2006, 2009 and 2010; and B & Co. were warned for non-compliance with securities-related laws in connection with the audited financial statements of Y Ltd. for the years ended 30 June 2008, 2009 and 2010. Notably, B & Co. is one of the big four companies in Bangladesh. This shows that not only small CA firms but also the big four firms have violated the SEC rules. Further, the SEC restricted access to the documentation on one CA firm on the SEC websites. The released information was a 'Disposal of review petition against Penalty Order. In connection with auditor's qualifications and Commission's observations on the audited financial statements of Z Ltd. for the year ended June 30, 2006',[6] M/S C & Co.[7] It also evident that the CA firms were retained for more than three years, but the SEC did not penalise the companies. An example of this would be the auditors of XX Ltd.[8] This evidence raises a question as to why these corrupt practices are repeated. According to the perceptions of the interviewees, the ICAB interprets the matter in favour of the CA firms. Another possible explanation suggested by the interviewees is that the SEC suffers from a lack of professionals, and therefore they cannot identify the CA firms' violations or act upon these if they are discovered.

This study also finds that the SEC's enforcement actions against CA firms do not convince companies to change auditors. Table 7.4 indicates that the ramifications of enforcement actions did not go beyond the impact of press releases. Further, the SEC did not identify any CA firms' violations of auditing standards. Hence, the evidence in this study indicates that the SEC's actions have no other market and economic consequences. One SEC official mentioned that when the SEC identifies any corrupt firms it then seeks comments from the ICAB. But the ICAB does not reply to the SEC on time. There is a quality assurance committee of the ICAB for overseeing CA firms' activities, but this committee is possibly not active in this regard. Another significant finding is that the identified CA firms are able to continue their work because of a culture of non-punishment for violating rules. This indicates the absence of any reliable exercising of due care or professional ethics in Bangladesh. It also raises questions around the quality of annual reports and investors' trust in the annual reports presented to them.

Low/high levels of corruption: 1st round interviews

The interviewees are asked: How would you regard corruption as an issue in implementing IFRS effectively? Twenty one interviewees comment regarding corruption in relation to IFRS implementation (see Table 7.5). They feel that a high level of corruption is a big threat to the implementation of IFRS.

Six interviewees from the policymaking group do not feel that corruption is a big problem (see Table 7.5). The majority of interviewees think that corruption is embedded in three sectors: government bodies; audit firms and professional bodies; and private companies. Ten out of the 21 interviewees feel that financial reporting practices are affected by the wide spread corrupt practices of governmental bodies. Respondents agree that the governmental bodies have become the epitome of corruption, given the close relation between the business elite and the political class. The only PM comments that:

> I think [that] the government does not want to implement IFRS fully. *The government knows very well about the corrupt practices of its regulatory bodies but is reluctant to take action against them because of their political connections.*

(PM5)

Table 7.5 Negative perceptions of corruption from four groups of interviewees (1st round interviews)

Corruption by:	PM	AP	US	AR	Total	%
Governmental bodies	1 [PM5]	5 [AP1, AP4, AP7, AP8, AP12]	2 [US3, US4]	2 [AR1, AR2]	10/21	47
Audit firms and professional bodies	0	5 [AP2, AP5, AP6, AP10, AP11]	1 [US2]	0	6/21	29
Companies	0	2 [AP3, AP9]	3 [US1, US5, US6]	0	5/21	24
Total	1	12	6	2	[21/27]*	78

Note: *Six interviewees from the total of 27 do not feel that corruption is a threat to the implementation of IFRS.

Further, the regulatory bodies are themselves involved with corrupt practices. The interviewees express frustration regarding the regulators' role in monitoring financial reporting practices. For instance, one AP said:

> Sometimes, inspectors from the regulatory bodies like the SEC and the National Audit Office visit our office to verify our accounts. They ask some irrelevant questions on IFRS but do not even give us an opportunity to explain things in detail. *I have a feeling that they have no background in accountancy at all (e.g. they might have an MA in History, or an MA in Sociology) and simply want bribes. It seems like whatever you explain to them they will respond NO but if you bribe them, they will respond YES.*
>
> (AP7)

Respondents express that the corrupt auditors and professional bodies' members can continue their activities because of their close links to politicians. Respondents also agree that implementers of IFRS (i.e. the ICAB, the SEC, the Ministry of Finance, and the Ministry of Commerce) are not necessarily honest and are likely to have high levels of corruption. None of the auditors comment on their corrupt practices. The following comments are representative of this issue:

> The professional bodies have not taken any action against corrupt auditor(s) since the independence of Bangladesh.
>
> (US2)

> *You know, the rating agency decides the credit ratings through bribery.* So, financially, the company is not strong enough but their credit rating is very high. How is this possible?
>
> (AP10)

Finally, corrupt practices are often found in companies. Five interviewees (two AP and three US) believe that there is history of a considerable number of large-scale frauds which have been carried out by managers and directors of listed companies (see Table 7.5). According to a group of respondents, some companies hide true information to evade taxes, and the tax authority is satisfied with bribery. One interviewee from the AP group in particular commented:

The directors are very influential. So, *the annual reports are being prepared according to the wishes of the directors. We are more concerned about the stability of our jobs and family than about IFRS and honesty.* If we lose our jobs then who will feed our family? You know [that] the *tax authority does not care about IFRS either and they are satisfied with bribery when it comes to IFRS compliance.*

(AP9)

The 2nd round interviews

The interviewees are asked: Q6. How does corruption affect effective IFRS implementation? Nine out of 12 interviewees feel that corruption is impeding the IFRS implementation process (see Table 7.6). Apart from the PM group, all the interviewees in the other groups (i.e. AP, US and AR) agree with this view. One interviewee sums this up:

To convince the Tax authority that you are complying with regulatory requirements, you have to bribe them.

(US5)

The findings of the 2nd round of interviews are similar to that seen in the 1st round of interviews. For example, PM1, PM2 and PM4 feel that corruption is not a big issue in the implementation of IFRS. PM1, PM2 and PM4 are linked with the Ministry of Commerce and the Ministry of Finance respectively. Consequently they tend not to comment on governmental bodies' corruption. According to the perceptions of the interviewees, during mid-2011 the country's capital market experienced major turbulence which resulted in the collapse of several companies, and led to the attrition of investors' confidence, leading to shareholder distrust and low confidence. Only one PM is very critical about the corruption issue and expresses the opinion that:

Recently, I chaired the quality assurance board of the ICAB. I saw [that] *many CA firms were identified as violating professional ethics,* but they were not fined or penalised . . . *the ICAB are taking membership fees* from the violators. It means [that] they can carry out their job legally. *It is a culture in Bangladesh to violate the rules because criminals know that nothing will happen to them.* I do not know where it will end so *how do you expect IFRS implementation and transparency to be achieved?*

(PM5)

Table 7.6 Negative perceptions of corruption in relation to IFRS implementation (2nd round interviews)

Corruption by:	PM	AP	US	AR	Total	%
Governmental body	1 [PM5]	4 [AP5, AP6, AP10, AP12]	2 [US4, US5]	2 [AR1, AR2]	9/12	75

Documentary analyses

This section of the present chapter examines enforcement releases during the period 1998–2010. More specifically, violations across various industries and court cases, with reference to corruption, are examined.

Violations across various industries

The distribution of enforcement actions across various industries on the DSE list is shown in Tables 7.7–7.9. These tables were created based on overall enforcement actions from 1998 to 2010 as depicted in Appendix 7.1. Table 7.7 shows that 19 industries violated the SEC rules; that the number of occurrences has increased from 2006 onwards; and specifies the number of years over which the wrongdoing took place. Most notably, in 2006, 174 companies were subject to a total of 326 enforcement actions. This is possibly a reflection of the fact that, during the period 2001 to 2005, Bangladesh was officially the most corrupt country in the world (TIB, 2005; see Chapter 4). As soon as the military-backed government took over from the democratic government, they tried to reduce corruption levels. For example, Transparency International Bangladesh (TIB, 2007) stated that corruption in Bangladesh was ranked seventh, whilst in 2006 it had been ranked third. TIB (2007, p. 2) mentioned some reasons for the improvement of Bangladesh's position by stating:

> It is quite likely that a perceived sense of insecurity and uncertainty that is widely believed to have prevailed among the business community in the wake of the post 1/11 [military-backed government]'s anti-corruption drive in Bangladesh may have prevented the possibility of a better score.

Table 7.8 shows that the highest number of occurrences was among Food and Allied, Pharmaceuticals and Chemicals, Textiles and Miscellaneous industries. These industries are dominated by politicians. On average, 186% (1,647/887) occurrences are reported in 19 industries from 1998 to 2010. This represents the fact that the effort of IFRS implementation may be slower if this practice is continual.

Table 7.9 shows the number of occurrences in relation to IFRS by industry. What is apparent from this table is that no occurrences in relation to violations of IFRS were reported during the period 1998 to 2005. In total there were 42 enforcement actions by 40 companies, and two companies had multiple violations. The main violations included major failure to disclose information, false statements, and issues with true and fair views. The largest number of cited companies belonged to the Food and Allied, Pharmaceuticals and Chemicals, Textiles, and Miscellaneous industries – which is consistent with the results for overall violations by industry, as mentioned in Table 7.8. Despite the fact that a limited number of enforcement releases were regarding IFRS issues, it should be noted that Food and Allied and Textiles had instances of non-compliance with IFRS. One important observation is that the highest number of enforcement releases regarding IFRS violations was seen in 2009, whilst the most enforcement releases with reference to SEC laws violations were seen in 2006. This is possibly because the SEC officials have become more concerned about IFRS compliance in recent years than they had been in the past.

Court cases of enforcement actions

The number of court cases regarding enforcement actions has been increasing year by year on a cumulative basis from 1999 to 2010 (see Figure 7.1). Table 7.10 shows that during 1999,

Table 7.7 Industry-wise total number of occurrences by year (1998–2010)

Industry	2010		2009		2008		2007		2006		2005		2004		2003		2002		2001		2000		1999		1998	
	O	C	O	C	O	C	O	C	O	C	O	C	O	C	O	C	O	C	O	C	O	C	O	C	O	C
Cement	3	2	0	0	2	1	10	2	5	3	0	0	0	0	3	3	0	0	0	0	0	0	1	0	0	0
Ceramics	5	3	4	1	2	1	9	2	7	4	3	1	0	0	0	0	0	0	3	3	0	0	0	0	0	0
Engineering	12	6	4	4	5	5	10	7	10	10	10	7	1	0	0	0	0	0	3	3	1	1	2	2	1	1
Food and Allied	36	19	21	10	14	5	28	12	58	23	19	13	4	4	4	4	5	2	1	1	0	0	2	2	1	1
Fuel and Power	13	6	5	5	7	5	5	4	3	3	3	3	6	6	0	0	4	1	2	2	0	0	0	0	0	0
Jute	2	2	2	5	1	1	26	6	10	3	6	1	1	0	1	1	0	0	0	0	0	0	0	0	0	0
Paper and Printing	9	4	14	6	4	4	6	4	12	6	2	2	6	3	0	0	0	0	1	0	0	0	1	1	1	0
Pharmaceuticals and Chemicals	20	9	7	6	11	7	21	11	21	12	15	6	3	2	2	1	6	3	2	2	2	2	5	5	1	1
Services and Real Estate	0	0	0	1	2	2	6	4	5	2	1	1	2	1	0	0	0	0	0	0	0	0	0	0	0	0
Tannery	4	3	8	4	6	4	17	6	13	4	2	1	1	1	2	2	0	0	0	0	1	2	0	0	0	0
Textile	44	21	36	14	21	9	59	23	60	25	17	9	6	6	22	5	4	2	1	0	2	2	6	5	3	3
Miscellaneous	19	9	9	4	6	5	32	10	19	10	8	4	1	1	5	3	5	5	0	0	0	0	49	13	50	17
IT	5	1	6	1	4	2	8	2	3	2	0	0	0	0	0	1	0	0	0	0	0	0	0	0	0	0
Bank	5	4	4	4	14	10	10	7	26	6	9	7	5	4	3	3	0	0	0	0	1	0	0	0	0	0
Brokerage	33	25	14	13	27	8	14	7	30	21	12	7	13	7	9	8	4	4	11	10	2	2	11	11	3	3
Insurance	8	7	20	14	28	9	8	7	9	9	7	5	7	1	1	1	0	0	0	0	0	0	0	0	0	0
Financial Institutions	5	4	6	4	5	1	2	2	8	7	1	0	0	2	2	2	2	1	0	0	0	0	0	0	0	0
CA firms	3	3	8	8	3	3	6	4	8	6	2	2	2	2	3	2	1	0	0	0	0	0	0	0	0	0
CDBL	13	9	0	0	12	1	4	0	19	18	18	16	11	0	0	0	0	0	0	0	0	0	0	0	0	0
Total year wise	239	137	172	101	176	83	281	120	326	174	135	86	62	38	57	36	29	14	24	22	10	10	77	40	59	26

Total number of occurrences of enforcement actions (1998–2010) : 1,647; Total number of companies: 887

Note: O = number of occurrences; C = number of companies.

Table 7.8 Total number of occurrences by industry (1998–2010)

Industry	No. of Occurrences	No. of Companies	Occurrences by Industry (%)
Cement	24	12	200
Ceramics	30	12	250
Engineering	59	47	126
Food and Allied	*194*	*97*	*200*
Fuel and Power	48	33	145
Jute	52	17	306
Paper and Printing	55	31	177
Pharmaceuticals and Chemicals	*115*	*67*	*172*
Services and Real Estate	16	11	145
Tannery	54	25	216
Textile	*281*	*126*	*223*
Miscellaneous	*204*	*77*	*265*
IT	27	9	300
Bank	78	47	166
Brokerage	183	126	145
Insurance	83	54	154
Financial Institutions	29	21	138
CA firms	38	31	123
CDBL	77	44	175
Total	**1,647**	**887**	**186**

Note: The italics indicate the highest number of occurrences by industry.

Table 7.9 Number of occurrences in relation to IFRS by industry (2006–2010)

Industry	2010		2009		2008		2007		2006		Total	
	O	C	O	C	O	C	O	C	O	C	O	C
Cement	1	1	0	0	0	0	1	1	0	0	2	2
Engineering	1	1	0	0	0	0	0	0	0	0	1	1
Food and Allied	*4*	*4*	*2*	*2*	*3*	*2*	*5*	*5*	*1*	*1*	*15*	*14*
Jute	0	0	1	1	0	0	0	0	0	0	1	1
Paper and Printing	1	1	0	0	1	1	0	0	0	0	2	2
Pharmaceuticals and Chemicals	*1*	*1*	*3*	*3*	*0*	*0*	*0*	*0*	*0*	*0*	*4*	*4*
Tannery	0	0	1	1	1	1	1	1	0	0	3	3
Textile	*1*	*1*	*6*	*5*	*1*	*1*	*1*	*1*	*0*	*0*	*9*	*8*
Miscellaneous	*0*	*0*	*1*	*1*	*0*	*0*	*3*	*3*	*0*	*0*	*4*	*4*
Insurance	0	0	0	0	1	1	0	0	0	0	1	1
Total year wise	9	9	14	13	7	6	11	11	1	1	42	40

Notes: O = number of occurrences; C = number of companies. The italics indicate the highest number of occurrences by industry.

43 court cases took place, whereas in 2010 the total reached about 332. It also shows that in the last three years, these cases have increased dramatically. One cautionary note is that these court cases are concerned with violations of the SEC's rules. I tried to find out how many cases were specifically related to IFRS. However, the SEC did not provide any information. My interpretation is that these cases, as indicated in Table 7.10, include IFRS-related

Table 7.10 SEC court cases of enforcement actions (1999–2010)

Sl.	Court	2010	2009	2008	2007	2006	2005	2004	2003	2002	2001	2000	1999
1	Supreme Court of Bangladesh Appellate Division	6	9	6	4	3	3	3	4	4	17	14	12
	High Court Division	*116*	*99*	*77*	*73*	*71*	*66*	*55*	*53*	*46*	*37*	*27*	*21*
2	District Judge Court, Dhaka	1	0	1	0	0	0	0	0	0	0	1	0
3	2nd Addl. Metropolitan Session Judge Court, Dhaka	0	0	0	0	0	0	0	0	0	1	1	1
4	8th Asst. Judge Court, Dhaka	0	1	0	0	0	0	0	0	0	0	0	0
5	9th Asst. Judge Court, Savar, Dhaka	1	0	0	0	0	0	0	0	0	0	0	0
6	6th Asst. Judge Court, Dhaka	0	1	2	2	3	3	2	0	2	2	2	2
7	4th Asst. Judge Court, Dhaka	1	0	0	0	0	0	0	0	0	0	1	1
8	1st Addl. Asst. Judge Court, Dhaka	0	0	0	0	0	0	5	0	1	1	0	0
9	*Chief Metropolitan Magistrate Court, Dhaka*	*10*	*9*	*6*	*7*	*6*	*6*	*0*	*4*	*4*	*7*	*0*	*0*
10	Metropolitan Session Judge Court	6	6	6	6	6	6	9	3	3	0	0	0
11	1st Asst. Metropolitan Session Judge Court, Dhaka	1	1	1	0	0	0	0	0	0	0	0	0
12	1st Joint District Judge Court, Dhaka.	0	0	0	0	0	0	0	1	0	0	0	0
13	*5th Joint District Judge Court, Dhaka*	*8*	*8*	*9*	*8*	*8*	*8*	*9*	*10*	*4*	*4*	*3*	*3*
14	4th Joint District Judge Court, Dhaka	1	1	0	0	0	0	0	0	0	0	0	0
15	1st Asst. Judge Court, Dhaka.	0	0	0	0	0	1	1	1	0	0	0	0
16	2nd Asst. Judge Court, Dhaka.	0	0	0	1	0	0	0	1	0	0	0	0
17	Asst. Judge Court, Savar, Dhaka.	0	0	1	0	0	0	0	0	0	0	0	0
18	*General Certificate Court, Dhaka*	*181*	*138*	*94*	*74*	*46*	*32*	*21*	*17*	*16*	*6*	*5*	*3*
	Total	**332**	**274**	**204**	**174**	**143**	**125**	**105**	**94**	**80**	**75**	**54**	**43**
	Cumulative increase by year	58	70	30	31	18	20	11	14	5	21	11	[54–43]

Notes: Data for 1998 was not available; italics indicate the highest number of court cases in various courts.

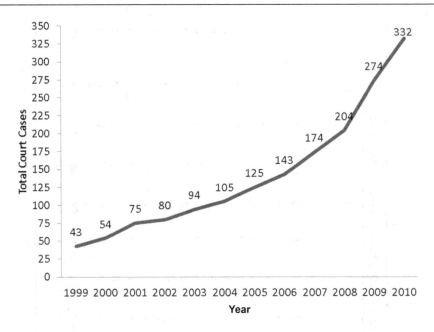

Figure 7.1 Court cases of enforcement actions, 1999–2010

violations (see Chapter 8). The cumulative increase in court cases weakens the SEC's enforce-ment motivations. Companies can appeal regarding the SEC's enforcement and go through various courts. Most cases are judged in the High Court Division, the Chief Metropolitan Magistrate Court, the 5th Joint District Judge Court, and the General Certificate Court. But there are no specialised courts (lower/higher court) regarding SEC enforcements. In the High Court and the District Judge Court, a money laundering bench exists, but there are no SEC-related benches and no parliamentary Acts have been passed since the emergence of the SEC. The common scenario in Bangladesh is that the guilty companies are reluctant to pay the penalty because the court cases normally take a long time to complete. This is not limited to the SEC's enforcement-related court cases but also applies to other cases.[9] After a case is filed in the court, nobody knows when it will end (Daily Star, 2007). Barrister Moudud Ahmed (former Law Minister) argues that the present judicial system in Bangladesh is old-fashioned, traditionalist, and corrupt and needs reform; and that, under existing procedures, 100 years will be required for the disposal of 10 million cases (Daily Star, 2007).

Corruption in the judicial system is a well-known phenomenon. Transparency International Bangladesh in its *Global Corruption Report* mentioned that:

> Bangladesh failed to ensure full independence of the judiciary and the politicisation of the judiciary is one of the major reasons behind judicial corruption . . . Two thirds of the people who used a court in 2004 paid bribes, with the typical bribe amounting to 25 per cent of average annual income.

> (TIB, 2007, p. 15)

This judicial corruption allows criminals (e.g. corrupt companies) to go unpunished. Accord-ing to the former Chief Justice, 'the corruption in the judiciary system has taken a turn into blood cancer and it will not be eradicated if nepotism and favouritism are not stopped' (Daily Star, 2007). The politicisation of the judiciary strengthens judicial corruption (Daily Star, 2004; Bhattacharjee, 2007). Under the provision of Article 94(4) of the Constitution of Bangladesh, the Chief Justice and the other judges shall be independent in the exercise of their judicial functions. However, in reality, their appointments are not determined solely by their abilities, experience or professionalism, but by the extent to which they have served the pecuniary and political benefit of the appointing party and supported its leaders and workers (Dainik Ittefaq, 2007). Therefore, the outcome of the cases regarding SEC rules or IFRS non-compliance violation may be influenced by the political executive. It also may weaken the SEC's enforcement effort towards IFRS implementation in Bangladesh.

Comparison of Interviewees' Perceptions

I have summarised the 1st and 2nd round interviewees' attitudes to IFRS implementation after reading and reflecting on the transcripts. The view of each interviewee on a given topic is represented by one answer. This approach requires making a judgement about the interviewee's primary opinion about a topic (i.e. whether he/she expresses positive/negative/no comment). This comparison of interviewees' attitudes helps to establish whether the interviewee's background characteristics, such as work experience and qualifications, are related to their expressed attitudes. However, there is no association between the interviewees' work experience/qualifications and their attitudes.

The evidence of the study reveals that there is a link between training opportunities in the accounting profession and corruption (Q5, Q6 and Q7: professional syllabus, training opportunities and corruption). In relation to policymaking groups, the four policymakers who are unhappy with the current professional syllabus and lack of provision of any training opportunities feel that corruption is not a big factor affecting the implementation process (see Table 7.11). But there are some contradictory comments observed. For example, although three policymakers (PM1, PM2 and PM5) are satisfied with the professional syllabus, two of these three (PM1 and PM2) are providing training and feel that corruption is not an important factor. One possible observation is that PM1 and PM2 are highly placed officials in the ICAB, and the ICAB is within the Ministry of Commerce. Therefore they are disinclined to provide negative views on the ICAB's professional syllabus, training issues or possible corruption. PM1 and PM2's answers represent their personal views rather than an institutional view. PM5 is an official of the World Bank and is therefore able to talk freely about corrupt activities. The respondent is happy with the professional syllabus because the respondent is chairing quality assurance boards of the ICAB. Table 7.11 also shows that 67% of the respondents feel that the professional syllabuses are not good enough to implement IFRS; 52% of interviewees are not providing or attending training; and 78% of respondents feel that corruption is impeding the implementation process.

With respect to the AP group, those who feel that the professional syllabus is up to date enough have attended training on IFRS and feel that corruption is a problem (see Table 7.11). The only AP (AP3) who has not attended any training on IFRS from his audit firms is happy with the professional syllabus. This is possibly because of his affiliation with the standards-setting body of the ICAB. Those who perceive that the professional syllabus is not up to date have not attended training on IFRS and view corruption as impeding the implementation process.

But the majority of the APs are not getting access to any training opportunities. The findings of the study reveal that the big four audit firms and large companies have more training opportunities in Bangladesh than average, but the smaller ones do not see themselves as

Table 7.11 Quantification of interviewee perceptions (1st round interviews, n = 27)

Code	Training Opportunities in the Accounting Profession, and Corruption			
	Q5	5(a)	Q6	Q7
PM1	1	1	1	1
PM2	1	1	1	1
PM3	0	1	0	1
PM4	0	1	0	1
PM5	1	1	0	0
PM6	0	1	0	1
PM7	0	1	0	1
AP1	1	1	1	0
AP2	0	1	0	0
AP3	1	1	0	0
AP4	0	1	0	0
AP5	0	1	0	0
AP6	0	1	0	0
AP7	0	1	0	0
AP8	0	1	0	0
AP9	0	1	0	0
AP10	1	1	1	0
AP11	0	1	0	0
AP12	1	1	1	0
US1	1	1	1	0
US2	0	1	1	0
US3	0	1	1	0
US4	0	1	1	0
US5	0	1	1	0
US6	1	1	1	0
AR1	0	1	1	0
AR2	0	1	1	0
Positive perceptions	33% [9/27]	100% [27/27]	48% [13/27]	22% [6/27]
Negative perceptions	67% [18/27]	0%	52% [14/27]	78% [21/27]
Total	100%	100%	100%	100%

Notes: '0' = negative perceptions, '1' = positive perceptions. Q5: '0' = professional syllabus is not suitable and '1' = professional syllabus is suitable to implement IFRS; Q5(a): '0' = university syllabus should not include IFRS contents and '1' = university syllabus should include IFRS contents; Q6: '0' = not providing training/not attending training/ training is not essential and '1' = providing training/attending training/training is essential; Q7: '0' = corruption by government, audit firms and professional bodies and companies; '1' = no corruption; Q8 (other country-specific factors) and Q9 (comments/suggestions) cannot be quantified due to the nature of the questions and the perceptions of the interviewees.

training facilitators and/or best-practice companies. The main point here is that the smaller companies' managements are not worried about disclosure policy, and therefore their directors' attitudes toward training are vague. From the US and AR groups, it is important to mention that (except for US1 and US6), a majority of the respondents are dissatisfied with the professional syllabus and also strongly believe that training opportunities are essential and that corruption is holding back the implementation of IFRS. One possible interpretation is that US1 and US6 may be heavily linked with the ICAB. In particular, the affiliated banks, Brac Bank (US1) and the Mercantile Bank (US6), have been awarded the 11th ICAB National

Table 7.12 Quantification of interviewee perceptions (2nd round interviews, n=12)

Code	Training Opportunities in the Accounting Profession, and Corruption	
	Q5	Q6
PM1	0	1
PM2	0	1
PM4	0	1
PM5	0	0
AP5	0	0
AP6	0	0
AP10	0	0
AP12	0	0
US4	0	0
US5	0	0
AR1	0	0
AR2	0	0
Positive perceptions	0%	25% [3/12]
Negative perceptions	**100%** [12/12]	**75%** [9/12]
Total	100%	100%

Notes: '0' = negative perceptions; '1' = positive perceptions. Q5: '0' = professional and university syllabuses are not suitable; '1' = professional and university syllabuses are suitable to implement IFRS. Q6: '0' = corruption by governmental body; '1' = no corruption. Q7 (other country-specific factors): cannot be quantified due to the nature of the question and the perceptions of the interviewees.

Awards for best published accounts and reports as well. Therefore, these two interviewees provide no comment on politics.

The purpose of the 2nd round of interviews is to test the interviewees' attitudes after a further year of the present democratic government has passed, i.e. its third year (see Chapter 5). The perceptions of the interviewees in the 2nd round of interviews are quite similar to previous responses (Table 7.12). PM1, PM2, PM5, AP10 and AP12 were positive about the professional syllabus in the 1st round interviews, but in the 2nd round they were more critical about it. This could be because there is a very low pass rate in the professional exams and there are very few qualified accountants in Bangladesh. Further, agreement in 2009 that the ICAEW should update the professional curricula in Bangladesh may suggest that these five interviewees changed their minds on professional syllabus issues (Siddiqui, 2010). Some differences in the interviewees' perceptions are observed. For instance, the 2nd round interviewees only mention corruption by government, while in the 1st round the interviewees had pointed out corruption in various bodies (e.g. audit firms and professional bodies, and in companies). It is unsurprising that PM1, PM2 and PM4 held the opinion that corruption is not an important factor. This is possibly due to the fact that these interviewees are heavily involved with the government and hence are hesitant to talk about government corruption. Table 7.12 also shows that 100% of the interviewees opine that professional and university syllabuses are not suitable for the implementation of IFRS, and 75% of respondents feel that corruption within the government is slowing down implementation. None of the interviewees provided 'no comment' on training opportunities in the accounting profession and corruption (see Tables 7.11 and 7.12).

Reflecting on interviewees' attitudes

The findings show that training opportunities in the accounting profession and corruption have a negative influence on implementation of IFRS in Bangladesh under the conditions of (a) deficiencies in the training opportunities in the accounting profession and (b) high levels of corruption.

In relation to condition (a), the effectiveness of accounting profession, the findings confirm that deficiencies in training opportunities in the accounting profession in Bangladesh inhibit the implementation process, rendering it ineffective. The findings suggest that the professional syllabus contains limited content on IFRS, and lacks practical examples and applications; meanwhile, the interviewees are not aware of the universities' curricula content (or lack of it) on IFRS. The interviewees' attitudes suggest a generally negative perception of the structure of accounting education. Interviewees' responses are also negative about the provision of training opportunities by policymakers and companies. Only the ICAB provides training facilities to its members. Some of the interviewees think that the regulators have very little knowledge of IFRS, and they cannot therefore identify those companies who are failing to comply with IFRS. This is because the SEC has a lack of professionals. Preparers with no training are preparing annual reports, and these annual reports do not reflect IFRS. The 2nd round of interviews confirms that the current professional syllabus of the ICAB and the universities' curricula are not effective enough to support the implementation of IFRS. The number of accountants has not substantially increased over the last 15 years. The findings from the documentary analysis suggest that true interpretations of IFRS may be rare, although the accountancy profession has moved with the help of the ICAEW to increase the number of CAs with knowledge of IFRS in recent years. Questions also arise around why a very low number of CA firms were penalised during the period 1998–2010; why the corrupt firms are continuing to operate freely; and, finally, why none of these firms paid any penalty. In my opinion, these practices may influence prospective accountants in Bangladesh towards the same corrupt practices.

With respect to low/high levels of corruption (condition b), a high level of corruption in Bangladesh is seen to be slowing down the implementation process. The findings suggest that the widespread corruption evident in governmental bodies, audit firms, and professional bodies and companies is a significant obstacle to the implementation of IFRS in Bangladesh. Corruption is widespread in both the public and private sectors. The reason for this in Bangladesh is that there has been an established history of corruption ever since the country's independence. Indeed, Bangladesh was ranked as the most corrupt country in the world for five consecutive years.

A further point from the interview findings is that almost all government agencies – including ministerial bodies, tax authorities and regulators – seem to be involved to some extent in corrupt practices. The 2nd round of interviews also provides strong evidence that corruption is impeding the IFRS implementation process: 75% of the respondents in the 2nd round of interviews only mentioned corruption by governmental bodies (see Table 7.6). However, the policymakers do not express any belief that corruption is hindering the implementation process, either in the 1st or the 2nd round of interviews. From the documentary analysis, it is evident that the highest number of SEC rule violations, including IFRS-related violations, was among the Food and Allied, Pharmaceuticals and Chemicals, Textiles, and Miscellaneous industry sectors. Since these industries tend to be owned by politicians, political influence possibly slows down the effective implementation process. In addition, the increasing number of court cases and the corruption in (and politicisation of) the judicial system may impede the effective implementation of IFRS.

In comparing interviewees' perceptions and reflecting attitudes, links between professional syllabuses, training opportunities and corruption are evident. The majority of members of the policymaking group who were interviewed do not provide training and are dissatisfied with the professional syllabus, but they also feel that corruption is not a major issue. Their views are understandable because the policymakers want to be seen to be supporting their government's activities. Only account preparers from the big four and large companies are given access to training opportunities.

Influences of other country-specific factors: 1st Round interviews

The interviewees were asked: What are the main problems of effective implementation of IFRS in Bangladesh? Different groups emphasised different problems, including a lack of qualified accountants; lack of interest in IFRS by managers of some companies; a culture of secrecy; lack of research; public sector dominance; and a predominantly family-based private sector, in order.

Lack of qualified accountants

According to most interviewees (18 out of 27), the root of many problems in implementing IFRS can be pinpointed to one principal issue: a lack of qualified accountants (see Table 7.13). There are not enough CAs to meet the needs of the country. Without adequate numbers of qualified CAs, it is nearly impossible even to consider implementing IFRS. There would be no one to physically implement the regulations of IFRS. Several factors can be attributed as causes for the small number of CAs, including low salary, an absence of desire in students

Table 7.13 Perceptions of other factors impacting on implementing IFRS in Bangladesh (1st round interviews)

Problems of Implementing IFRS	PM	AP	US	AR	Total	%	Rank
Lack of qualified accountants	2 [PM5, PM6]	9 [AP1,AP2,AP3, AP4,AP5,AP6, AP7,AP10, AP11]	5 [US1, US2, US4, US5, US6]	2 [AR1,AR2]	18/27	67	I
Lack of interest in IFRS by managers of some companies	3 [PM3, PM5, PM6]	4 [AP1,AP5, AP10,AP12]	3 [US1, US4, US5]	2 [AR1,AR2]	12/27	44	II
Culture of secrecy	3 [PM1, PM4, PM7]	4 [AP1,AP8, AP9,AP12]	3 [US3, US5, US6]	1 [AR1]	11/27	41	III
Lack of research	2 [PM1, PM5]	0	0	2 [AR1,AR2]	4/27	15	IV
Public sector dominance	1 [PM3]	0	0	2 [AR1,AR2]	3/27	11	V
Family-based private sector	1 [PM2]	0	0	2 [AR1,AR2]	3/27	11	VI

wanting to pursue a CA career, as well as the societal perception of CAs. The comment below represents this issue:

> In Bangladesh, we have only 700–800 qualified accountants, whereas we have more than 80,000 companies. *Without qualified CAs, it is a dream to implement IFRS.*
>
> (AR2)

Further, many students choose to pursue alternative careers to CA because they feel the services a CA provides are not properly compensated. They also feel the salary of a CA is insufficient. One of the main reasons for this is the unwillingness of companies to pay a decent salary to CAs. As a result of low salary levels, society in general views a career as a CA to be inferior to others and that CAs are incapable of supporting themselves and their families. One interviewee's thoughts on this debate are given below:

> There is a lack of qualified professionals because *the companies don't want to pay the same as those in a developed country would. The low level of audit fees demotivates students from becoming CAs.*
>
> (AP1)

Despites the barriers and odds there are a few students who choose to study CA. These students, however, have a difficult time throughout their education because of the inconsistencies among the assessment criteria and the difficulty of the curricula. As a result, many students who choose to study CA do not pass national exams. These students feel they are at a disadvantage. There is a continuous cycle of small numbers of students studying CA, and from those an even smaller number of students actually pass exams and become CAs. This cycle is an overwhelming factor that causes an ongoing shortage in CAs to meet the needs of the country. One interviewee states his opinion on this issue:

> The pass rate for CAs is very low due to the lack of transparency in the assessment criteria. It creates a *real frustration for us in studying CA.* Although nepotism plays a big role, the majority of the students still fail.
>
> (US5)

Lack of interest in IFRS by managers of some companies

Twelve out of 27 interviewees express that in order to implement IFRS effectively the companies' management have to take a wide and in-depth interest first (see Table 7.13). One of the main reasons companies lack interest is due to the fact that costs override benefits. One interviewee states:

> The company thinks that there won't be any benefit in complying with IFRS because the tax department won't trust them. They also think [that] training and development costs will be higher in implementing IFRS.
>
> (PM3)

Two policymakers hold the belief that directors do not fully understand the underlying meaning of IFRS and its usefulness. One PM comments:

> I would say [that] . . . *business directors think [that] if IFRS are implemented, they will be unduly controlled and monitored* . . . Their attitude is, *if the old system is working then why implement a new one [e.g. IFRS].*
>
> (PM6)

Another core problem with the implementation of IFRS is a lack of initiative by management with regard to auditing and the costs associated with it. In order to save on costs, management often opt out of being audited by one of the big four. This issue is highlighted by one interviewee:

> In the UK or other developed countries, about 95–96% of the listed companies are audited by the Big Four. Conversely, *in Bangladesh, about 95–96% of companies are audited by Tom, Dick and Harry, and only 4% by the Big Four. This is because companies' management are not interested in spending money on being audited by one of the Big Four.*
>
> (AP12)

Culture of secrecy

The interviewees also emphasised another topic constituting a central problem in the effective implementation of IFRS as being corporate practice: 11 of the 27 interviewees mention that current corporate practice in Bangladesh allows for hiding and copying of information, as well as a lack of knowledge among shareholders (see Table 7.13). The two interviewees from the PM group state:

> Bangladesh is a closed society in terms of disclosure, as *hiding of information is a natural phenomenon.* Therefore, being in a closed society, the disclosure level is not [as] per expectations.
>
> (PM1)

> Our company's culture is to hide income or profit for different purposes. They don't want to reveal the actual [or] true picture of the company.
>
> (PM4)

Interviewees also feel that it is easy for accountants to copy extracts from the notes to the financial statements (e.g. accounting policies) of big companies' financial statements. This type of practice occurs because of a lack of enforcement of laws and a lack of punishment. The thoughts of one interviewee are given below:

> The *'copying culture'* in our country is a very common phenomenon. For example, *one of my friends is an accountant in another company who copied one particular standard practice from British American Tobacco.* But this is very ironic, as BAT and his company are completely two different entities.
>
> (AP8)

According to the respondents, the culture of Bangladesh is such that shareholders are not concerned about whether accounts are prepared in accordance with IFRS or not; the culture allows for companies to neglect the following of IFRS. One interviewee states:

> The first, immediate and direct users of accounting information are shareholders. However, *shareholders are not concerned with whether the accounts have been prepared in accordance with IFRS. How will the present culture of (non-)compliance with IFRS change if the users are not demanding that change?*
>
> (AP9)

Lack of research

According to the interviewees, lack of research has been found to be another fundamental problem in the implementation of IFRS. The interviewees feel that research is not only important but also necessary to further current knowledge about accounting and finance. One reason for the small amount of research being done in accounting and finance could be the lack of funds provided by the government. One of the interviewees' thoughts on the issue are given below:

> You know in Bangladesh, *there is a paucity of research with respect to financial reporting in particular. There has been a handful of research done on voluntary disclosure.* Therefore, the government and the professional bodies should encourage researchers by providing more funds to conduct research on IFRS issues.
>
> (AR1)

Further, respondents (in particular, policymakers) think that not only does the government have an apparent lack of interest in research but academia also fails to give research any significance in Bangladesh. Two interviewees state:

> Do the university academics care about research? No, they don't, because of a lack of incentives to conduct research. Without research, how do we inform the policymakers of what is happening and what to do?
>
> (PM1)

> The *World Bank and the IMF are helping to carry out research on accounting issues.* I think [that] more research papers should be conducted by development partners and academics.
>
> (PM5)

Public sector dominance and family-based private sector

Public sector dominance and a family-based private sector play key roles in the problems associated with the implementation of IFRS. According to the respondents, the public sector has always had an overwhelming dominance in Bangladesh. During the 1980s, the private sector increased to vast numbers of companies, but the majority of these are family based (see Chapter 4). The interviewees suggest that in order to effectively implement IFRS, there should be a decrease in the public sector and an increase in the private sector – one that is not primarily family-oriented. The following three comments below from policymakers and academics highlight the conflicting issue of public versus private sector:

> Since the *beginning of the country,* the public sector used to dominate industry in Bangladesh. According to the *financial system* (equity-based finance, bank finance and state finance), the public sector was/is not equity based. But you know, in the US, about 65% of companies are equity based and disclosure is much needed for them. *The capital market in Bangladesh is very small in size, which is an inherent weakness of the economy of Bangladesh. 'The structure of the Bangladeshi economy does not permit disclosure'.*
>
> (PM3)

> If the government sector does not follow the IPSAS, why should the private sector follow IFRS?
>
> (AR1)

> The private sector is gradually rising from the late eighties, but those private sector companies are mostly family based. More than 70,000–80,000 registered companies are small size private companies where there is no disclosure and no corporate governance practices are observed.
>
> (AR2)

The 2nd round interviews

The interviewees are asked: Q7. What are the main problems in the effective implementation of IFRS? In the 2nd round of interviews, interviewees emphasise four major issues, including a lack of qualified accountants; lack of interest in IFRS by managers of some companies; a culture of secrecy; and higher costs of IFRS compliance with lower benefits for small companies according to ranking. All of the issues except the cost-benefit problems emerged in the 1st round of interviews according to ranking. Firstly, 11out of 12 interviewees respond that there is a lack of qualified accountants in Bangladesh (see Table 7.14). They strongly point out that without qualified accountants the implementation process is *more rhetoric than reality*. An AR opines that:

> *Of course, the lack of qualified accountants (is important)* . . . Additionally, the professional accountants do not know how to properly follow these IFRS in the preparation and auditing of the annual reports of the companies and in practice; they are copying others' annual reports!
>
> (AR1)

Secondly, 83% of the interviewees (against 44% in the 1st round interviews, Table 7.13) believe that companies in Bangladesh have a lack of interest in IFRS implementation issues. PM5, AP5, AP10, AP12, US4, US5, AR1 and AR2 shared the same perceptions in the 1st round of interviews. PM2 thinks that the accounting standard-setting and adoption process will be useless if companies are not interested in following it. Interviewees feel that 'A-category' companies (i.e. large and profitable ones) are not employing qualified accountants, meaning that other companies do not bother about qualified accountants either. AP6 comments that:

> *We are trying to implement IFRS, in particular depreciation and inventory issues* . . . *We are a loss-making company and follow a conservative approach. Therefore, we can't follow IFRS fully. I think [that] if a company fully complies with IFRS, then its weaknesses will be visible to its competitors.*

Thirdly, 66% of interviewees (41% in the 1st round, Table 7.13) argue that general corporate practice in Bangladesh is to hide information, resulting in a lack of transparency (see

Table 7.14 Perceptions of other factors causing problems in the implementation of IFRS in Bangladesh (2nd round interviews)

Problems of Implementing IFRS	PM	AP	US	AR	Total	%	Rank
Lack of qualified accountants	3 [PM1, PM2, PM5]	4 [AP5, AP6, AP10, AP12]	2 [US4, US5]	2 [AR1, AR2]	11/12	92%	I
Lack of interest in IFRS by managers of some companies	2 [PM2, PM5]	4 [AP5, AP6, AP10, AP12]	2 [US4, US5]	2 [AR1, AR2]	10/12	83%	II
Culture of secrecy	3 [PM1, PM4, PM5]	2 [AP10, AP12]	1 [US5]	2 [AR1, AR2]	8/12	66%	III
Higher costs of IFRS compliance with lower benefits for small companies	4 [PM1, PM2, PM4, PM5]	3 [AP5, AP6, AP12]	0	0	7/12	58%	IV

Table 7.14). In the first phase, PM5, AP10 and AR2 do not provide any comment on this, but they are sceptical in the second phase. The interviewees' view is that companies are inclined to hide information, and that this is facilitated by their political connections. In addition, directors are aware of the fact that the regulators will not question their non-complying activities because they themselves are corrupt. This culture makes it difficult to implement IFRS. One accountant from a multinational company explains that:

> As a multinational company, we strictly follow *IFRS* because we have global guidance to follow them. The orientation is also bigger than that of the local companies in Bangladesh. As a matter of fact, *the culture of multinational companies is to be transparent, far more than the in local companies.*
> (AP10)

Finally, 58% of the interviewees view that cost-benefit is a significant factor in the implementation of IFRS (see Table 7.14). This issue has been raised only by the PM and AP groups. The US and AR groups are not involved in the implementation process and therefore they are not aware of the cost-benefit issues.

Respondents point out that university graduates from various backgrounds (e.g. History, Marketing, Management, Finance, Accountancy etc.) are working as company accountants in small companies. These graduates have a very limited technical knowledge of accounting standards. The AP group criticised the regulators' policy of the implementation of IFRS by all listed companies. They believe that the regulators are only concerned about large companies. A partner of an audit firm expresses his sentiments in the following way:

> First of all, *size does matter*. For example, *a small company cannot employ a CA because the costs would not be bearable.* Further, companies are not well equipped to comply with IFRS.
> (AP12)

Reflecting on other country-specific factors

These findings reveal that other factors (i.e. a lack of qualified accountants; lack of interest in IFRS by managers of some companies; a culture of secrecy; lack of research; public sector dominance; and a predominantly family-based private sector) – all ranked in order of dominance; see Table 7.13 – are playing a part in slowing down the IFRS implementation process in Bangladesh. For example, a lack of qualified accountants is one of the key problems in implementing IFRS in Bangladesh. The majority of the interviewees suggest that company managers in Bangladesh are hesitant to comply with IFRS. Respondents think that normal practice is that most companies copy big companies' reporting styles. Shareholders do not bother to acquaint themselves with what is happening through annual reports, e.g. whether or not their companies are complying with IFRS. The purpose of IFRS is therefore questionable, if even shareholders do not care about this compliance. The interviews reveal that the government is not providing enough funding to conduct research into IFRS issues. As mentioned in Chapter 4, the government has not conducted any research into accounting standards issues over the last 10 years. Moreover, the public sector's dominance is apparent, and the family-based private sector is not inclined to comply with IFRS.

The 2nd round of interviews indicate that a lack of qualified accountants, lack of interest in IFRS by managers of some companies, and a culture of secrecy are hindering the implementation process. Interviewees from the 2nd round of interviews express beliefs that the government and donor agencies should plan solutions in order to enable small companies to comply with IFRS. Small companies in Bangladesh are not usually in a position to employ a qualified accountant, and the cost of doing so would be a major issue for them. As a result, although some of these companies may be interested in complying with IFRS, the reality is that the costs involved do not permit them to do so.

Conclusion

The purpose of the present chapter is to discuss the influences of (a) training opportunities in the accounting profession, and corruption; and (b) other country-specific factors on the implementation of IFRS in Bangladesh. With respect to training opportunities and corruption, Proposition P_{IIIA} and P_{IIIB} are examined. The evidence from the interviews suggests that training opportunities in the accounting profession and corruption exert a negative influence on implementation of IFRS in Bangladesh.

In relation to the effective/ineffective development of training opportunities in the accounting profession – condition (a), P_{IIIA} – the findings show that in Bangladesh, deficiencies in training opportunities are impeding IFRS implementation. Respondents who are directly or indirectly linked with the ICAB (e.g. as members or on any of its committees) display positive attitudes towards the professional syllabus. However, most of the respondents feel that the syllabus should be brought up to date. Additionally, IFRS course content is not incorporated into the universities' syllabuses. All of the interviewees agree that IFRS should be included so that prospective accountants will be aware of the benefits of complying with IFRS. Similarly, training opportunities are seen to be very limited for accountants. The findings reveal that training opportunities are a serious, inherent weakness with regard to compliance with IFRS. This is because policymakers are not providing training and companies' managements are not encouraging it – or to some extent are not helpful in supporting their accountants towards attending some training on IFRS. Perhaps because of this, account preparers generally come to feel that the training is not essential, since their companies are not concerned about it.

With respect to low/high levels of corruption – condition (b), P_{IIIB} – the evidence in the study finds that high levels of corruption in Bangladesh have a negative influence on implementation of IFRS. According to respondents, corruption is an everyday problem in Bangladesh. As mentioned in Chapter 4, Bangladesh was top of the list of the most corrupt countries in the world for five consecutive years. It is part of the established culture for companies to violate regulations, confident that the regulators (e.g. the SEC and tax officials) can be controlled through bribery. The enforcement evidence collected in this study suggests that a combination of a lack of professional ethics, the existence of corruption in the judiciary and political motivations impedes the implementation of IFRS in Bangladesh. Hence, the evidence in this study confirms that implementation may not be effective in a corrupt country such as Bangladesh.

In terms of comparing interviewees' perceptions and attitudes, the study finds that a link exists between professional syllabuses, training opportunities and corruption. It is found that the views of the users, academics and researchers do not significantly vary, while the policymakers and account preparers provide opinions contrary to the aforementioned grouping. In the 2nd round of interviews, all the interviewees, with the exception of the policymaking group, agree that corruption in the government is hindering the effective implementation of IFRS in Bangladesh. It is worth noting that the interviewees in the 1st round allude to corruption in various areas (e.g. by governmental bodies, audit firms and professional bodies and companies). The interviewees were not satisfied with the democratic government's slow move towards IFRS implementation. Nothing has changed in the policymakers' attitudes, possibly because they are representing their respective government institutions. According to the perceptions of the interviewees, the policymaking group did not provide any training except by the ICAB. The respondents also mentioned that training opportunities were limited to the 'big four' and large companies, while the majority of companies did not bother with providing IFRS training for their accountants.

In relation to the influences of other factors on implementing IFRS, the evidence suggests that there are country-specific factors which are also slowing down the implementation process in Bangladesh. Based on the respondents' comments, the other factors were ranked in the following order of dominance: a lack of qualified accountants; a lack of interest in IFRS by managers of some companies; a culture of secrecy; lack of research; public sector dominance; and a predominantly family-based private sector. It is evident that Bangladesh's lack of an adequate number of qualified accountants is unhelpful in effectively implementing IFRS. Several reasons are likely for the low number of CAs; for example, that the salary structure of CAs is much lower than in other comparable South Asian countries such as India, Pakistan or Sri Lanka (see Chapter 4). Students are perhaps less interested in studying CA because the pass rate is very low. Despite donor agencies' efforts to assist in this regard, state institutions seem to be inactive in doing anything to rectify the problem. It has also been argued that companies' managements are reluctant to comply with IFRS, while the norm for many companies in Bangladesh is to copy the format of other companies' annual reports. The underlying issue therefore remains that if shareholders care about the quality of their annual reports, then the quality of those reports (including their compliance with IFRS) will increase. Again, because of a lack of any significant research by the government and donor agencies, the real motivations of companies towards IFRS remain unknown. No policy documents or consultation papers on IFRS have been published by the government over the last decade.

Negative responses are found regarding state-owned enterprises' non-compliant activities. Respondents strongly indicate that the SEC allows non-compliance with IFRS because of its government affiliations. In a similar environment, most of the companies listed on the stock exchange are family-led businesses which often have close connections to various members of the government. This encourages these companies to hide information and any evidence of corrupt activities. In the 2nd round interviews, the findings reveal that small companies are interested in compliance with IFRS, but that following this through (e.g. by hiring qualified accountants) is not possible because the costs of doing so override the benefits.

Notes

1 Bangladesh topped the list of the most corrupt nations in the world for five consecutive years from 2001 to2005 (Transparency International Bangladesh, 2005).
2 As in Chapter 6, italics in an interview quote indicate that the interviewee strongly emphasised the specific issue.
3 With the agreement between the ICAB and the ICAEW in 2009, the syllabus changed from 2010 onwards (http://www.icab.org.bd/index.php?option=com_content&view=article&id=54&Item id=64, accessed 12 February 2012) (see Chapter 4also).
4 Source: http://www.ugc.gov.bd/reports/Part-2.pdf (accessed 12 February 2012).
5 This question was asked of the PM groups. The AP groups were asked: what training and development did you attain to cope with IFRS? The US and AR groups were asked a question regarding the importance of training and development.
6 http://www.secbd.org/List%20of%20Enforcement%20Actions%20for%20the%20month%20 of%20February%202010.htm (accessed 12 February 2012).

7 (http://www.secbd.org/April-27.2010%20_Ms%20Mowla%20Mohammad%20&%20Co_.pdf (accessed 12 February 2012).
8 (http://www.secbd.org/Keya%20Cosmetics%20Ltd.%2026.04.11–458.pdf (accessed 12 February 2012).
9 There are approximately 10million cases pending in different courts:4,946 in the Appellate Division; 127,244 in the High Court Division; 344,518 civil cases and 95,689 criminal cases in the Judges' courts; 296,862 cases with Magistrate courts; and 99,004 cases with the Metropolitan Magistrate courts (*Daily Star*, 2003).

Chapter 8

Theory of the role of the state in the implementation of IFRS

Introduction

The objective of this chapter is to present the results of research question three – RQ-3: How does a study of implementing IFRS help to build an understanding of a theory of the role of the state in accounting change in a developing country such as Bangladesh? In particular, the findings of Chapters 6 and 7 will be discussed in light of the theory of the role of the state. Based on the findings of the interviews and documentary analyses, I discuss institutional dynamics in order to explain how external and internal forces (i.e. the state–society relationship) have influenced IFRS implementation, as an example of accounting change in Bangladesh. I also discuss the state level (i.e. the role of the state); the organisational field level (although this level has not been researched in this study); and 13 case studies of IFRS non-compliance in order to explore the relationship between the state level and the individual organisational level in terms of individual organisations' tendencies towards non-payment of monetary fines. This analysis of the social and political dimensions of the IFRS implementation process in Bangladesh may yield insights that will assist understanding of the way in which standards are developed and diffused from the state level to the individual organisation level. I will also offer a possible explanation of the extended Weberian view of the theory of the role of the state and accounting change. Finally, a summary of this chapter is discussed.

As mentioned in Chapter 2, the drivers of accounting change (i.e. the most frequently discussed issues on the role of the state and accounting change) are accounting regulatory frameworks, politico-institutional factors, and cultural factors (e.g. [i] training opportunities in the accounting profession and [ii] corruption). In terms of accounting regulatory frameworks (P_I), the findings of the study reveal that accounting regulatory frameworks have a negative influence on accounting change in Bangladesh under the conditions of low-quality investor protection laws; stakeholders' non-participation in the standard-setting process; and looser enforcement of the laws. With respect to politico-institutional factors (P_{II}), the findings of the study suggest that politics has a negative influence on accounting change under the conditions of a higher level of government intervention; a higher level of donor agencies' pressure; and a higher level of political lobbying. The absence of co-operation among institutional bodies is slowing down the effective implementation process in Bangladesh. Regarding cultural factors (P_{III}), the study reveals that deficiencies in training opportunities in the accounting profession and high levels of corruption have a negative influence on accounting change in Bangladesh.

Institutional dynamics: links between the role of the state and individual organisations

As mentioned in Chapter 3, none of the state theorists have explored the theoretical aspects of the state–society relationship in accounting literature. Most studies have employed Weber's works in developed countries in focusing on external forces. Further, very few studies employed case studies to explain their theoretical framework. Hence, in this study I have employed Dillard et al. (2004)'s model of institutional dynamics. This model's implications in Bangladesh are shown in Figure 8.1. This model has three levels: the state; the organisational field; and the individual organisation level.

State level: the role of the state

In terms of the state level, the roles of the state (external forces) negatively influence accounting change, as asserted by 'N' (negative) in Figure 8.1. The state institutions employ an unfavourable distribution of power which may very well prevent manifestations of negative outcomes of accounting change in Bangladesh. In the external forces (E), the state level (directly) and the donor agencies (indirectly) influence accounting change. Based on the drivers of accounting change, I also find that accounting regulatory frameworks, politico-institutional factors, accounting profession, and corruption have a negative influence on accounting change (as indicated by 'N' in Figure 8.1).

Based on the findings of drivers of accounting change (see Chapters 6 and 7), in this section I discuss the roles of the state in determining the outcomes of IFRS implementation as an example of accounting change in Bangladesh.

The state approves experts to write rules

The findings in this study indicate that the interplay between state institutions and politics in the Bangladeshi context is a story shaped by the complexity of accounting change (as indicated by 'N' in Figure 8.1). It is found that a higher level of government intervention in the accounting regulatory process negatively influences accounting change in Bangladesh. The present democratic government has not yet passed the Financial Reporting Act (FRA) which was proposed during the military-backed government of 2006–08. The findings reveal that the delayed process is due to the political interests of the government, because some politicians simply do not want to assist any Act which implements IFRS. The ruling parties transform the core decision-making structure of the government into a political club. This political club is glued tightly together, and thus politics plays an instrumental role in pulverising state institutions' competence in implementing IFRS. Hence, continuous interference by politics renders the state dysfunctional and unaccountable to the people, and corruption encompasses the judiciary. The state in Bangladesh as a manager of the market system does not reach an equilibrium of the state-society's interest for the betterment of accounting change because continual intervention and politicisation create complexities in the regulatory process and, of course, conflicts of interest. Since state institutions should be democratic in general, the ultimate question is whether the state in Bangladesh needs to answer to its stakeholders. To minimise state intervention, the state should create an independent body like the Financial Reporting Council (FRC) to ensure the effectiveness of the regulatory process.

The state consults with various stakeholders

The findings of the present study reveal that the state does not engage stakeholders in the standard-setting process in Bangladesh (as indicated by 'N' in Figure 8.1). National accounting has been characterised as being intimately linked to the exercise of national power in Bangladesh. Due to a lack of co-operation, the state's actions are considered as 'taken for

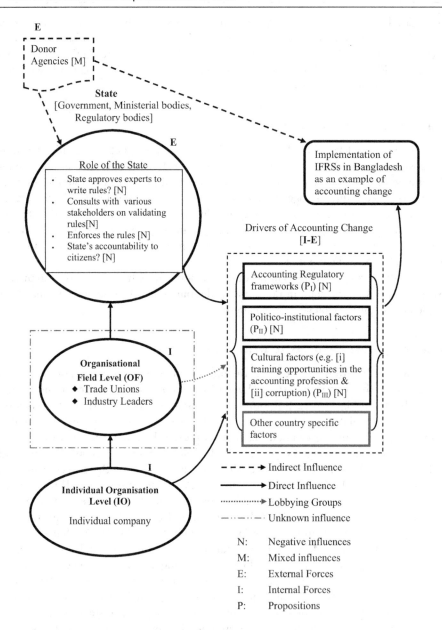

E

Donor
Agencies [M]

State
[Government, Ministerial bodies,
Regulatory bodies]

E

Role of the State
- State approves experts to
  write rules? [N]
- Consults with various
  stakeholders on validating
  rules[N]
- Enforces the rules [N]
- State's accountability to
  citizens? [N]

Implementation of
IFRSs in Bangladesh
as an example of
accounting change

Drivers of Accounting Change
[I-E]

Accounting Regulatory
frameworks (P_I) [N]

Politico-institutional factors
(P_{II}) [N]

Cultural factors (e.g. [i]
training opportunities in the
accounting profession &
[ii] corruption) (P_{III}) [N]

Other country specific
factors

**Organisational
Field Level (OF)**
♦ Trade Unions
♦ Industry Leaders

I

**Individual Organisation
Level (IO)**

Individual company

I

- - - - ➔ Indirect Influence
————➔ Direct Influence
············➔ Lobbying Groups
— ··— ··— Unknown influence

N: Negative influences
M: Mixed influences
E: External Forces
I: Internal Forces
P: Propositions

Figure 8.1 Theoretical framework in relation to Bangladesh (based on Figure 3.2)

granted', and individual organisations are legally restricted to following these rules. It is found that interested parties are working for their own interests and engaging in continual political connections. For example, tension exists between two professional bodies, provoked by the apparent lack of consultation with members of the ICAB, ICMAB and the SEC. Even the standard-setting body is very much unknown to the stakeholders. High levels of government intervention and a blame culture are also observed in Bangladesh, because existing state institutions are maintaining individualistic approaches. These institutions are reluctant to undertake collective action, and therefore tussles between different actors' interests take place. If politics, actors' interests, and heavy involvement of the government exist within a regulatory process, then the process will suffer from overwhelming credibility problems when trying to establish an efficient regulatory system and gain public trust in Bangladesh. In contrast to DiMaggio (1988), the state actors in Bangladesh attempt to pursue their self-interests.[1] Therefore, the interrelations between accounting and the role of the state in Bangladesh need to be depoliticised, establishing a strengthened and engagement-based regulatory process in order to build effective regulatory systems. Standard-setting bodies in Bangladesh have to respond to political forces and strike a balance between the needs of interested parties, in a process that is inescapably political in nature.

The state enforces outcomes

The findings in this study show that the lack of regulatory enforcement has a negative influence on accounting change because of the inefficacy of the judicial system and a lack of punitive penalties/fines (as indicated by 'N' in Figure 8.1). As documented in Chapter 4, Bangladesh has a lower rate of enforcement than India and Pakistan (see Tables 4.4–4.7, using World Bank Governance Indicators Data, 2010). This is because Bangladesh has higher levels of corruption, which eventually weakens enforcement. The documentary analyses confirm that the enforcement mechanisms are vague and that regulatory loopholes may hinder the effective implementation of IFRS. There is also a concern over issues of political influence on enforcing accounting standards (e.g. that the Ministry of Finance is closely linked with the SEC) because the state enforces the standards. In this case, since the state fails to enforce the standards, the establishment of an independent FRC to enforce the standards may help to produce better outcomes of accounting change. The military-backed government proposed an FRC in 2008, but was unable to follow through because of parliamentary systems' unavailability in the military period. The present democratic government was less interested and failed to put out a consultation paper to even initiate the creation of such an independent institution. This raises a question: why is the democratic government not interested in establishing the FRC for better outcomes of accounting change?

The state is accountable to its citizens

Although in this study the state's accountability has not been implicitly examined, the three propositions may inform whether the state is accountable to its citizens in Bangladesh in terms of accounting change. As mentioned in Chapter 2, according to the World Bank's Governance Indicators (1996–2010), voice and accountability was lower during the democratic government in 2004. In terms of quality of investor protection laws and stakeholder participation/ non-participation in the standard-setting process, the interviewees suggest that an independent Financial Reporting Council and the enforcement of accounting standards through a Financial Reporting Act (FRA) may create an effective framework of accountability. Since accounting regulatory frameworks, politico-institutional factors, [i] training opportunities in the accounting profession and [ii] corruption have negative influences on accounting change, then this may call the state's accountability into question in Bangladesh (as indicated by 'N' in Figure 8.1). It is found that due to a lack of political independence, IFRS practices are very poorly developed in Bangladesh. Since its independence in 1971, the country has frequently been ruled by military dictators. As the military-backed government has ruled for 19 out of 40 years of independence, the political freedom of the country has not been smoothly developed. In both democratic and in military eras there has been an absence of stakeholder participation in the standard-setting and regulatory processes. Further, certain political groups' incentives are seen as more important by those with political power and/or connections than the common interests of the citizens of Bangladesh. Therefore, democratic and military governments' efforts in reforming accounting systems may also provide insights into the role of the state in a developing country such as Bangladesh.

The role of donor agencies

In this study, the findings in the first round of interviews evidence the critical role of the donor agencies in Bangladesh. In the second round of interviews, the respondents did not provide any comments on the donor agencies' political pressure. Therefore, the donor agencies' influence in Bangladesh regarding accounting change is indicated by 'M' (mixed) in Figure 8.1. The donor agencies are providing funding for the reform of accounting in Bangladesh. There is no doubt that these reforms are essential for the effective implementation of IFRS. However, their collaboration with the state raises some issues: firstly, that funding is possibly not being used effectively by the state for its intended purpose. It has also been found that donor agencies are aware of this fact but do nothing to stop the evident practices. This research is unable to reveal why this is the case and what the true intentions of the donor agencies are. Hence, the donor agencies must presumably take a long-term view of their aid commitments, and their aid funding should not involve government intervention. Secondly, the processes of IFRS adoption and implementation in Bangladesh are likely to involve taken for granted norms without considering the engagement of societal values and norms. In my opinion, the donor agencies should not impose any reforms without considering the local or national culture, since Bangladesh's culture is more secretive in nature.

Discussion of the state level: the role of the state

At the state level, the role of the state has been discussed in explaining the diffusion of good practice – when donor agencies (such as the World Bank, the IMF and the EU) come to accept IFRS as a legitimate form of international best practice, and later adopters then follow in adopting it (especially developing countries like Bangladesh) in order to secure legitimacy; provide meaning; facilitate communication; underpin social action; and, often, to reflect political and economic ideologies. In terms of the state–society argument, all roles of the state are seen to have negative influences on accounting change in Bangladesh. Power and politics create complex processes of accounting change in Bangladesh because the state constitutes rule and a power resource towards IFRS implementation. The state as a social agent acts in its own interests. In contrast to general arguments put forth by Friedland and Alford (1991) in relation to western developed countries,[2] the state and professions share common interests in Bangladesh because the professional bodies are under the Ministries of Finance and Commerce, and bureaucratic arrangements are in place among various state institutions. Subsequently, state actors are more likely to create and maintain social beliefs (in particular, stakeholders' non-participation) within a society, and this may ultimately impede the effective implementation of IFRS.

Organisational field level

In the organisational field, lobbying groups' activities towards influencing IFRS implementation are unknown in this research (see Figure 8.1, indicated as 'unknown influence'). One caution is that lobbying groups were not interviewed, and the interviewees in this research argued about the influence of ministerial bureaucracy and political lobbying rather than about industry leaders' and trade unions' lobbying. This is because, in Bangladesh, the fulfilment of political functions and election manifestos are seemingly deemed more important than societal and economic fitness. This is likely to create conflicts of interest, within which accounting choice could be a major factor at the organisational field level. It can be argued that political factionalism, derived from family politics, essentially undermines the rule of law and the independent effectiveness of institutions by maintaining loyal political supporters in various positions within key institutions in Bangladesh. This phenomenon can also be thought of as 'personification of the state institutions' in Bangladesh.

Individual organisation level

At the individual organisation level, the evidence presented in this study shows that the majority of individual organisations may negatively influence outcomes of accounting change, given the presence of political lobbying, family businesses, a lack of training facilities, and corruption. The individual organisation level directly (as indicated by internal forces 'I' in Figure 8.1) influences accounting change. This section examines case studies in the form of 13 enforcement notices regarding IFRS non-compliance during the period 1998–2010 in order to explain the individual organisation's tendency not to pay a fine or a penalty in Bangladesh. Table 8.1 shows that there were 1,647 violations of SEC rules including IFRS non-compliance between 1998 and 2010. Only 42 violations were IFRS related and the IFRS-related enforcement actions represent only 2.56% (42/1,647) of total enforcement actions. The analysis in this study is limited to 13 violations for 12 companies. This is because these 13 companies have been identified as having perpetrated similar types of IFRS non-compliance, but were then penalised differently. The case study of 13 enforcement notices signifies 31% (13/42) with reference to IFRS non-compliance. In the following subsections, I will discuss these enforcement notices, classifying them into four categories (see Table 8.2).

Table 8.1 Total enforcement actions including IFRS (1998–2010)

Year	Total Enforcement	Total %	IFRS-Related Enforcements	IFRS %	Case Study	Case Study %
1998	59	3.6	0	0	0	0
1999	77	4.7	0	0	0	0
2000	10	0.6	0	0	0	0
2001	24	1.5	0	0	0	0
2002	29	1.8	0	0	0	0
2003	57	3.5	0	0	0	0
2004	62	3.8	0	0	0	0
2005	135	8.2	0	0	0	0
2006	326	19.7	1	2.4	0	0
2007	281	17.1	11	26.2	5	38.5
2008	176	10.7	7	16.7	2	15.4
2009	172	10.3	14	33.3	2	15.4
2010	239	14.5	9	21.4	4	30.8
Total	**1,647**	100 [1,647/1,647]	**42**	100 [42/42]	**13**	100 [13/13]

Cases on depreciation-related violations (N=7)

Seven companies were subject to depreciation-related violations (see Table 8.2). Of the seven companies, five were 'Z' category[3] companies and all were politically connected and family ownership based. There were also variations of the fines/penalties applied to those companies. For example, the minimum amount was Tk. 0.60 million and the maximum was Tk. 1.4 million. To explore the variations of fines imposed, I examine the detailed nature of the violations. It is found that six companies failed to charge depreciation on fixed assets, and one company did not provide the method of depreciation used in the financial statements. The SEC provided information about five companies regarding whether the fine had been paid or not, and hence information for two of the companies was unknown for the present study. Of the five companies, one of the companies was warned, meaning that no fine was imposed by the SEC. A question can be raised as to why this particular company was warned rather than penalised (i.e. monetary penalty). The rest of the four companies' cases are still pending.

Cases on qualified audit opinion (n=2)

The SEC issued enforcement actions against H Ltd. and I Ltd. because these two companies provided qualified opinions, but their financial statements for the year ended 30 June 2007 and 30 June 2003 respectively did not reflect a 'true and fair view'. The details of the violations were not provided by the SEC, but the fine varied – e.g. Tk. 0.60 million and Tk. 3.5 million (see Table 8.2). H Ltd. (public shareholding 23%) did not hold an AGM in 2008 and I Ltd. allegedly earned an abnormal return on shares of 6.57% in 2003; however, at the time the SEC failed to take action on these two companies (Independent, 2003).

Cases on disclosures as prescribed by the ICAB (n=2)

Two companies were issued with enforcement actions because their financial statements, for the year ended 30 June 2007 (J Ltd.) and 30 June 2006 (I Ltd.) respectively, were not prepared in accordance with IFRS and notes as prescribed by the ICAB. The SEC provided details on the nature of the violations for J Ltd. but not for I Ltd. Although I Ltd. is in the 'A' category,[4] the study reveals that there is no relationship between the company category and fine amount (see Table 8.2). Then the question may arise: on what basis does the SEC impose penalty amounts? As mentioned in this chapter, I Ltd. was issued with enforcement actions in 2007. Further, J Ltd. has not paid listing fees to the DSE, amounting to Tk. 0.09 million, since 2003 (Financial Express, 2008). These companies are repeatedly violating the rules, but the SEC did not provide any further information regarding the settlement of their fines.

Cases on half-yearly audited reports (n=2)

The SEC issued enforcement actions to two companies for violating SEC rules regarding half-yearly audited statements, including balance sheet, income statement, cash flow statement and changes in equity. K Ltd. is a 'B' category company[5] (public shareholdings only 12.5%) and was fined Tk. 0.80 million, whereas L Ltd. (public shareholdings 50%), a 'Z' category company, was fined Tk. 0.70 million (see Table 8.2). The study did not find any information on whether L Ltd. paid its fine or not, and K Ltd.'s court case is pending. Both companies have violated the same regulations by failing to provide half-yearly financial statements in accordance with BAS/IFRS. These two companies are part of the K-I Group and have a regular record of violating SEC rules. For instance, neither of the companies held an AGM in 2000 and 2001 respectively, or paid any dividend to its shareholders (Financial Express, 2004).

How to avoid a penalty imposed by the SEC

Generally, there are two ways to avoid incurring a financial penalty in Bangladesh. Firstly, a company may challenge the SEC's enforcement action, and can file a case in courts of Bangladesh (see Figure 8.2). Three courts handle most of the cases.[6] The cost of filing a case in these courts is generally lower than the penalty amount ordered. For instance, the minimum penalty is Tk. 100,000 (approximately £1,000), but the minimum cost of going to the Supreme Court – including the writ petition/court order and filing a case etc. – is approximately Tk. 40,000–50,000 (£400–500). In my opinion, this regulatory loophole may make companies less likely to pay a penalty. It is also understandable that the company may think that paying a penalty results in a bad record for the company (which may lose their investors' faith and confidence). Therefore, a company may feel that the safer option is to file a case rather than pay a penalty. Secondly, as mentioned above, all 13companies had political connections or political affiliations which might impede the enforcement actions of the SEC. The court(s) may favour these companies, and decisions can be classed as 'pending' for seemingly unlimited periods of time (i.e. stay order permission from the Supreme Court of Bangladesh, High Court Division). I was unable to find out whether the six companies' fines were paid or not because the SEC did not provide any information on this, raising the question of how many companies are paying the fines (see Table 8.2). Again, the enforcement notices had no effect on the share prices, e.g. earnings per share (EPS), of the 12 companies (see Table 8.3). Since the enforcement notices have no market implications in Bangladesh, the companies may not care about the level of fine imposed on them.

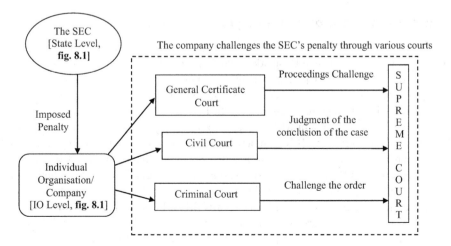

Figure 8.2 The procedure for a company to avoid a penalty

Table 8.2 Non-disclosure violations in relation to IFRS (n = 13)

Violation	Company	Year	Industry	Category[a]	Politics[b]	Family[c]	Fine (Tk.)/ Warning	Fine Paid/ Not Paid
Depreciation (n = 7)	A Ltd.	2010	Cement	Z	√	√	1,400,000	Pending
	B Ltd.	2010	Paper and Printing	Z	√	√	1,000,000	Pending
	C Ltd.	2010	Engineering	Z	√	√	1,000,000	Not known
	D Ltd.	2009	Textile	A	√	√	900,000	Pending
	E Ltd.	2008	Tannery	Z	√	√	800,000	Pending
	F Ltd.	2007	Tannery	Z	√	√	600,000	Not known
	G Ltd.[d]	2007	Miscellaneous	Z [A]	√	√	Warning	N/A
Qualified audit opinion (n = 2)	H Ltd.	2009	Textile	Z	√	√	600,000	Not known
	I Ltd.	2007	Food and Allied	A	√	√	3,500,000	Not known
Disclosures as prescribed by the ICAB (n = 2)	J Ltd.	2010	Pharmaceuticals/ Chemicals	Z	√	√	500,000	Pending
	I Ltd.	2008	Food and Allied	A	√	√	1,000,000	Not known
Half-yearly audited report (n = 2)	K Ltd.	2007	Food and Allied	B	√	√	800,000	Pending
	L Ltd.	2007	Food and Allied	Z	√	√	700,000	Not known

Notes: Fine paid: pending = 6 (i.e. court cases); not known = 6 (i.e. the SEC did not provide any information); warning = 1 (i.e. N/A). Company names have been anonymised. Detailed information is available on request from the author.

a   'A' category companies are regular in holding current AGMs and have declared a dividend at the rate of 10% or more in the last calendar year; 'B' companies hold regular AGMs but have failed to declare a dividend at the rate of 10%; 'Z' companies have failed to hold current AGMs or have failed to declare any dividend (DSE, 2009–10).
b   √ indicates that the company is politically connected.
c   √ indicates that the company is predominantly family owned.
d   G Ltd. was renamed Z Ltd. after an amalgamation in August 2008. Then it became an 'A' category company, from 'Z' previously.

Discussion of the individual organisation level

This section demonstrates that at an individual organisation level, the outcome of accounting change is likely to be negative in Bangladesh. Weber (1968, pp. 67–8) emphasises the state's role in politico-cultural terms in shaping a particular form of society. The efficiency of the role of the state depends on how power and interests are transmitted from the state level to the individual organisation level (Dillard et al., 2004, p. 512). In Bangladesh, the state actors (i.e. state institutions, ministers, and government MPs) are unable to restrict or modify the behaviour of individual organisations regarding IFRS implementation. Such behaviour is accepted as resulting from social norms. Interviewees have indicated that state institutions in Bangladesh are politically motivated regarding IFRS implementation. The individual organisations researched in this section are shown to be politically connected to state institutions and appear to be free to carry out corrupt activities, including non-compliance with IFRS and falsification of financial statements. This is also likely because actors in individual organisations (e.g. the directors) and their interests are likely to centre on the pursuit of profits, to the exclusion of compliance with the law.

Several other factors are impeding the implementation of IFRS. These include a lack of qualified accountants; a lack of interest in IFRS by managers of some companies; a culture of secrecy; and a predominantly family-based private sector of individual organisations. To minimise the

Table 8.3 Earnings per share (EPS) of 12 companies (2006–2011)

Violation	Company	Month[a]	Year[b]	Industry	EPS (Taka)					
					2011	2010	2009	2008	2007	2006
Depreciation (n = 7)	A Ltd.	Jan.	2010	Cement	0.36	1.93	0.18	-2.97	-10.74	-10.60
	B Ltd.	June	2010	Paper and Printing	0.06	0.04	0.04	0.02	0.19	-0.66
	C Ltd.	Sept.	2010	Engineering	0.04	0.013	-7.20	-8.50	-34.97	1.70
	D Ltd.	Nov.	2009	Textile	1.81	1.37	10.59	18.61	13.97	10.62
	E Ltd.	Sept.	2008	Tannery	0.69	0.62	0.19	0.67	-0.17	-2.59
	F Ltd.	May	2007	Tannery	-15.22	-62.73	-66.31	-98.21	-121.19	-56.79
	G Ltd.	Nov.	2007	Miscellaneous	7.36	8.23	66.57	23.41	N/A	N/A
Qualified audit opinion (n = 2)	H Ltd.	Jan.	2009	Textile	N/A	N/A	N/A	N/A	-47.43	-3.03
	I Ltd.	Dec.	2007	Food and Allied	1.57	3.11	1.01	0.10	-0.14	-0.14
Disclosures as prescribed by the ICAB (n = 2)	J Ltd.	Jan.	2010	Pharmaceuticals and Chemicals	N/A	N/A	N/A	N/A	-28.00	-20.11
	I Ltd.	Oct.	2008	Food and Allied	1.57	3.11	1.01	0.10	-0.14	-0.14
Half-yearly audited report (n = 2)	K Ltd.	Sept.	2007	Food and Allied	-4.43	0.59	0.55	-10.21	-14.46	-1.35
	L Ltd.	Sept.	2007	Food and Allied	-0.63	-1.64	-1.02	-1.84	-0.03	-1.00

Notes:
a Month of enforcement releases;
b year of enforcement releases; N/A information 'not available'. Company names have been anonymised. Detailed information is available on request from the author.

current tensions and struggles within IFRS practices in Bangladesh, effective implementation of IFRS will depend on individual organisations' attitudes to the power which has been developed by the state through engaging stakeholders, and non-political connectedness.

I conclude that in terms of the relationship between the state level and the individual organisation level, political connectedness and corruption are the strongest, most dominant factors, something which brings the role of the state regarding the effective implementation of IFRS in Bangladesh into serious question.

Conclusion

As a result of this study, I can now make the following statements about the theory of the role of the state. Firstly, with respect to the state level (the role of the state), this study reveals that power struggles among state institutions may have negative outcomes on accounting change in Bangladesh. The state acts as a social agent in Bangladesh to fulfil its own interests rather than the interests of the stakeholders regarding IFRS implementation. This study discussed the following roles of the state based on the findings of interviews and documentary analyses:

> The state approves experts to write rules [N].
> The state consults with various stakeholders [N].
> The state enforces outcomes [N].
> The state is accountable to its citizens [N].

It is evident that all of the state's roles have negative influences (as indicated by 'N') on IFRS implementation. This is because of a higher level of government intervention and the political interests of the government in approving experts to write rules; the state's actions regarding IFRS implementation take for granted the non-engagement of stakeholders in the decision-making process (i.e. the ICAB and the SEC are fulfilling their own interests); higher levels of corruption and political influence on enforcing accounting standards exist (e.g. the Ministry of Finance's close links with the SEC); a lack of political independence from the emergence of an independent Bangladesh onwards (i.e. regular intervals of military intervention, 19 years of military-backed government in 40 years of independence) are impeding accounting reforms and hence the state's accountability to its citizens may not be guaranteed. However, the roles of the donor agencies have mixed influences (as indicated by 'M' in Figure 8.1') in accounting change. According to the first round of interviews, the interviewees suggest that donor agencies' aid funds are transformed through government ministries, and those funds are not being utilised efficiently in progressing IFRS implementation in Bangladesh. In the second round of interviews, the interviewees ignored the donor agencies' critical role because the interviewees were frustrated with the current democratic government in terms of its failures so far to approve the IFRS Act or establish the Financial Reporting Council (see Chapter 6).

Secondly, in relation to the organisational field level, the influence of industry leaders' or trade unions' lobbying is unknown in this research. This is one of the limitations of this research (see also Chapter 9). I was unable to conduct interviews with any members of these groups because they were not interested in taking part in this study, despite being invited to do so. Additionally, the findings from the interviews and documentary analyses did not reveal any particular influence of these groups in implementing IFRS (see Chapters 6 and 7). The interviewees in this study were keen to comment on politics and corruption at state level and individual organisation level rather than at the organisational field level.

Thirdly, in terms of the individual organisation level, the study has shown that the outcomes of accounting change can be negative. Individual organisations are regarded as being

politically connected to state institutions and this political connectedness may generate negative outcomes of accounting change. This is possibly also because the directors of individual
organisations have links to state institutions, ministers, and government MPs in carrying out
activities which are non-compliant with IFRS without being penalised. In addition, many
directors are not inclined to train their company accountants to comply with IFRS (see
Chapter 6). Furthermore, a lack of qualified accountants, a lack of interest by companies'
management, poor corporate practice, and a predominance of family businesses among individual organisations are also slowing down the implementation of IFRS (see Chapter 7). It is
strikingly evident that 13 violations by 12 companies were penalised, but that none of these
companies then paid the financial penalty imposed on them. The findings also show that all
of these companies were politically connected family businesses and were penalised differently.
The links between state institutions (i.e. the SEC and the Supreme Court of Bangladesh) and
individual organisations are so politicised in a developing country like Bangladesh that the
effective implementation of IFRS may be difficult to put into practice.

Focusing on the institutional dynamics (i.e. the state–society relationship), the results show
that the reasons for the slow implementation of IFRS in Bangladesh can be observed at the
state and individual organisation field levels, and especially at the state level. One limitation is
that the influence of the organisation field level is unknown in this research. As has been mentioned in Chapter 3, according to Weber, cultural values explain 'why different actors make
different choices even in similar situations' (Swidler, 1986, p. 274). The findings of this study
extend the Weberian (1958)[1904], (1968)[1922] view of the state–society relationship. In the
case of Bangladesh, within the state, various political regimes have behaved in different ways
towards IFRS implementation. More specifically, under a democratic government, politico-
institutional factors and corruption (as indications of societal values) may be more important
and concentrated factors than for a state under a military-backed government in terms of
impeding IFRS implementation.

Notes

1 DiMaggio (1988, p. 4) argues the importance of norms or taken for granted assumptions 'that make
   actors unlikely to recognize or to act upon their interests'.
2 Friedland and Alford (1991) argue that the state and professions will not share the same interests.
3 Companies which have failed to hold current annual general meetings or have failed to declare any
   dividend (DSE, 2009–10).
4 Companies which have regularly held annual general meetings in recent years and have declared a
   dividend at a rate of 10% or more in the last calendar year (DSE, 2009–10).
5 Companies which have regularly held annual general meetings in recent years but have failed to
   declare a dividend at a rate of 10%or more in the last calendar year (DSE, 2009–10).
6 *(a) The General Certificate Court (GCC):* This court is for SEC ordinance violation related cases. If the SEC
   identifies any violations, then they issue show-cause cum-hearing. If the SEC is satisfied at the hearing,
   no further action is taken against the companies; otherwise the SEC imposes a penalty. To recover the
   penalty/revenue (Public Demands Recovery Act 1913), the SEC stands by the decision of the officer
   of the GCC. If the company opposes the GCC's decision of a payable penalty, the company may
   appeal to the Supreme Court of Bangladesh. This court is the highest court in Bangladesh and has
   two divisions, namely the Appellate Division and High Court Division. *(b) The Civil Court:* The
   Company may also appeal against the SEC's decision in the civil court. If the outcome of the civil
   court goes against the company, then the company may appeal to the Supreme Court. *(c) The Criminal
   Court:* If any pending case is heard in the criminal court, then before disposal/judgement in the
   criminal court, the company may also appeal to the Supreme Court challenging the order of the
   criminal court.

Chapter 9

Conclusions

The purpose of this chapter is to summarise the results of the study, discuss the theory involved, make recommendations, and offer suggestions about future research. The motivating research question of this book was to examine what factors have been affecting the implementation of IFRS in Bangladesh from 1998 to 2010. To answer this motivating question, three more specific questions are studied in this research, which are:

RQ-1: What is the relative impact of accounting regulatory frameworks and politico-institutional factors on the implementation of IFRS in Bangladesh as an example of a developing country?

RQ-2(a): How do (i) training opportunities in the accounting profession and (ii) the state of corruption, as outcomes of culture in Bangladesh, affect the implementation of IFRS?

RQ-2(b): What other country-specific factors are affecting implementation of IFRS?

RQ-3: How does a study of implementing IFRS help build an understanding of a theory of the role of the state in accounting change in a developing country such as Bangladesh?

These questions have been answered by applying mixed methods (i.e. interviews and documentary analyses; see Chapter 5).

The following section summarises the findings and original contributions of this book. The subsections reflect original contributions in relation to RQ-1, RQ-2 and RQ-3. Then, the limitations of the study and suggestions for future research are discussed.

Summary of findings

The relative impact of accounting regulatory frameworks and politico-institutional factors

This study contributes regarding the relative impact of accounting regulatory frameworks and politico-institutional factors on the implementation of IFRS in a developing country such as Bangladesh, and it also has important implications for other developing countries in general.

With respect to accounting regulatory frameworks, the evidence suggests that the accounting regulatory frameworks in Bangladesh have a negative influence on the implementation of IFRS (see Chapter 6). This is for several reasons, including low-quality investor protection laws in Bangladesh which are hindering the effective implementation of IFRS; stakeholders' non-participation in the standard-setting process; and relatively looser enforcement of the laws. As mentioned in Chapters 4 and 6, the Companies Act 1994 has not been updated regarding IFRS since 1994, and contradictions exist between local laws and the requirements of the IFRS (World Bank, 2003, 2009; Siddiqui, 2010). Unlike the findings of prior studies on developing countries (Boross et al., 1995; Saudagaran and Diga, 1997; Taplin et al., 2002; Banerjee, 2002) on professional bodies' engagement with stakeholders, the ICAB is responsible for accounting standard-setting in Bangladesh but does not engage the stakeholders in the setting of standards; there has even been a lack of any published exposure drafts and/ or consultation papers on standards. This is possibly because the ICAB is directly linked with the Ministry of Commerce, and their decisions are political and based on closed-door policymaking rather than being engagement based. Prior studies argue that government agency is in a prime position to enforce accounting regulations effectively (Belkaoui, 1983; Parker, 1986; Watts and Zimmerman, 1986; Zeff, 1988; Tower, 1993). But, in Bangladesh, continual political lobbying and government intervention in the SEC are impeding the operation of a stringent enforcement process. A lack of effective penalty criteria calls into question the SEC's role regarding tightening enforcement mechanisms in Bangladesh.

In terms of politico-institutional factors, the findings suggest that these factors have a negative influence on the implementation of IFRS in Bangladesh (see Chapter 6). This is due to a higher level of government intervention, a higher level of pressure from donor agencies and a higher level of political lobbying. Similar to previous studies (Leuz and Oberholzer-Gee, 2006; Siddiqui, 2010; Faccio, 2010), the evidence in this research confirms that government intervention and political lobbying are hindering the effective implementation of IFRS. It is found that companies are often not penalised, because of their political connections with the government. In addition, a lack of co-operation among institutional bodies is hindering the implementation of IFRS in Bangladesh. This is because of an absence of participatory rights for the stakeholders and an undemocratic government (McKinnon, 1984). The study finds a lack of co-operation to be evident among the institutional bodies in both democratic and undemocratic governments. It is important to mention that military-backed government in Bangladesh was effective in comparison to democratic government in terms of taking action against companies identified as being corrupt. Although the blame culture has previously been limited to developed countries (Hood, 2007, 2009; O'Neill, 2002), the state institutions and professional bodies in Bangladesh (as an example of a developing country) are blaming each other regarding the IFRS implementation process. This could be because the 'blame game' may be aimed at attempting to remove power and responsibility from other institutions in order to facilitate the legitimacy and increase the scope of government.

Prior research argues that common-law origin is more transparent in terms of setting accounting standards (La Porta et al., 1998; Kothari, 2000; Ball et al., 2000, 2003; Leuz et al., 2003). However, in this study, common-law origin has little or no influence on implementing IFRS in Bangladesh (see Chapter 6). This is possibly because Bangladesh contains an unique environment which may be explained via several factors – e.g. training opportunities in the accounting profession, corruption and other country-specific factors (see Chapter 7). The legal origins (common-law vs. code-law) argument in this study raises a question as to why a country with common-law origins has no influence on the implementation of IFRS or has moved toward code-law regarding the implementation of IFRS. This may require further investigation.

This study also finds that politico-institutional factors are stronger and more dominant factors than accounting regulatory frameworks in inhibiting the implementation of IFRS (see Chapter 6). The findings suggest that policymakers are keen to comment on donor agencies' political influence, while denying the existence of government intervention or political lobbying. This is because the policymakers appointed by the government represent different government institutions and want, therefore, to be seen to support the government. By contrast, the account preparers and professionals seemed hesitant to talk about government intervention, and it is possible that the account preparers and professionals feel under pressure because they are fearful of losing their jobs if they become involved in commenting on politics.

Training opportunities in the accounting profession, corruption and country-specific factors

The evidence in this research suggests that training opportunities in the accounting profession and corruption have a negative influence on implementing IFRS in Bangladesh (see Chapter 7). As mentioned in Chapter 2, two factors are investigated in the present research: (a) training opportunities in the accounting profession and (b) corruption. With respect to the training opportunities in the accounting profession, this study finds that deficiencies in the training opportunities in accounting profession are inhibiting IFRS implementation. The majority of respondents feel that the curricula should be brought up to date and that IFRS course content is not incorporated into the universities' curricula. The respondents affiliated with the ICAB (e.g. as a member of the ICAB or by chairing any of its committees) were positive regarding the professional curricula of the ICAB. In addition, the limited training facilities for accountants are an issue of concern in compliance with IFRS. Although the policymakers argued for the necessity of IFRS-related training facilities, they are not providing any training. With the exception of 'big four' and other large companies, a majority of companies are reluctant to provide training for their company accountants. These findings are in disagreement with prior studies in developing countries (Parry and Groves, 1990; Abayo and Roberts, 1993; Ahmed and Nicholls, 1994; Haniffa and Cooke, 2002) that argue that the training opportunities in the accounting profession are not an important factor in explaining levels of corporate disclosure. However, training opportunities in the accounting profession are an important factor in Bangladesh as an example of a developing country in explaining issues with the implementation of IFRS.[1]

This research also finds that high levels of corruption in Bangladesh have a negative influence on implementing IFRS (see Chapter 7). As mentioned in Chapter 4, Bangladesh was top of the list of the most corrupt countries in the world from 2001 to 2005. The interview respondents feel that corruption is deeply rooted in Bangladeshi society. Listed companies can violate the SEC's regulations, including IFRS non-compliance, and can satisfy the relevant authorities (e.g. the SEC, tax officials etc.) through their political connections. It is found that a perceived lack of professional ethics among auditors and company accountants is inhibiting effective IFRS implementation. It is not surprising that the policymakers and users who have links with the ICAB and state institutions were in agreement that corruption is not an important issue in implementing IFRS, while for a majority of account preparers, users and academics corruption is a big threat in a developing country like Bangladesh to effectively implementing IFRS.

The findings in this research are somewhat similar to Hofstede et al. (2010)'s index of Bangladesh (see Chapter 4), in which Bangladesh has the highest Power Distance score, indicating a high level of inequality of power and wealth within its society. In addition, Bangladesh has a more secretive culture than India or Pakistan (Mir and Rahaman, 2005). Hence, company managements are less likely to pursue a high level of disclosure. Moreover, using data from the World Bank's Governance Indicators (2010) and La Porta et al. (1998) (see also Leuz et al., 2003 and Han et al., 2012), the present study reveals a lower rate of enforcement in Bangladesh compared with India and Pakistan. This is due to higher levels of corruption, a factor which weakens enforcement of the laws. The study also finds that Bangladesh and Pakistan's secrecy scores and enforcement scores are relatively similar compared to India. This is due to the fact that both Bangladesh and Pakistan have experienced political instability due to military intervention. Levels of corruption were noticeably lower in Bangladesh during the military-backed government. Although the government established the Anti-Corruption Bureau to tackle corruption in Bangladesh, the government's involvement and the political appointment of the chairman and the staff of that bureau mean that the independence of this institution must seriously be questioned (Choudhury, 2008; Knox, 2009; IMF, 2005, 2010; Huque, 2010).

In relation to the influence of other factors on implementing IFRS, this study finds that country-specific factors – e.g. a lack of qualified accountants; a lack of interest in IFRS by managers of some companies; a culture of secrecy; higher costs of IFRS compliance with lower benefits for small companies; a lack of research; public sector dominance; and a predominantly family-based private sector (all ranked in order of dominance) – are also impeding the implementation process in Bangladesh (see Chapter 7). The study reveals reasons for the lack of qualified accountants: (i) the poor salary structure of Chartered Accountants in Bangladesh compared with India, Pakistan or Sri Lanka; and (ii) the low pass rate needed to become a CA. Hence, students are not interested in studying Chartered Accountancy (Var, 1976; Perera, 1989). Companies' managements are not inclined to comply with IFRS, while a majority of companies are copying extracts from the notes to the financial statements (e.g. accounting policies) of big companies' financial statements (i.e. a culture of secrecy). Again, state companies are relaxed about IFRS compliance (Jones and Sefiane, 1992; Abu-Nassar and Rutherford, 1995). As seen in prior studies in Bangladesh (Uddin and Hopper, 2001, 2003; Akhtaruddin, 2005; Farooque et al., 2007; Khan et al., 2011), the interviewees comment that most listed companies in Bangladesh are family-led businesses which tend to follow non-compliance with IFRS. It is important to add that small companies' IFRS compliance is an issue of concern because for them the costs of complying with IFRS will exceed the benefits. According to interviewees, if the shareholders do not care about, or demand, higher-quality annual reports, then the effectiveness of the implementation process remains questionable in Bangladesh.

In summary, effective implementation may require the depoliticising of state institutions and the establishment of an independent Financial Reporting Council. Since managers and directors in Bangladesh conventionally strive to reap maximum benefits from political relationships and tend to follow a secretive culture, the state should pursue a stringent enforcement of the laws. In this regard, the state should make sure that politicians and their associates are not abusing their powers in order to violate the SEC rules. The current democratic government has acknowledged the need to introduce a culture of transparency in the public and private sectors through the Anti-Corruption Bureau, the Financial Reporting Act and the Financial Reporting Council. To date, though, these remain more promising rhetoric than concrete reality.

The theory of the role of the state in the implementation of IFRS

As has been mentioned in Chapters 3 and 8, the aim of this study is to discuss the literature on the role of the state and accounting change in a developing country and to link the findings with theories of the role of the state. The theoretical contribution of this study in response to RQ-3 is fourfold, as is outlined below.

Firstly, the study contributes to literature on accounting change studies in developing countries such as Bangladesh by applying a Weberian view of the theory of the role of the state (see Chapters 3 and 8). Through this, the study has been able to show that different outcomes of accounting change in Bangladesh can be explained by the most frequently discussed issues in the literature, i.e. drivers of accounting change.

Secondly, the study takes into consideration how external and internal forces influence accounting change. The prior research which employed the Weberian framework to both developed and developing countries did not consider the state–society relationship (see Chapter 3). In this study, the adoption of institutional dynamics has allowed a broader understanding of the theory of the state, and to overcome some of the limitations of previous studies by considering accounting change on at least two levels (i.e. external and internal forces). In particular, outcomes of accounting change in Bangladesh are observed from the state level and the individual organisation level. However, the influence of the organisational field level is unknown in this research because industry lobbying groups were not interviewed. Extending Weber's (1958)[1904], (1968)[1922]] argument on state-society, the study finds that for a state in an era of democratic government, politico-institutional factors and corruption (as indications of societal values) may be more important and concentrated factors than for a state under a military-backed government in terms of impeding IFRS implementation.

Thirdly, as has been mentioned, very limited research has been conducted on the theory of the role of the state, and the roles of the state are vague in the prior research (see Chapter 3). I have discussed roles of the state (i.e. the state approves experts to write rules; it consults with various stakeholders; it enforces outcomes; it is accountable to its citizens; and it engages with donor agencies) in a developing country's experience during the process of change. The study reveals that all roles of the state have negative influences on accounting change. Several consequences arise from this. Accounting regulatory frameworks have not been updated to include IFRS requirements, and a contradiction exists between the Companies Act and IFRS. Stakeholders' participation is not guaranteed in the standard-setting process in Bangladesh. Political pressure by the government, and in particular by successive democratic governments, inhibits the IFRS implementation process. A lack of co-operation among state institutions and professional bodies negatively impacts the outcomes of accounting change.

Finally, corruption (as a societal value) is one of the major contributing factors in impeding IFRS implementation (see Chapters 6 and 7). However, interviewees' initial concerns about the roles of donor agencies are transformed into concerns about the democratic government's failure to implement IFRS.

The new understanding which emerges from my book regarding the theory of the role of the state can be summarised as follows:

> For Weber (1958, p. 113) [1904], the social sources of the role of the state may change. However, in Bangladesh, individuals in society follow consistent societal values (i.e. continuous corruption) because corruption is considered to be natural and is widely accepted by the country's society (see Chapter 7).
>
> Weber (1968, p. 72)[1922] argues that different actors make different choices, and stresses that power is exercised over the state's citizens, who have a duty to obey, and the state's power (e.g. compliance with laws) becomes the objective of social action. In Bangladesh, different actors (in different democratic governments) have been seen to make the same choices in terms of not effectively implementing IFRS. Some specific observations can be made regarding IFRS implementation: the state tends to be politicised, with a looser enforcement of laws which allows corruption and pays scant attention towards actual, effective implementation. Nevertheless, the present study raises major questions around how effective implementation can be achieved, given the state's ongoing failure to initiate and enable it over the past 13 years or more (see Chapter 6).
>
> Weber (1968, pp. 156-7)[1922] saw that a democratic state, by means of elections and a parliamentary process, can reduce tension and struggles for power. Weber predicted that the essential role of the state is to make and enforce rules. In my opinion, Weber did not allow in his argument for the consequences of a developing country's experiences. In a developing country like Bangladesh, regulatory frameworks are often unenforceable in the presence of strong political connectedness, and obligations to the state become insignificant in the face of obligations to political connectedness. In particular,

successive democratic eras in Bangladesh have been marked by inhibited IFRS implementation in comparison to the military era (see Chapter 6). Weber (1968, p. 156) [1922] argues for the creation of meaning in everyday life, and that power is ultimately social through the parliamentary process and democracy. In the case of Bangladesh, the parliamentary process and democracy do not guarantee power to all citizens, meaning that power may not be ultimately social because of politicisation and continuum corruption within a state (see Chapter 8).

Limitations of the study

The following limitations are inherent in this study. Firstly, some limitations exist in conducting interviews (both in the 1st and 2nd round of interviews) in a developing country such as Bangladesh. As mentioned in Chapter 5, some of the interviewees cancelled their appointments, and in some cases the waiting time was too long. Another limitation was in relation to translating and transcribing the interviews. Although the interviews were conducted in English, the interviewees responded mostly in Bengali and to some extent a mixture of Bengali and English. Further, respondents were often reluctant to explain much or talk extensively (e.g. offering only 'yes/no/no comment'), and some of the Bengali words used by the interviewees have the same meaning, a different meaning or no equivalent meaning in English. Researchers like Miles and Huberman (1994) and Williamson (2011) argue that coding and interpretation is dependent on the knowledge and skill of the researcher. As the present researcher is fluent in Bengali and English, the experience and knowledge of the researcher (in sharing the cultural background of the participants)in terms of translating and transcribing interview data could minimise any interpretation bias.

Secondly, another limitation of the research is the small sample size of the interviews. It may be argued that conducting more interviews could have obtained a deeper insight into the issues at hand. Miles and Huberman (1994) suggest that six to eight interviews are enough to justify the results of a study. This study purposively selected interviewees likely to be able to help the researcher understand the specific problems and the research question (Street, 2002; Creswell, 2007). Accordingly, 27 interviews were conducted in the 1st round of interviews consisting of four groups – i.e. (a) policymakers [PM]; (b) accounts preparers and professionals [AP]; (c) users [US]; and (d) academics/researchers [AR] (see Chapter 5). According to Myers and Newman (2007), representing a variety of voices can overcome various biases. However, in the 2nd round only 12 out of 27 agreed to participate. In particular, interviewees in the AP and US groups were disinclined to participate (representing 33% of the sample when comparing the 2nd round to the 1st round of interviews). Patton (2001) argues that qualitative research does not necessarily suggest a large number of participants. Nevertheless, two rounds of interview data were available to be used for the generalisation of the findings of this study.

Thirdly, the leaders of the industry groups (e.g. BAB, BAPLC, BGMEA, BIGUF, BTMA, DCCI, FBCCI and NGWF) were not interviewed. Although this group of people are undeniably important to the effective implementation of IFRS, it is not easy to interview this group in Bangladesh. The researcher contacted those leaders several times but they were not interested in participating in the study. In addition, during the period of this research, Bangladesh experienced some trade union turbulence, making it even more difficult to set up interviews with this group. The researcher decided to use other sources of information instead, such as documentary analyses. Hence, the activities of these individuals and groups towards influencing IFRS implementation remain unknown in this research and the theoretical framework in this study limits the generalisation of the findings, in particular at the organisational field level.

Fourthly, the state's accountability to its citizens has not been implicitly examined in this study. The findings of the three propositions may offer insights as to whether the state is accountable to its citizens in Bangladesh in terms of accounting change. Nevertheless, the World Bank's Worldwide Governance Indicators (1996–2010); interviewees' comments on the quality (or lack of it) of investor protection laws; and stakeholders' participation/non-participation in the standard-setting process all illustrate why the state is not accountable to its citizens in Bangladesh.

Finally, with respect to documentary analyses, some limitations were observed (see Chapter 5). For instance, parts of some of the enforcement notices are illegible; some of the notices were not available on websites; the releases contain repeated information on the same enforcement actions (Bremser et al., 1991; Feroz et al., 1991; Campbell and Parker, 1992; Files, 2012); the bandwidth of the SEC website is very low; no full record of enforcement documents was available (i.e. data related to 13 years ago were not available); there was a tendency to frequently cancel meetings with the researcher; and dealing with the lack of co-ordination among various departments in the SEC and collecting data in a developing country like Bangladesh from state institutions (such as the SEC) is generally time-consuming. Further, the study follows a subjective analysis of the SEC enforcement releases because the material does not lend itself to quantitative analysis. Nonetheless, this limitation is mitigated by the fact that a substantial number of enforcement releases are analysed.

Avenues for future research

Several suggestions can be made as to possible avenues for further research which arise from this study's focus and findings.

Firstly, in accounting literature, different researchers have applied a Weberian view in different ways. Future research could be conducted on the Weberian perspective of accounting change in broader terms. This theory could help a researcher understand how and why some states are more successful than others in relation to the outcomes of their accounting change, and in particular, in terms of their implementation of IFRS.

Secondly, this study focuses on theory of the role of the state. According to the findings of this study, agency theory is one possible theory which might explain effective implementation of IFRS. Therefore, for future research, researchers may gain more insight by utilising agency theory in their studies.

Thirdly, this study does not include interviews with industry leaders due to the limitations mentioned in Chapter 5. For future research, it would be interesting to study the perspectives of industry leaders and trade unions towards IFRS implementation. This kind of further research may consider how best to encourage these particular groups (if the groups remain reluctant to participate in the research) to explain the theoretical framework involved in the study. It would also be interesting to compare these groups across various developing countries.

Fourthly, this study does not focus on social values or beliefs to explain cultural values; instead, training opportunities in the accounting profession and corruption are discussed. Cultural theory – as proposed by Hofstede (1980), Hofstede et al. (2010) and Gray (1988) – is not discussed in detail in this research because cultural theory is seen as the opposite of the Weberian view of the state. For future research it would be interesting to study social values or beliefs and their effects on accounting change using Hofstede's or Gray's model. The findings in this study are discussed in the reflection section in the context of South Asian culture (comparing India, Pakistan and Bangladesh) using Hofstede's (2010) scores, the World Bank Governance Data (2010) and La Porta et al. (1998)'s scores.

Fifthly, future research could be conducted which defines corruption as an institutional factor in the implementation of IFRS in developing countries.

Finally, it is suggested that the theoretical perspectives, interviews and the documentary analyses embraced within this broader study could be replicated in studies of another developing country, or for a group of developing countries, in order to determine and compare the outcomes of accounting change, and in particular the different levels of effectiveness seen in the implementation of IFRS.

Note

1 See similar findings in other developing countries: Wickramasinghe and Hopper (2005) in Sri Lanka, and Zeghal and Mhedhbi (2006) in other countries.

References

Abayo, A.G. and Roberts, C.B. (1993). 'Does training more accountants raise the standard of accounting? Further evidence from Tanzania'. *Research in Third World Accounting*, 2: 259–80.

Abd-Elsalam, O.H. and Weetman, P. (2003). 'Introducing international accounting standards to an emerging capital market: Relative familiarity and language effect in Egypt'. *Journal of International Accounting, Auditing and Taxation*, 12(1): 63–84.

Abdelsalam, O.H. and Weetman, P. (2007). 'Measuring accounting disclosure in a period of complex changes: the case of Egypt'. *Advances in International Accounting*, 20: 75–104.

Abdullah, A.B.M., Boyle, S. and Joham, C. (2011). 'Cultural factors in workforce management: The case of multinational companies operating in Bangladesh'. *International Review of Business Research*, 7(2): 196–211.

Abu-Nassar, M. and Rutherford, B.A. (1995). 'Preparers' attitudes to financial reporting in less developed countries with moderately sophisticated capital markets: The case of Jordan'. *International Journal of Accounting*, 30(2): 129–38.

Ahmad, M. (1976). 'The historical perspective of public sector enterprises in Bangladesh'. *Journal of Management Business and Economics*, 2(3): 252–94.

Ahmad, N. (1950). 'Industrial development in East Bengal (East Pakistan)'.*Economic Geography*, 26(3): 183–95.

———. (2002). Corruption and government regulations: An empirical analysis. *Bangladesh Development Studies*, 28(4): 29–51.

Ahmed, E. (1998). 'The military and democracy in Bangladesh', in May, R.J. and Selochan, V. (eds), *The Military and Democracy in Asia and the Pacific*. Bathurst, NSW: Crawford, 102–13.

———. (2003). *Democracy in Crisis: The Case of Bangladesh*. Islamabad: Sustainable Development Policy Institute, 2003.

Ahmed, K. (1996). 'Disclosure policy choice and corporate characteristics: A study of Bangladesh'. *Asia-Pacific Journal of Accounting*, 3(1): 183–203.

———and Nicholls, D. (1994). 'The impact of non-financial company characteristics on mandatory disclosure compliance in developing countries: The case of Bangladesh'. *International Journal of Accounting*, 29(3): 62–77.

Ahmed, N. (2010). 'Party politics under a non-party caretaker government in Bangladesh: The Fakhruddin interregnum (2007–09)'. *Commonwealth and Comparative Politics*, 48(1): 23–47.

Akhtaruddin, M. (2005). 'Corporate mandatory disclosure practices in Bangladesh'. *International Journal of Accounting*, 40(4): 399–422.

Akkas, S.A. (2004). *Independence and Accountability of Judiciary: A Critical Review*. Dhaka: Center for Rights and Governance (CriG).

Al-Akra, M., Ali, M.J. and Marashdeh, O. (2009). 'Development of accounting regulation in Jordan'. *International Journal of Accounting*, 44(2): 163–86.

Al-Akra, M., Eddie, I.A. and Ali, M.J. (2010). 'The influence of the introduction of accounting disclosure regulation on mandatory disclosure compliance: Evidence from Jordan'. *British Accounting Review*, 42(3): 170–86.

Alamgir, J. (2009). 'Bangladesh's fresh start'. *Journal of Democracy*, 20(3): 41–55.

Alexander, D. and Archer, S. (2000). 'On the myth of "Anglo-Saxon" financial accounting'. *International Journal of Accounting*, 35(4): 539–57.

Alexander, D. and Servalli, S. (2010). 'The state and/of accounting regulation'. *Paper presented at the 6th Accounting History International Conference (6AHIC), Wellington, New Zealand, 18–20 August.*

Alexander, D. and Micallef, M. (2011). 'Accounting regulation in Malta'. *Accounting in Europe*, 8(1): 1–21.

Ali, M.J., Ahmed, K. and Henry, D. (2004). 'Disclosure compliance with national accounting standards by listed companies in South Asia'. *Accounting and Business Research*, 34(3): 183–99.

Al-Shammari, B., Brown, P. and Tarca, A. (2008). 'An investigation of compliance with international accounting standards by listed companies in the Gulf Co-Operation Council member states'. *International Journal of Accounting*, 43(4): 425–47.

Al-Shiab, M. (2003). *Financial Consequences of IAS Adoption: The Case of Jordan.* Unpublished PhD thesis, Newcastle University Business School, UK.

Amer, M.B. (1969). 'Impact of public ownership on the U.A.R. accounting profession'. *International Journal of Accounting Education and Research*, 4(2): 49–61.

Anechiarico, F. and Jacobs, J. (1995). 'Panopticism and financial controls: The anticorruption project in public administration'. *Crime, Law and Social Change*, 22(4): 361–79.

Archer, M.S. (2002). 'Realism and the problem of agency'. *Alethia/Journal of Critical Realism* 5(1): 11–20.

Arikan, G.G. (2004). 'Fiscal decentralization: A remedy for corruption?' *International Tax and Public Finance*, 11(2): 175–95.

Armstrong, P. (1987). 'The rise of accounting controls in British capitalist enterprises'. *Accounting, Organizations and Society*, 12(5): 415–36.

Ashraf, J. and Ghani, W.I. (2005). 'Accounting development in Pakistan'. *International Journal of Accounting*, 40(2): 175–201.

Asian Development Bank (ADB). (2001). *Corporate Governance and Finance in East Asia: A Study of Indonesia, Republic of Korea, Malaysia, Philippines, and Thailand.* Available at:http://www.adb.org/Documents/Books/Corporate_Governance/Vol2/default.asp [accessed: 8 June 2010].

Asian Development Bank (ADB). (2005). *Capital Market Development Program (Loan 1580-BAN[SF]) in Bangladesh.* Available at: http://www.oecd.org/dataoecd/19/26/35253322.pdf [accessed: 11 November 2009].

Asian Development Bank (ADB). (2007). *Asian Development Outlook 2007: Bangladesh.* Available at: http://www.adb.org/Documents/Books/ADO/2007/update/BAN.pdf [accessed: 8 June 2010].

Askary, S. (2006). 'Accounting professionalism: – A cultural perspective of developing countries'. *Managerial Auditing Journal*, 21(1): 102–11.

Avineri, S. (1972). *Hegel's Theory of the Modern State.* Cambridge: Cambridge University Press.

Azizuddin, A.B.M. (2006). 'IAS/IFRS: – Overview, status, adoption, challenges, implementation and future dimensions'. *Paper presented at CPE Seminar Series, The Institute of Chartered Accountants of Bangladesh, Dhaka, 17 May.*

Baber, W.R. (1990). 'Toward a framework for evaluating the role of accounting and auditing in political markets: The influence of political competition'. *Journal of Accounting and Public Policy*, 9(1): 57–73.

Baek, J., Kang, J. and Park, K. (2002). '*Corporate Governance and Firm Value: Evidence from the Korean Financial Crisis*'. Available at: http://globaledge.msu.edu/KnowledgeRoom/FeaturedInsights/0031.pdf [accessed: 30 October 2010].

Ball, R. (2001). 'Infrastructure requirements for an economically efficient system of public financial reporting and disclosure', in Litan, R. and Herring, R. (eds), *Brookings-Wharton Papers on Financial Services.* Washington, DC: Brookings Institution Press, 127–83.

Ball, R. (2006). 'International financial reporting standards (IFRS): pros and cons for investors'. *Accounting and Business Research*, 36(special issue): 5–27.

Ball, R. (2009). 'Market and political/regulatory perspectives on the recent accounting scandals'. *Journal of Accounting Research*, 47(2): 277–323.

Ball, R., Kothari, S.P. and Robin, A. (2000). 'The effect of international institutional factors on properties of accounting earnings'. *Journal of Accounting and Economics*, 29(1): 1–51.

Ball, R., Robin, A. and Wu, J. (2003). 'Incentives versus standards: Properties of accounting income in four East Asian countries, and implications for acceptance of IAS'. *Journal of Accounting and Economics*, 36(1–3): 235–70.

Banerjee, A. and Iyer, L. (2005). 'History, institutions, and economic performance: The legacy of colonial land tenure systems in India'. *American Economic Review*, 95(4): 1190–213.

Banerjee, B. (2002). *Regulation of Corporate Accounting and Reporting in India*. Calcutta: World Press.

Bangladesh Bank (2006–07). Annual Report.

Barkat, A., Hoque, M. and Chowdhury, Z.H. (2004). 'State capacity in promoting trade and investment: The case of Bangladesh'. UNDESA, Dhaka, 25 February.

Baskerville, R.F. (2001). 'Taylor's legacy in international accounting research'. *Third Asian Pacific Interdisciplinary Research in Accounting Conference, July*.

———. (2003). 'Hofstede never studied culture'. *Accounting, Organizations and Society*, 28(1): 1–14.

———. 'A research note: the unfinished business of culture'. *Accounting, Organizations and Society*, 30(4): 389–91.

Bealing, W.E. Jr, Dirsmith, M.W. and Fogarty, T. (1996). 'Early regulatory actions by the SEC: An institutional theory perspective on the dramaturgy of political exchanges'. *Accounting, Organizations and Society*, 21(4): 317–38.

Beardsworth, A. and Keil, T. (1992). 'The vegetarian option: Varieties, conversions, motives and careers'. *Sociological Review*, 40: 253–93.

Belkaoui, A. (1983). 'Economic, political, and civil indicators and reporting and disclosure adequacy: empirical investigation'. *Journal of Accounting and Public Policy*, 2(3): 207–19.

———. (1985). *Public Policy and the Problems and Practices of Accounting*. Westport, CT: Quorum Books.

———. (2004). *Accounting Theory*. 5thedn. London: Thomson.

Bennell, P. (1997). 'Privatisation in sub-Saharan Africa: Progress and prospects during the 1990s'. *World Development*, 25(11): 1785–803.

Bennett, A. and Braumoeller, B. (2006). 'Where the model frequently meets the road: Combining statistical, formal, and case study methods'. *Working Paper, Departments of Government, Georgetown University, USA*.

Benston, G.J. (1976). 'Public (US) compared to private (UK) regulation of corporate financial disclosure'. *The Accounting Review*, 51(3): 483–98.

Beresford, D. (2001): 'Congress looks at accounting for business combinations'. *Accounting Horizons*, 15(1): 73–86.

Berger, A. (2010). 'The development and status of enforcement in the European Union'. *Accounting in Europe*, 7(1): 15–35.

Beyme, K.V. (1986). 'The contemporary relevance of the concept of the state' .*International Political Science Review/Revue internationale de science politique*, 7(2): 115–19.

Bhaskar, R. (1978). *A Realist Theory of Science*. 2nd edn. Hassocks: Harvester Press.

Bhattacharjee, J. (2007). 'Politicisation major reason for judicial graft in Bangladesh'. Observer Research Foundation, 21 May. Available at: http://www.orfonline.org/cms/sites/orfonline/modules/news-brief/NewsBriefDetail.html?cmaid=7471&mmacmaid=7472&volumeno=I&issueno=18[accessed: 12 February 2012].

Bloom, R., Fuglister, J. and Myring, M. (1998). 'The state of accounting in Armenia: A case'. *International Journal of Accounting*, 33(5): 633–54.

Boross, Z., Clarkson, A.H., Fraser, M. and Weetman, P. (1995). 'Pressures and conflicts in moving towards harmonization of accounting practice: The Hungarian experience'. *European Accounting Review*, 4(4): 713–37.

Boyatzis, R. (1998). *Transforming Qualitative Information: Thematic Analysis and Code Development*. Thousand Oaks, CA/London: Sage.

Braun, M. and Raddatz, C. (2010). 'Banking on politics: When former high-ranking politicians become bank directors'. *World Bank Economic Review*, 24(2): 234–79.

Bremser, W.G., Licata, M.P. and Rollins, T.P. (1991). 'SEC enforcement activities: A survey and critical perspective'. *Critical Perspectives on Accounting*,2(2): 185–99.

Briston, R.J. (1978). 'The evolution of accounting in developing countries'. *International Journal of Accounting Education and Research*, 14(2): 105–20.

———. (1990). 'Accounting in developing countries: Indonesia and the Solomon Islands as case studies for regional co-operation'. *Research in Third World Accounting*, 1: 195–216.

Briston, R.J. and Hadori, Y. (1993). 'Role and training of accounting technicians: IFAC's IEG no. 7 and its relevance for South East Asia'. *Research in Third World Accounting*, 2: 245–58.

Brown, P. and Tarca, A. (2001), Politics, processes and the future of Australian accounting standards. *Abacus*, 37(3): 267–96.

Brown, P. and Tarca, A. (2005). 'A commentary on issues relating to the enforcement of international financial reporting standards in the EU'. *European Accounting Review*, 14(1): 181–212.

Bryman, A. (2008). *Social Research Methods*. 3rd edn. Oxford: Oxford University Press.

Bryman, A. and Bell, E. (2007). *Business Research Methods*. Oxford: Oxford University Press.

Buchanan, D. and Badham, R. (1999). *Power, Politics and Organizational Change: Winning the Turf Game*. London: Sage.

Buchanan, J.M. (1962). 'Politics, policy, and the Pigouvian margins'. *Economica*, 29(113): 17–28.

Burchell, S., Clubb, C., Hopwood, A., Hughes, J. and Nahapiet, J. (1980).'The roles of accounting in organizations and society'. *Accounting, Organizations and Society*, 5(1): 5–27.

Burns, J. (1996). *The Routinization and Institutionalization of Accounting*. Unpublished PhD thesis, University of Manchester, UK.

Burns, J. and Scapens, R.W. (2000). 'Conceptualizing management accounting change: An institutional framework'. *Management Accounting Research*, 11: 3–25.

Bushman, R. and Landsman, W.R. (2010). 'The pros and cons of regulating corporate reporting: A critical review of the arguments'. *Accounting and Business Research*, 40(3): 259–73.

Bushman, R. and Piotroski, J. (2006). 'Financial reporting incentives for conservative accounting: The influence of legal and political institutions'. *Journal of Accounting and Economics*, 42(1/2): 107–48.

Butler, J. (1997). *The Psychic Life of Power: Theories In Subjection*. Stanford, CA: Stanford University Press.

Cairns, D. (1990). 'Aid for the developing world'. *Accountancy*, March: 82–5.

Campbell, D.R. and Parker, L.M. (1992). 'SEC communications to the independent auditors: An analysis of enforcement actions'. *Journal of Accounting and Public Policy*, 11(4): 297–330.

Campbell, D.T. and Fiske, D.W. (1959). 'Convergent and discriminant validation by the multitrait-multimethod matrix'. *Psychological Bulletin*, 56(2): 81–105.

Caramanis, C.V. (2002). 'The interplay between professional groups, the state and supranational agents: Pax Americana in the age of "globalisation"'. *Accounting, Organizations and Society*, 27(4–5): 379–408.

Carnoy, M. (1984). *The State and Political Theory*. Princeton: Princeton University Press.

Carpenter, V.L. (1991). 'The influence of political competition on the decision to adopt GAAP'. *Journal of Accounting and Public Policy*, 10(2): 105–34.

Carpenter, V.L. and Feroz, E.H. (2001). 'Institutional theory and accounting rule choice: An analysis of four US state governments' decisions to adopt generally accepted accounting principles'. *Accounting, Organizations and Society*, 26 (7–8): 565–96.

Cascino, S. and Gassen, J. (2010). 'Mandatory IFRS adoption and accounting comparability'. *SFB 649 Discussion Paper, No. 2010–046, Humboldt-Universität zu Berlin, Germany*.

Cassese, S. (1986). 'The rise and decline of the notion of state'. *International Political Science Review/Revue internationale de science politique*, 7(2): 120–30.

Central Intelligence Agency (CIA) (2008). *The World Factbook*. Available at: https://www.cia.gov/library/publications/the-world-factbook/ [accessed: 11 January 2009].

Chabod, F. (1964). 'Was there a Renaissance state?', in Lubasz, H. (ed.), *The Development of the Modern State*. New York: Macmillan, 27–36.

Chabod, F. (1967). 'Alcuni questioni di terminologia: stato, nazione, patria nel linguaggio del Cinquecento', in Chabod, F. (ed.), *Scritti sul Rinascimento* (translated version). Turin: Einaudi.

Chamisa, E.E. (2000). 'The relevance and observance of the IASC standards in developing countries and the particular case of Zimbabwe'. *International Journal of Accounting*, 35(2): 267–26.

Chand, P., Cummings, L. and Patel, C. (2012). 'The Effect of accounting education and national culture on accounting judgments: A comparative study of Anglo-Celtic and Chinese culture'. *European Accounting Review*, 21(2): 153–82.

Chandler, J.S. and Holzer, H.P. (1984). 'Accounting in the third world', in Holzer, H.P. et al. (eds), *International Accounting*. New York: Harper and Row, 453–81.

Chandler, R.A. (1992). 'The international harmonization of accounting: In search of influence'. *International Journal of Accounting*, 27(3): 222–33.

Chaney, P.K., Faccio, M. and Parsley, D.(2011). 'The quality of accounting information in politically connected firms'. *Journal of Accounting and Economics*, 51(1–2): 58–76.

Chen, G., Firth, M., Gao, D.N. and Rui, O.M. (2005). 'Is China's securities regulatory agency a toothless tiger? Evidence from enforcement actions'. *Journal of Accounting and Public Policy*, 24(6):451–88.

Chen, S., Sun, Z., Tang, S. and Wu, D. (2011). 'Government intervention and investment efficiency: Evidence from China'. *Journal of Corporate Finance*, 17(2): 259–71.

Cheng, R.H. (1992). 'An empirical analysis of theories on factors influencing state government accounting disclosure'. *Journal of Accounting and Public Policy*, 11(1): 1–42.

Chiapello, E. and Medjad, K. (2009). 'An unprecedented privatization of mandatory standard-setting: The case of European accounting policy'. *Critical Perspectives on Accounting*, 20(4): 448–68.

Choi, F.D.S. (1979). 'ASEAN Federation of Accountants: A new international accounting force'. *International Journal of Accounting Education and Research*, 15(1): 53–75.

Choi, F.D.S. and Mueller, G.G. (1978). *An Introduction to Multinational Accounting*. Englewood Cliffs, NJ: Prentice Hall.

———. (1984). *International Accounting*. Englewood Cliffs, NJ: Prentice Hall.

Choi, J.S. (2002). 'Financial crisis and accounting reform: A cultural perspective'. *Journal of Accounting and Finance*, 1: 77–93.

Chowdhury, A. (2002). 'Politics, society and financial sector reform in Bangladesh'. *International Journal of Social Economics*, 29(12): 963–88.

Christensen, H.B., Hail, L. and Leuz, C. (2010). 'Capital-market effects of securities regulation: The role of implementation and enforcement'. *Working Paper No. 241, George J. Stigler Center for the Study of the Economy and the State, University of Chicago, USA*.

Chua, W.F. and Taylor, S.L. (2008). 'The rise and rise of IFRS: An examination of IFRS diffusion'. *Journal of Accounting and Public Policy*, 27(6): 462–73.

Coad, A.F. and Herbert, I.P., (2009). 'Back to the future: New potential for structuration in evolutionary theories of management accounting?' *Management Accounting Research*, 20(3): 177–92.

Coffee, J.C., Jr. (2007). 'Law and the market: The impact of enforcement'. *Columbia Law and Economics Working Paper No. 304*. Available at: http://ssrn.com/abstract=967482 [accessed: 21 January 2010].

Cohen, J.E. and Hamman, J.A. (2003). 'Interest group PAC contributions and the 1992 regulation of cable television'. *Social Science Journal*, 40(3): 357–69.

Colignon, R. and Covaleski, M. (1991). 'A Weberian framework in the study of accounting'. *Accounting, Organizations and Society*, 16(2): 141–57.

Constable, P. and Kuasirikun, N. (2007). 'Accounting for the nation-state in mid nineteenth-century Thailand'. *Accounting, Auditing and Accountability Journal*, 20(4): 574–619.

Cooke, T.E. and Wallace, R.S.O. (1990). 'Financial disclosure regulation and its environment: A review and further analysis'. *Journal of Accounting and Public Policy*,9(2): 79–110.

Cooper, C. (1995). 'Ideology, hegemony and accounting discourse: A case study of the National Union of Journalists'. *Critical Perspectives on Accounting*, 6(3): 175–209.

Cooper, D.J. and Robson, K. (2006). 'Accounting, professions and regulation: Locating the sites of professionalization'. *Accounting, Organizations and Society*, 31(4–5): 415–44.

Cottle, T.J. (1977). *Private and Public Accountants*. New York: New Viewpoints.

Covaleski, M.A. and Dirsmith, M.W. (1988). 'An institutional perspective on the rise, social transformation, and fall of a university budget category'. *Administrative Science Quarterly*, 33: 562–87.

Creswell, J.W. (2007). *Qualitative Inquiry and Research Design: Choosing Among Five Approaches*.3rd edn. Thousand Oaks, CA/London: Sage.

Creswell, J.W. and Miller, D.L. (2000). 'Determining validity in qualitative inquiry'. *Theory into Practice*, 39(3): 124–31.

Dahawy, K., Merino, B.D. and Conover, T.L. (2002). 'The conflict between IAS disclosure requirements and the secretive culture in Egypt'. *Advances in International Accounting*, 15: 203–28.

Davie, S.S.K. (2007). 'A colonial "social experiment": Accounting and a communal system in British-ruled Fiji'. *Accounting Forum*, 31(3): 255–76.

Dawson, P. (1994). *Organizational Change: A Processual Approach*. London: Chapman.

De Vaus, D. (2001). *Research Design in Social Research*. London: Sage.

Deloitte and Touche Tohmatsu. (2007). *IAS Plus Bangladesh*. Available at: http://www.iasplus.com/country/banglade.htm [accessed: 22 December 2009].

Dillard, J.F., Rigsby, J.T., and Goodman, C. (2004). 'The making and remaking of organization context: Duality and the institutionalization process'. *Accounting, Auditing and Accountability Journal*, 17(4): 506–42.

Dima, B. and Cristea, S.M. (2009). 'Discussion on new cultural variables and IFRSs' Implementation'. *Cahiers de Recherche, Working Paper No. 11: 103–30*.

DiMaggio, P.J. (1988). 'Interest and agency in institutional theory', in Zucker, L.G. (ed.), *Institutional Patterns and Organizations: Culture and Environment*. Cambridge, MA: Ballinger, 3–22.

Ding, Y., Jeanjean, T. and Stolowy, H. (2005). 'Why do national GAAP differ from IAS? The role of culture'. *International Journal of Accounting*, 40(4): 325–50.

Dobosiewicz, Z. (1992). *Foreign Investment in Eastern Europe*. London: Routledge.

Doidge, C., Karolyi, G. and Stulz, R. (2004). 'Why are foreign firms listed in the U.S. worth more?' *Journal of Financial Economics*, 71(2): 205–38.

Douglas, M. (1982). 'Cultural bias', in Douglas, M. (ed.), *In the Active Voice*. London: Routledge & Kegan Paul, 183–254.

Doupnik, T.S. and Salter, S.B. (1995). 'External environment and accounting practice: A preliminary test of a general model of international accounting development'. *International Journal of Accounting*, 30(2): 189–207.

Downs, A. (1957). *An Economic Theory of Democracy*. New York: Harper and Row.

Dhaka Stock Exchange (DSE) (2009–10). Annual Report.

Dubois, A. and Gadde, L.-E. (2002). 'Systematic combining: An abductive approach to case research'. *Journal of Business Research*, 55(7): 553–60.

Dumontier, P. and Raffournier, B. (1998). 'Why firms comply voluntary with IAS: An empirical analysis with Swiss data'. *Journal of International Financial Management and Accounting*, 9(3): 216–45.

Dunne, T.M., Fifield, S.G.M., Fox, A.M., Hannah, G.M., Veneziani, M., Power, D.M., Finningham, G. and Helliar, C.V. (2008). 'The implementation of IFRS in the UK, Italy and Ireland'. *Research Report, Institute of Chartered Accountants of Scotland*.

Dusza, K. (1989). 'Max Weber's conception of the state'. *International Journal of Politics, Culture, and Society*, 3(1): 71–105.

Easterby-Smith, M., Thorpe, R., and Lowe, A. (2002). *Management Research: – An Introduction*. London: Sage.

Edwards, R. (1998). 'A critical examination of the use of interpreters in the qualitative research process'. *Journal of Ethnic and Migration Studies*, 24(2): 197–208.

Elliot, D. and Judy, E. (1997). *Research Ethics: A Reader*. Hanover, NH: University Press of New England.

Enikolopov, R. and Zhuravskaya, E. (2007). 'Decentralization and political institutions'. *Journal of Public Economics*, 91(2): 2261–90.

Enthoven, A.J.H. (1965). 'Economic development and accountancy'. *Journal of Accountancy*, August: 29–35.

Ernstberger, J., Stich, M. and Vogler, O. (2010). 'Economic consequences of accounting enforcement reforms: The case of Germany'. Available at: http://ssrn.com/abstract=1321674 [accessed: 28 January 2011].

Esposito, N. (2001). 'From meaning to meaning: The influence of translation techniques on non-English focus group research'. *Qualitative Health Research*, 11(4): 568–79.

Esterberg, K.G. (2002). *Qualitative Methods in Social Research*. Boston, MA: McGraw-Hill.

Evans, P. and Rauch, J.E. (1999). 'Bureaucracy and growth: A cross-national analysis of the effects of 'Weberian' state structures on economic growth'. *American Sociological Review*, 64(5): 748–65.

Ezzamel, M., Xiao, J.Z. and Pan, A. (2007). 'Political ideology and accounting regulation in China'. *Accounting, Organizations and Society*, 32(7–8): 669–700.

Faccio, M. (2002). *Politically-Connected Firms: Can They Squeeze the State?* Association of Financial Economists, Washington, DC. Available at: http://ssrn.com/abstract=305099 [accessed: 29 November 2010].

Faccio, M. (2010). 'Differences between politically connected and nonconnected firms: A cross-country analysis'. *Financial Management*, 39(3): 905–28.

Fan, C.S., Lin, C. and Treisman, D. (2009). 'Political decentralization and corruption: Evidence around the world'. *Journal of Public Economics*, 93(1–2): 14–34.

Farooque, O.A., Zijl, T.V., Dunstan, K.L. and Karim, A.K.M.W. (2007). 'Corporate governance in Bangladesh: Link between ownership concentration and financial performance'. *Corporate Governance: An International Review*, 15(6): 1453–68.

Fekete, S., Matis, D. and Lukács, J. (2008). 'Factors influencing the extent of corporate compliance with IFRS: The case of Hungarian listed companies'. *Annales Universitatis Apulensis Series Oeconomica*, 1(10): 1–12.

Feroz, E.H., Park, K. and Pastena, V.S. (1991). 'The financial and market effects of the SEC's accounting and auditing enforcement releases'. *Journal of Accounting Research*, 29(Supplement): 107–42.

Files, R. (2012). 'SEC enforcement: Does forthright disclosure and cooperation really matter?' *Journal of Accounting and Economics*, 53(1–2): 353–74.

Fogarty, T.J. (1992). 'Financial accounting standard setting as an institutionalized action field: Constraints, opportunities and dilemmas'. *Journal of Accounting and Public Policy*, 11(4): 331–55.

Foucault, M. (1977). *Discipline and Punish: The Birth of the Prison*. Translated by A. Sheridan. London: Penguin.

Frey, B.S. and Stutzer, A. (2001). 'Beyond Bentham-measuring procedural utility'. *CESifo Working Paper Series No. 492, IEER Working Paper No. 76*.

Friedland, R., and Alford, R.R. (1991). 'Bringing society back in: Symbols, practices and institutional contradictions', in Powell, P.D. (ed.), *The New Institutionalism in Organizational Analysis*, Chicago: University of Chicago Press, 232–63.

Fuentes, C.M.M. (2008). 'Pathways from interpersonal violence to sexually transmitted infections: A mixed method study of diverse women'. *Journal of Women's Health*, 17: 1591–603.

Fukui, H. (1981). 'Bureaucratic power in Japan', in Drysdale, P. and Hironobu, K. (eds), *Japan and Australia: Two Societies and Their Interactions*, Canberra: Australian National University Press, 275–303.

Geddes, B. and Ribeiro-Neto, A. (1999). 'Institutional sources of corruption in Brazil', in Rosenn, K.S. and Downes, R. (eds), *Corruption and Political Reform in Brazil*. Miami: North-South Center Press of the University of Miami, 21–48.

Georgiou, G. (2004): 'Corporate lobbying on accounting standards: Methods, timing and perceived effectiveness'. *Abacus*, 40(2): 219–37.

Gernon, H. and Wallace, R.S.O. (1995). 'International accounting research: A review of its ecology, contending theories and methodologies'. *Journal of Accounting Literature*, 14: 54–106.

Gernon, H., Meek, G. and Mueller, G. (1987). *Accounting: An International Perspective*. Homewood, IL: Irwin.

Gernon, H., Purvis, S.E.C. and Diamond, M.A. (1990).'An analysis of the implications of the IASC's comparability project'. *Topical Issues Studies: Study No. 3, School of Accounting, University of California*.

Ghafur, A. (1976). 'On the nationalised industrial sector controversy: Political economy'. *Journal of Bangladesh Economic Association*, 2(1): 5–10.

Ghazali, N.A.M. and Weetman, P. (2006). 'Perpetuating traditional influence: Voluntary disclosure in Malaysia following the economic crisis'. *Journal of International Accounting, Auditing and Taxation*, 15(2): 226–48.

Gibbs, G. (2008). *Analyzing Qualitative Data*. London: Sage.

Giroux, G. (1989). 'Political interests and governmental accounting disclosure'. *Journal of Accounting and Public Policy*, 8(3): 199–217.

Glaum, M. and Street, D.L. (2003). 'Compliance with the disclosure requirements of Germany's new market: IAS versus US GAAP'. *Journal of International Financial Management and Accounting*, 14(1): 64–100.

Grace, M., Ireland, A. and Dunstan, K. (1995). 'Board composition: Non-executive directors' characteristics and corporate financial performance'. *Asia-Pacific Journal of Accounting*, 2: 121–37.

Graf, W. (1995). 'The state in the third world'. *Socialist Register*, 140–62.

Gray, S.J. (1988). 'Towards a theory of cultural influence on the development of accounting systems internationally'. *Abacus*, 24(1): 1–15.

Grieco, M. and Holmes, L. (1999). 'Tele options for community business: An opportunity for economic growth in Africa'. *Africa Notes* (October): 1–3.

Habermas, J. (1988). 'Law and Morality' (translated by K. Baynes), in McMurrin, S.M. (ed.), *The Tanner Lectures on Human Values*. Salt Lake City: University of Utah Press, 217–79.

Hagigi, M. and Williams, P.A. (1993). 'Accounting, economic and environmental influences on financial reporting practices in third world countries: The case of Morocco'. *Research in Third World Accounting*, 2: 67–84.

Hail, L., Leuz, C. and Wysocki, P. (2010). 'Global accounting convergence and the potential adoption of IFRS by the U.S. (Part II): Political factors and future scenarios for U.S. accounting standards'. *Accounting Horizons*, 24(4): 567–88.

Halim, M.A. (2008). *The Legal System of Bangladesh*. Dhaka: Children's Charity Bangladesh (CCB) Foundation.

Haller, A., Ernstberger, J. and Froschhammer, M. (2009). 'Implications of the mandatory transition from national GAAP to IFRS: – Empirical evidence from Germany'. *Advances in Accounting*, 25(2): 226–36.

Hambrick, D.C. and Mason, P.A. (1984). 'Upper echelons: The organization as a reflection of its top managers'. *Academy of Management Review*, 9(2): 193–206.

Han, S., Kang, T. and Yoo, Y.K. (2012). 'Governance role of auditors and legal environment: Evidence from corporate disclosure transparency'. *European Accounting Review*, 21(1): 29–50.

Haniffa, R.M. and Cooke, T.E. (2002). 'Culture, corporate governance and disclosure in Malaysian corporations'. *Abacus*, 38(3): 317–50.

Hardy, C. (1996). 'Understanding power: Bringing about strategic change'. *British Journal of Management*, 7(1): 3–16.

Harrison, G.L. and McKinnon, J.L. (1986). 'Culture and accounting change: A new perspective on corporate reporting regulation and accounting policy formulation'. *Accounting, Organizations and Society*, 11(3): 233–52.

Hasan, T., Karim, W. and Quayes, S. (2008). 'Regulatory change and the quality of compliance to mandatory disclosure requirements: Evidence from Bangladesh'. *Research in Accounting Regulation*, 20: 193–203.

Hay, C. (1996). 'Marxist theories of the state: Horses for courses?' *Muirhead Working Paper, University of Birmingham, UK*.

Hayes, N. and Walsham, G. (2001). 'Participation in groupware-mediated communities of practice: A socio-political analysis of knowledge working'. *Information and Organization*, 11(4): 263–88.

Healey, M.J. (1991). 'Obtaining information from business', in Healey, M.J. (ed.), *Economic Activity and Land Use*. Harlow: Longman, 193–251.

Henslin, J.M. (1995). 'What is sociology?', in Henslin, J.M. (ed.), *Down to Earth Sociology: Introductory Readings*. New York: The Free Press, 8–18.

Hesse-Biber, S. (2010). 'Qualitative approaches to mixed methods practice'. *Qualitative Inquiry*, 16(6): 455–68.

Hitz, J-M., Ernstberger, J. and Stich, M. (2012). 'Enforcement of accounting standards in Europe: Capital-market-based evidence for the two-tier mechanism in Germany'. *European Accounting Review*, 21(2): 253–81.

Hoarau, C. (1995). 'International accounting harmonisation: American hegemony or mutual recognition with benchmarks?' *European Accounting Review*, 4(2): 217–33.

Hodgdon, C., Tondkar, R.H., Adhikari, A. and Harless, D.W. (2009). 'Compliance with international financial reporting standards and auditor choice: New evidence on the importance of the statutory audit'. *International Journal of Accounting*, 44(1): 33–55.

Hoffman, J. (1995). *Beyond the State*. Cambridge: Polity Press.

Hofstede, G. (1980). *Culture's Consequences: International Differences in Work-Related Values*. Beverly Hills, CA: Sage.

Hofstede, G. (1987). 'The cultural context of accounting', in Cushing, B.E. (ed.), *Accounting and Culture*. New York: American Accounting Association, 1–11.

Hofstede, G. (2001). *Culture's Consequences: Comparing Values, Behaviors, Institutions and Organizations Across Nations*. 2nd edn. Thousand Oaks, CA/London: Sage.

Hofstede, G., Hofstede, G.J. and Minkov, M. (2010). *Cultures and Organizations: Software of the Mind*. 3rd edn. New York: McGraw-Hill.

Holthausen, R.W. (2009). 'Accounting standards, financial reporting outcomes, and enforcement'. *Journal of Accounting Research*, 47(2): 447–58.

Hood, C. (2004). 'Institutions, blame avoidance and negativity bias: Where public management reform meets the blame culture'. *Paper presented at CMPO Conference on Public Organisation and the New Public Management, 19 March, University of Bristol, UK.*

Hood, C. (2007). 'What happens when transparency meets blame-avoidance?' *Public Management Review*, 9(2): 191–210.

Hood, C. (2009). 'Risk management and blame-avoidance: A political science perspective'. *Paper presented at Managing the Social Impacts of Change from a Risk Perspective, SCARR, Beijing Normal University, ESRC, RCUK, University of Kent, 15–17 April.*

Hood, C., Scott, C., James, O., Jones, G.W. and Travers, T. (1999). *Regulation inside Government: Waste-Watchers, Quality Police and Sleaze-Busters*. Oxford: Oxford University Press.

Hoogvelt, A.M.M. and Tinker, A.M. (1978). 'The role of colonial and post-colonial states in imperialism: A case-study of the Sierra Leone development company'. *Journal of Modern African Studies*, 16(1): 67–79.

Hope, O.K. (2003). 'Disclosure practices, enforcement of accounting standards and analysts' forecast accuracy: An international study'. *Journal of Accounting Research*, 41(3): 235–72.

Hope, T. and Gray, R. (1982). 'Power and policy making: The development of an R&D standard'. *Journal of Business Finance and Accounting*, 9(4): 531–58.

Hopper, T. and Major, M. (2007). 'Extending institutional analysis through theoretical triangulation: Regulation and activity-based costing in Portuguese telecommunications'. *European Accounting Review*, 16(1): 59–97.

Hopwood, A.G. (1976). 'Editorial: the path ahead'. *Accounting, Organizations and Society*, 1(1): 1–4.

———. (1990). 'Accounting and organisation change'. *Accounting, Auditing and Accountability Journal*, 3: 7–17.

———. (1994). 'Some reflections on the harmonization of accounting within the EU'. *European Accounting Review*, 3(2): 241–53.

———. (1999). 'Situating the practice of management accounting in its cultural context: An introduction'. *Accounting, Organizations and Society*, 24(5–6): 377–78.

Houqe, M.N., Van Zijl, T., Dunstan, K. and Karim, A.K.M.W. (2012). 'The effect of IFRS adoption and investor protection on earnings quality around the world'. *International Journal of Accounting*, 47(3): 333–55.

Hossain, M.A. (1999). *Disclosure of Financial Information in Developing Countries: A Comparative Study of Non-financial Companies in India, Pakistan and Bangladesh*. Unpublished PhD thesis, University of Manchester, UK.

Hove, M. (1989). 'The inappropriateness of international accounting standards in less developing countries: The case of international accounting standard number 24 related party disclosure concerning transfer prices'. *International Journal of Accounting Education and Research*, 24(2): 81–100.

Hove, M.R. (1986). 'Accounting practices in developing countries: Colonialism's legacy of inappropriate technologies'. *International Journal of Accounting Education and Research*, 22(1): 81–100.

Huque, A.S. (2010). 'Extra-bureaucratic accountability mechanisms and governance in Bangladesh'. *Paper presented at the 14th IRPSM Conference in Berne, Switzerland, 7–9 April.* Available at: http://www.irspm2010.com/workshops/papers/31_extrabureaucratic.pdf [accessed: 12 June 2011].

Hussein, M.E., and Ketz, J.E. (1980). 'Ruling elites of the FASB: A study of the big eight'. *Journal of Accounting and Public Policy*, 10(1): 59–81.

ICAB (1998–99). Annual Report, the Institute of Chartered Accountants of Bangladesh.

ICAB (2010–11). Annual Report, the Institute of Chartered Accountants of Bangladesh.

ICAEW (2008). *Fighting Poverty*. October. Available at: http://www.icaew.com/~/media/Files/About-ICAEW/Newsroom/Accountancy/Features/Accountancy_oct_2008_IFRS_in_Bangladesh.ashx [accessed: 19 May 2010].

IFAD (2006). *A Country Report on Bangladesh*. United Nations, International Fund for Agricultural Development.

Illés, K., Weetman, P., Clarkson, A.H. and Fraser, M. (1996). 'Change and choice in Hungarian accounting practice: An exploratory study of the Accounting Law of 1991'. *European Accounting Review*, 5(3): 523–43.

Imam, O. and Malik, M. (2007). 'Firm performance and corporate governance through ownership structure: Evidence from Bangladesh stock market'. *International Review of Business Research Papers*, 3(4): 88–110.

Inchausti, B. (1997). 'The influence of company characteristics and accounting regulation on information disclosed by Spanish firms'. *European Accounting Review*, 6(1): 45–68.

International Monetary Fund (IMF) (2005). *Bangladesh: Report on the Observance of Standards and Codes – Fiscal Transparency Module: – Update*. IMF Country Report No. 05/328, September.

International Monetary Fund (IMF). (2010) *Bangladesh: Financial System Stability Assessment*. IMF Country Report No. 10/38, February.

Irvine, H. (2008). 'The global institutionalization of financial reporting: The case of the United Arab Emirates'. *Accounting Forum*, 32(2): 125–42.

Jaggi, B. and Low, P.Y. (2000). 'Impact of culture, market forces, and legal system on financial disclosures'. *International Journal of Accounting*, 35(4): 495–519.

Jaggi, B. and Low, P.Y. (2011). 'Joint Effect of investor protection and securities regulations on audit fees'. *International Journal of Accounting*, 46(3): 241–70.

Jaggi, B.L. (1975). 'The impact of the cultural environment on financial disclosures'. *International Journal of Accounting Education and Research*, 11: 75–84.

Jahan, R. (2003). 'Bangladesh in 2002: Imperilled democracy'. *Asian Survey*, 43(1): 222–9.

———. (2005). *Bangladesh Politics: Problems and Issues*. Dhaka: University Press (UPL).

Jalal, A. (1995). *Democracy and Authoritarianism in South Asia*. Cambridge: Cambridge University Press.

Jankowicz, A.D. (2005). *Business Research Projects*. 4th edn. London: Thomson Learning.

Jensen, M.C. and Meckling, W.H. (1976). 'Theory of the firm: Managerial behavior agency costs, and ownership structure'. *Journal of Financial Economics*, 3(4): 305–60.

Jepperson, R. (1991). 'Institutions, institutional effects and institutionalism', in Powell, W. and DiMaggio, P. (eds), *The New Institutionalism in Organizational Analysis*, Chicago: University of Chicago Press, 143–64.

Jessop, B. (1977). 'Recent theories of the capitalist state'. *Cambridge Journal of Economics*, 1(4): 353–73.

———. (1990). 'Regulation theories in retrospect and prospect'. *Economy and Society*, 19(2): 153–216.

Jick, T. (1979). 'Mixing qualitative and quantitative methods: Triangulation in action'. *Administrative Science Quarterly*, 24(4): 602–11.

Jones, C.S. and Sefiane, S. (1992). 'The use of accounting data in operational decision making in Algeria'. *Accounting, Auditing and Accountability Journal*, 5(4): 71–83.

Jones, E. (1981). *Accountancy and the British Economy 1840–1980: The Evolution of Ernst and Whinney*. London: Batsford.

Jones, M.J. (2010). 'Sources of power and infrastructural conditions in medieval governmental accounting'. *Accounting, Organizations and Society*, 35(1): 81–94.

Jonsson, S. (1991). 'Role making for accounting while the state is watching'. *Accounting, Organizations and Society*, 16(5–6): 521–46.

Karampinis, N.I. and Hevas, D.L. (2011). 'Mandating IFRS in an unfavorable environment: The Greek experience'. *International Journal of Accounting*, 46(3): 304–32.

Kaufmann, D., Kraay, A. and Mastruzzi, M. (2010). *The Worldwide Governance Indicators: A Summary of Methodology, Data and Analytical Issues*. World Bank Policy Research Working Paper No. 5430. Available at: http://siteresources.worldbank.org/INTMACRO/Resources/WPS5430.pdf [accessed: 2 January 2011].

Kelly-Newton, L. (1980). 'A sociological investigation of the U.S.A. mandate for replacement cost disclosures'. *Accounting, Organizations and Society*, 5(3): 311–21.

Khan, A.R., Hossain, D.M., and Siddiqui, J. (2011). 'Corporate ownership concentration and audit fees: The case of an emerging economy'. *Advances in Accounting, Incorporating Advances in International Accounting*, 27(1): 125–31.

Khan, M.M. and Husain, S.A. (1996). 'Process of democratization in Bangladesh'. *Contemporary South Asia*, 5(3): 319–34.

Klumpes, P. (1998). 'Competition among pressure groups for political influence over the determination of accounting standards'. *Working Paper No. 1998/013, Lancaster University Management School, UK*. Available at: http://www.lums.lancs.ac.uk/publications/viewpdf/000086/ [accessed: 25 October 2009].

Knowles, S. and Garces, A. (2000). 'Measuring government intervention and estimating its effect on output: With reference to the high performing Asian economies'. *CREDIT Research Paper No. 00/14, Centre for Research in Economic Development and International Trade, University of Nottingham*. Available at: http://www.nottingham.ac.uk/credit/documents/papers/00–14.pdf [accessed: 25 October 2009].

Knox, C. (2009). 'Dealing with sectoral corruption in Bangladesh: Developing citizen involvement'. *Public Administration and Development*, 29(2): 117–32.

Königsgruber, R. (2010). 'A political economy of accounting standard setting'. *Journal of Management and Governance*, 14(4): 277–95.

Kothari, S.P. (2000). 'The role of financial reporting in reducing financial risks in the market', in Rosengren, E.S. and Jordan, J.S. (eds), *Building an Infrastructure for Financial Stability*. Boston, MA: Federal Reserve Bank of Boston, 89–112.

Krzywda, D., Bailey, D. and Schroeder, M. (1995). 'A theory of European accounting development applied to accounting change in contemporary Poland'. *European Accounting Review*, 4(4): 625–57.

Kurunmaki, L., Lapsley, I. and Miller, P. (2011).'Accounting within and beyond the state'. *Management Accounting Research*, 22(1): 1–5.

Kvaal, E. and Nobes, C. (2012). 'IFRS Policy changes and the continuation of national patterns of IFRS practice'. *European Accounting Review*, 21(2): 343–71.

Kvale, S. (1996). *Interviews: An Introduction to Qualitative Interviewing*. London: Sage.

La Porta, R., Lopez-de-Silanes, F., Shleifer, A. and Vishny, R. (1998). 'Law and finance'. *Journal of Political Economy*, 106(6): 1113–55.

La Porta, R., Lopez-de-Silanes, F., Shleifer, A., and Vishny, R.W. (1999). 'Corporate ownership around the world'. *Journal of Finance*, 54(2): 471–518.

Lama, M.D.V., Sánchez, H.M. and Sobrino, J.N.R. (2011). 'Disclosure level and compliance in IFRS and the conception of reliability: An empirical investigation in Spain and the United Kingdom'. *Paper presented at XIII Accounting and Auditing Congress (ACIM), Porto, Portugal, 18–20 May*.

Lange, M.K. (2004). 'British colonial legacies and political development'. *World Development*, 32(6): 905–22.

Larson, R. (1993). 'International accounting standards and economic growth: An empirical investigation of their relationship in Africa'. *Research in Third World Accounting*, 2: 27–43.

Larson, R. and Kenny, S. (1995). 'An empirical analysis of international accounting standards, equity markets, and economic growth in developing countries'. *Journal of International Financial Management and Accounting*, 6(2): 130–57.

Laskar, S.I. (2007). *Bangladesh: Justice in Disarray. Transparency International (TI) Global Corruption Report 2007*. Available at: http://www.ti-bangladesh.org/Documents/Bangladesh%20-%20justice%20in%20disarray.pdf [accessed: 24 October 2009].

Laughlin, R. (2007). 'Critical reflections on research approaches, accounting regulation and the regulation of accounting'. *British Accounting Review*, 39(4): 271–89.

Lederman, D., Loayza, N.V. and Soares, R.R. (2005). 'Accountability and corruption: Political institutions matter'. *Economics and Politics*, 17(3): 1–35.

Lee, G.M. (1997). *Three Articles on the Relevance of Cultural Factors on the Development of National Accounting Systems*. Unpublished PhD thesis, University of Utah, USA.

Lehmbruck, G. and Schmitter, P.C. (1982). *Patterns of Corporatist Policy Making*. London: Sage.

Lessmann, C. and Markwardt, G. (2010). 'One size fits all? Decentralization, corruption, and the monitoring of bureaucrats'. *World Development*, 38(4): 631–46.

Leuz, C. (2010). 'Different approaches to corporate reporting regulation: How jurisdictions differ and why'. *Accounting and Business Research*, 40(3): 229–56.

Leuz, C. and Oberholzer-Gee, F. (2006). 'Political Relationships, global financing, and corporate transparency: Evidence from Indonesia'. *Journal of Financial Economics*, 81(2): 411–39.

Leuz, C. and Wysocki, P. (2008). 'Economic consequences of financial reporting and disclosure regulation: A review and suggestions for future research'. *Working Paper, Massachusetts Institute of Technology*. Available at: http://mit.edu/wysockip/www/papers/LW2008.pdf [accessed: 18 September 2009].

Leuz, C., Nanda, D. and Wysocki, P.D. (2003). 'Earnings management and investor protection: An international comparison'. *Journal of Financial Economics*, 69(3): 505–27.

Leuz, C., Pfaff, D. and Hopwood, A. (2004). *The Economics and Politics of Accounting: International Perspectives on Research, Trends, Policy, and Practice*. Oxford: Oxford University Press.

Lewin, Y.D., Mitrani, Y., Fischer, Y.D. and Hoffman, A. (2010).'Freedom, alienation and identity in Hegel's theory of the modern state'. *Working Paper, Faculty of the Social Sciences Department of Political Science, The Hebrew University of Jerusalem*.

Liguori, M. and Steccolini, I. (2012). 'Accounting change: Explaining the outcomes, interpreting the process'. *Accounting, Auditing and Accountability Journal*, 25(1): 27–70.

Lincoln, Y. and Guba, E. (1989). 'Ethics: The failure of positivist science'. *Review of Higher Education*, 12: 221–40.

Llewellyn, S. (2007). 'Case studies and differentiated realities'. *Qualitative Research in Accounting and Management*, 4: 53–68.

Loft, A. (1994). 'Accountancy and the First World War', in Hopwood, A.G. and Miller, P. (eds), *Accounting as Social and Economic Practice*. Cambridge: Cambridge University Press.

Lopez, J.J. (1998). 'Private investment response to neoliberal reform in a delegative democracy: Reflections on Argentina'. *Quarterly Review of Economics and Finance*, 38(3): 441–57.

Lowe, E.A., Puxty, A.G. and Laughlin, R.C. (1983). 'Simple theories for complex processes: Accounting policy and the market for myopia'. *Journal of Accounting and Public Policy*, 2(1): 19–42.

Mann, M. (1986). *The Sources of Social Power: A History OF Power from the Beginning to A.D. 1760 (Vol. 1)*. Cambridge: Cambridge University Press.

Manzetti, L. (2000). 'Market reforms without transparency', in Tulchin, J.S. and Espach, R.H. (eds), *Combating Corruption in Latin America*. Washington, DC: Woodrow Wilson Center Press, 130–72.

Masel, L. (1983). 'The future of accounting and auditing standards'. *Australian Accountant*, 53(8): 541–49.

Matthieson, T. (1997). 'The viewer society: Michel Foucault's "panopticon" revisited'. *Theoretical Criminology*, 1(2): 215–34.

Maxwell, J.A. and Loomis, D. (2003). 'Mixed methods design: An alternative approach', in Tashakkori, A. and Teddlie, C. (eds), *Handbook of Mixed Methods in Social and Behavioral Research*. Thousand Oaks, CA: Sage.

McGee, R. (1999). 'The problem of implementing international accounting standards: A case study of Armenia'. *Journal of Accounting, Ethics and Public Policy*, 2(1): 38–41.

McKee, A.J., Williams, P.F. and Frasier, K.B. (1991). 'A case study of accounting firm lobbying: Advice or consent'. *Critical Perspectives on Accounting*, 2(2): 273–94.

McKinnon, J.L. (1984). *The Historical Development and Operational Form of Corporate Reporting Regulation in Japan*. Unpublished PhD thesis, Macquarie University. Australia.

McKinnon, J.L. and Harrison, G.L. (1985).'Cultural influence on corporate and governmental involvement in accounting policy determination in Japan'. *Journal of Accounting and Public Policy*, 4(3): 201–23.

McLeay, S., Ordelheide, D. and Young, S. (2000). 'Constituent lobbying and its impact on the development of financial reporting regulations: Evidence from Germany'. *Accounting, Organizations and Society*, 25(1): 79–98.

Meckling, W.H. (1976). 'Values and the choice of the model of the individual in the social sciences'. *Swiss Journal of Economics and Statistics*, 112(4): 545–60.

Merchant, K.A., Chow, C.W. and Wu, A. (1995). 'Measurement, evaluation, and reward of profit center managers: A cross-cultural field study'. *Accounting, Organizations and Society*, 20(7/8): 619–38.

Merryman, J.H. (1985). *The Civil Law Tradition*. Stanford, CA: Stanford University Press.

Mezias, S.J. (1990). 'An institutional model of organizational practice: Financial reporting at the Fortune 200'. *Administrative Science Quarterly*, 35(3): 431–57.

Miles, M.B. and Huberman, A.M. (1994). *Qualitative Data Analysis*.2nd edn. Thousand Oaks, CA: Sage.

Miliband, R. (1969). *The State in Capitalist Society*. New York: Basic Books.

Miller, M.C. (1996). 'Accounting regulation and the roles assumed by the government and the accounting profession: The case of Australia'. *Paper presented at the 19th Annual Congress of the European Accounting Association NHH, Bergen, Norway, 2–4 May*.

Miller, P. (1986). 'Accounting for progress – national accounting and planning in France: A review essay'. *Accounting, Organizations and Society*, 11(1): 83–104.

Miller, P. (1990). 'On the interrelations between accounting and the state'. *Accounting, Organizations and Society*, 15(4): 315–38.

Miller, P. (1994). 'Accounting as social and institutional practice: an introduction', in Hopwood, A.G. and Miller, P. (eds), *Accounting as Social and Institutional Practice*. Cambridge: Cambridge University Press, 1–39.

Miller, P. and Redding, R. (1988). *The FASB: The People, the Process, and the Politics*. Homewood, IL: Irwin.

Ministry of Law, Justice and Parliamentary Affairs, Bangladesh. Available at: http://www.minlaw.gov. bd/ [accessed: 12 February 2012].

Mintzberg, H. (1983). *Power in and Around Organization*. Englewood Cliffs, NJ: Prentice Hall.

Mir, M.Z. and Rahaman, A.S. (2005). 'The adoption of international accounting standards in Bangladesh: An exploration of rationale and process'. *Accounting, Auditing and Accountability Journal*, 18(6): 816–41.

Miranti, P. (1986). 'Associationism, statism and professionalization regulation: Public accountants and the reform of the financial markets, 1896–1940'. *Business History Review*, 60(3): 438–69.

Mitnick, B.M. (1980). *The Political Economy of Regulation: Creating, Designing, and Removing Regulatory Forms*. New York: Columbia University Press.

Mitton, T. (2002). 'A cross-firm analysis of the impact of corporate governance on the East Asian financial crisis'. *Journal of Financial Economics*, 64(2): 215–41.

Modell, S. (2005). 'Triangulation between case study and survey methods in management accounting research: An assessment of validity implications'. *Management Accounting Research*, 16(2): 231–54.

Modell, S. (2010). 'Bridging the paradigm divide in management accounting research: The role of mixed methods approaches'. *Management Accounting Research*, 21(2): 124–9.

Mollah, M.A.H. (2008). 'Judiciary and good governance in Bangladesh'. *South Asian Survey*, 15(2): 245–62.

Mommsen, W. (1987). 'Personal conduct and societal change', in Whimster. S. and Lash. S. (eds), *Max Weber, Rationality and Modernity*, London: Allen & Unwin, 35–51.

Moonitz, M. (1974). *Obtaining Agreement on Standards: Studies in Accounting*. Sarasota, FL: American Accounting Association.

Moran, M. (2002). 'Understanding the regulatory state'. *British Journal of Political Science*, 32(2): 391–413.

———. (2010). 'The political economy of regulation: Does it have any lessons for accounting research?' *Accounting and Business Research*, 40(3): 215–25.

Mueller, G.G. (1967). *International Accounting*. New York: Macmillan.

Murphy, A. (1999). 'Firm characteristics of Swiss companies that utilize international accounting standards'. *International Journal of Accounting*, 34(1): 121–31.

Myers, M.D. and Newman, M. (2007). 'The qualitative interview in IS research: Examining the craft'. *Information and Organization*, 17: 2–26.

Naciri, A. and Hoarau, C. (2001). 'A comparative analysis of American and French financial reporting philosophies: The case for international accounting standards'. *Advances in International Accounting*, 14: 229–47.

Nair, R.D. (1982). Empirical guidelines for comparing international accounting data. *Journal of International Business Studies*, 13: 85–98.

Nair, R.D. and Frank, W.G. (1980). 'The impact of disclosure and measurement practices on international accounting classifications'. *The Accounting Review*, 55(3): 426–50.

———. (1981). 'The harmonization of international accounting standards 1973–1979'.*International Journal of Accounting Education and Research*, 17(1): 61–77.

Napier, C. and Noke, C. (1992). 'Accounting and the law: An historical overview of an uneasy relationship', in Bromwich, M. and Hopwood, A.G. (eds), *Accounting and the Law*. London: Prentice Hall.

Napier, C.J. (2006). 'Accounts of change: 30 years of historical accounting research'. *Accounting, Organizations and Society*, 31(4/5): 465–507.

Narayanaswamy, R. (1996). 'Voluntary US GAAP disclosure in India: The case of Infosys Technology Limited'. *Journal of International Financial Management and Accounting*, 7(2): 137–66.

Needles, B.E. Jr. (1976). 'Implementing a framework for the international transfer of accounting technology'. *International Journal of Accounting Education and Research*, 12(1): 45–62.

Neu, D., Gomez, E.O., Graham, C. and Heincke, M. (2006).'Informing technologies and the World Bank'. *Accounting, Organizations and Society*, 31(7): 635–62.

Neuman, W. (2000). *Social Research Methods: Qualitative and Quantitative Approaches*. Boston, MA: Allyn and Bacon.

Newman, D.P. (1981). 'An investigation into the distribution of power in the APB and FASB'. *Journal of Accounting Research*, 19(1): 247–62.

Nobes, C. (1984). *International Classification of Financial Reporting*. London: Croom Helm.

———. (1998). 'Towards a General model of the reasons for international differences in financial reporting'. *Abacus*, 34(2): 162–87.

Nobes, C.W. and Zeff, S.A. (2008). 'Auditors' affirmations of compliance with IFRS around the world: An exploratory study'. *Accounting Perspectives/Perspectives Comptables*, 7(4): 279–92.

North, D. (1990). *Institutions, Institutional Change and Economic Performance*. Cambridge: Cambridge University Press.

Norton, S.D. (2012). 'Judicial interpretation of the will of the state: A Hegelian perspective in the context of taxation'. *Critical Perspectives on Accounting*, 23(2): 117–33.

O'Neill, O. (2002). *A Question of Trust (The 2002 Reith Lectures)*. Cambridge: Cambridge University Press.

Oehr, T. and Zimmermann, J. (2012). 'Accounting and the welfare state: The missing link' *Critical Perspectives on Accounting*, 23(2): 134–52.

Omar, B. and Simon, J. (2011). 'Corporate aggregate disclosure practices in Jordan'. *Advances in Accounting, Incorporating Advances in International Accounting*, 27(1): 166–86.

Ordelheide, D. (2004). 'The politics of accounting: A framework', in Leuz, C., Pfaff, D. and Hopwood, A. (eds), *The Economics and Politics of Accounting*. Oxford: Oxford University Press, 269–85.

Organisation for Economic Co-operation and Development (OECD) (2001). *Citizens as Partners: OECD Handbook on Information, Consultation and Public Participation in Policy-Making*. Paris: OECD.

Ostrom, E. (1990). *Governing the Commons: The Evolution of Institutions for Collective Action*. New York: Cambridge University Press.

Oxford Economics (2008). *Bangladesh: Country Briefing*. Oxford: ABI/Inform Global/Oxford University.

Panday, P.K. and Mollah, M.A.H. (2011). 'The judicial system of Bangladesh: An overview from historical viewpoint'. *International Journal of Law and Management*, 53(1): 6–31.

Parker, R.H. (1986).'Accounting standards and the law: An Australian experiment'. *Working Paper No. 18, University of Sydney Accounting Research Centre*.

Parker, R.H and Nobes, C.W. (1994). *An International View of True and Fair Accounting*. London: Routledge.

Parkinson, J.M. (1984). '"Economic, political, and civil indicators and reporting and disclosure adequacy: Empirical investigation": A Comment'. *Journal of Accounting and Public Policy*, 3(3): 239–48.

Parry, M.J. (1989). *The Role of Accounting in the Economic Development of Bangladesh*. Unpublished PhD thesis, University of Wales.

Parry, M.J. and Groves, R.E. (1990). 'Does training more accountants raise the standard of accounting in third world countries?' *Research in Third World Accounting*,1: 3–54.

Patton, M.Q. (1999). 'Enhancing the quality and credibility of qualitative analysis'. *Health Services Research*, 34(5 Pt 2): 1189–208.

Patton, M.Q. (2001). *Qualitative Research and Evaluation Methods*. 2nd edn. Thousand Oaks, CA: Sage.

Peltzman, S. (1976). 'Towards a more general theory of regulation'. *Journal of Law and Economics*, 19(2): 211–40.

Peng, S. and Bewley, K. (2009). 'Adaptability of fair value accounting in China: Assessment of an emerging economy converging with IFRS'. *Paper presented at the CAAA Annual Conference, August*. Available at: http://ssrn.com/abstract=1326004 [accessed: 17 January 2010].

Perera, H. (1989). 'Towards a framework to analyse the impact of culture on accounting'. *International Journal of Accounting*, 24: 42–56.

Perera, H., Cummings, L. and Chua, F. (2012). 'Cultural relativity of accounting professionalism: Evidence from New Zealand and Samoa'. *Advances in Accounting*, 28(1): 138–46.

Perera, M.H.B. (1975). 'Accounting and its environment in Sri Lanka'. *Abacus*, 11(1): 85–96.

———. (1985). 'The relevance of international accounting standards to developing countries'. *Working Paper 85–8, School of Financial Studies, University of Glasgow, UK*.

Perry, J. and Nölke, A. (2006). 'The political economy of international accounting standards'. *Review of International Political Economy*, 13(4): 559–86.

Pettigrew, A. (1973). *The Politics of Organizational Decision Making*. London: Tavistock Publications.

———. (1990). 'Longitudinal field research on change: theory and practice'. *Organizational Science*, 1(3): 267–92.

Pettigrew, A. and McNulty, T. (1995). 'Power and influence in and around the boardroom'. *Human Relations*, 48(8): 845–73.

Pfeffer, J. (1981). *Power in Organizations*. Cambridge, MA: Ballinger.

Points, R. and Cunningham, R. (1998). 'The application of international accounting standards in transitional societies and developing countries'. *Advances in International Accounting*, 1(Supplement): 3–16.

Posner, R.A. (1974). 'Theories of economic regulation'. *Bell Journal of Economics and Management Science*, 5(2): 335–58.

Poulantzas, N. (1975). *Classes in Contemporary Capitalism*. London: New Left Books.

———. (1978). *State, Power, Socialism*. London: Verso.

Power, M.K. (1997). *The Audit Society: Rituals of Verification*. Oxford: Oxford University Press.

Previts, G. and Merino, B. (1998). *A History of Accountancy In the United States: The cultural Significance of Accounting*. Columbus: Ohio State University Press.

Previts, G.J. (1975). 'On the subject of methodology and models for international accountancy'. *International Journal of Accounting Education and Research*, 18(2): 1-12.

Pushkin, A.B. and Pariser, D.B. (1991). 'Political and economic forces shaping regulatory accounting for troubled debt restructuring'. *Critical Perspectives on Accounting*, 2(2): 127–43.

Puxty, A.G., Willmott, H.C., Cooper, D.J. and Lowe, T. (1987). 'Modes of regulation in advanced capitalism: Locating accountancy in four countries'. *Accounting, Organizations and Society*, 12(3): 273–91.

Radebaugh, L.H. (1975). 'Environmental factors influencing the development of accounting objectives, standards and practices in Peru'. *International Journal of Accounting Education and Research*, 11: 39–56.

Rahaman, A. (1997). *Public Sector Accounting and Financial Management in the Context of a Developing Country: An Empirical Study of the VRA in Ghana*. Unpublished PhD thesis, University of Waikato, New Zealand.

Rahman, M.Z. (2000). 'Accounting standards in the East Asia region'. *Paper presented at the Second Asian Roundtable on Corporate Governance on the role of disclosure in strengthening corporate governance and accountability, 31 May–2 June, Hong Kong, OECD and World Bank*.

Rajan, R. and Zingales, L. (2000). 'The great reversals: The politics of financial development in the 20th century'. *Unpublished Working Paper, University of Chicago*.

Ramanna, K. (2008). 'The implications of fair-value accounting: Evidence from the political economy of goodwill accounting'. *Journal of Accounting and Economics*, 45(2–3): 253–81.

Reischauer, E.O. (1977). *The Japanese*. Cambridge MA: Harvard University Press.

Riaz, A. (2006). 'Bangladesh in 2005: Standing at a crossroads'. *Asian Survey*, 46(1): 107–13.

Richardson, A.J. (1987). 'Accounting as a legitimating institution'. *Accounting, Organizations and Society*, 12(4): 341–55.

Risse, T. (2004).'Global governance and communicative action'. *Government and Opposition*. 39(2): 288–313.

Roberts, R.W. and Kurtenbach, J.M. (1998). 'State regulation and professional accounting education reforms: An empirical test of regulatory capture theory'. *Journal of Accounting and Public Policy*, 17(3): 209–26.

Robertson, R. (1990). 'Mapping the global condition: Globalization as the central concept'. *Theory, Culture and Society*, 7(2): 15–30.

Rock, M.T. and Bonnett, H. (2004). 'The comparative politics of corruption: Accounting for the East Asian paradox in empirical studies of corruption, growth and investment'. *World Development*, 32(6): 999–1017.

Rollins, T.P. and Bremser, W.G. (1997). 'The SEC's enforcement actions against auditors: An auditor reputation and institutional theory perspective'. *Critical Perspective on Accounting*, 8(3): 191–206.

Rose, N. (1991). 'Governing by numbers: Figuring out democracy'. *Accounting, Organizations and Society*, 16(7): 673–92.

Rose, N. and Miller, P. (1992). 'Political power beyond the state: Problematics of government'. *British Journal of Sociology*, 43(2): 173–205.

Rose, N. and Miller, P. (2010). 'Political power beyond the state: Problematics of government'. *British Journal of Sociology*, 61(s1): 271–303. Special issue: 'The BJS: Shaping sociology over 60 years'.

Rosser, A. (2003). 'Globalisation, international norms, and the politics of accounting reform in Indonesia', in Underhill, G. and Zhang, X. (eds), *What Is to Be Done? Global Economic Disorder and Policies for a New International Financial Architecture*. Cambridge: Cambridge University Press.

Ryan, B., Scapens, R.W. and Theobald, M. (2002). *Research Method and Methodology in Finance and Accounting*. 2nd edn. London: Thomson.

Ryan, C., Dunstan, K. and Stanley, T. (1999). 'Constituent participation in the Australian public sector accounting standard-setting process: The case of ED 55'. *Financial Accountability and Management*, 15(2): 173–200.

Samuel, S. and Manassian, A. (2011). 'The rise and coming fall of international accounting research'. *Critical Perspectives on Accounting*, 22(6): 608–27.

Samuels, J.M. and Oliga, J.C. (1982). 'Accounting standards in developing countries'. *International Journal of Accounting Education and Research*, 18(1): 69–88.

Sandbrook, R. (1993). *The Politics of Africa's Recovery*. Cambridge: Cambridge University Press.

Sandholtz, W. and Koetzle, W. (2000). 'Accounting for corruption: Economic structure, democracy, and trade'. *International Studies Quarterly*, 44(1): 31–50.

Saudagaran, S.M. (2009). *International Accounting: A User Perspective*. Chicago: CCH.

Saudagaran, S.M. and Diga, J.G. (1997). 'Accounting regulation in ASEAN: A choice between the global and regional paradigms of harmonization'. *Journal of International Financial Management and Accounting*, 8(1): 1–32.

Saudagaran, S.M. and Diga, J.G. (1998). 'Post colonial accountancy regulation in ASEAN: accounting ideology in an international context'. *Working Paper, Santa Clara University, USA*.

Saudagaran, S.M. and Diga, J.G. (2000). 'The institutional environment of financial reporting regulation in ASEAN'. *International Journal of Accounting*, 35(1): 1–26.

Sayer, A. (2004). 'Foreword: Why critical realism?', in Fleetwood, S. and Ackroyd, S. (eds), *Critical Realist Applications in Organisation and Management Studies*. London: Routledge.

Scapens, R.W. (1994). 'Never mind the gap: Towards an institutional perspective on management accounting practices'. *Management Accounting Research*, 5(3/4): 301–21.

Schipper, K. (2005). 'The introduction of international accounting standards in Europe: Implications for international convergence'. *European Accounting Review*, 14(1): 101–26.

Schneider, B.R. (2002). 'Why is Mexican business so organized?' *Latin American Research Review*, 37(1): 77–118.

Scott, W. (1987). 'The adolescence of institutional theory'. *Administrative Science Quarterly*, 32(4): 493–511.

Securities and Exchange Commission (SEC) (2004–05). Annual Report, Bangladesh.

Seidler, L.J. (1969). 'Nationalism and international transfer of accounting skills'. *International Journal of Accounting Education and Research*, 5: 35–46.

Shleifer, A. and Vishny, R.W. (1993). 'Corruption'. *Quarterly Journal of Economics*, 108(3): 599–617.

Siddiqui, J. (2010). 'Development of corporate governance regulations: The case of an emerging economy'. *Journal of Business Ethics*, 91(2): 253–74.

Simon, W.H. (1983). 'Legality, bureaucracy, and class in the welfare system'. *Yale Law Journal*, 92(7):1198–269.

Skocpol, T. (1985). 'Bringing the state back in: Strategies of analysis in current research', in Evans, P.B., Rueschemeyer, D. and Skocpol, T. (eds), *Bringing the State Back In*. Cambridge: Cambridge University Press,3–37.

Smith, M.A. (2000). *American Business and Political Power*. Chicago: University of Chicago Press.

Sobhan, F. and Werner, W. (2003). *A Comparative Analysis of Corporate Governance in South Asia: Charting a Roadmap for Bangladesh*. Dhaka: Bangladesh Enterprise Institute.

Solaiman, S.M. (2006). 'Recent reforms and the development of the securities market in Bangladesh'. *Journal of Asian and African Studies*, 41(3): 195–228.

Solomons, D. (1978). 'The politicization of accounting'. *Journal of Accountancy*, 146(5): 65–72.

Stigler, G.J. (1971). 'The theory of economic regulation'. *Bell Journal of Economics*, 2(1): 3–21.

Stiglitz, J.E. (1993). *The Role of the State in Financial Markets*. Washington, DC: World Bank.

Stoddart, E.K. (2000). 'Political influences in changes to setting Australian accounting standards'. *Critical Perspectives on Accounting*, 11(6): 713–40.

Streeck, W. and Schmitter, P.C. (1985). 'Community, market, state – and associations? The prospective contribution of interest governance to social order'. *European Sociological Review*, 1(2): 119–38.

Street, D.L. (2002). 'Large firms envision worldwide convergence of standards'. *Accounting Horizons*, 16(3): 215–18.

Street, D.L. and Bryant, S.M. (2000). 'Disclosure level and compliance with IASs: A comparison of companies with and without US listings and filings'. *International Journal of Accounting*, 35(3): 305–29.

Street, D.L., Gray, S.J. and Bryant, S.M. (1999). 'Acceptance and observance of international accounting standards: An empirical study of companies claiming to comply with IASs'. *International Journal of Accounting*, 34(1): 11–48.

Street, D.L., Nichols, N. and Gray, S.J. (2000). 'Assessing the acceptability of international accounting standards: An empirical study of the materiality of US GAAP reconciliations by non-US companies complying with IASC standards'. *International Journal of Accounting*, 35(1): 27–63.

Stulz, R.M. and Williamson, R. (2003). Culture, openness, and finance. *Journal of Financial Economics*, 70(3): 313–49.

Sudarwan, M. and Fogarty, T.J. (1996). 'Culture and accounting in Indonesia: An empirical examination'. *International Journal of Accounting*, 31(4): 463–81.

Sunder, S. (1988). 'Political economy of accounting standards'. *Journal of Accounting Literature*, 7: 31–41.

———. (2002). 'Regulatory competition among accounting standards within and across international boundaries'. *Journal of Accounting and Public Policy*, 21(3): 219–34.

———. (2005). 'Minding our manners: Accounting as social norm'. *British Accounting Review*, 37(4): 367–87.

Sunder, S. (2010). 'Adverse effects of uniform written reporting standards on accounting practice, education, and research'. *Journal of Accounting and Public Policy*, 29(2): 99–114.

Sutton, T.G. (1984). 'Lobbying of accounting standard-setting bodies in the U.K. and the U.S.A.: A Downsian analysis'. *Accounting, Organizations and Society*, 9(1): 81–95.

Swidler, A. (986). 'Culture in action: Symbols and strategies'. *American Sociological Review*, 51(2): 273–86.

Taplin, R., Tower, G. and Hancock, P. (2002). 'Disclosure (discernibility) and compliance of accounting policies: Asia-Pacific evidence'. *Accounting Forum*, 26(2): 172–90.

Tarrow, S. (2004). 'Bridging the quantitative–qualitative divide', in Brady, H.E. and Collier, D. (eds), *Rethinking Social Inquiry: Diverse Tools, Shared Standards*. Lanham, MD: Rowman &Littlefield, 21–50.

Taylor, C. (1975). *Hegel*. Cambridge: Cambridge University Press.

Taylor, P. and Turley, S. (1986). *The Regulation of Accounting*. Oxford: Blackwell.

Tilly, C. (1973). 'Reflections on the history of European state-making', in Tilly, C. (ed.), *The Formation of National States in Western Europe*. Princeton: Princeton University Press, 3–83.

Tinker, A.M. (1980). 'Towards a political economy of accounting: An empirical illustration of the Cambridge controversies'. *Accounting, Organizations and Society*, 5(1): 147–60.

Tinker, A.M. (1984). 'Theories of the state and the state of accounting: Economic reductionism and political voluntarism in accounting regulation theory'. *Journal of Accounting and Public Policy*, 3(1): 55–74.

Tower, G.D. (1993). 'A public accountability model of accounting regulation'. *British Accounting Review*, 25(1): 1–25.

Transparency International Bangladesh (TIB) (2005). *Corruption Perceptions Index 2005*. Available at: http://www.transparency.org/policy_and_research/surveys_indices/cpi/2005 [accessed: 12 June 2010].

———. (2007). *Global Corruption Report*. Dhaka: TIB.

Trott, E. (2009). 'Keep politics out of accounting standards: Advice for the Financial Crisis Advisory Group'. *CPA Journal*, May: 19–20.

Tsalavoutas, I. (2009). *The Adoption of IFRS by Greek Listed Companies: Financial Statement Effects, Level of Compliance and Value Relevance*. Unpublished PhD thesis, University of Edinburgh Business School, UK.

Tsalavoutas, I. (2011). 'Transition to IFRS and compliance with mandatory disclosures: What is the signal?' *Advances in Accounting, Incorporating Advances in International Accounting*, 27(2): 390–405.

Tweedie, D. (2007). 'The European Parliament, before the Economic and Monetary Affairs Committee of the European Parliament', 10 April 2007.Available at: http://www.ifrs.org/news/iasb+chairman+addresses+european+parliament.htm [accessed: 12 April 2010].

Tyrrall, D., Woodward, D. and Rakhimbekova, A. (2007). 'The relevance of international financial reporting standards to a developing country: Evidence from Kazakhstan'. *International Journal of Accounting*, 42(1): 82–110.

Uddin, S. and Choudhury, J. (2008). 'Rationality, traditionalism and the state of corporate governance mechanisms: Illustrations from a less-developed country'. *Accounting, Auditing and Accountability Journal*, 21(7): 1026–51.

Uddin, S. and Hopper, T. (2001). 'A Bangladesh soap opera: Privatisation, accounting, and regimes of control in a less developed country'. *Accounting, Organizations and Society*, 26(7–8): 643–72.

Uddin, S. and Hopper, T. (2003).'Accounting for privatisation in Bangladesh: Testing World Bank claims'. *Critical Perspectives on Accounting*, 14(7): 739–74.

UNCTAD (2008). *World Investment Report 2008*. Available at:http://www.unctad.org/Templates/webflyer.asp?docid=10502&intItemID=2068&lang=1 [accessed: 7 January 2009].

UNFPA (2008). *About Bangladesh*. Available at: http://www.unfpa-bangladesh.org/php/about_bangladesh.php [accessed: 7 January 2009].

Uphoff, N. (1989). 'Authority and legitimacy: Taking Max Weber at his word by using resources-exchange analysis'. *Polity*, 22(2): 295–322.

Var, T. (1976). 'The current accounting education and practice in Turkey'. *International Accountant*, 4: 8–12.

Verma, S. and Gray, S.J. (2009). 'The development of company law in India: The case of the Companies Act 1956'. *Critical Perspectives on Accounting*, 20(1): 110–35.

Wagenhofer, A. (2011). 'Towards a theory of accounting regulation: A discussion of the politics of disclosure regulation along the economic cycle'. *Journal of Accounting and Economics*, 52(2–3): 228–34.

Walker, R.G. (1985). 'The ASRB: Policy formation, political activity and "research"'. *Paper presented at the Accounting and Finance Association of Australia and New Zealand Annual Conference (AFAANZ), 17–20 August, Sydney*.

Walker, R.G. (1987). 'Australia's ASRB: A case study of political activity and regulatory "capture"', *Accounting and Business Research*, 17(67): 269–286.

———. (1990). 'Reforms: Some fundamental flaws'. *Australian Accountant*, 50 (10): 16–19.

———. (1992). 'Interactions between government and the profession in the regulation of financial reporting: The Australian experience', in Bromwich, M. and Hopwood, A.G. (eds), *Accounting and the Law*. London: Prentice Hall.

Walker, R.G. and Robinson, P. (1993). 'A critical assessment of the literature on political activity and accounting regulation'. *Research in Accounting Regulation*, 7: 3–40.

Wallace, R.S.O. (1988). Corporate financial reporting in Nigeria. *Accounting and Business Research*, 18 (72): 352–62.

———. (1993). 'Development of accounting standards for developing and newly industrialised countries'. *Research in Third World Accounting*, 2: 121–65.

Wallace, R.S.O. and Briston, R.J. (1993).'Improving the accounting infrastructure in developing countries'. *Research in Third World Accounting*, 2: 201–24.

Walton, P. (2009). *French Politicians Want More Control of Standards*. ESSEC Business School, France. Available at: http://www.essec-kpmg.net/us/docs/observatory/other-matters/French-politicians-want-more-control.pdf [accessed: 9 January 2010].

Wang, Q., Wong, T.J. and Xia, L. (2008). 'State ownership, the institutional environment, and auditor choice: Evidence from China'. *Journal of Accounting and Economics*, 46(1): 112–34.

Watts, R.L. (1977). 'Corporate financial statements: A product of market and political processes'. *Australian Journal of Management*, 2(1): 53–75.

———. (1980). 'Beauty is in the eye of the beholder: A comment on John C. Burton's "The SEC and Financial Reporting: The Sand in the Oyster"', in Abdel-Khalik, R.A. (ed.), *Government Regulation of Accounting and Information*. Gainesville: University Presses of Florida, 96–103.

Watts, R.L. and Zimmerman, J.L. (1978).' Towards a positive theory of the determination of accounting standards'. *The Accounting Review*, 53(1): 112–37.

———. (1986). *Positive Accounting Theory*. Englewood Cliffs, NJ: Prentice Hall.

———. (1990). 'Positive accounting theory: A ten year perspective'. *The Accounting Review*, 65(1): 131–56.

Weber, M. (1958) [original publication 1904].*The Protestant Ethic and the Spirit of Capitalism*. English translation by Parsons, T. in Tawney, R.H. (ed.). New York: Scribner's Sons.

Weber, M. (1961) [original publication 1927].*General Economic History*. English translation by Knight, F.H. New York: Collier Books.

Weber, M. (1968) [original publication 1922]. *Economy and Society: An Outline of Interpretive Sociology (Vols1–3)*. English translation by Fischoff, E. in Roth, G. And Wittich, C. (eds). New York: Bedminster Press.

Wengraf, T. (2006). *Qualitative Research Interviewing*. London: Sage.

Weyland, K. (1998). 'The politics of corruption in Latin America'. *Journal of Democracy*, 9(2): 108–21.

Whitehead, L. (1989). 'On presidential graft: The Latin American evidence', in Heidenheimer, A.J., Johnston, M. and LeVine, V. (eds), *Political Corruption: A Handbook*. New Brunswick, NJ: Transaction Publishers, 781–800.

———. (2000). 'High-level political corruption in Latin America: a transitional phenomenon', in Tulchin, J.S. and Espach, R.H. (eds), *Combating Corruption in Latin America*. Washington, DC: Woodrow Wilson Center Press, 107–29.

Whittington, G. (2005). 'The adoption of international accounting standards in the European Union'. *European Accounting Review*, 14(1): 127–53.

Wickramasinghe, D. and Hopper, T. (2005). 'A cultural political economy of management accounting controls: A case study of a textile mill in a traditional Sinhalese village'. *Critical Perspectives on Accounting*, 16(4): 473–503.

Wijewardena, H. and Yapa, S. (1998). 'Colonialism of accounting education in developing countries: The experiences of Singapore and Sri Lanka'. *International Journal of Accounting*, 33(2): 269–81.

Wilkinson, T.L. (1965). 'United States accounting as viewed by accountants of other countries'. *International Journal of Accounting Education and Research*, 1(1): 3–14.

Williamson, O. (1985). *The Economic Institutions of Capitalism*. New York: The Free Press.

Williamson, D.L. (2011). 'Interpreter-facilitated cross-language interviews: A research note'. *Qualitative Research*, 11(4): 381–94.

Willmott, H.C., Puxty, A.G., Robson, K., Cooper, D.J. and Lowe, E.A. (1992). 'Regulation of accountancy and accountants: A comparative analysis of accounting for research and development in four advanced capitalist countries'. *Accounting, Auditing and Accountability Journal*, 5(2): 32–56.

Wolk, H.I., Francis, J.R. and Tearney, M.G. (1989). *Accounting Theory: A Conceptual and Institutional Approach*. Boston, MA: Kent Publishing.

World Bank. (1997). *The State in a Changing World: World Development Report*. Washington, DC: World Bank.

———. (2000). *ROSC: Review of Accounting and Auditing Practices*. Available at: http://www.imf.org/external/np/rosc/2000/stand.htm [accessed: 4 December 2009].

———. (2003). *Bangladesh: Report on the Observance of Standards and Codes: Accounting Auditing*. World Bank Country Report No. 35016, May 16. Available at: http://www.worldbank.org/ifa/rosc_aa_bgd.pdf [accessed: 4 December 2009].

———. (2009). *Report on the Observance of Standards and Codes: Corporate Governance Country Assessment: Bangladesh*. World Bank Country Report No. 62534. Available at: http://www.worldbank.org/ifa/rosc_cg_bgd09.pdf [accessed: 11 January 2010].

———. (2010). *Bangladesh: Country Assistance Strategy (FY 2011–2014)*. Available at: http://siteresources.worldbank.org/BANGLADESHEXTN/Resources/295759–1271081222839/6958908–1284576442742/BDCASFinal.pdf [accessed: 2 January 2011].

———. (2011). *Economic Policy and External Debt Data*. Available at: http://data.worldbank.org/topic/economic-policy-and-external-debt[accessed: 4 January 2012].

World Bank's Governance Indicators Data (2010). *The Worldwide Governance Indicators: A Summary of Methodology, Data and Analytical Issues*. World Bank Policy Research Working Paper No.5430. Available at: http://info.worldbank.org/governance/wgi/pdf/wgidataset.xls [accessed: 2 January 2011].

World Bank Newsletter (2009). 'Developing accounting and auditing profession in Bangladesh', *Bangladesh*. 29October.

Wrate, R.M., Rooney, A.C., Thomas, P.F. and Cox, J.L. (1985). 'Postnatal depression and child development. *British Journal of Psychiatry*, 146: 622–7.

Wu, X. (2005). 'Firm accounting practices, accounting reforms and corruption in Asia'. *Policy and Society*, 24(3): 53–78.

———. (2009). 'Determinants of bribery in Asia: Evidence from business environment survey'. *Journal of Business Ethics*, 87(1): 75–88.

Wu, W., Wu, C., Zhou, C. and Wu, J. (2012). 'Political connections, tax benefits and firm performance: Evidence from China'. *Journal of Accounting and Public Policy*, 31(3): 277–300.

Xiao, J.Z., Weetman, P. and Sun, M. (2004). 'Political influence and coexistence of a uniform accounting system and accounting standards: Recent developments in China'. *Abacus*, 40(2): 193–218.

Yeoh, J. (2005). 'Compliance with mandatory disclosure requirements by New Zealand listed companies'. *Advances in International Accounting*, 18: 245–62.

Yin, R. (2003). *Case Study Research: Design and Methods*. Thousand Oaks, CA: Sage.

Young, S.D. (1991). 'Interest group politics and the licensing of public accountants'. *The Accounting Review*, 66(4): 809–17.

Yunus, H. (1988). 'History of accounting in developing nations: The case of Indonesia'. *Working Paper, University of Birmingham, UK*.

Zafarullah, H. (1999). 'Consolidating democratic governance: One step forward, two steps back', in Alauddin, M. and Hasan, S. (eds), *Development, Governance and the Environment in South Asia: A Focus on Bangladesh*. London: Macmillan, 185–92.

Zafarullah, H. and Akhter, M.Y. (2000). 'Non-political caretaker administrations and democratic elections in Bangladesh: An assessment'. *Government and Opposition*, 35(3): 345–69.

Zarzeski, M.T. (1996). 'Spontaneous harmonization effects of culture and market forces on accounting disclosure practices'. *Accounting Horizons*, 10(1): 18–37.

Zeff, S.A. (1972). *Forging Accounting Principles in Five Countries: A History and an Analysis of Trends*. Champaign, IL: Stipes Publishing.

———. (1978). 'The rise of economic consequences'. *Journal of Accountancy*, 146(6): 58–63.

———. (1988). 'Setting accounting standards: Some lessons from the US experience'. *Accountant's Magazine*, 92 (1): 20–2.

———. (1993). 'The politics of accounting standards'. *Economia Aziendale*, August: 123–42.

———. (1995). 'A perspective on the U.S. public/private-sector approach to the regulation of financial reporting. *Accounting Horizons*, 9(1): 52–70.

———. (2002). 'Political lobbying on proposed standards: A challenge to the IASB'. *Accounting Horizons*, 16(1): 43–54.

———. (2006). 'Political lobbying on accounting standards: National and international experience', in Nobes, C. and Parker, R. (eds), *Comparative International Accounting*. London: Prentice Hall.

———. (2007). 'Some obstacles to global financial reporting comparability and convergence at a high level of quality'. *British Accounting Review*, 39(4): 290–302.

———. (2012). 'The evolution of the IASC into the IASB, and the challenges it faces'. *The Accounting Review*, 87(3): 807–37.

Zeghal, D. and Mhedhbi, K. (2006). 'An analysis of the factors affecting the adoption of international accounting standards by developing countries'. *International Journal of Accounting*, 41(4): 373–86.

Zimmerman, A. (1998). 'Legislating being: Words and things in Bentham's panopticon'. *European Legacy*, 3(1): 72–83.

Zülch, H. and Hoffmann, S. (2010). 'Lobbying on accounting standard setting in a parliamentary environment: A qualitative approach'. *HHL Working Paper No. 94, Leipzig Graduate School of Management, Germany*. Available at:http://www.hhl.de/fileadmin/texte/publikationen/arbeitspapiere/hhlap0094.pdf [accessed: 7 December 2010].

Newspapers

Ahmed, J. (2006). 'Roadmap for accountancy profession in Bangladesh'. *Financial Express*, 19 February.

———. (2010). 'Global branding of chartered accountancy profession in Bangladesh'. *Financial Express*, 8 March.

Bangladesh Observer (1991). 19 January.

Banglanews24.com (2012). 20 March.

Bloomberg (2008). 'Bangladesh stock market value to double, Dhaka bourse predicts', 3 September. Available at: http://www.bloomberg.com/apps/news?pid=newsarchive&sid=avxseaZENGFc [accessed: 12 February 2012].

Choudhury, S.U.S. (2008). 'Corrupts and corruption in Bangladesh'. *American Chronicle*, 16 May.

Daily Inquilab (1991). 'Editorial'. 2 January.

Daily Star (1996). 23 December.

———. (2003). 'Administration of judicial system in Bangladesh'. 20 January.

———. (2004). 15 January.

———. (2007). 25 May.

———. (2009). 6 July.

———. (2010). 29 April.

———. (2011). 'Corruption emerges as major threat to Bangladesh', 9September.

Dainik Ittefaq (2007). 25 May.

Economist (1997). 'Revenge of the innocents'. 10 April.

Financial Express (2004). 24 October.

———. (2008). 30 December.

———. (2011). 21 December. Available at: http://www.thefinancialexpress-bd.com/more.php?news_id=97591&date=2011–12–21 [accessed: 23 December 2011].

Guardian (2009). 27February.

Halim, A. (2005). 'Martial law and military intervention: role of the judiciary'. *Daily Star*,1 October.

Independent (2003). 21 January.

International Financing Review (2008). 12December.

Khan, A.A. (2011). 'The test case for development revisited'. *Daily Star*, 17 March.

New Age (2012). 8 March.

Siddiqui, J. (2011). 'The auditing profession in Bangladesh: Turning the tide'. *Financial Express*, 5 August.

Appendices

Abacus
Accounting and Business Research
Accounting and Finance
Accounting Education
Accounting Forum
Accounting Historians Journal
Accounting History
Accounting Horizons
Accounting in Europe
The Accounting Review
Accounting, Auditing & Accountability Journal
Accounting, Business and Financial History
Accounting, Organizations and Society
Advances in International Accounting
Auditing: A Journal of Practice and Theory
Behavioral Research in Accounting
British Accounting Review
British Tax Review
Contemporary Accounting Research
Critical Perspectives on Accounting
European Accounting Review
Financial Accountability and Management
Intelligent Systems in Accounting, Finance and Management
International Journal of Accounting
International Journal of Accounting Auditing and Performance Evaluation
International Journal of Accounting Information Systems
International Journal of Auditing
Issues in Accounting Education
Journal of Accounting and Economics
Journal of Accounting and Organizational Change
Journal of Accounting and Public Policy
Journal of Accounting Education
Journal of Accounting Literature
Journal of Accounting Research
Journal of Accounting, Auditing and Finance
Journal of Applied Accounting Research
Journal of Business Finance and Accounting
Journal of International Accounting Research

Journal of International Accounting, Auditing and Taxation
Journal of International Financial Management & Accounting
Journal of Management Accounting Research (AAA)
Management Accounting Research
Managerial Auditing Journal
Qualitative Research in Accounting and Management
Review of Accounting Studies

Appendix 2.2 Articles in relation to the role of the state and accounting change from Google Scholar

Accounting Perspectives/Perspectives Comptables
Australian Journal of Management
British Journal of Sociology
Economia Aziendale
European Sociological Review
Journal of Accountancy
Journal of Financial Economics
Journal of Management and Governance
Journal of Modern African Studies
Research in Accounting Regulation
Review of International Political Economy

Appendix 2.3 Combined articles in relation to role of the state and accounting change from ABS and Google Scholar

Abacus
Accounting and Business Research
Accounting Horizons
Accounting Perspectives/Perspectives Comptables
The Accounting Review
Accounting, Auditing & Accountability Journal
Accounting, Organizations and Society
Australian Journal of Management
British Accounting Review
British Journal of Sociology
Critical Perspectives on Accounting
Economia Aziendale
European Accounting Review
European Sociological Review
Financial Accountability and Management
International Journal of Accounting Education and Research *(retitled International Journal of Accounting, in 1989)*
Journal of Accountancy
Journal of Accounting and Public Policy
Journal of Accounting Literature
Journal of Financial Economics
Journal of International Financial Management & Accounting
Journal of Management and Governance
Journal of Modern African Studies
Management Accounting Research
Research in Accounting Regulation
Review of International Political Economy

Note: The journals in italics indicate articles from Google Scholar.

Appendix 2.4(a) Papers related to the role of the state in relation to regulatory frameworks, politico-institutional factors and cultural issues and accounting change

Author(s)	Article	Theory	Drivers of Accounting Change			
			R	P-I	C	O
Radebaugh (1975)	Environmental factors influencing the development of accounting objectives, standards and practices in Peru	Theory of culture on *secrecy and transparency*	R	–	C	E Pr
Watts (1977)	Corporate financial statements: A product of the market and political processes	– Agency theory – Economic regulation theory – Public choice theory	R	P-I	–	–
Hoogvelt and Tinker (1978)	The role of colonial and post-colonial states in imperialism: A case-study of the Sierra Leone development company	State theory	–	P	–	–
Solomons (1978)	The politicization of accounting	No theory	–	P	–	–
Burchell et al. (1980)	The roles of accounting in organizations and society	– Organisation theory – Institutional theory	R	P	C	–
Tinker (1980)	Towards a political economy of accounting: An empirical illustration of the Cambridge controversies	– Classical political economy theory – Neo-classical economics theory	R	P	–	–
Lowe et al. (1983)	Simple theories for complex processes: Accounting policy and the market for myopia	Positive accounting theory	R	P	C	–
Belkaoui (1983)	Economic, political, and civil indicators and reporting and disclosure adequacy: empirical investigation	No theory	R	P	C	–
Tinker (1984)	Theories of the state and the state of accounting: Economic reductionism political Voluntarism in accounting regulation theory	State theory	R	P	–	–
Sutton (1984)	Lobbying of accounting standard-setting bodies in the UK and the USA: A Downsian analysis	No theory [Cost-benefit framework of the Downsian voting model on lobbying]	R	P	–	–
McKinnon and Harrison (1985)	Cultural influence on corporate and governmental involvement in accounting policy determination in Japan	No theory	–	P	C	–
Streeck and Schmitter (1985)	Community, market, state – and associations?: The prospective contribution of interest governance to social order	– State theory – Organisation theory	R	P	–	–

Author(s)	Article	Theory	Drivers of Accounting Change			
			R	P-I	C	O
Miller (1986)	Accounting for progress – national accounting and planning in France: a review essay	No theory	–	P-I	C	–
Harrison and McKinnon (1986)	Culture and accounting change: A new perspective on corporate reporting regulation and accounting policy formulation	– Diffusion of innovation theory – Theory of culture	R	–	C	–
Puxty et al. (1987)	Modes of regulation in advanced capitalism: Locating accountancy in four countries	Theory of regulation	R	–	–	–
Armstrong (1987)	The rise of accounting controls in British capitalist enterprises	Economics theory (functions of capital)	R	–	–	Ca Pr
Walker (1987)	Australia's ASRB: A case study of political activity and regulatory 'capture'	Regulatory capture theory	R	P-I	–	–
Sunder (1988)	Political economy of accounting standards	Review of Economics theory	R	P		Ca
Giroux (1989)	Political interests and governmental accounting disclosure	Public choice theory (median voter model and the bureaucratic model)	–	P	–	–
Baber (1990)	Toward a framework for evaluating the role of accounting and auditing in political markets: The influence of political competition	Political competition theory	–	P	–	–
Cooke and Wallace (1990)	Financial disclosure regulation and its environment: A review and further analysis	– Environmental determinism theory – Agency theory – Macro-sociological theory of environmental dependency	R	P	C	E Pn Eg
Miller (1990)	On the interrelations between accounting and the state	State theory	R	P	–	–
Jonsson (1991)	Role making for accounting while the state is watching	– Cultural theory – Communicative theory – Role of the state	R	P	C	E
Young (1991)	Interest group politics and the licensing of public accountants	No theory	R	P	C	–
Pushkin and Pariser (1991)	Political and economic forces shaping regulatory accounting for troubled debt restructuring	Positive accounting theory	R	P	C	–

(Continued)

Appendix 2.4(a) (Continued)

Author(s)	Article	Theory	Drivers of Accounting Change			
			R	P-I	C	O
Rose (1991)	Governing by numbers: Figuring out democracy	Macroeconomic theory (Democracy)	R	P	–	–
Rose and Miller (1992/2010)	Political power beyond the state: Problematics of government	– Social theory – Theories of power – Role of the state	–	P	–	–
Cheng (1992)	An empirical analysis of theories on factors influencing state government accounting disclosure	– Positive accounting theory – Interest-group theory (Agency theory)	–	P-I	–	–
Walker (1992)	*Interactions between government and the profession in the regulation of financial reporting: The Australian experience*	No theory	–	P	–	E
Napier and Noke (1992)	*Accounting and the law: An historical overview of an uneasy relationship*	Positive accounting theory	R	–	C	–
Stiglitz (1993)	*The Role of the State in Financial Markets*	No theory	R	P	–	–
Zeff (1993)	The politics of accounting standards	No theory	R	P	–	–
Walker and Robinson (1993)	A critical assessment of the literature on political activity and accounting regulation	No theory	R	P	–	–
Miller (1994)	*Accounting as social and institutional practice: an introduction*	– Institutional theory – Political economy	–	P-I	–	–
Boross et al. (1995)	Pressures and conflicts in moving towards harmonization of accounting practice: the Hungarian experience	No theory	R	P	C	–
Krzywda et al. (1995)	A theory of European accounting development applied to accounting change in contemporary Poland	State theory (Max Weberian concept)	R	P	–	–
Zeff (1995)	A perspective on the U.S. public/private-sector approach to the regulation of financial reporting	No theory	R	P	–	–
Zarzeski (1996)	Spontaneous harmonization effects of culture and market forces on accounting disclosure practices	– Theory of culture – Resource dependency theory	–	–	C	Ca
Saudagaran and Diga (1997)	Accounting regulation in ASEAN: A choice between the global and regional paradigms of harmonization	No theory	R	P	–	E
Saudagaran and Diga (1998)	*Post Colonial Accountancy Regulation in ASEAN: Accounting Ideology in an International Context*	No theory	R	P	–	–

Author(s)	Article	Theory	Drivers of Accounting Change			
			R	P-I	C	O
Nobes (1998)	Towards a general model of the reasons for international differences in financial reporting	– Theory of culture – Positive accounting theory	R	P-I	C	Ca La
Roberts and Kurtenbach (1998)	State regulation and professional accounting education reforms: An empirical test of regulatory capture theory	– Theories of economic regulation – Capture theory – Predatory capture theory	R	P	–	E
Klumpes (1998)	Competition among pressure groups for political influence over the determination of accounting standards	– Agency theory – Economic theory of regulation	R	–	–	–
Ryan et al. (1999)	Constituent participation in the Australian public sector accounting standard-setting process: The case of ED 55	No theory	R	P-I	–	–
McLeay et al. (2000)	Constituent lobbying and its impact on the development of financial reporting regulations: evidence from Germany	No theory	R	P	–	–
Stoddart (2000)	Political influences in changes to setting Australian accounting standards	No theory	R	P	–	–
Uddin and Hopper (2001)	A Bangladesh soap opera: Privatisation, accounting, and regimes of control in a less developed country	Labour process theory	R	P	–	Pr
Brown and Tarca (2001)	Politics, processes and the future of Australian accounting standards	Interest group theory	R	P	–	–
Zeff (2002)	Political lobbying on proposed standards: A challenge to the IASB	No theory	–	P	–	–
Faccio (2002)	Politically-connected firms: Can they squeeze the state?	No theory	–	P	–	–
Caramanis (2002)	The interplay between professional groups, the state and supranational agents: Pax Americana in the age of 'globalisation'	State theory	R	P	–	–
Sunder (2002)	Regulatory competition among accounting standards within and across international boundaries	No theory	R	–	–	–
Xiao et al. (2004)	Political influence and coexistence of a uniform accounting system and accounting standards: Recent developments in China	No theory	R	P	C	Ca Pn

(Continued)

Appendix 2.4(a) (Continued)

Author(s)	Article	Theory	Drivers of Accounting Change			
			R	P-I	C	O
Ordelheide (2004)	The politics of accounting: A framework	No theory	–	P	C	–
Sunder (2005)	Minding our manners: Accounting as social norm	Theory of culture	R	–	C	–
Leuz and Oberholzer-Gee (2006)	Political Relationships, Global Financing, and Corporate Transparency: Evidence from Indonesia	No theory	R	P	–	–
Cooper and Robson (2006)	Accounting, professions and regulation: Locating the sites of professionalization	– Public choice theory – Theory of hegemony – Actor network theory	R	P	–	Pr E
Ball (2006)	International financial reporting standards (IFRS): Pros and cons for investors	No theory	R	P	–	–
Zeghal and Mhedhbi (2006)	An analysis of the factors affecting the adoption of international accounting standards by developing countries	No theory	R	P	C	Eg E Pn Ca
Zeff (2006)	Political lobbying on accounting standards: National and international experience	No theory	R	P	–	–
Perry and Nölke (2006)	The political economy of International Accounting Standards	No theory	–	P	–	–
Napier (2006)	Accounts of change: 30 years of historical accounting research	– Labour process theory – Positive accounting theory – Institutional theory review – Theory of accounting change	R	P	C	–
Constable and Kuasirikun (2007)	Accounting for the nation-state in mid nineteenth-century Thailand	State theory	–	P	C	–
Ezzamel et al. (2007)	Political ideology and accounting regulation in China	Capitalist accounting theory	R	P	–	–
Zeff (2007)	Some obstacles to global financial reporting compara-bility and convergence at a high level of quality	No theory	R	P	C	Au La
Ramanna (2008)	The implications of fair-value accounting: Evidence from the political economy of goodwill accounting	Theory of regulation	R	P	–	Mn

Author(s)	Article	Theory	Drivers of Accounting Change			
			R	P-I	C	O
Leuzand Wysocki (2008)	Economic consequences of financial reporting and disclosure regulation: A review and suggestions for future research	– Theory of disclosure regulation – Institutional economics – Agency theory	R	P	–	–
Nobes and Zeff (2008)	Auditors' affirmations of compliance with IFRS around the world: An exploratory study	No theory	R	P	–	–
Königsgruber (2010)	A political economy of accounting standard setting	No theory	–	P	–	–
Sunder (2010)	Adverse effects of uniform written reporting standards on accounting practice, education, and research	Agency theory	R	–	C	Pn E
Zülch and Hoffmann (2010)	Lobbying on accounting standard setting in a parliamentary environment: A qualitative approach	No theory	R	P	–	–
Jones (2010)	Sources of power and infrastructural conditions in medieval governmental accounting	Social theory of Michael Mann (power framework)	R	R	C	–
Moran (2010)	The political economy of regulation: does it have any lessons for accounting research?	– State theory – Political theory	R	P-I	C	–
Alexander and Servalli (2010)	The State and/of Accounting Regulation	State theory	R	P	C	–
Wagenhofer (2011)	Towards a theory of accounting regulation: A discussion of the politics of disclosure regulation along the economic cycle	– Theory of accounting regulation	R	P-I	–	–
Kurunmaki et al.(2011)	Accounting within and beyond the state	– Institutional theory – Structuration theory – Role of the state	–	P-I	–	–
Liguori and Steccolini (2012)	Accounting change: explaining the outcomes, interpreting the process	– New-institutional theory – Archetype theory – Role of the state	R	–	C	–
Norton (2012)	Judicial interpretation of the will of the state: A Hegelian perspective in the context of taxation	– Critical accounting theory – Social contract theory – Role of the state	R	P	–	–
Oehr and Zimmermann (2012)	Accounting and the welfare-state: The missing link	– State theory – Neo-institutional theory	R	P	–	–
	Total 79 articles		62	68*a	27	

Notes: R = Accounting regulatory frameworks; P-I = politico-institutional factors; P = politics; C = cultural factors; O = other country-specific factors [E = accounting education; Pn = accounting profession; Ca = capital markets; Pr = privatisation; Eg = economic growth; Mn = manipulation of accounting; Au = auditing; La = language].
* Italics indicate working papers, book chapters and a research report is also included.
*a 58 papers are based on politics and 10 papers are based on politico-institutional factors [58+10 = 68].

Summary of Articles: (i) Total 79 articles; (ii) 15 are based on the theory of the role of the state: [Hoogveltand Tinker (1978); Tinker (1984); Streeck and Schmitter (1985); Miller (1990); Jonsson (1991); Rose and Miller (1992/2010); Krzywda et al. (1995); Caramanis (2002); Constable and Kuasirikun (2007); Moran (2010); Alexander and Servalli (2010); Kurunmaki et al. (2011); Liguori and Steccolini (2012); Norton (2012);Oehr and Zimmermann (2012)]; (iii) 34 other theories; and (iv) 30 no theories.

Appendix 2.4(b) Theory and non-theory based papers in relation to developing vs. developed countries

Theory based papers

Developing country	Developed country
• Ezzamel et al. (2007): China	• *Liguori and Steccolini (2012): Italy*
• *Constable and Kuasirikun (2007):Thailand*	• *Norton (2012):The UK and the USA*
• Uddin and Hopper (2001): Bangladesh	• *Alexander and Servalli (2010):The EU and the IASB*
• *Krzywda et al. (1995): Poland*	• *Moran (2010):The USA and the UK*
• *Hoogvelt and Tinker (1978): Sierra Leone*	• Jones (2010): Medieval country
• Radebaugh (1975): Peru	• Sunder (2010):The USA and the EU
	• *Oehr and Zimmermann (2012): Germany, Canada and the UK*
	• Leuz and Wysocki (2008):The USA
	• Ramanna (2008):The USA
	• Cooper and Robson (2006):The UK
	• Sunder (2005):The USA
	• *Caramanis (2002): Greece*
	• Brown and Tarca (2001):Australia
	• Klumpes (1998):Australia
	• Roberts and Kurtenbach (1998):The USA
	• Zarzeski (1996): France, Germany, Hong Kong, Japan, Norway, the UK and the USA
	• Napier and Noke (1992):The UK and New Zealand
	• Cheng (1992):The USA
	• *Rose and Miller (1992/2010):The UK and the USA*
	• *Jonsson (1991): Sweden*
	• Rose (1991):The USA
	• Pushkin and Pariser (1991):The USA
	• *Miller (1990): France*
	• Giroux (1989):The USA
	• Sunder (1988):The USA
	• Walker (1987):Australia
	• Armstrong (1987):The UK
	• Puxty et al. (1987): Germany, the UK, Sweden and the USA
	• Harrison and McKinnon (1986): Japan
	• Lowe et al.(1983):The UK and the USA
	• Tinker (1980):The UK

Theory based papers

Developing country	*Developed country*

Both developed and developing countries
- Nobes (1998)
- Cooke and Wallace (1990)

General theory (theory based only)
- *Kurunmaki et al. (2011)*
- *Wagenhofer (2011)*
- Napier (2006)
- Miller (1994)
- Baber (1990)
- *Streeck and Schmitter (1985)*
- *Tinker (1984)*
- Burchell et al. (1980)
- Watts (1977)

Non-theory based papers

Developing country	*Developed country*
• Leuz and Oberholzer-Gee (2006): Indonesia	• Zülch and Hoffmann (2010): Germany
• Zeghal and Mhedhbi (2006)	• Königsgruber (2010): The EU and the USA
• Xiao et al. (2004): China	• Perry and Nölke (2006): The EU and the USA
• Saudagaran and Diga (1998): ASEAN, Malaysia, Philippines, Indonesia, Thailand and Singapore [except Singapore all are developing countries]	• Zeff (2006): The USA, the UK, Canada and Sweden
	• Zeff (2002): The USA, the UK and Australia
	• Sunder (2002): The USA
	• Stoddart (2000): Australia
• Saudagaran and Diga (1997): ASEAN, Malaysia, Philippines, Indonesia, Thailand and Singapore [except Singapore all are developing countries]	• McLeay et al. (2000): Germany
	• Ryan et al. (1999): Australia
	• Zeff (1995): The USA
• Boross et al. (1995): Hungary	• Zeff (1993): The USA
	• Walker (1992): Australia
	• Young (1991): The USA
	• Miller (1986): France
	• McKinnon and Harrison (1985): Japan
	• Sutton (1984): The UK and the USA
	• Solomons (1978): The USA

Both developed and developing countries
- Nobes and Zeff (2008)
- Zeff (2007)
- Ball (2006)
- Ordelheide (2004)
- Faccio (2002)
- Walker and Robinson (1993)
- Belkaoui (1983)

Note: Italics indicate papers relating to the theory of the role of the state.

Appendix 5.1 Semi-structured interview schedule

Interviewee type: _____

Interview date: _____

Time: _____

Name of the interviewee: _____

Company: _____

Job title: _____

Work experience (in years): _____

Qualification: _____

Date of qualification: _____

Interview preamble:

This interview is about the implementation of IFRS in Bangladesh. You have been invited to participate in this study based on your involvement in the policymaking/accounts preparing/using/researching of accounting arenas in Bangladesh.

All responses to this interview are absolutely confidential and results will be presented in an anonymous form.

With your permission, I would like to record the interview to ensure that I do not miss any important points. I will make the transcript available if you wish. (Yes/No)

Would you like me to acknowledge your support in my thesis? (Yes/No)

Do you have any questions before we commence?

Interview questions

Background information: The definition of 'implementation' regarding my research is: The actual observed outcomes of introducing and monitoring the standards. These outcomes will include the action of the government, SEC, ICAB, ICMAB, DSE, Bangladesh Bank.

Drivers of accounting change	Policymakers		Preparers/ Professionals		Academics		Users	
[A] Accounting regulatory frameworks (RQ-1)	1.	How would you describe the accounting regulatory frameworks in relation to the existing laws for investor protection, standard-setting process and enforcement issues in Bangladesh?	1.	How would you describe the accounting regulatory frameworks in relation to the existing laws for investor protection, standard-setting process and enforcement issues in Bangladesh?	1.	How would you describe the accounting regulatory frameworks in relation to the existing laws for investor protection, standard-setting process and enforcement issues in Bangladesh?	1.	How would you describe the accounting regulatory frameworks in relation to the existing laws for investor protection, standard-setting process and enforcement issues in Bangladesh?
	2.	Who really regulates accounting issues in the country today?	2.	Who really regulates accounting issues in the country today?	2.	Who really regulates accounting issues in the country today?	2.	Who really regulates accounting issues in the country today?
[B] Politico-institutional factors (RQ-1)	3.	Is there any higher/lower level of political pressure (e.g. government intervention, donor agencies' pressure and political lobbying) to implement or not implement IFRS?	3.	Is there any higher/lower level of political pressure (e.g. government intervention, donor agencies' pressure and political lobbying) to implement or not implement IFRS?	3.	Is there any higher/lower level of political pressure (e.g. government intervention, donor agencies' pressure and political lobbying) to implement or not implement IFRS?	3.	Is there any higher/lower level of political pressure (e.g. government intervention, donor agencies' pressure and political lobbying) to implement or not implement IFRS?
	4.	Do you feel the institutional and professional bodies can work together to better implement IFRS?	4.	Do you feel the institutional and professional bodies can work together to better implement IFRS?	4.	Do you feel the institutional and professional bodies can work together to better implement IFRS?	4.	Do you feel the institutional and professional bodies can work together to better implement IFRS?

(Continued)

Drivers of accounting change	Policymakers		Preparers/ Professionals		Academics		Users	
[C] Cultural factors (e.g. training opportunities in the accounting profession and corruption) (RQ-2a)	5.	Do you feel that the current syllabus of the professional accountancy qualification is suitable to implement IFRS effectively?	5.	Do you feel that the current syllabus of the professional accountancy qualification is suitable to implement IFRS effectively?	5.	Do you feel that the current syllabus of the professional accountancy qualification is suitable to implement IFRS effectively?	5.	Do you feel that the current syllabus of the professional accountancy qualification is suitable to implement IFRS effectively?
	5(a)	Will the IFRS be included in the universities' curricula?	5(a)	Should the IFRS be included in the universities' curricula?	5(a)	Should the IFRS be included in the universities' curricula?	5(a)	Do you know whether the IFRS will be included in the universities' curricula?
					5(b)	Is there any lack of research in this sector?		
	6.	What kind of training and development you are offering them (the preparers and professionals) to cope with IFRS?	6.	What are the training and development you attained to cope with IFRS?	6.	What do you think about what kind of training and development they (the preparers and professionals) needed to cope with IFRS?	6.	Would you feel that the preparers and professionals need training and development to cope with IFRS?
	7.	How would you regard corruption as an issue in implementing IFRS effectively?	7.	How would you regard corruption as an issue in implementing IFRS effectively?	7.	How would you regard corruption as an issue in implementing IFRS effectively?	7.	How would you regard corruption as an issue in implementing IFRS effectively?
[C] Other country-specific factors (RQ-2b)	8.	What are the main problems of effective implementation of IFRS in Bangladesh?	8.	What are the main problems of effective implementation of IFRS in Bangladesh?	8.	What are the main problems of effective implementation of IFRS in Bangladesh?	8.	What are the main problems of effective implementation of IFRS in Bangladesh?
	9.	Are there any other comments you would like to make regarding the implementation of IFRS?	9.	Are there any other comments you would like to make regarding the implementation of IFRS?	9.	Are there any other comments you would like to make regarding the implementation of IFRS?	9.	Are there any other comments you would like to make regarding the implementation of IFRS?

Appendix 5.2 Detailed summary of the interviewees (1st round)

Category	Code	Company/ Organisation	Work Experience	Highest Qualification	Date and Time of Interviews		Recorded/ Not Recorded*
					Date	Time	
A. Policymakers	PM1	ICAB (Institute of Chartered Accountants of Bangladesh)	26 years	PhD	12/06/10	9:30–10:43	Not recorded
	PM2	ICAB	10 years	ACA	14/06/10	11:23–12:39	Recorded
	PM3	ICMAB (Institute of Cost and Management Accountants of Bangladesh)	30 years	FCMA	23/06/10	15:00–16:00	Recorded
	PM4	SEC (Securities and Exchange Commission of Bangladesh)	11 years	MBA	24/06/10	14:30–15:20	Not recorded
	PM5	World Bank	14 years	FCA	30/06/10	16:00–17:12	Not recorded
	PM6	Bangladesh Bank [The Central Bank]	40 years	PhD	16/06/10	12:00–13:10	Recorded
	PM7	Ministry of Finance	16 years	MA	01/07/10	9:00–10:20	Not recorded
B. Preparers and professionals	AP1	Big four accountancy firm in Bangladesh	32 years	ACA	04/07/10	9:00–10:00	Not recorded
	AP2	Pharmaceutical company	24 years	ICMA (Part)	05/07/10	9:00–9:55	Recorded
	AP3	Big four accountancy firm in Bangladesh	9 years	ACA	06/07/10	14:00–15:15	Not recorded
	AP4	Small accountancy firm	10 years	ACA	11/07/10	12:00–13:10	Recorded
	AP5	Bank	10 years	MCom	14/07/10	9:00–10:15	Not recorded
	AP6	Engineering company	8 years 2 months	MBA	17/07/10	10:00–11:30	Not recorded
	AP7	Bank	15 years	MCom	18/07/10	11:00–12:15	Recorded
	AP8	Small accountancy firm	5 years	ACA	19/07/10	9:00–10:17	Not recorded
	AP9	Small accountancy firm	20 years	FCA	21/07/10	15:00–16:20	Recorded
	AP10	Multinational company	11 years	ACMA	22/07/10	10:00–10:49	Recorded
	AP11	Pharmaceutical company	7 years	ACA	27/07/10	16:00–16:53	Not recorded
	AP12	Big four accountancy firm in Bangladesh	15 years	FCMA, FCA	29/07/10	13:00–14:15	Not recorded

(Continued)

Appendix 5.2 (Continued)

Category	Code	Company/ Organisation	Work Experience	Highest Qualification	Date and Time of Interviews		Recorded/ Not Recorded*
					Date	Time	
C. Users	US1	Bank	10 years	MBA	02/08/10	10:45–11:38	Recorded
	US2	Stockbroker and Central Depository Bangladesh Ltd (CDBL)	9 years	MA	05/08/10	9:00–9:47	Not recorded
	US3	Financial institution and CDBL	8 years 7 months	MBA	08/08/10	9:00–10:11	Recorded
	US4	Bank	10 years	CMA (Part)	09/08/10	13:00–14:02	Recorded
	US5	Credit Rating Agency of Bangladesh (CRAB	5 years 10 months	MBA	12/08/10	11:00–11:52	Not recorded
	US6	Bank	18 years	MCom	13/08/10	15:00–16:07	Recorded
D. Academics and Researchers	AR1	Private university, Bangladesh	21 years	PhD	16/08/10	9:00–10:12	Recorded
	AR2	Public university, Bangladesh	10 years	MBA	19/08/10	13:15–14:27	Recorded

Note:
* 13 interviewees declined to record the interviews.

Appendix 5.3 Interview guide of the study

Introduction
- Welcome to the interviewee for participating in this research.
- The introduction and the general purposes of the topic are discussed for few minutes.
- I explain the use of recording equipment to the interviewee.
- I also address the issue of ethical guidelines (e.g. anonymity and confidentiality).
- Finally, I read a protocol summary to the interviewee.

Interview
After the introduction the questions relevant to the topics are put to the interviewees. They are given some opportunities to provide some examples relevant to the questions which may bring forth their opinions that they have been waiting to share.

Closing remarks
Those are all the questions I have, and thank you very much for participating in this research.

Appendix 5.4 The 2nd round interview questions

Drivers of Accounting Change	PM, AP, AR and US
[A] Accounting regulatory frameworks (RQ-1)	1(a). How would you describe the accounting regulatory process in Bangladesh?
	1(b). How would you describe the accounting standard-setting process in Bangladesh?
	2. How effective is the enforcement mechanism in implementing IFRS?
[B] Politico-institutional factors (RQ-1)	3. How do you regard the political pressure to implement or not implement IFRS?
	4. How important is institutional co-operation to implementing IFRS effectively?
[C] Cultural factors (e.g. training opportunities in the accounting profession and [corruption) [RQ-2(a)]	5. How effective are accounting education and training opportunities in implementing IFRS?
	6. How does corruption affect effective IFRS implementation?
[C] Other country-specific factors [RQ-2(b)]	7. What are the main problems in the effective implementation of IFRS?

Appendix 6.1 IFRS/BFRSs*related enforcement, 1998–2010(n= 42–41 penalty/fine, 1 warning)

Year	Month	SJ**	Industry	Violation Type	Relevant Accounting Standard(s)	Relevant Regulations	Actions
2010	January	50	Cement	Non-application of depreciation on fixed assets, true and fair view	IAS 1, IAS 16	SEC Ordinance 1969 S. 18, Rule 12(2) of SEC Rule 1987	Fine[†] [1,400,000]
	January	51	Food and Allied	Going concern; selling, distribution and sales promotion; sales/turnover; falsification; true and fair view	IAS 1	SEC Ordinance 1969 S. 18, Rule 12(2) of SEC Rule 1987	Fine [300,000]
	January	57	Food and Allied	Provision for bad and doubtful debts, unreliability of unconfirmed balance of debtors, true and fair view	IAS 1, IAS 39	SEC Ordinance 1969 S. 18, Rule 12(2) of SEC Rule 1987	Fine [1,200,000]
	January	58	Textile	Inventory, financial expenses, advance and deposits, deferred expenses, tax holiday reserve, true and fair view	IAS 1, IAS 2, IAS 12, IAS 23	SEC Ordinance 1969 S. 18, Rule 12(2) of SEC Rule 1987	Fine [800,000]
	May	19	Pharmaceuticals and Chemicals	Going concern (machines were non-operative from 2006); provision for bad and doubtful debts	IAS 1, IAS 39	SEC Ordinance 1969 S. 18, Rule 12(2) of SEC Rule 1987	Fine [1,500,000]
	May	20	Food and Allied	Most of the amounts of inventories have not been changed over the years	IAS 2, IAS 36	SEC Ordinance 1969 S. 2(g), Rule 12(2) of SEC Rule 1987	Fine [1,200,000]
	June	29	Paper and Printing	No appropriate method was followed in charging depreciation of other fixed assets	IAS 16	SEC Ordinance 1969 S. 2(g), Rule 12(2) of SEC Rule 1987	Fine [1,000,000]
	September	7	Engineering	No depreciation has been charged	IAS 16	SEC Ordinance 1969 S. 2(g), Rule 12(2) of SEC Rule 1987	Fine [1,000,000]
	November	4	Food and Allied	Closing stock of the inventories does not assure the balance of inventories	IAS 1, IAS 2	SEC Ordinance 1969 S. 2(g), Rule 12(2) of SEC Rule 1987	Fine [100,000]

Year	Month	No.	Sector	Issues	Accounting standards	Regulation	Action
2009	January	14	Textile	True and fair view and qualified audit opinion	IAS 1	SEC Ordinance 1969 S. 18, Rule 12(2) of SEC Rule 1987	Fine [600,000]
	January	15	Pharmaceuticals and Chemicals	No detailed notes as prescribed by the ICAB and true and fair view	IAS 1	SEC Ordinance 1969 S. 18, Rule 12(2) of SEC Rule 1987	Fine [500,000]
	June	6	Textile	Financial expenses, non-declaration of the date of AGM, true and fair view	IAS 1	SEC Ordinance 1969 S. 18, Rule 12(2) of SEC Rule 1987	Fine [400,000]
	July	1	Textile	Accounts receivable and non-payment of dividend, true and fair view	IAS 1	SEC Ordinance 1969 S. 18, Rule 12(2) of SEC Rule 1987	Fine [15,000,000]
	July	7	Food and Allied	Inventory, deferred liabilities, financial expenses, loans from associated companies and loan from other parties, true and fair view	IAS 1, IAS 2	SEC Ordinance 1969 S. 18, Rule 12(2) of SEC Rule 1987	Fine [300,000]
	July	8	Food and Allied	True and fair view, no disclosure of income from insurance of damaged goods	IAS 1	SEC Ordinance 1969 S. 18, Rule 12(2) of SEC Rule 1987	Fine [400,000]
	July	12	Tannery	No disclosure of amount due by directors of the company or associate concerns, true and fair view	IAS 1	SEC Ordinance 1969 S. 18, Rule 12(2) of SEC Rule 1987	Fine [2,400,000]
	August	5	Pharmaceuticals and Chemicals	Inventory valuation, deferred expenditure, amortisation, true and fair view	IAS 1, IAS 2	SEC Ordinance 1969 S. 18, Rule 12(2) of SEC Rule 1987	Fine [6,000,000]
	August	6	Textile	Inventory valuation, deferred expenditure, amortisation, provision for taxation, falsification, true and fair view	IAS 1, IAS 2	SEC Ordinance 1969 S. 18, Rule 12(2) of SEC Rule 1987	Fine [6,000,000]
	August	7	Miscellaneous	Inventory valuation, deferred expenditure, amortisation, true and fair view	IAS 1, IAS 2	SEC Ordinance 1969 S. 18, Rule 12(2) of SEC Rule 1987	Fine [6,000,000]
	August	9	Jute	Taxation, contingent liabilities, stock of finished goods, sundry debtors, provident fund, interim unpaid dividend, true and fair view	IAS 1, IAS 2, IAS 12, IAS 37	SEC Ordinance 1969 S. 18, Rule 12(2) of SEC Rule 1987	Fine [1,600,000]
	November	1	Pharmaceuticals and Chemicals	Creditors for expense and accruals, creditors for finance, custom debenture, true and fair view	IAS 1, IAS 37	SEC Ordinance 1969 S. 18, Rule 12(2) of SEC Rule 1987	Fine [400,000]
	November	11	Textile	Depreciation on revalued amount of fixed assets, true and fair view	IAS 1, IAS 16	SEC Ordinance 1969 S. 18, Rule 12(2) of SEC Rule 1987	Fine [900,000]
	November	12	Textile	Inter-company current account, true and fair view	IAS 1, IAS 24	SEC Ordinance 1969 S. 18, Rule 12(2) of SEC Rule 1987	Fine [600,000]

(Continued)

Appendix 6.1 (Continued)

Year	Month	Sl**	Industry	Violation Type	Relevant Accounting Standard(s)	Relevant Regulations	Actions
2008	April	12	Food and Allied	Old loan, true and fair view	IAS 1, IFRS 7	SEC Ordinance 1969 S. 18, Rule 12(2) of SEC Rule 1987	Fine [100,000]
	April	13	Food and Allied	Administrative expenses, turnover and other income, selling and distribution expenses, collection from turnover and other income, payment for cost and expenses, loan received and loan repaid, true and fair view	IAS 1	SEC Ordinance 1969 S. 18, Rule 13(A) of SEC Rule 1987	Fine [100,000]
	July	6	Textile	Accounts receivables, true and fair view	IAS 1, IFRS 7	SEC Ordinance 1969 S. 18, Rule 12(2) of SEC Rule 1987	Fine [1 million]
	September	8	Tannery	Property plant and equipment, true and fair view	IAS 1, IAS 16	SEC Ordinance 1969 S. 18, Rule 12(2) of SEC Rule 1987	Fine [800,000]
	October	4	Insurance	Receivables, advance business expenses, no accounting for deferred taxation, IAS, true and fair view	IAS 1, IAS 12	SEC Ordinance 1969 S. 18, Rule 12(2) of SEC Rule 1987	Fine [4,200,000*] Waived
	October	6	Food and Allied	No detailed disclosures as prescribed by the ICAB, true and fair view	IAS 1	SEC Ordinance 1969 S. 18, Rule 12(2) of SEC Rule 1987	Fine [1 million]
	October	7	Paper and Printing	Fixed asset, no justification of physical inventory	IAS 2, IAS 16	SEC Ordinance 1969 S. 18, Rule 12(2) of SEC Rule 1987	Fine [1,000,000]
2007	March	19, 20, 21, 22, 23, 24	Miscellaneous	True and fair view, non-disclosure of loan default and information about selling of mortgages in annual report	IAS 1, IFRS 7	SEC Ordinance 1969 S. 18, Rule 12(3) of SEC Rule 1987	Fine [600,000]
	May	17, 18, 19, 20, 21, 22	Tannery	Intangible assets, depreciation on factory assets, lease	IAS 16, IAS 17, IAS 38	SEC Ordinance 1969 S. 18, Rule 12(2) of SEC Rule 1987	Fine [600,000]
	May	23, 24, 25, 26	Textile	Chance of error and omission in internal control procedures; cost of goods sold; not adopting an appropriate accounting system of controlling inventory; true and fair view	IAS 1, IAS 2	SEC Ordinance 1969 S. 18, Rule 12(2) of SEC Rule 1987	Fine [400,000]

Year	Month	SI.	Company type	Description	IAS reference	Regulation	Penalty
2007	May	27, 28, 29, 30, 31, 32, 33	Cement	Full details and locations of all individual assets in fixed assets not shown	IAS 16	SEC Ordinance 1969 S. 18, Rule 12(2) of SEC Rule 1987	Fine [700,000]
	May	52, 53, 54, 55, 56, 57	Miscellaneous	Balance sheet and change in equity not prepared in accordance with IAS	IAS 34- Para 20(a) and (c)	SEC Ordinance 1969 S. 18, Rule 13(A) of SEC Rule 1987	Fine [600,000]
	July	25	Food and Allied	No stock register for auditors' verification; no provision for employee leave pay and gratuity	IAS 19, IAS 2-Para 36(a)	SEC Ordinance 1969 S. 18, Rule 12(2) of SEC Rule 1987	Fine [600,000]
	September	6	Food and Allied	Deficiency in internal control, lack of detailed record of fixed assets, biological assets, current and non-current assets; presentation of biological assets; no double entry cash book maintained; true and fair view	IAS 41, IAS 1	SEC Ordinance 1969 S. 18, Rule 12(2g) of SEC Rule 1987	Fine [400,000]
	September	7	Food and Allied	ISA, half yearly audited report, balance sheet, income statement, cash flow statement, change in equity	IAS 34- Para 20(a), (b), (c) and (d)	SEC Ordinance 1969 S. 18, Rule 13(A) of SEC Rule 1987	Fine [800,000]
	September	8	Food and Allied	ISA, half yearly audited report, balance sheet, income statement, cash flow statement, change in equity	IAS 34- Para 20(a), (b), (c) and (d)	SEC Ordinance 1969 S. 18, Rule 13(A) of SEC Rule 1987	Fine [700,000]
	November	1	Miscellaneous	Depreciation, deferred tax	IAS 12, IAS 16	SEC Ordinance 1969 S. 18, Rule 12(2) of SEC Rule 1987	Warning
	December	13	Food and Allied	Qualified audit opinion; true and fair view	IAS 1	SEC Ordinance 1969 S. 18, Rule 12(2) of SEC Rule 1987	Fine [3,500,000]
2006	October	19–26	Food and Allied	Direct and indirect cash flow method	IAS 34- para 20(a): Part ii, 20(c): Part iii, schedule-sub Para 1 A(1)	SEC Ordinance 1969 S. 18, Rule 13(A) of SEC Rule 1987	Fine [800,000]

Notes:
* IFRS and BFRSs are used interchangeably.
** SI. – the serial number of the SEC's monthly enforcement notices.
†The values are given in the Bangladeshi currency, i.e. the Taka (Tk.). The exchange rate on 31 March 2012 was Tk. 1 = £0.0083 (or £1 = Tk. 119.815), source: http://www.hmrc.gov.uk/exrate/bangladesh.htm (accessed 12 February 2012).

Appendix 6.2 The Companies Act 1994 regarding penalties in Bangladesh

---

Section 190. Copy of balance-sheet, etc. to be filed with Registrar:
(1) After the balance sheet and profit and loss account or the income and expenditure account, as the case may be, have been laid before a company at an annual general meeting as aforesaid, there shall be filed with the Registrar, within thirty days from the date on which the balance sheet and the profit and loss accounts were so laid, or where the annual general meeting of a company for any year has not been held, there shall be filed with the Registrar within thirty days from the last day on which that meeting should have been held in accordance with the provisions of this Act three copies of the balance-sheet, and of the profit and loss account or the income and expenditure account, as the case may be signed by the managing director, managing agent, a manger or secretary of the company or if there be none of these, by a director of the company, together with three copies of all documents which are required by this Act to be annexed or attached to such balance-sheet or profit and loss account or income and expenditure account: Provided that in the case of a private company, which is not an subsidiary of a public company, no person other than a member of the company shall be entitled to inspect or to obtain copies of the profit and loss account of that company.
(2) If the annual general meeting of a company before which a balance-sheet is laid as aforesaid does not adopt the balance-sheet or, if the annual general meeting of a company for any year has not been half, a statement of that fact and of the reasons there for shall be annexed to the balance-sheet and to the copies thereof required to be file with the Registrar.
(3) If a company makes default in complying with the requirements of this section, it shall be liable *to a fine not exceeding one hundred taka for every day* during which the default continues, and every office of the company who knowingly and wilfully authorises or permits the default shall be liable to the like penalty.

Statement to be published by Banking and certain other companies:
Section 192. Certain companies to publish statement in schedule:
(1) Every company being a limited Banking company or an insurance company for a deposit, provident or benefit society shall, before, it commences bushiness, and also on the first Monday in February and the First Monday in August in every year during which it carries on business make a statement herein after referred to as the said statement in the form as in Schedule XII, or as near thereto as circumstances will admit.
(2) If a company makes default in complying with the requirements of this section, it *shall be liable to a fine not exceeding one hundred taka for everyday* during which the default continues; and, also every officer of the company who knowingly and wilfully authorises or permits the default shall be liable to the like penalty.
Section 332. Penalty for falsification of book. – I[f] any director, manager, officer or contributory of any company being wound up destroys, mutilates, alters o[r] falsifies or fraudulently secret[e]s any books papers or securities or makes or is privy to the making of any false or fraudulent entry in any register book of account or document belonging to the company with intent to defraud or deceive any person, he *shall be liable to imprisonment for a term which may extend to seven years, and shall also be liable to fine.*
Section 334. Penalty for false evidence. – If any person, upon any examination authorised under this Act, or in any affidavit, depositing or solemn affirmation, in or about the winding up of any company under this Act, or otherwise in or about any matter arising under this Act intentionally give[s] false evidence, he *shall be liable to imprisonment for a term which may extend to seven years, and shall also be liable to find.*
Section 397. Penalty for false statement. – Whoever in any return, report, certificate balance-sheet or other documents, required by or for the purposes of any of the provisions of this Act, wilfully makes a statement false in any material particular, knowing it to be false, *shall be punishable with imprisonment of either description for a term which may extend to five years, and shall also be liable to fine.*

Appendix 6.3 The SEC Act 1993 regarding penalties in Bangladesh

---

Section 19. Cognizance. –

(1) No Court other than a *Session Court* shall take cognizance of any offence under this Act.

(2) No offence under this Act shall be taken cognizance of except on a *complaint in writing made by the Commission or any person authorised by the Commission.*

Section 20. Offences by companies. – If the person contravening any of the provisions of this Act is a company, *the owner, director, manager, secretary or any other officer or agent of the company shall be deemed guilty* of the contravention of the provision, unless he proves that the contravention was committed without his knowledge or that he exercised all due diligence to prevent the contravention.

Section 21. Appeal. –

(1) Any person aggrieved by an order passed by any member or officer in accordance with this Act, the rules or regulations may, within such period as may be specified by regulation, prefer an appeal to the Commission against such order and the decision of the Commission there upon shall be final.

(2) No appeal filed after the expiration of the specified period shall be acceptable, but *if the appellant satisfies the Commission to the effect that there existed reasonable grounds for the appeal not to have been filed within the specified period, the Commission may accept* an appeal filed after the expiration of the specified period.

(3) An appeal under this section shall be made in such form, and shall be accompanied by such fee, as may be specified by regulation and shall be filed together with a copy of the order against which it has been filed.

(4) Every appeal shall be decided on in such manner as may be specified by regulation; and no appeal shall be decided on without giving reasonable opportunity for hearing to the appellant.

(5) The Commission may, at its *own instigation or in the light of any application, reconsider any matter already decided upon and in this case the decision of the Commission shall be final.*

Appendix 6.4 Comparison of perceptions of interviewees based on Q1–4 [1st round interviews, n=27]

Code	Accounting Regulation		Politico-Institutional		Work Experience (years)	Qualification
	Q1	Q2	Q3	Q4		
PM1	(Need regulation)	ICAB and SEC	Yes (PD)	Yes (Need co-operation)	26 years	PhD
PM2	(Enforcement)	ICAB, SEC and BB	Yes (PG)	Yes (Need co-operation)	10 years	ACA
PM3	– (Need regulation)	ICAB, ICMAB and MOC	Yes (PG)	Yes (Need co-operation)	30 years	FCMA
PM4	– (Need regulation)	ICAB, MOF	No (PG)	Yes (Need co-operation)	11 years	MBA
PM5	– (Enforcement)	ICAB, ICMAB and SEC	Yes (PG)	Yes (Need co-operation)	14 years	FCA
PM6	– (Need regulation)	ICAB, SEC and BB	Yes (PG)	Yes (Need co-operation)	40 years	PhD
PM7	+ (Satisfactory)	ICAB	Yes (PD) and No (PG)	Yes (Need co-operation)	16 years	MA
AP1	– (Need regulation)	ICAB, SEC and BB	Yes (PD) andIP (PG)	Yes (Need co-operation)	32 years	ACA
AP2	+ (Satisfactory)	ICAB	Yes (PD) and Yes (PG)	Yes (Need co-operation)	24 years	ICMA (Part)

(Continued)

Appendix 6.4 (Continued)

Code	Accounting Regulation		Politico-Institutional		Work Experience (years)	Qualification
	Q1	Q2	Q3	Q4		
AP3	– (Standard setting)	ICAB	No comment	Yes (Need co-operation)	9 years	ACA
AP4	– (Enforcement)	ICAB	No comment	Yes (Need co-operation)	10 years	ACA
AP5	– (Need regulation)	ICAB and ICMAB	IP (PG)	Yes (Need co-operation)	10 years	M.Com.
AP6	– (Standard setting)	ICAB and DSE	No comment	Yes (Need co-operation)	8 years 2 months	MBA
AP7	– (Enforcement)	ICAB and BB	No comment	Yes (Need co-operation)	15 years	M.Com
AP8	– (Enforcement)	ICAB	No comment	Yes (Need co-operation)	5 years	ACA
AP9	+ (Satisfactory)	ICAB, SEC	No comment	Yes (Need co-operation)	20 years	FCA
AP10	– (Standard setting)	ICAB, SEC	No comment	Yes (Need co-operation)	11 years	ACMA
AP11	– (Enforcement)	ICAB	No comment	Yes (Need co-operation)	7 years	ACA
AP12	– (Enforcement)	ICAB	IP (PG)	Yes (Need co-operation)	15 years	FCMA, FCA
US1	– (Need regulation)	ICAB and ICMAB	No comment	Yes (Need co-operation)	10 years	MBA
US2	– (Enforcement)	ICAB	Yes (PG)	Yes (Need co-operation)	9 years	MA
US3	– (Need regulation)	ICAB	Yes (PG)	Yes (Need co-operation)	8 years 7 months	MBA
US4	– (Need regulation)	ICAB	No comment	Yes (Need co-operation)	10 years	CMA (Part)
US5	– (Enforcement)	ICAB and SEC	Yes (PG)	Yes (Need co-operation)	5 years 10 months	MBA
US6	– (Enforcement)	SEC	No comment	Yes (Need co-operation)	18 years	M.Com
AR1	– (Standard setting)	ICAB and SEC	Yes (PD)	Yes (Need co-operation)	21 years	PhD
AR2	– (Enforcement)	ICAB and SEC	No comment	Yes (Need co-operation)	10 years	MBA

Notes: Interviewee codes – PM: Policymaker; AP: Preparers and professionals; US: Users; and AR: Academics and researchers

Q1: '–' a negative (non-satisfactory) perception of accounting regulation (e.g. need for high-quality investor protection regulations, standard-setting and enforcement); '+' a positive (satisfactory) perception of accounting regulation.

Q2: ICAB: The Institute of Chartered Accountants of Bangladesh; SEC: Securities and Exchange Commission of Bangladesh; ICMAB: Institute of Cost and Management Accountants of Bangladesh; DSE: Dhaka Stock Exchange; BB: Bangladesh Bank; MOC: Ministry of Commerce; MOF: the Ministry of Finance.

Q3: Yes (PD): political pressure from donor agencies; Yes (PG): political lobbying and the government intervention; No (PG): no politics (i.e. no political pressure) by the government; IP (PG): indirect politics by the government; and No comment: no comment on politics.

Q4: Yes (Need co-operation): co-operation among institutional bodies is essential to implement IFRS.

Appendix 6.5 Comparison of perceptions of interviewees based on Q1–4 [2nd round interviews, n=12]

Code	Accounting Regulation			Politico-Institutional		Work Experience (years)	Qualifications
	Q1(a)	*Q1(b)*	*Q2*	*Q3*	*Q4*		
PM1	– Need regulation	+ Standard setting	– Enforcement	Yes (PG)	Yes (Need co-operation)	26 years	PhD
PM2	– Need regulation	+ Standard setting	– Enforcement	Yes (PG)	Yes (Need co-operation)	10 years	ACA
PM4	+ Need regulation	- Standard setting	+ Enforcement	Yes (PG)	Yes (Need co-operation)	11 years	MBA
PM5	– Need regulation	- Standard setting	– Enforcement	Yes (PG)	Yes (Need co-operation)	14 years	FCA
AP5	– Need regulation	- Standard setting	– Enforcement	Yes (PG)	Yes (Need co-operation)	10 years	M.Com.
AP6	– Need regulation	- Standard setting	– Enforcement	No comment	Yes (Need co-operation)	8 years 2 months	MBA
AP10	– Need regulation	- Standard setting	– Enforcement	No comment	Yes (Need co-operation)	11 years	ACMA
AP12	– Need regulation	- Standard setting	– Enforcement	No comment	Yes (Need co-operation)	15 years	FCMA, FCA
US4	– Need regulation	- Standard setting	– Enforcement	Yes (PG)	Yes (Need co-operation)	10 years	CMA (Part)
US5	– Need regulation	- Standard setting	– Enforcement	Yes (PG)	Yes (Need co-operation)	5 years 10 months	MBA
AR1	– Need regulation	- Standard setting	–Enforcement	Yes (PG)	Yes (Need co-operation)	21 years	PhD
AR2	– Need regulation	- Standard setting	–Enforcement	Yes (PG)	Yes (Need co-operation)	10 years	MBA

Notes:

Q1(a): '– *Need regulation*': non-satisfactory perception of accounting regulation and therefore need for high quality investor protection regulations; '+ *Need regulation*': satisfactory perception of accounting regulation and therefore no need to introduce more regulations.

Q1(b): '– *Standard setting*': non-satisfactory perception of the standard setting process; '+ *Standard setting*': satisfactory perception of the standard setting process.

Q2:   '– *Enforcement*': non-satisfactory perception of enforcement; '+*Enforcement*': satisfactory perception of enforcement.

Q3:   *Yes (PG)*: political lobbying and the government intervention; *No comment*: no comment on politics.

Q4:   *Yes (Need co-operation)*: co-operation among institutional bodies is essential to implement IFRS.

Appendix 7.1 Enforcement actions comparison, by year (1998–2010)

	2010	2009	2008	2007	2006	2005	2004	2003	2002	2001	2000	1999	1998
Total enforcement actions	**239**	**172**	**176**	**281**	**326**	**135**	**62**	**57**	**29**	**24**	**10**	**77**	**59**
Violation type													
Price-sensitive information (PSI) related violations	29	8	16	42	11	4	1	1	0	2	4	0	0
Non co-operation with SEC appointed auditors	50	60	68	58	45	37	14	3	5	1	2	13	0
Non/delayed submission of half-yearly/interim financial statements	4	2	0	11	25	0	0	0	0	0	0	0	0
Non/delayed submission of yearly audited financial statements	4	8	5	11	22	21	15	2	4	1	0	0	0
Non submission of capital and shareholding position	0	1	0	7	40	0	0	0	0	0	0	0	0
Non holding/delay of AGM	36	12	19	22	27	12	2	1	0	5	0	10	7
Non submission of audio visual recording of AGM	0	10	0	0	0	0	0	0	0	0	0	0	0
Trading related violations by securities companies	1	0	0	12	17	5	6	1	1	3	0	8	0
Violation related to corporate governance guidelines	24	0	12	0	12	1	5	41	10	5	0	2	27
Non/delayed payment of dividend to the shareholder	11	0	0	0	0	0	0	0	0	0	0	0	2
Non-compliance with SEC rules/laws/ notifications/ordinance	15	15	8	23	1	0	0	0	0	0	0	0	0
Violation relating to auditor qualification	3	0	0	0	8	0	0	0	0	0	0	0	0
Non-compliance with IFRS	**9**	**14**	**7**	**11**	**1**	**0**	**0**	**0**	**0**	**0**	**0**	**0**	**0**
Retention of auditors for more than three consecutive years	1	0	6	0	15	18	0	0	0	0	0	0	0
Non/delayed payment of beneficiary owners'(BO) A/C maintenance Fee	0	3	0	0	0	3	0	0	0	0	0	0	0
Violation of depository (CDBL) regulations by its members	0	0	1	3	0	0	0	0	0	0	0	0	0
Cancellation of irrevocable declaration for buy/sell of shares	0	0	0	1	0	4	0	0	4	0	0	0	0
IPO related violations	0	0	0	16	11	2	0	3	0	0	1	0	0
Non-payment of interest and principal against debenture	0	0	0	4	0	0	0	0	0	0	0	0	0
Falsification/misrepresentation/failure to present 'true and fair view'	0	0	0	0	15	0	0	0	0	0	0	0	0

Failure to audit by SEC recommended partnership firms	0	0	0	0	0	22	0	0	1	0	0	0	0
Failure to provide explanation of SEC enquiry	14	20	13	20	17	3	3	2	1	2	1	44	23
Non-payment of auditors' remuneration	20	8	11	15	14	4	1	1	0	2	0	0	0
Others	18	11	10	25	23	21	15	1	4	3	0	0	0
By report type													
Annual report	53	60	68	58	45	49	24	3	5	1	2	13	0
Interim report	22	8	16	42	11	4	1	1	0	2	4	0	0
Type of Enforcement Action(s)													
Warning	135	71	106	110	194	75	42	47	4	13	3	63	50
Waiver/exemption from imposed penalty	11	11	9	22	13	2	3	1	0	0	0	0	0
Upholding the imposed penalty/rejection of appeal	24	7	3	0	10	0	1	1	7	0	0	0	0
Penalty/fine	62	63	53	128	88	56	14	3	17	6	7	14	9
Payment of penalty by instalments	0	1	0	12	7	0	0	0	0	0	0	0	0
Disposal of alleged matter	7	3	1	5	3	0	0	0	0	0	0	0	0
Registration/licence cancellation/suspension of trading facilities	0	2	2	0	1	1	2	2	1	5	0	0	0
Others	0	14	2	4	10	1	0	3	0	0	0	0	0

Index

Note: figures and tables are denoted with italicized page numbers; end note information is denoted with an n following the page number.

enforcement related to 156, *158*, *159*; IFRS requirements for 2, 61; politico-institutional factors in relation to 28; training/education level correlation with 34–5
donors *see* foreign aid

Economic Management Technical Assistance Programme (EMTAP) 7, 64–5, 107, 125
education *see* training
Egypt: country-specific factors in 39, 40; cultural factors in 32; disclosure in 34; IFRS implementation in 2, *3*
enforcement of IFRS: accounting regulatory frameworks for 23–5, 97–102, *101, 208–11*, 212–13; avoiding penalties associated with 157, *157*; in Bangladesh 2, 9, 10–11, 73, *73*, 88–9, 97–102, *101*, 114–15, *114–15*, 116, 128–9, 132–7, 153, *155*, 155–7, *157, 158, 159*, 161n6, 168, *208–11*, 212–13, *216–17*; company-specific violations in *116, 128*, 128–9, *155*, 155–7, *157, 158*; corruption impacting 10, 136–7, 153; court cases in 132, 134, *135, 136*, 136–7, 161n6; cultural factors impacting 73, *73*; depreciation-related violations in 156, *158, 159*; in developing countries 2, 10–11 (*see also in Bangladesh* subentry); disclosure-related issues in 156, *158, 159*; global 25; half-yearly audited report issues in 156–7, *158, 159*; industry-specific violations in 132, *133, 134, 216–17*; literature review on 23–5; penalties associated with 102, 157, *157*, 212–13; politico-institutional factors impacting 114–15, *114–15*; preventive mechanisms for 24; punitive mechanisms for 24–5 (*see also penalties* subentry); qualified audit opinion issues in 156, *158, 159*; research consideration of 9, 10–11, 23–5, 48–9, 73, *73*, 88–9, 97–102, *101*, 114–15, *114–15, 116*, 128–9, 132–7, 153, *155*, 155–7, *157, 158, 159*, 161n6, 168, *208–11*, 212–13, *216–17*; role of state in 48–9, 153, *155*, 155–7, *157, 158, 159*, 161n6; South Asian 73, *73*
Ershad, H. M. *57*, 58
ethical issues, with research 84–5
European Union (EU): enforcement in 25; IFRS adoption in 1–2, 12n2; politico-institutional factors in 29; standard setting process and implementation in 22–3; theory of role of state applied to 47; *see also specific countries*

Family Courts Ordinance, 1985 59
FASB (Financial Accounting Standards Board) 53
FDI (foreign direct investment) 5, 39
Fiji: country-specific factors in 37
Financial Accounting Standards Board (FASB) 53
Financial Institutions Act, 1993 59
Financial Reporting Ordinance, 2008 60
Financial Sector Reform Programme (FSRP) 59
foreign aid: cultural factors considered for 74; donor agencies' pressure as

politico-institutional factor related to 106–8; donor agencies' role with state in 49, 154; literature review on 38–9
foreign direct investment (FDI) 5, 39
France: colonial influences of 37; country-specific factors in 38; standard setting process and implementation in 22; theory of role of state applied to 47
FSRP (Financial Sector Reform Programme) 59

Germany: enforcement in 24; IFRS implementation in 2; politico-institutional factors in 28, 29; standard setting process and implementation in 22; theory of role of state applied to 47
globalisation 4–5
government intervention 26–8, 30–1, 104, *104, 105–6, 106*
Greece: enforcement in 25; IFRS implementation in 2
Gulf Cooperation Council states 2, *3*

Hasan, K.M. 58
Hasina, Sheik *57*, 58, 59
Hungary: IFRS implementation in 2, *3*

IASB (International Accounting Standards Board): enforcement authority of 1; ICAB membership in 59, 64; IFRS of (*see* IFRS implementation)
ICAB (Institute of Chartered Accountants of Bangladesh): accounting regulatory framework for 5, 6, 7, 64–5, *96*, 96–7; cooperation with other institutional bodies by 111–15; enforcement by 10–11, 99; establishment of 59; standard-setting process role of 66–8, *67*; status of adopted standards under 68, *68–70*, 70; Technical and Research Committee of 66–8, *67*, 77nn17–18; training role of 125, 128
ICAEW (Institute of Chartered Accountants of England and Wales) 7, 64–5
ICMAB (Institute of Cost and Management Accountants of Bangladesh) 59, 65, 112–13
IFAC (International Federation of Accountants) 7, 64
IFRS implementation: accounting regulatory frameworks impacting (*see* accounting regulatory frameworks); adoption and 1–2; corporate governance regulations impacting 2; corruption impacting (*see* corruption); cost-benefit analysis of 2, 11, 142–3, 145, *145*, 146; cultural factors impacting (*see* cultural factors); developing countries' (*see* Bangladesh; developing countries); disclosure requirements with (*see* disclosure); enforcement of (*see* enforcement of IFRS); language issues with (*see* language); literature review on (*see* literature review); overview of challenges of, in developing countries 1–12, 162–9;

to *4*, 4–5, *5*, 61, 65; Securities and Exchange
Commission regulating (*see* Securities and
Exchange Commission)
Switzerland: IFRS implementation in 2

Tanzania: disclosure in 35
taxes: corruption related to 130–1; Income Tax
  Ordinance, 1984 on 59, 61, 62; National
  Board of Revenue role in collecting 59, 66
technology transfers 38–9
Thailand: country-specific factors in 37; politico-
  institutional factors in 30; training and
  professional standing in 34
theory of role of state: accountability of state to
  citizens in 49, 153–4; in Bangladesh 150–61,
  165–7; donor agencies' role in 49, 154;
  enforcement of outcomes by state in 48–9,
  153, *155*, 155–7, *157, 158, 159*, 161n6; experts
  writing rules in 46–7, 151; external forces in
  45–6, 51–3; individual organisational level
  dynamics in 154–5, 158, *159*, 160; institutional
  dynamics in 51–3, 150–4; internal forces in
  51–3; key papers on 45–50; neo-liberal states
  in 48; organisational field level dynamics
  in 154–5; overview of 45, 55, 150, 160–1;
  proposed theoretical models for 50, *50*, 53–4,
  54, 83, 152; research methodology related
  to 45–55, 83, *83*, 150–61, 165–7; research
  question related to 45, 150; stakeholder
  consultation with state in 47–8, 151–3; state
  level dynamics in 151, 154–8; state-society
  relationship in 51–4, 154, 161, 165–7; welfare
  states in 47–8
training: disclosure practices correlation with
  34–5; Economic Management Technical
  Assistance Programme ("Twinning Project")
  providing 7, 64–5, 107, 125; effectiveness

of development of 124, 127–8, *128*; lack
  of qualified accountants and 142; literature
  review on 33–5; overview of 12; professional
  and university curricula for *125*, 125–6, 127–8;
  professional development and 126–7, *127*;
  professional standing and 33–4, 142; research
  on IFRS related to 7, 10–11, 12, 33–5, 36,
  64–5, 123–8, 137–41, *138, 139*, 142, 147–8,
  164; research propositions on 36, 124, 147
Turkey: training and professional standing in 34
Twinning Project 7, 64–5, 107, 125

United Arab Emirates (UAE): theory of role of
  state applied to 49
United Kingdom: colonial influences of 37, 38,
  44n34; enforcement in 24; ICAEW in 7, 64–5;
  IFRS implementation in 2; theory of role of
  state applied to 47
United States: country-specific factors in 38;
  cultural factors in 33; enforcement in 24, 25;
  politico-institutional factors in 26, 28, 29;
  standard setting process and implementation in
  22–3; theory of role of state applied to 47

Weber, Max, on state 17, 51–3, 79, 150–1, 161,
  166–7
World Bank: adjustment programmes of 59;
  Economic Management Technical Assistance
  Programme ("Twinning Project") 7, 64–5,
  107, 125; foreign aid from 38–9, 49, 74,
  107–8; Governance Indicators by *60, 73*, 76n2,
  168; legitimacy and influence of 38; public
  sector dominance opposition by 40; training
  initiatives of 7, 34, 64–5, 107, 125, 126, 128
World Trade Organization (WTO) 71

Zia, Khaleda *57*, 58